W9-ADD-991

STUDIES IN THE ENGLISH RENAISSANCE

John T. Shawcross, General Editor

JOHN MILTON

The Self and the World

JOHN T. SHAWCROSS

THE UNIVERSITY PRESS OF KENTUCKY

Copyright © 1993 by The University Press of Kentucky

Scholarly publisher for the Commonwealth,
serving Bellarmine College, Berea College, Centre
College of Kentucky, Eastern Kentucky University,
The Filson Club, Georgetown College, Kentucky
Historical Society, Kentucky State University,
Morehead State University, Murray State University,
Northern Kentucky University, Transylvania University,
University of Kentucky, University of Louisville,
and Western Kentucky University.

Editorial and Sales Offices: Lexington, Kentucky 40508-4008

Library of Congress Cataloging–in–Publication Data

Shawcross, John T.
    John Milton : the self and the world / John T. Shawcross.
        p.   cm.—(Studies in the English Renaissance)
    Includes bibliographical references and index.
    ISBN 0–8131–1808–5
    1. Milton, John, 1608–1674—Biography—Psychology.   2. Poets,
English—Early modern, 1500–1700—Psychology.   3. Psychoanalysis and
literature.   4. Self in literature.   I. Title.   II. Series.
PR3581.S5   1993
821'.4—dc20   92–22037

Contents

Acknowledgments

Chapter 3 is revised from "Milton and Diodati: An Essay in Psychodynamic Meaning" in *Eyes Fast Fixt*, ed. Albert C. Labriola and Michael Lieb, extra issue of *Milton Studies* 7 (1975): 127-63. Chapter 4 is revised from "Milton's Decision to Become a Poet," *Modern Language Quarterly* 24 (1963): 21-30. Parts of Chapters 8 and 9 were first printed in "Milton and Covenant: The Christian View of Old Testament Theology" in *Milton and Scriptural Tradition: The Bible into Poetry*, ed. James H. Sims and Leland Ryken (Columbia: Univ. of Missouri Press, 1984), 160-91.

For various informative discussions, help and encouragement, I sincerely thank my good friends and colleagues Joan Heiges Blythe, Virginia Blum, and Michael Lieb.

Abbreviations

CD   *De doctrina christiana* ("Of Christian Doctrine")

CM   The Columbia Milton: *The Works of John Milton*. Frank Patterson, gen. ed. New York: Columbia University Press, 1931-38.

CPB   Milton's Commonplace Book

DDD   *The Doctrine and Discipline of Divorce*

ME   *A Milton Encyclopedia*. William B. Hunter, gen. ed. Lewisburg, Penn.: Bucknell University Press, 1978-83.

PL   *Paradise Lost*

PR   *Paradise Regain'd*

SA   *Samson Agonistes*

YP   The Yale Prose: *Complete Prose Works of John Milton*. Don M. Wolfe, gen. ed. New Haven: Yale University Press, 1954-82.

1

The Roots of Being: Some Problems in Milton's Biography

Problems still loom large over a biography that is so much more replete than that of comparable writers of the age, such as Spenser, Shakespeare, Donne, or Marvell, or anyone else from those more than a hundred years. So much is known about the biography of John Milton that attention has narrowed to details: Did he die before or after midnight on November 8/9, 1674? Was *The Reason of Church-Government* published in January or February 1642? When did he live on Jewin Street, early 1661 through sometime in 1669? Was his sister Anne alive when he returned from the Continent in August 1639? The evidence for his life comes from the usual documents of genealogical and literary research—parish records, taxation lists, legal writs and deeds, printing house data—as well as from the less usual personal memoirs and the rare contemporary or near-contemporary biographical accounts. Not just one but five such accounts exist from within twenty-five years of his death. In the second half of the nineteenth century, David Masson's indispensable *Life of Milton*[1] incorporated four of these lives, at least seven later important biographies, and the findings of the preceding two hundred years. Masson's magisterial biography radiated out into the political, historical, intellectual, religious, and literary contexts of Milton's times. Then, after years of careful searching by many people, a milestone narrative came forth from William Riley Parker,[2] with new and voluminous details, that deliberately rejected the inclusion of the contemporaneous handled so well by Masson. There seems to be no need to redo Parker's life record, since it has been amplified or altered only here and there in the last twenty-five years. Yet there are some problems or questions in Milton's biography, not just further details, that we would like to have engaged, topics that have been too little studied. The chapters of this

book attempt to raise some of these issues and provide rational conclusions, based less on "factual" evidence than on logical analysis of what we
do know about the man and the work.

In a review of a popular life of Milton I questioned, passingly, its
chronological organization because its treatment seemed to me to suggest that a different organization might have been wiser—or is chronological organization a necessity in a life? When asked about the current
book as I pursued it over the last few years, I would talk of a "biography,"
a word originally intended to appear in its title. Perhaps "biographical
study" would be more accurate, for this book does not reexamine the
vital statistics one would expect in a biography (for which we thankfully
have the excellent work of Masson and Parker), nor does it formulate
itself as an expected chronological account. While I was pursuing my
text, a talk on William Faulkner's *Absalom, Absalom!* by Professor Alessan-
dro Portelli of the University of Rome presented narrative techniques
that I saw as pertinent to the challenge of my endeavor. Oral narrative
with its similarity in Faulkner's prose is built on two particularly interesting techniques of presentation, which Portelli had found to be natural
patterns in accounts of people about their lives. The first is the nonchronological presentation of material, a mixture of times and a triggering of
remembrances from various time frames without time differentiations.
While the application of this natural narrative pattern is clear in fiction,
does it have use in such nonfictional work as biography? My conclusion
is yes, that it is a meaningful technique depending on the specific material to be presented, and I have thus been emboldened to retain what
was becoming nonchronological and moving through various time
frames. For such nonchronological presentation makes clear that an act
or a point in time within a person's biography always develops out of
prior acts and points in time while developing into other times and acts
in the future. To see such points of time and act together rather than
with the intervention of nonpertinent narrative—nonpertinent, that is,
to a particular context being discussed—is to enhance their significance
for the person emerging biographically in the prose. While some chronological sense remains, a relentless year-by-year ordering should not be
required and could indeed be antagonistic to an understanding of Milton's mind and psyche.

A difficulty that this arrangement creates is frequency of repetition.
But Portelli also pointed out that we speak, tell stories, build impressions
through incremental repetition, just as his interviewees and Rosa Cold-
field were doing. As in epic, such repetitions create a communication of
significance, of revision, and of convergence of action or thought. This
second narratological technique of repetition which keeps expanding

with each new context is useful in nonfictional biography, as I hope my reader will agree. Such incremental repetitions are akin to what Jacques Lacan calls nodes.[3] For the sense of the person and that person's mind, emotional world, and even factual context is never only what hindsight is able to state in a declarative and unmodified sentence. A repetend "condenses" the gist of a point being made, and the incrementalization allows that point to offer multiple signifying representations.

Thus, while each chapter of this biography (limited in specific content and scope though it is) proceeds in roughly chronological arrangement, each chapter itself may range in time and act, offering a view of the author not only in being but in process of being: a "different" biography of John Milton from what might more usually be expected by such classification.

The problems or questions or considerations that I believe need further treatment in a biography of Milton are those of his religion, his career decisions and career activities, his conceptions of himself as talented and as writer, his governmental work, his real achievements in the realms of thought, his psychological being, and his personal life, particularly his marriages. Though it goes without saying, these are all interrelated, and we cannot treat one without treating another. But further, beneath any discussion of a literary figure will also be a reading of the works, and such reading can and should delve into the biographical, the ideological contextualizations, and the exclusively literary. Some of Milton's poetry—such as the Latin poems—is usually read only in terms of biographical contexts, or—like *Samson Agonistes*—is reduced by the critic's conviction that it was written wholly as a result of Milton's life experience, the ideological and definitely the literary being obscured. The prevalence of the history of ideas, significant as such an approach is for contextualization, has often obliterated a work as composition, stylistic achievement, and somewhat disembodied literary artifact.[4] There is no need to note such "historical" studies; generally these have been excellent and most worthwhile for what they anchor as ideological concerns for Milton or a specific work.

In this biography of John Milton, "religious" poet and political advocate, I examine, among other matters, Milton's religion. Parker indexes it about ten times, yet the closest he gets to presenting that subject is to write: "Undisturbed by any perverse notions of natural goodness, [Milton] knew that man is born into this world with the taint of original sin, and that sinful boys and young men are naturally attracted neither to good morals nor to good literature. Standing squarely on the experience of the human race, he hoped through continued Christian education to amend his own depraved nature" (22). Parker noted further:

In the latter part of his life, John Toland tells us, Milton 'was not a professed member of any particular sect among Christians, he frequented none of their assemblies, nor made use of their peculiar rites in his family.' He had developed his own Christian Doctrine, which he hoped some day to publish to the world, and in it he had expressed his conviction that neither a pious man nor a profane should be forced into any given church or be compelled to attend public worship. Since the individual believer enjoys divine guidance, the illumination of the Holy Spirit, he possesses the right to interpret the Scriptures for himself, and civil power should not force religious conformity upon him. These had come to be Milton's profound beliefs, and he lived them. [579]

These latter remarks are not so much statements of Milton's religion as attitudes toward religion's administration.

Less attention has been paid to Milton's career as poet than one might have expected, as well, partially, I suppose, because he did become a poet and so no need has been felt to examine the career, and because most critics have not differentiated vocation and avocation. A detailed study of two aspects of Milton's decision to be a poet—the Trinity MS and the Commonplace Book—has not been adequately probed. There has been some detailed attention to these works in articles, but what did Milton do specifically in those early months of decision? What are the evidences of his thinking and planning? Milton is far from the occasional poet Donne, or the coterie poet Carew, or the personal poet Herbert, and at the same time far from a careerist like Jonson or Dryden. A general statement is the frequent one: "From childhood Milton's scholarly tastes and talents had marked him out, in his elders' eyes and his own, for a clerical career, but in his own mind that idea must have weakened before he left Cambridge; when he reached a definite decision we do not know. The reason he later gave, hostility toward the prelatical church, was doubtless combined with a growing sense of his poetic vocation."[5]

As part of his other, more public career, A.N. Wilson's description of Milton's governmental secretaryship is brief, and usual: "To outward appearances, it seems a fairly tame appointment, more worthy of the talents of a trained diplomat than of an artist. It was to be his task to sit in, as an interpreter and adviser, during meetings with foreign powers. He was to translate letters for the Council, and compose them, at their dictation."[6] Perhaps the most curious position related to one aspect of that secretaryship, most particularly curious for a biographer, is Parker's: "I must warn my reader," he admits, "that I have not attempted to do much with the letters of state in the following notes, chiefly because I believe that to do so would contribute little to biography, but partly because my efforts to learn all the facts about several dozen of them resulted in lengthy and complicated documentation for each" (952).

Related are such issues as Milton's conception of himself as a poet or as a polemicist, with the attendant question of his abilities as a thinker. To this we can add the tensions we all feel from time to time between intention and achievement, and achievement and its aftermath. My conclusions may not convince everyone, for they are not always in agreement with traditional views. But being an idealist—like Milton—I keep hoping that people will weigh the arguments without worrying that they may be in conflict with formerly learned and held opinions. My arguments ask the reader to proceed logically, as if greeting each piece of the narrative not with preconceptions about Milton and his life nor with prior judgment of what Milton's works *say*, but for the first time. The arguments are incremental, building by repetitions and reconsiderations of Milton's life and inner being. For the past is always the present in some way.

The trend of this biography is psychological—Milton as anal personality, Milton conditioned by oedipal influences, and Milton as one caught in conflict between his self and his world. As readers we should recognize the presence of an author as craftsperson in the work being discussed, and at the same time we should stay with and generally within the text—to deconstruct it without jargon, as it were. Yet it seems to me that most readers do not allow themselves to enter the work as they should: they do not bring their own experience into the text—its words, its constructions, its ideas—and they do not bring into the text their understanding of the author through their own experience. An example of this is the much discussed question of "virginity" and "chastity" in "Comus," where we have allowed certain critics to bring apparently *their* (but not mine and I hope not my reader's) experiences with these words into their reading. The psychodynamic aspects of the self that involve sexual attitudes and experiences and gender matters are basic to an understanding of an author, whose work may both reveal and hide that self. Yet biographies of Milton have generally shied away from the psychological. Milton's self greeting the various worlds through which he moved makes more meaningful that external world one finds in a more usual biography. Much of the literary author's self is found in the creative work produced, nagging the reader into interpreting and delving more deeply into that creative work than most other biographical studies of Milton have allowed.

Many critics have employed the terms "virginity" and "chastity" interchangeably and yet condemn Milton for confusion, not admitting that equivalency in the terms exists for many people. Indeed, dictionaries, *reflecting usage,* give as a definition of "chaste" the irrelevant word "celibate"! Even William Kerrigan confuses "virginity" and "virtue" and sees the Lady meaning "virginity" when she says "chastity."[7] An added problem, of course, is that, indefensibly, the terms are usually applied to women only, by women as well as by men, so that even in our supposedly liberated world the nonvirgin female has immediately became unchaste, and the nonvirgin male, "experienced." A simple check of Milton's use of the words indicates the *he* knew that "virgin" in sexual terms means one who has not experienced sexual intercourse physically and that "chaste" means one who is morally pure and virtuous in sexual matters.[8] For one example: in *Animadversions* he refers to "a chast Matron" (21).

"Comus," with the Castlehaven scandal in the background, and perhaps with the Margery Evans case in some of the audience's minds,[9] is concerned with potential rape, and argues that one's becoming nonvirginal physically does not make one unchaste. The Lady calls on Faith, Hope, and Chastity "To keep [her] life and honour unassail'd," that is, unraped, but it is the Elder Brother who states the main point for the Bridgewater audience to understand: "no goblin, or swart faery of the mine / Has hurtfull power o'er true virginity" (436-37). The most important words here are "hurtful" and "true": the goblin may have power o'er virginity and execute a rape, but that does not mean that the true virgin, that is, the one who is chaste of mind and intent, will thereby alter or be altered into an unchaste being. The Lady says her honor will be unassailed through her faith in God's goodness and omnipotence, through her hope that any action will not cause an alteration in her life in terms of honor, and through her chastity of mind and intent, which do not join in such rape. Surely our experience with forcible rape in our own times proclaims that the victim has not become unchaste by the action of a perverted psychopath, even though the victim (female or male) be no longer physically virginal.

An accurate reading of "Comus" can lead to an accurate understanding of Milton, and these both in turn can color our reactions to the divorce tracts and to the narratives involving Adam and Eve. Attention here in Chapter 1, a kind of prospectus and introduction, prepares us for many of the issues to be discussed later and certainly for a view of Milton that has too often been misrepresented in critical inquiry. Though his highminded, virtuous ideal of sexual intercourse seems to have repressed schoolboy affairs (as we see from the Sixth Prolusion) and libido (as in "Elegia prima"), the divorce tracts, with the same kind of highminded virtue within their fabric, assume chasteness on the part of each marriage partner and recognize incompatibilities other than sex as a reason for divorce. The highminded ideal is rapturously depicted for the unfallen Adam and Eve, and its replacement is lust in the fallen pair. We do not see a Milton in any of these works idealizing virginity (although "Epitaphium Damonis" raises the issue); rather, it is chastity that drives "Comus" and an assumed chastity that underlies the divorce tracts and *Paradise Lost.*

The psychological Milton also accounts for the religious and political Milton, the son of his father, and this underpins the creation of the master poetry. Milton believed in God, and he believed that the Bible was the Word of God. He also believed, however, that the Bible demanded interpretation and was not always literally true. He recognized that there were two accounts of the creation of humans and tried to reconcile them but came up with indistinct conclusions, accepting basically the second, more specific account of God's creation of man in his image and then God's creation of woman out of man. Paul "ends the controversie," he writes, "by explaining that the woman is not primarily and immediately the image of God, but in reference to the man" (*Tetrachordon*, 3). Written in 1645, this statement is still valid in the later years when Milton finished *Paradise Lost,* but it is qualified to reject some masculinist inferences, just as numerous other masculinist positions are rejected in the poem. There is a continuance and a growth. "Nevertheless man is not to hold her as a servant," his next sentence in *Tetrachordon* reads, "but receives her into a part of that empire which God proclaims him to, though not equally, yet largely, as his own image and glory: for it is no small glory to him, that a creature so like him, should be made subject to him. Not but that particular exceptions may have place, if she exceed her husband in prudence and dexterity, and he contentedly yeeld, for then a superior and more naturall law comes in, that the wiser should govern the lesse wise, whether male or female."

By the 1650s or 60s, expansion has put the first Genesis account of creation, that of the Elohim narrator (1:26-28), into the mouth of Raphael (VII, 519-34) and the second Genesis account, that of the Yahweh narrator (2:5-25), into the mouth of Adam (VIII, 437-99), a subtle distinction that has missed a number of Milton's antagonistic critics. Raphael's account, which stressed both sexes ("So God created man in his own image, in the image of God created he him; male and female created he them. And God blessed them, and God said unto them, Be fruitful, and multiply, and replenish the earth, and subdue it") takes on the appearance of God's creation and intent. Adam's account, which stresses man over woman ("And the Lord God formed man of the dust of the ground, and breathed into his nostrils the breath of life; and man became a living soul. . . . And the Lord God, said, It is not good that the man should be alone; I will make him a help meet for him. . . . And the Lord God caused a deep sleep to fall upon Adam, and he slept; and he took one of his ribs, and closed up the flesh instead thereof. And the rib, which the Lord God had taken from man, made he a woman, and brought her unto the man. And Adam said, This is now bone of my bones, and flesh of my flesh: she shall be called Woman, because she was taken out of Man") takes on the appearance of a masculine inter- pretation. It is this reading of the creation that dominates Adam's think- ing and feeling when he partakes of the fruit of the tree of good and evil ("he scrupl'd not to eat / Against his better knowledge, *not deceav'd*, / But fondly overcome with Femal charm" [IX, 997-99]). The presentation of Adam and his "reasoning" is subtle; it suggests a growth and expansion of Milton's thought from the mid-1640s, and the relation between the sexes in the epic takes on religious/philosophic beliefs, with a critical analysis of humankind and specifically of the man.

I should mention here something that is not really an aside. Various pieces of evidence for Milton's positions on these religious and sociolog- ical points have come from his *De doctrina christiana*, not from the Latin in which the work is written but through a translator's inadequate language.[10] For example, in *De doctrina christiana*, I.vii.36 (in the Colum- bia Edition), Milton writes of the creation of "hominem," which means basically in Latin "a human being," the "human race"; the meaning "a man" came later. Milton goes on to say "that it was not the body alone that was then made but the soul also [although the translations add "the soul of man also"], in which our likeness to God principally consists." The discussion in Latin does not make distinctions between man and woman except to cite that the mother of mankind was fabricated "ex simplici costa." The word "man" or even "human being" is not used, although "from the first created" is implied from Genesis 2, which is cited. In Chapter X, quoting Genesis 2 again, Milton talks of marriage as being instituted for the mutual love, society, help, and comfort of "viri et ux- oris" (the man and the wife): "iure licet viri potiore" (that is, reading the biblical text, "it is lawful that the greater or stronger or preferable right is the man's"). The stress in the word *potior* in Latin is on *preferable*, but definitely does not say *superior rights*, as Charles Sumner has it, or even quite *greater authority* (a much better translation), as John Carey has it. Milton goes on to cite the Hebrew meaning as both husband and lord and then two decidedly male-oriented, but biblical, texts: 1 Peter 3:6 and 1 Timothy 2:12-14.

Milton's thinking about the relationship of husband and wife (of man and woman) rests on his understanding of the relationship of the divine Father and the Son, seen as well in that of his own father and himself. The doctrine of subordinationism is explored in *De doctrina christiana* and underlies *Paradise Lost*. Early commentators had no diffi- culty in seeing God the Son as God the Father's agent in effecting the defeat of Satan and his cohorts, in creating the universe and its inhabitants, in pronouncing the Judgment—all major actions of the poem expressed as acts of the surrogate. With the discovery of Milton's theological tractate and its publication in 1823-25, charges of Arianism arose and persist today in the minds of imprecise critics who seem neither to know what Arianism is (what they mean is anti-Trinitarianism) nor to have read the Latin of the treatise. Evidence for these charges seems to originate from the translation rather than from what Milton actually wrote. What Milton describes in the theological work and in the poem is a subordination of everything, including the Son, to the Father, who is "Father" only in reference to the "Son." The godhead is a triune god, with "God" implying that trinity and connoting all the attributes of God the Father. Prior to the denunciation of Arius, subordinationism was not a heresy for the Church fathers. Just as the Son has an independent being (essence), so has Milton the son and so has Eve (woman); just as the Father is he who has omnipotence, omniscience, and omnipresence, which he may grant to his Son in his stead, so Milton's father has certain controls over his son, and so has Adam (man) a "preferable right" over Eve (woman). Man and woman are not the same; they have their own essences, as do the Father and the Son. But there is a kind of hierarchy in Milton's way of thinking (drawn from and repeatedly underscored by the Bible, from Pauline but other texts as well). Milton extends the doctrine of subordinationism to the angels, who are subordinate to God the Father and God the Son, and to humankind, who are subordinate to God, and thence to the sexes, since the man was created first in the image of God and the woman second, from the man.

There are many today who do not like this conclusion—or at least we enlightened ones do not—yet many others still refuse to recognize the Bible as a male-oriented and human-generated attempt to explain existence and generation. But if one accepts the Bible as truth, as Milton did, even if in need of interpretation, subordination of the sexes is a conclusion that can be inferred. The concept is encased in the much-discussed line "Hee for God only, shee for God in him" (*PL* IV, 299). This has been and is a commonplace in our world, which world has generally been patriarchal. The Bible was written down within a Hebrew context, and Hebrew culture has been and often still is male-oriented, with the wife in a subordinate position to the husband. The Bible naturally reflects its culture, and its culture was patriarchal. The Bible should not be used (but is) as "proof" that man is woman's superior. The confusion in the accounts of Genesis probably resulted from two strata of the story of creation, written at different times, which story attempts to make cogent the existence that surrounded the peoples who produced the text and who finally wrote down what had become traditionally "logical." (One should note that some rabbinical writers and modern scholars advance the idea that the Exodus is the basic historical event and that the accounts leading up to that point in Hebraic history were devised to make sense of existence and the state of existence at the time of the Exodus. The leaving of Eden is thus cast as an earlier form of the Exodus; indeed, it can be construed as an explanation of birth from the womb into the uncertain world lying before the child, the Israelites, and Adam and Eve.)

That word "superior" illustrates the difficulties of language, or rather of our reading of language, in such a discussion as this. The word does suggest an opposite—"inferior"—and both suggest certain attitudes and relationships. Adam in recounting the creation of Eve to Raphael employs the language and concepts of subordination and of superior/inferior. His parallel thinking rests on his understanding of the animal world around him:

> here passion first I felt,
> Commotion strange, in all enjoyments else
> Superior and unmov'd, here onely weak
> Against the charm of Beauties powerful glance.
> Or Nature faild in mee, and left some part
> Not proof enough such Object to sustain,
> Or from my side subducting, took perhaps
> More then enough; at least on her bestow'd
> Too much of Ornament, in outward shew
> Elaborate, of inward less exact.
> For well I understand in the prime end
> Of Nature her th'inferiour, in the mind
> And inward Faculties, which most excell,
> In outward also her resembling less
> His Image who made both, and less expressing
> The character of that Dominion giv'n
> O're other Creatures. [VIII, 530-46]

The ideas are those the reader heard from the narrative voice, first viewing the human pair: "For contemplation hee and valour formd, / For softness shee and sweet attractive Grace, / Hee for God only, shee for God in him" (IV, 297-99) and then from Eve: "thy gentle hand / Seis'd mine, I yeilded, and from that time see / How beauty is excelld by manly grace / And wisdom, which alone is truly fair" (IV, 488-91).

These various passages define the subordinationism underlying Milton's view of humankind, but one that fits into a full range of being from God the Father down to the lowest of animal life. Further, of course, it attempts to offer some prototypical ways of looking at man—given to mental and physical activity—and at woman—beautiful and passive. We do not like such stereotyping as this implies, and we know these stereotypes do not hold up, either for the man or for the woman. Yet they have been and are very generally accepted by numerous people, male and female both, Milton among them. Part of this prototypical description lies in the physicality of man, who is often larger and more muscular and who is often made to exercise that physicality in sports and war and employment, and in the physicality of woman, who is often prettier and less muscular and who has too often been made to consider herself less capable in areas of thought and creative achievements (other than motherhood). But part of this prototypical description also derives from sexual observation. Man in sexual relationship is observed as active, aggressive, forceful, while woman is seen as receptive, submissive, passive (despite situations and people clearly refutable of such common observation). And in coition it is usually the man who is "superior" in position, actively pursuing and effecting sexual intercourse, and the woman who is receptive, supposedly less active, in position beneath and thus "inferior." Milton seems not to have examined such explanations of the myths that have grown up around human beings, nor to have questioned such genderizations very thoroughly. But he does in the divorce tracts recognize that the man is not always the wise one or the one worthy of dominance.

The simile in *Paradise Lost* likening Adam and Eve to the Greek divine rulers of the heavens is most apt here:

> he in delight
> Both of her Beauty and submissive Charms
> Smil'd with superior Love, as *Jupiter*
> On *Juno* smiles, when he impregns the Clouds
> That shed *May* Flowers; and press'd her Matron lip
> With kisses pure . . . [IV, 497-502]

The double entendres of physicality in these words iterate the concepts set out in the previous paragraph. Certainly Adam is not being said to be experiencing "better" love or "purer" love: his love, rather, is active while Eve is receptive; his love involves impregnation like Jupiter's creating in the clouds the rain that will fall on the receptive earth to bring forth flowers; his love (or loving) is physically "over" the "Beauty" and "submissive Charms" of Eve. When just before Eve says that these "marly" attributes "excel" "beauty," she is concluding that activity excels passivity.

If we can understand this paralleling of subordinations on divine and human levels, we can see Milton placing man in a "superior" position to woman, as the "head," as the dominant in the relationship of husband and wife, unless other circumstances appertain, as qualified in the divorce tracts. Proceeding from this thought, whether we agree with it or not, we can recognize in Milton's thinking that woman is her own essence, that she is not "inferior" in the usual connotations of that word (just as the Son is not "inferior"), that she is a "helpmeet" and that thus a union is emphasized even as a hierarchy is implied. The Son can be seen as a "helpmeet" to the Father, their union being emphasized even as a hierarchy is implied. Indeed, *Paradise Lost* explores a parallel of the Son and Eve as well as paralleled contrasts of the Son and Satan, Eve and Sin. Adam, unfortunately, has little in common with the Son, more in common with Satan, and is contrastively metaphorized with Death.

These gender differences should be emphasized in reading *Paradise Lost* only where we see them leading to the concept of the androgyne, that form of human duality (as there is the duality of God the Father and God the Son, producing God the Holy Spirit to create the Trinity) yielding oneness. The image of the pair "hand in hand," which will be explored later in this biography, as will many of the other matters here raised, epitomizes that androgenous concept—that oneness, that "amiable knot," that mutual love—while each whose hand is so joined remains a separate essence, a man and a woman, each independent and worthy, each contributing a complementary quality to that union. The divorce tracts have set the stage for the development of such a conclusion, although it is not reached until later—the late 1650s? the early 1660s? The biographical Milton and the psychological Milton led to these ideas in the mid-1640s—in his own family, his father and mother's relationship, his relationship with his father, his homoerotic tendencies, his shyness and "effeminate" interests and compassions. The changing biography and psychology of the ensuing years will lead to the mutuality, the raised consciousness toward the woman (seen through Eve), the indictment of the man given to war and to self-gratification, the catalysts lying in the experience of marriage and family, of governmental hopes and their repulse.

As I read Milton's treatment of the biblical story and the commentaries that had grown up around it, I see him interpreting it to castigate man, not woman—thus countering the cliché that Eve brought about man's destruction. Feminist criticism has not picked up on this. The narrative in *Paradise Lost* indicates a male bias, for the world was lost for man not by a woman but by man himself. Milton rejects the standard male-oriented story of woman's "weakness" as full agency for the Fall, for she falls deceived and Adam falls not deceived. Though man is endowed with wisdom (having been made for "contemplation"), he rejects mind in favor of self. But Milton's irony has been lost on male and female commentators alike. Milton rejects condemning woman, and in its place stresses the idea that man himself created his Fall, an actually more male-oriented interpretation, proceeding to put faith in woman as the means to redemption. It is only Eve who is tempted by Satan and his fraudulence, and thus, because temptation has been achieved through fraud, God the Father will allow mercy. The fraud that takes in Uriel in Book III, shortly before, and the statement that only God can recognize hypocrisy are there to explain, not to excuse, Eve's succumbing to Satan's wiles. Adam falls by conscious will and knowledge of what he does in Milton's version of the story. This two-stage Fall, as I have called it, must be reversed to reestablish worthiness for mercy, and it is therefore through woman that redemption will come. Narratively, it is through the incarnation that the example is shown and the redemption will be made: internally—psychologically—individually it is through love (the sum of obedience and those virtues Michael talks of at the end of Book XII).

The position of Eve and thus of woman in the Fall of man (and thence of humankind) and in the means to salvation is in extremely sharp contrast in Milton to that in other writers, philosophic, religious, or creative. Look at Donne for a married author; look at Marvell for one unmarried. Both Milton's and their views are male-centered, but in Milton woman is *not* blamed and is the means by which man can hope to correct his error of willful disobedience. Woman's status is much higher in Milton's works than other writers', but—as the Bible tells us, particularly its Pauline component—she is not man's equivalent. It is Eve who speaks last in the poem, a significant position, in lines that stress the protevangelium, yielding hope and putting the focus on the woman's role in life. What position Milton's mother and his wives had in helping to develop his readings of such epistemological and ontological matters we can try to explore.

Individuation for the son is a function, it would seem, of his relationship with the mother which, when broken, enables a fuller individuation from the father. In Milton's case the death of his mother in April 1637 seems to have set in motion action that would lead to assertion of the self from his father. The sense of self that we may with hindsight interpret from Milton's school and university years seems to have been repressed during those years and outwardly manifested only as the end of 1637 approached. That sense of self emerges in the self-esteem of "Ad Patrem" and keeps emerging as we move through his more public career, both in his prose and in his poetic endeavors. We can understand Milton's early selfobject as that which responds to and confirms his "sense of vigour, greatness and perfection," the mirroring selfobject; later as assertion of an individuation develops in the studious retirement, Milton's selfobject is that to whom he "can look up and with whom he can merge as an image of calmness, infallibility and omnipotence," the idealized general parent imago.[11]

Narcissistic personality disorders manifest themselves as depression, hypersensitivity to slights, and a lack of zest,[12] the kinds of reaction Milton felt toward attacks upon him, especially in 1645 after the publication of *Tetrachordon* and *Colasterion* on 4 March. His reaction was to withdraw from public controversy, to immerse himself in his studies and writing, and to retreat to poetry again, the first collection of the shorter poems being licensed on 6 October. It is also interesting to note the apparently psychosomatic effect of personal troubles upon his eyesight at various times in his life (noted elsewhere in this biography). "Failures in the responses of the mirroring and the idealized selfobjects," Kohut and Wolf write, "lead to the gradual replacement of the selfobjects and their functions by a self and its functions" (416). Such a self for Milton emerges fully in the later 1650s after blindness, the death of his first wife and his son, and the vituperation of critics against his political views through personal slander, as he returns to his earlier hopes for fame and great ethical achievement for humankind, the seeming interference of public duty discharged by the left hand now understood as fulfillment of those hopes as well. The function of this self—the talent that Milton often alludes to—has transformed the acquisitions of his ego (his narcissism) through creativity, through the ability to be empathic, through the capacity to contemplate his own impermanence, and through his wisdom.[13]

Milton's great purpose in life as he expressed it early and often is the major thread of this biography. It demands attention to the catalysts that fashioned that purpose, to the actions taken once that purpose was formulated and circumstances allowed its pursuit, to the alterations of understanding of that purpose and its achievement, and to the personality behind the author and the characterizations, like Eve's, which inscribe that purpose for the fit audience. While Eve has been viewed in terms of narcissistic behavior, commentators seem not to have recognized the antithesis to narcissism that she exhibits as *Paradise Lost* ends (what may be epitomized as Milton's message to the world): that is, object love.[14] We can observe the pertinency of mother identification for Eve (as her own mother figure), for the Son of *Paradise Regain'd*, and for Milton in Kohut's statement: "Just as the child's *primary empathy* with the mother is the precursor of the adult's ability to be empathic, so his *primary identity* with her must be considered as the precursor of an expansion of the self, late in life, when the finiteness of individual existence is acknowledged."[15]

In 1637 Milton's delayed reaction to the death of Edward King, in "Lycidas," records the beginning of that acknowledgment of the finiteness of his own individual existence. The expansion of Milton's self finally reaches calmness, as in the idealized mother imago, with the discharge of his masterworks, *Paradise Lost* and *Paradise Regain'd*. It reaches wisdom (implying an acceptance of limitations of physical, intellectual, and emotional powers[16]), as in the realistic father imago, with the completion and resolution of *Samson Agonistes*. In the continued pursuit and completion of these three works and the publication of early prose ventures during that "calm" following 1665, we see "not the revival of the original anal stage but the reactivation of the regressive return to anality in early latency after the retreat from shattering oedipal castration anxieties."[17]

This biography studies Milton's self in the world he encountered, exploring issues usually given only cursory prose, detailing undoubtedly more than the reader wants to know about preparations to undertake the great purpose of his life and about the significance and influence of some of the fruits of that purpose. The movement will be somewhat chronological but there will be repetitions and incremental buildings of being. What should loom large, finally, is a Milton above us all and yet one of us, human and real, a reminder that each person can have an independence of worth.

2

A Biographical and Literary Overview to 1645

John Milton is one of the world's foremost writers, largely as author of *Paradise Lost* and other poems and of *Areopagitica,* his tract arguing against prepublication censorship, as well as other prose works influential in the development of republicanism in England, the United States, and France. His presence can be felt in educational theory and reform, in the arguments for the separation of church and state, in religious toleration of schismatic or dissenting sects, in the need for accountability of political leaders and for control of government in the hands of the people, and in arguments for divorce on the grounds of incompatibility. Some later writers (such as Samuel Johnson), in strong disagreement with his antimonarchical and social stands, have tried to cast his prose into oblivion and have even extended their negative attitudes to the poetry (Hilaire Belloc, for example, who was incensed by Milton's anti–Roman Catholic position). His deep and extensive influence on the poetry of the late seventeenth century and after lies in his revisions of generic structures and forms, in his prosodic innovations, in his style and language (somewhat Latinate but much less so than was formerly thought), in his "sublimity," and in his poetry's philosophic/moral content.

His poetic influences have been both positive—through inspiration of and emulation by other major writers such as Pope, Gray, Blake, Wordsworth, Tennyson, and Joyce—and negative, through dreary superficial and repetitive imitation and appropriation of language, imagery, and prosody. The inadequacies of such poets as the eighteenth-century William Mason or Mark Akenside have been the source of some twentieth-century indictments against Milton and his influence, as well as the masterful achievements of "Romantic" poets such as Shelley, impugned by such twentieth-century critics as Pound, Eliot, and Babbitt.

Much detail is known about Milton's life, not only through documentary sources but also through his own recountings of his activities and hopes (particularly in *The Reason of Church Government* and *Pro Pop-*

ulo Anglicano Defensio Secunda), and, most unusual for the times, through near-contemporary biographies. These include a brief, anonymous life (probably by his former student, amanuensis, and friend Cyriack Skinner), minutes for a life compiled by the antiquarian John Aubrey, biographical entries by Anthony Wood in *Athenæ Oxonienses,* and fairly full biographies by his older nephew, Edward Phillips (1694), and John Toland (1698).

Milton was born on December 9, 1608, on Bread Street in Cheapside, London, near St. Paul's Cathedral, to Sara (Jeffrey) and John Milton, Sr., a scrivener and well-known composer, whose business involved ownership of numerous properties and the extending of loans. The younger Milton lived most of his life within the compass of the cathedral bells and, aside from a period of private tutoring and his government service during the Interregnum, did not pursue remunerative employment. He attended St. Paul's School, under Alexander Gill, and then (in 1625) Christ's College, Cambridge, receiving the bachelor's degree in 1629 and the master of arts in 1632. An early private tutor was Thomas Young, the TY of the antiprelatical acronym SMECTYMNUUS, who apparently was instrumental in bringing Milton into the controversy that led to his first prose publications in 1641. An older sister, Anne, mother of his two nephews, Edward and John Phillips, and a younger brother, Christopher, survived into adulthood. His closest friend from days at St. Paul's School was Charles Diodati, to or about whom he wrote both letters and poems; Diodati died in 1638 while Milton was in Italy.

Milton's years at Christ's College saw him rusticated to his family home in London in 1626, apparently through some altercation with his tutor, William Chappell, and given the sobriquet "The Lady of Christ's," perhaps for his youthful looks, more probably for his high moral attitude and lack of participation in his classmates' social and athletic activities. His course of study was ministerial, and his signing the Subscription Books in 1629 and 1632 indicates that this vocational intention had not yet altered, as it perhaps had by 1637 or so. (Among the Articles of Religion he subscribed to were the liturgy and doctrines of the Church of England and royal supremacy.)

Upon graduation he lived at his parents' home in Hammersmith and then in Horton, Bucks—his "studious retirement"—probably because of their increasing dependency. His mother died in 1637. A living arrangement for his father with his brother and his brother's wife enabled him to tour France and Italy, with a servant, in 1638-39. Upon his return he began schoolteaching, his two nephews being his first boarding students, with others joining as day-students. In 1642, at thirty-three, he married sixteen-year-old Mary Powell, who returned to her parents' home in Oxford soon afterward, not returning to her husband until 1645. Her family was Royalist, and the marriage seems to have been arranged, apparently because of her father's indebtedness to Milton's father. During this period Milton wrote and published various prose works, some, however, being published later or posthumously. It was also during this period that *Paradise Lost* and perhaps the other two major poems were begun, or so it has been speculated.

Milton's poetry written during these years, 1624-45, was gathered into his first volume of shorter poems, entered in the Stationers' Register on October 6, 1645, and perhaps published in late December. The poems are divided between English and Latin texts, and subdivided into thematic or generic categories. Three poems from this period were omitted but are included in the second edition of 1673, and two Latin fragments were discovered in 1874 with his Commonplace Book. Whether further texts were produced (such as additional translations of psalms or an alleged third poem on Hobson, the coachman, who provided travel between London and Cambridge) is uncertain.

These shorter poems, such as the Gunpowder Plot poems or the Latin poems on deceased Cambridge personages, find their sources in college exercises. Others were written in commemoration, including "An Epitaph on the Marchioness of Winchester" and the two canonical Hobson poems. Still others arise from personal experience (other of the Latin elegies or the sonnets), in writing tasks set for himself—"On the Morning of *Christs* Nativity" or the so-called English odes ("On Time," "Upon the Circumcision," "At a Solemn Music"), or in commissioned work—"Arcades" and "A Mask." ("A Mask" was revised in 1738 by John Dalton, with music by Thomas Arne, incorporating verses and the character of Euphrosyne from "L'Allegro." Its refocussing of action and treatment henceforth popularly renamed the poem "Comus.")

The earliest extant completed poem is "A Paraphrase on Psalm 114," dated 1624, prior to Milton's entry into Christ's. It is an important work for an understanding of Milton and his craft because of its subject matter and its treatment. While the commonplace school method of learning foreign languages and "composition" was translation from Greek and Latin into English and its reversal (the psalms providing the more usual vehicle), this particular paraphrase (only one other early rendition of a psalm was preserved, "Psalm 136") treats the miraculous delivery of the Israelites out of bondage in Egypt through the parting of the Red Sea. Delivered into a new wilderness, Canaan, the chosen people are to proceed to glory through faith under the guidance of God. The lines ending *Paradise Lost*, which recall another Passover psalm, Psalm 107, stress the same belief in God's Providence, the Exodus from the life of "bondage" and ease of the immediate past (Pharaoh was equated with Satan by interpreters of the Bible), the potential for salvation in the new world that lies before humankind, and especially the miracles that God will bring to pass for his faithful servants. Indeed, had Adam had faith in God and "miraculous" solution to the dilemma he faced in eating or not eating of the fruit of the Tree of Knowledge, he would not have been disobedient, for he was "not deceav'd." Adam's action, not Eve's, ordains human fate in the poem. Milton's treatment of the Genesis story of the Fall, while he could not reverse its biblical narrative and outcome, pits a human Adam against the potential human who would have believed that the Lord "glassy flouds from rugged rocks can crush, / And make soft rills from fiery flint-stones gush." The thought and the belief encased in this paraphrase—that God will save the faithful as the "miracle" of his bringing water from the rock metaphorizes—lie at the base of everything Milton wrote, though human despair may occasionally enter for a brief moment.

But the psalm paraphrase also exhibits another basic concept for Milton and illustrates an attitude (and compositional approach) that emerges elsewhere. In the first line Milton renders "the house of Jacob" as "the blest seed of *Terah*'s faithfull Son"; that is, Jacob, who was the son of (faithful) Abraham, who was the son of Terah. The emphasis on the father and his passage of faith and inspiration to the son is the keystone of Milton's "Ad Patrem" (which should be read as "To My Father," not "To His Father"), of the relationship between God the Father and God the Son in *Paradise Lost* (and we should note particularly that the Son ascends to defeat Satan and his cohorts in the War in Heaven in the "Chariot of Paternal Deity," the only use of this epithet for Ezekiel's chariot in biblical discourse), and of the way we read *Samson Agonistes*. In the latter dramatic poem, Samson's father, Manoa, is not presented as a father figure adequate for emulation; Samson, instead, must learn truly to have faith in his Divine Father, and once achieving this he is able to become the Great Deliverer he was prophesied to be. He goes to the Feast of Dagon saying, not unlike the Faithful traversing the Red Sea, "Happ'n what may, of me expect to hear / Nothing dishonourable, impure, unworthy / Our God, our Law, my nation, or my self, / The last of me or no I cannot warrant" (1423-26).

Milton's concept of God as Father sets up, on the one hand, doctrinal beliefs and acceptance of God's ways toward humankind, for "All is, if [he] has grace to use it so, / As ever in [his] great task-maisters eye" (Sonnet 7). On the other hand, it is a concept that helps separate the father figure proffered as the king by such political writers as Sir Robert Filmer in *Patriarcha* as no father, or as a false father at best. The psychological significance for Milton that can be read into such positive emphasis on the father is manifest. It is not what has become the standard Freudian oedipal complex; for Milton the emulation does not involve envy and overgoing, but praise and imitation.

What Milton demonstrates in this paraphrase of Psalm 114 is the need to interpret or to render meaningful for a human audience the truths of the Bible. In *De doctrina christiana* he asserted that the truths of the Bible should stand forth with literal meaning (4-5), but the numerous and conflicting readings that others had propounded make him realize that, as he said in *The Reason of Church Government*, the minister and the poet need to dress Truth elegantly so that "those especially of soft and delicious temper . . . will . . . look upon Truth herselfe" (38). His remarks to Young, an exiled Anglican minister, in *Elegia quarta*, iterate the point when he talks of those "whom provident God himself has sent . . ., and who bring joyous messages from heaven, and who teach the way which leads beyond the grave to the stars" (ll. 92-94). In the psalm paraphrase he adds lines 2, 4, 8, and 10, and compresses in lines 13-14 the four lines of verses 5 and 6. His Greek translation of this same psalm in 1634 puts the sixteen lines of Hebrew into twenty-two lines of Greek while keeping closer to the original than the earlier rendition did. The added lines of the paraphrase stress the toil of the past, the strength of the Almighty's hand, and the power of God over the foe with a biblical allusion to Revelation 6:16.

Throughout his poetry and prose Milton rendered the truths of the Bible not only by citation and paraphrase but by interpretation, as would a minister in the pulpit, and by imaginative dressing of Truth, whether it meant creating angelic characters like Abdiel (in *Paradise Lost*) or antagonists like Harapha (in *Samson Agonistes*) or expanding the threefold Temptation of Jesus in the Wilderness (in *Paradise Regain'd*) to involved subdivisions of the three basic motifs and to imaginary "action," such as Jesus's dream or his endurance of a night of storm. As well, the burden of some of the prose—*Tetrachordon* is a good example—is the interpretation of the Bible for those he felt incapable of reading it cogently: in his divorce tract of 1645 he presented "Expositions upon the foure chief places in Scripture, which treat of Mariage, or nullities in Mariage. . . . Wherin the Doctrine and Discipline of Divorce, as was lately publish'd, is confirm'd by explanation of Scripture. . . . "

The 1645 collection of Milton's shorter poems has as frontispiece a portrait by William Marshall, a badly drawn representation perhaps based on another portrait (the so-called [Arthur] Onslow portrait, from its eighteenth-century owner) showing a very youthful-looking twenty-one-year-old. Below the portrait medallion, around which are four of the muses, one in each corner, is a poem in Greek script jocularly criticizing the artist for his "bad imitation" of an unrecognized "modelled face." The muses pictured point to the nature of the poetry of the volume: Erato, lyric; Clio, historical (and personal); Urania, sacred; and Melpomene, tragic. In the background, out a window, is a pastoral scene depicting another division of the poems. First are sacred texts, beginning with "On the morning of *Christs* Nativity" (1629) and including "The Passion" and the English odes. "The Passion" appears, although "the Author" found the subject "to be above the yeers he had, when he wrote it, and nothing satisfi'd with what was begun, left it unfinisht," because Milton, as true child of God, was offering up a full record of his achievements and ambitions, successful or not. Presented is an eight-stanza proem (in contrast to the four-stanza proem of the Nativity poem) but a text on the crucifixion is missing. The commonplace double vision of the poet (compare John Donne's "The Annunciation and Passion") prompted Milton's attempt to write this poem in spring 1630 as companion to the Nativity "ode" (as he calls it in l. 24).

Created as four stanzas in a variation of rime royal[1] (appropriate for the King of Peace), followed by twenty-seven uniquely structured stanzas of "The Hymn," the Nativity ode treats the significance of the birth of Jesus and its effect upon the world. It does not narrate the birth. Major motifs in the poem are light (since the Son is "that Light unsufferable," "that far-beaming blaze of Majesty") and dark, and music (including the hymn itself, which joins "the Angel Quire") and silence (as in the silencing of the Oracles and the "hideous humm" with the binding of "Th'old Dragon underground"). The hymn moves to its central point in stanza 14 when, through the redemption of Christ, "speckl'd vanity," "leprous sin," and "Hell it self" will have passed away. Thus the proem depicts the eternal world of God's heaven, now taking on a human dimension in the Incarnation, followed by a song of praise beginning in the "Winter wilde" of the Nativity, progressing to the Apocalypse, when God's children will be saved and Satan will be chained underground, and then returning to the Nativity scene (stanza 27), where "the Virgin blest, / Hath laid her Babe to rest," after the 'historical' effect of Peace in the world has been enounced.

The poem was being composed in December 1629 when Milton wrote a Latin elegy to his friend Charles Diodati, who was vacationing in the north country. Here in "Elegia sexta" he contrasts what a later age will label the Dionysian poet (that is, Diodati) and the Apollonian poet (Milton), "singing the King, bringer of peace by his divine origin, / and the blessed times promised in the sacred books." It has long been recognized that the Nativity ode encapsulates Milton's steady beliefs and concerns, particularly in *Paradise Lost* (this comparison manifesting the major "message" and intentionality of the epic), and is built upon those elements that will reemerge in other works, such as the catalogue of false gods and their destruction, its biblical allusiveness,[2] and its employment of myth while maintaining unswerving belief in the truth of the monomyth of Christ. The disengagement of a text from its companion poetical texts has been a heritage of twentieth-century critical stances, but to privilege in this way is to read Milton inadequately and at times inaccurately. The interpretation and amplification of the Bible that was noted before is evidenced again here and repeatedly.

The Nativity ode also provides the kind of experimentation with form and structure discussed earlier. The distanced window the proem provides for the hymn is not dissimilar to the perspective that the leave-taking of "Lycidas" creates for its ten verse paragraphs or to the first book of *Paradise Regain'd* read against the remainder of the brief epic, with a frame provided by the new induction in Book II and the final verse paragraph assigned to the narrative voice in Book IV. The progression to the apex of stanza 14, noted above, is similar to the progression in the diffuse epic to the defeat of Satan by the Son, in the Chariot of Paternal Deity (*PL* VI, 762). The beginning of *Paradise Lost* gives us Satan and his cohorts just before action is taken to achieve "revenge" and bring Sin and Death into the human world, and ends with the human pair just before the action of goodness and evil (shown representatively in Books XI and XII) will take place in the human world, outside the womb of Eden.

The mystical significance of numbers (created ultimately by God and illuminating His ubiquitous divine presence) can be seen in the four seven-line stanzas of the proem (three being the number of divinity and four the number of humankind, seven becomes the number of creation), as well as the eight-line stanzas of the hymn (eight signifying the age of Christ after the seven ages of human life have passed). Further, the *third* line of the poem presents a chiasmus, a chi, X, the sign of Christ: "Of wedded Maid, and Virgin Mother born." In *Paradise Lost* the Council in Heaven occurs in Book III, Adam and Eve are introduced in Book IV, the Creation takes place in Book VII, and Sin and Death enter the narrative in the duplicitous Book II as the originals of the two beasts in Revelation (chapter 13), with Death specifically being introduced at line 666. The unique stanza of the hymn—eight lines in 6, 6, 10, 6, 6, 10, 8, 12 syllables and rhyming a a b c c b d d—exemplifies the kind of prosodic variation Milton will continue to pursue in the English odes, "Lycidas," and the blank verse (or decasyllabic lines without rhyme) of the epics. The poet is "overgoing" his predecessors (and there are many who are influential from classical and more recent times) in examining the fundamental aspect of the subject and in its treatment, in his poetic structuring and in its prosodic lumber, and in his employment of mythic/ mystical concepts that manifest the presence of godhead.

The English odes, like the poems already discussed, evidence a poet concerned with "standard" religious beliefs, based upon Scripture, though it is in need of interpretation, and with the artifact itself in its form and metric; they present a believer who accepts mythic substructs while in no way casting that myth out of Truth; and they give further testimony to the preacher/teacher concept and category for the poet. They reflect a study of Italian canzoni, specifically of the poetry of Giovanni della Casa, whose *Rime e Prose* Milton purchased in December 1629. (The volume, which also binds a copy of the *Sonetti* of Benedetto Varchi, is owned by the New York Public Library.) Perhaps around spring 1630 Milton wrote a brief sonnet sequence, five sonnets and a canzone in Italian, and the three odes may have been written some time after 1633 and by 1637, the probable date of the third. "On Time" and "Upon the Circumcision" (working on the importance of sacred time and on the Feast of the Circumcision, January 1) again incorporate eschatological thought, with a double vision of birth and redemption. "At a Solemn Music," which is composed in the important poetic notebook called the Trinity MS, specifically engages salvation for those who follow God and plays upon the harmoniousness of true servants on Earth (and represented by the poet) and of the saved singers before the throne of God (Revelation 7:9). This is the only poem worked out in the manuscript, all others being transcriptions to begin with, although most are revised therein. The manuscript is owned by the Trinity College (Cambridge) Library, probably having been deposited there by Milton's last amanuensis, Daniel Skinner, who became a fellow of the College after Milton's death. It also records a letter to an unknown friend (Young?) and its revision, and subjects and brief outlines for various dramas drawn from the Bible, British history, and Scotch history. The manuscript could not have been begun before 1634 (the date of "Arcades" and "Comus") but more likely dates, as has been argued, from autumn 1637. It records short original poems in English written through 1658(?), the last ones being written down by amanuenses.

The three odes indicate a few other matters of biographical significance: they show a Milton who is consciously experimenting with form and prosody, they evidence a continued tinkering with his poems, and they suggest a concern with the writing of poetry as bid to fame, not observable in works prior to his leaving Cambridge in 1632. The prosodic experimentation will triumph in the meters and rhyming of the verse paragraphs of "Lycidas" (November 1637). It takes advantage of a relationship with meaning—as in the minimizing trimeters of ll. 6-8 of

"On Time" and in the alexandrine of its last line: "Triumphing over Death, and Chance, and thee O Time." In rhyming schemes of the odes, meaning is seen in the way less ordered rhyme becomes ordered (becomes "harmonious" through couplets). The linkages of trimeters (thirteen) and pentameters in the pastoral elegy, the seemingly disordered rhyme and unrhymed lines (ten within verse paragraphs), which are transcended by the ottava rima of the leave-taking (a form, significantly, almost achieved at the beginning of the last, the tenth, verse paragraph), demonstrate that a more "harsh din" can be replaced by the "undiscording voice" of those whose "motion sway'd / In perfect Diapason" through the love of "thir great Lord" upon them ("At a Solemn Music," 20, 17, 22-23). The miraculous God is always in Milton's thoughts.

Two of the odes evidence the same kind of tinkering with poems that the second edition of *Paradise Lost* exhibits (there is more change than simply the revision from ten books into twelve) and that lines 143-44 of the Nativity ode show in its second edition of 1673. First, in "Upon the Circumcision" ll. 13-14 and 27-28 are each given as one in the Trinity MS and then are divided (after 1640 the handwriting shows, perhaps when the 1645 edition was being prepared) into the printed two. Second, in the three and a half manuscript drafts of "At a Solemn Music" the last line appears four times, rather shockingly, as "To live & sing with him in endlesse morne of light." The revision of the 1645 printing corrects the doctrinal error: "To live with him, and sing in endles morn of light." God, of course, does not join the palmers in their singing before His throne! In other words, Milton is a creative artist who may keep revising his texts to "improve" them metrically, imagistically, structurally, and even substantively. One should not be surprised to find revisions between versions of "Comus" or "Lycidas" or the sonnets or *Paradise Lost*, nor in the two other major poems, were there more than one version of them. Unlike Charles Lamb, who, when he saw the Trinity MS, was dismayed that "Lycidas" did not come full blown from the author's mind, readers should recognize the anal personality who is not always certain that his work is quite as he wishes it, and who thus is retentive and somewhat secretive. There is a kind of perfectionism in Milton toward his studies and writing and ordering of his life, a lack of satisfaction with what is done and its interruption. Accompanying such a subconscious is the strong ego domination of privilege and dismissal of the purportedly inferior. (Compare ll. 79-80 of "Ad Patrem" and the sonnet "A book was writt of late call'd *Tetrachordon*" for this sociological attitude.)

The next group of poems in the 1645 edition are mixed, although four are elegiac pieces, including the two humorous and somewhat "metaphysical" Hobson poems and "On Shakespear," written in 1630 and published—the first poem by Milton in print—in the Second Folio of the *Workes* without authorial indication. This poem was revised before it was reprinted in Milton's collection (it had also appeared in Shakespeare's 1640 *Poems,* where it is assigned to "I. M."). It has come in for deconstructed readings in recent years, under the sway of "the anxiety of influence" or its rebuttal. The poem is a tissue of likenesses to other poems on Shakespeare that Milton could have known, and it would not be considered remarkable or memorable did it not interface the two major poets of England. Joining these four poems are "Song. On *May* Morning" and the companion pieces, "L'Allegro" and "Il Penseroso," all of which were written during Milton's college years. The other elegiac poem, "An Epitaph on the Marchioness of Winchester," written around April 1631, offers iambic tetrameter couplets, some of which are headless, the basic meter of the companion poems. These somewhat "pastoral" poems are therefore usually dated 1631 and generally in the summer vacation of that year, before Milton's graduation. They have been exceedingly popular over the years, and their meter (as well as their dialectic) influenced unrelentingly the poetry of the eighteenth century (and beyond) through the development of the octosyllabic couplet form for general lyrics, pastorals, and odes.

"Il Penseroso," which is a bit longer, is considered the better poem, "L'Allegro" perhaps showing the less confident accomplishment often necessary as preparation for a more sustained art. The overreading that has been extended to the companion poems has made them biographical statements of the "Happy Man, L'Allegro," that side of Milton's personality revelling in the countryside, the daytime, "comic" literature and drama, and the like, or of the "Contemplative Man, Il Penseroso," that side of Milton's personality given to study, night hours, serious works, and the like. ("Il Penseroso," being longer and better, of necessity becomes the better representation of Milton in this interpretation.) Of course, even a superficial reading of the poems indicates that the dichotomies of place, time, and activity are not present exclusively in either one, although the dialectic of the "Happy" or the "Contemplative" human provides the basic imagery of humour description. The ten-line proems to each poem indicate that the first expels Melancholy so that Mirth can be fully described, and the second expels "vain deluding joyes" so that Melancholy can be fully described.

The proems, the basic substance of the poems, and their impetus lie in Robert Burton's *Anatomy of Melancholy* (1621), which begins with an influential preliminary poem. "The Author's Abstract of Melancholy. A Dialogue" offers some similar images, the oppositions between "pleasing thoughts" and "a thousand pleasures," and "All my joys besides are folly, / None so sweet as Melancholy," and octosyllabic couplets. The meter and imagery of the proems derive from a song in John Fletcher's *Nice Valour* ("Hence, all you vain delights, / As short as are the nights / Wherein you spend your folly, . . . But only melancholy, / Oh, sweetest melancholy," etc.). The last two lines of each poem reprise Christopher Marlowe's "Come live with me and be my love." The companion poems are not biographical indices to Milton's personality nor products of the career poet; they are wonderful poetic exercises for a coterie; they are a piling up of images that can be seen to delineate two personality types; and they reflect the close imitation of other writers, as do "On Shakespear," "On the Death of a fair Infant dying of a Cough" (added in 1673), and such Latin poems as "Elegia quinta."

The sonnets are printed next in 1645—the first ten, that is, which include the nightingale poem and the Italian sequence. Milton's sonnets take the Petrarchan, or Italianate, form: an octave and a sestet, with the volta (or turn) occurring at the end of the eighth line, and with a rhyme scheme most frequently a b b a a b b a   c d e c d e. Later sonnets will alter the position of the volta, exhibit some rhyme variation (as here in Sonnet 8, where the sestet is c d c d c d), and will increase enjambment. The form indicates a background in the octave with its resolution in the sestet, which thus becomes the more meaningful section. For example, in the seventh sonnet, which was apparently written shortly after his twenty-third birthday (December 1631) the poet presents what seem to be discrepancies between his age and his being: his late spring has shown no bud or blossom (which might become a fruit); his semblance suggests a younger person; his inward maturity shows much less than in others of his age. Out of this set of circumstances comes the realization—his main point of importance to himself, and perhaps to others—that his lot will be that to which he is brought by Time and by the will of Heaven: as long as he has grace upon him, all will be as God has foreseen.

One way of looking at the poem is as rationalization of a life that has as yet accomplished little, if anything. But a more cogent understanding is Milton's acceptance of the almighty and miraculous God of the Psalm 114 paraphrase. This is a Calvinistic God who has predestinated humankind, has shed his grace upon some, and is a taskmaster for all believers. The statement is reassurance for Milton, about to be graduated from Christ's College with a master's degree, a time when he would have wondered what his future would achieve. (The title made up for this poem by Elijah Fenton in 1725, "On His Having Arriv'd at the Age of Twenty-Three," is useful though susceptible of misdirection to the reader.) The poem is not concerned with any specific career ("bud" and "blossom" do not refer to literary works, as early commentators, through hindsight, urged).

The seemingly biographical love-sonnet sequence of 1630(?), in which the narrative line has Milton falling in love with a girl from the Italian community, we shall look at in Chapter 3. More than a decade intervenes between the first seven sonnets, written during his college years, and sonnets 8-10, dated 1642-44?, and much has happened to Milton in his way of life, his experiences, his "vocation," and his writing activities. In these years there is the "studious retirement," so frequently referred to, the Italian journey, and the return to London, where he set up a school and began his public career as a prose writer in opposition to prelacy and censorship and in favor of divorce and reformed education.

The sonnets from number eight onward often fuse the political with the personal, the epideictic with the parænetic. While the potential soldier at his door in the first of the Civil Wars (November 1642) is praised, he is also admonished not to lift his spear "against the Muses Bowre." While the might of the spear (or sword) is acknowledged, it is the pen that is mightier, that brings fame "o're Lands and Seas, / What ever clime the Suns bright circle warms." Milton is now a determined poet as his bid to fame. The war and its performers bring destruction; poetry— Pindar's, Euripides', the author's—brings a lasting name, avoids ruin bare. While much of Milton's poetry is political, it should not be delimited to only some of the narrower concerns of current historicist literary critics.

In Sonnet 8 the personal emerges in several ways: there is the ego reinforcement in the author's coupling himself with Pindar and Euripides (which also has some of the ludicrous about it); there is the derision of the ignorant force that by "chance" may come to *his* door, though he represents no counterforce of battle (a political image through its disparagement of power); and there is the fear that indeed this could come to pass, creating but a mute, inglorious Milton for aftertimes. Behind this last perception, of course, is Milton's personal context: he was then, in 1640 through 1642, engaged in work on his great poem, for which the Trinity MS records four distinct outlines (one even being so revised that it takes on almost separate identity). In the serious context of the poem lies the abortive life depicted in "Lycidas" as well as that poem's answer to despair and cynicism: God's Judgment of His true servants. The question of power is at the base of the sonnet, but it is inextricably woven with the personal.

Sonnet 9 both praises some young lady for her moral being (identifications have been offered without any foundation other than the zeal of the conjecturer) and gives advice, though subtly. Continue in your narrow path (Matthew 7:14) is the message, and the implication is the experiential one that that is very difficult to do in this our life. Many "fret their spleen" at her "growing vertues," and though "No anger" has yet been provoked, only "pity and ruth," an unstated warning can be heard. Why Milton was known as "The Lady of Christ's" is discerned by reading this sonnet: one does not need to rush into marriage because one is coming to an age that society assigns as a boundary for the unmarried. This Milton counsels when he is thirty-four, having married at thirty-three. In his wifeless life he may be regretting his succumbing to societal demands even at his "older" age. And the next sonnet, addressed to Lady Margaret Ley, praises her through praise of her father, as he will praise Edward Lawrence through his father and Cyriack Skinner through his grandfather (Sonnets 20 and 21): the Father/Son relationship again shows itself fundamental to Milton's thinking.

The final three poems in the 1645 collections are commissioned and dramatic works, "Arcades" and "A Mask" ("Comus"), and a pastoral elegy, "Lycidas." Products of the studious retirement in 1634, the first two works came into being through the important musician Henry Lawes, perhaps a friend of Milton's father, and his position as music tutor to the children of John Egerton, Earl of Bridgewater. "Arcades" is "Part of an entertainment presented to the Countess Dowager of *Darby* at *Harefield*" on the occasion of her seventy-fifth birthday, May 4, 1634. Members of the family (probably her grandchildren) took part in pastoral costume, and Lawes performed the role of the Genius of the Wood, presenting songs and speech in a procession leading to the countess, seated in state. The first song (in four stanzas, the first being different from the others) reflects influence from Ben Jonson's masques; the Genius then appears and speaks (in couplets); and two more songs conclude Milton's contribution to the celebration. Sources also lie in Vergil's *Aeneid*, Greek mythology, and Platonic/Pythagorean cosmology, sources traceable in the Nativity ode as well. At this time Milton was living in Hammersmith, not in Horton, Bucks, as early critical accounts assumed, placing him nearer to the countess's residence in Harefield, near Uxbridge, Middlesex. The countess was Alice Spencer, to whom Edmund Spenser dedicated "Teares of the Muses" and praised as Amaryllis in "Colin Clouts Come Home Againe." She was the widow of Ferdinando Stanley, Lord Strange, Earl of Derby, and of Sir Thomas Egerton, Lord Ellesmere and Viscount Brackley, for whom John Donne had worked. Her daughter Frances married her step-son John Egerton, who became the Earl of Bridgewater; their three children, Lady Alice, John Lord Brackley, and Thomas, apparently took part in "Arcades" as they did in "Comus."

Milton's connection with aristocratic and titled people continues throughout his life, despite his political views and position and others' royalist sympathies. Likewise his relation to Anglicans persists despite his

Puritan views and argument against prelacy. Significant for "Arcades" is the liturgy for a date associated with its occasion according to the Anglican Book of Common Prayer (Milton himself having been a recent ministerial student ostensibly in the Church of England): 1 Kings 10:6-7, which underlies the second stanza.

In September of that same year, on Michaelmas eve, September 29, 1634, Milton's masque was presented at the installation at Ludlow Castle of the Earl of Bridgewater as Lord President of Wales. Again with music by Lawes, who played the Attendant Spirit/Thyrsis, and the three children, plus other actors as Comus, Sabrina, and various attendants or members of Comus's rout, the poem breaks out of the usual mold by engaging a "plot," being much longer than others of the genre, presenting rather long speeches by various characters, and reducing the music and dance in comparison with the speeches. Five songs have come down to us in two transcriptions (one by Lawes himself), suggesting that there was less dance and song than in works like Aurelian Townshend's "Tempe Restor'd" (1632). (There is a "Measure" indicated for Comus's crew for which there is no music; this was a dance "in a wild rude & wanton antick," as the Trinity MS has it.) The major difficulty in assessing the poem's generic alterations is that the received text (probably published in early 1638; the title page gives 1637, which is Old Style dating) is an expansion and revision of the text presented in 1634. A manuscript called the Bridgewater MS has often been taken as representing the text employed in 1634 (though it may not be); this is shorter and relates better to two of the extant songs than the basic version in the Trinity MS or the published version. This same difficulty casts questions on the interpretation and intent of the work, since the received text places stresses that do not appear so strongly in the basic Trinity MS or the Bridgewater MS transcriptions.

The plot presents a young lady and her two brothers who have lost their way in a dark forest one evening on the way to their father's house. The brothers leave the lady, who has become tired, to seek refreshment, and have not returned before Comus, son of Bacchus and Circe, has fraudulently offered to help her find her brothers and bring her "to a low / But loyal cottage, where [she] may be safe / Till furder quest." Instead he immanacles her in an enchanted chair, offers her refreshment, and attempts to seduce her, which she resists. His followers are likened to the swine into which Circe had transformed Ulysses' men; the Lady's succumbing to his temptations would place her among them "To roul with pleasure in a sensual stie." But the Attendant Spirit (a version of the Genius of the Wood of the earlier poem) takes on the guise of Thyrsis, a shepherd in the children's father's household, and intercepts the brothers, who have been talking of the dangers that might beset their sister left alone in this wood. He instructs them how to free their sister, to whom he takes them, but they do not snatch Comus's wand and thus they cannot free the Lady. Thyrsis then calls upon Sabrina, a virgin who holds sway over the Severn (a river of Wales), to free the Lady, which she does. The scene changes to Ludlow Town and the President's Castle, and the Attendant Spirit/Thyrsis leads the children to join others in procession to the parents who sit in state. (The ending has close affinities with the procession in the earlier poem.) The allegoric subtext is clear and will appear again in the three major poems. Its moral significance (particularly in terms of virginity and chastity) will be taken up further in Chapter 3.

This allegoric subtext goes to the heart of Milton's personal beliefs throughout his life, despite, always, the possibility that the journey may be cut short at any point before the quest has been fulfilled. Three years later Milton explored the latter subject in "Lycidas," galvanizing himself in his belief that the great taskmaster's eye will always be upon him. The allegoric temptation motif provides the plotting of *Paradise Regain'd,* supports the three central episodes of *Samson Agonistes,* and is shown originating in Eve's seduction by Satan in *Paradise Lost.* Milton's allegoric mind employs this motif, as well as the quest theme, as lesson for his readers, in all four poems.

The first volume of Milton's shorter poems also includes "Lycidas," written in November 1637 and published in a memorial volume for Edward King, former fellow student at Christ's College, in 1638, and the Latin poems. The pastoral elegy will be discussed in Chapter 4: it represents the resolution of his life in dedication to the Muse and preludes his trip to the Continent in April 1638 through August 1639 to be more fit for his chosen avenue to fame. The Latin poems for the most part record occasional poetry written while in college, some of which came about to commemorate a campus dignitary or resulted from a kind of assignment, and some of which (the elegies) offer more personal statements of a biographical or seemingly biographical nature. Such biographical dimensions will figure here and there in succeeding chapters. The Latin poems also record five poems written during his Italian sojourn (three of which are epigrams on the singer Leonora Baroni, the others being addressed to acquaintances from that sojourn) and his elegy on his friend Charles Diodati, who died during his time away from England. These and the tributes to his poetic ability communicated by various Italian friends prefacing the Latin poems will be looked at particularly in Chapters 3 through 5.

Upon his return to England, Milton began tutoring his two nephews, who came to reside with him, and other boys, who were day-students; involved himself in his poetic planning and activity, his vocational decision having been made and his great purpose determined; and found himself embroiled in various controversies through 1645, when disaffection from hostile antagonists led to retraction into a more private world and the publication of the poems as solid evidence of his conceived self.

The controversies moved from arguments against prelacy, not against the religion of those now being called Anglicans, to arguments for divorce and against prepublication censorship, and a prompted statement concerning education. These prose tracts will be discussed in ensuing chapters, particularly 6 and 7. Because Milton came to be associated with what is loosely labelled Puritanism, scholars seem to forget that he was educated toward a career in what would have been Anglicanism, until "church-outed," and that the first five prose works (or six if we assign the "Postscript" to the first 1641 Smectymnuan volume to him) are of the same religious persuasion as, for example, that espoused by Stephen Marshall, who was to become a leading Presbyterian in the Westminster Assembly, or by Edmund Calamy, who was later to serve as chaplain to Charles II. Some religious perceptions remain constant, but acceptance of much of the administrative form, with its regulating canons and hierarchies, undergoes change and development in Milton's thinking. Though he seems to accept Presbyterianism for a while, he later rejects it; though he seems influenced by the Independents and their Arminian stance, he does not become a thorough Independent or Arminian; though he shows an agreement with underlying principles of much in what will be Congregationalism and Quakerism and even antinomianism, he was none of these. The antiprelatical tracts offer largely historical argument against an administrative setup, presented through oratorical debate, rebuttal in kind and including invective, and personal defense.

The divorce tracts, which caused him to be labelled "fornicator" and with other such opprobrious terms, declare his opposition to forced outward "administrative form" when the inward being of marriage has dissolved. While his own married situation may have directed his public championing of divorce, the substance of his work reacts to the dissolution of the ideal of marriage and its false outward show just as the administrative form of religion had been seen as a let on inward faith. Again late to act, as he generally was in all things, Milton's expressing dismay at licensing—the Star Chamber decree of July 11, 1637, and the Parliamentary order of June 14, 1643, had been in effect well before he wrote *Areopagitica* in November 1644—iterates rejection of outward controls and fosters development of inward being, best attained by sallying forth to confront the adversary of right reason. The "message" is that of the three major poems, of course. *Areopagitica* was written during the period when he was continuing work and thinking on his great poem— the Plans in the Trinity MS are dated 1640-42—as time from tutoring and public debate allowed. Within the tract lies the general focus and concept of *Paradise Lost,* as Edward S. Le Comte has shown.[3]

Milton's statement concerning education in June 1644, prompted by his friend Samuel Hartlib and the movement for reform he, John Dury, and John Amos Comenius were advocating, completes what Milton would claim in the *Second Defense* as his arguments for that variety of liberty called "domestic or personal." This form of liberty "seemed to be concerned with three problems: the nature of marriage itself, the education of the children, and finally the existence of freedom to express oneself."[4] Whether this is hindsight or not, his attack on the reduction of ecclesiastical liberty, domestic liberty, and later civil liberty[5] does sustain our view of Milton as one recognizing the outward restrictions that delimit inward development of self and the need to develop that inward self to counter the "evil" forces that may impinge. We can appreciate such recognition as coming from a self that sees the world through that self or is not cognizant of the world around it until that world obtrudes upon the self. Interfering with Milton's great purpose for his life, thus, are aspects of the self crying out for liberty for itself when delimited by such disruptive forces as church administration and canons, personal unhappiness and restraint, and abrogation of thought and freedom. But for Milton such recognition arises from his own being, now tethered, implying a kind of narcissism, as well as a sense of the ideal possible though thwarted by others' selves.

3

The Lady of Christ's

At the conclusion of "Epitaphium Damonis," the Latin elegy on the death of his friend Charles Diodati, Milton makes a curious pagan-Christian collocation. Of Diodati's apotheosis he writes: "You, encircled around your glorious head with a shining crown / and riding in happy bowers entwined with palm leaves, / shall pursue eternally the immortal marriage / where song and mingled lyre rage with blessed dances, / and festal orgies revel under the thyrsus of Sion" (ll. 215-19).[1] Diodati, now an angel of pure air (ll. 203-4), is haloed and resident in the happy bowers of Paradise. Earthly bowers of bliss are made, we know from "Comus," from "hyacinth and roses" (male and female symbols); in contrast such bowers as Diodati's are created by "Flowers of more mingled hew," entwined with palm leaves—the palm of the victor in life's struggle, of the multitude singing before the throne of God (Revelation 7:9). But Diodati does not simply rest in his bower: he is "riding" (*gestans*). Whether we translate this as "being carried about" for pleasure or "riding," the word *gesto* takes on the obvious meaning of his spinning round in his heavenly orbit like all angelic intelligences, but also the commonplace physical meaning of sexual intercourse. The sexual meaning is evident from the association of "bowers" and "marriage," if nothing else. The imagery here has kinship with the allegoric lines of the epilogue to "Comus," in which Milton contrasts the bower of Adonis with that of Cupid and Psyche, "farr above in spangled sheen." Adonis "oft reposes" and Venus sits sadly on the ground, no continued coition being possible. On the other hand, the marriage of heart (or body) and soul after its "wandring labours long" will bring an eternal wedding (note that Psyche is Cupid's eternal *bride*, not *wife*), and through an immaculate birth ("from her fair unspotted side") will come "Youth" (immortality; without decline) and "Joy" (heavenly bliss). In his bower Diodati will pursue his immortal marriage with God,[2] one made possible through the love that is God and the perseverance of his soul (a female symbol) through the mazes of life. The expression of apotheosis as union with God is not unusual; yet the metaphor of human union to express that divine union, though frequent in such mystical writers as St. Teresa of Avila, has been little examined in literary work such as Milton's.

The psychodynamic propensities of this metaphor are major avenues of literary investigation. Man's creative act becomes the metaphor to explain God's creation, and man's closest form of oneness, the metaphor for unity with God. The realization that all men are female counterparts in the divine marriage (in "Comus" made obvious through Psyche, the soul) leads to awareness of many mortal symbols of worthiness: motherliness, celibacy, love, tears, music, aesthetic leanings, charity, humanitarianism, etc. Further, man as supine receiver of God's insemination helps explain the antiheroic view of life, although Milton would stress that this is a union, demanding reciprocal action by both partners for consummation.[3] The initial failings of Satan can be explained as his refusal to submit to the demands of supineness, which is the prelude to fruitful union with God.[4] The antihero, who exhibits self-hate, cannot accept nonaction but wishes to assert his "maleness." When assertion of one's "maleness" is denied, it becomes the psychological source of self-hate similar to Freud's hypothesis concerning the female's "loss" of a penis as castration complex.

It should be noted, of course, that such concepts as the foregoing imply a male point of view only. Man in his inability to bring forth creation, since he is only an agent, develops a self-love of agency (the penis) and of action-driven life, involving "male" symbols of worthiness: heroism, sexual potency, war, nonsentimentalism ("emotional strength"), mechanical and technological leanings, etc. We can see in the preceding the sources of our commonplace separation of things in terms of sex: careers, sports, the activities one engages in, handwriting, attire, physical beauty, and so forth. Man's view of the female thus focuses on creation and the achievement of continuance (through birth and nurture, through love, through the arts), and, to counter such female qualities within himself, he praises destructive, mechanical, short-lived action. The male's inadequacy to generate and maintain develops self-hate, by reversal, when he is denied "male" command and dominance. Satan, as his interview with Chaos and Old Night in Book II of *Paradise Lost* makes clear, is dedicated not to *non*creation but to *un*creation, the reversal of what is created back to its "original" elements. As archetypal antihero he must nullify totally the achievement of the creative spirit. Unfortunately, since Judeo-Christian societies have been male-oriented, our philosophies, literatures, and other expressions have reflected only this male point of view.

In "Epitaphium Damonis" Diodati is worthy because of his "sweet and holy simplicity," his "radiant virtue," his "blushing modesty," his "youth without blemish," and because he did not taste of "the delight of marriage." The reward of virginity is salvation, according to Revelation 14:4: "These are they which were not defiled with women; for they are virgins. These are they which follow the Lamb withersoever he goeth." Likewise in his friendship for Milton, Diodati has shown his worthiness (ll. 37-56). The apotheosis is certain, to Milton, and implied when he cites the passing of the eleventh day. Diodati will not crumble to dust in an unwept sepulchre "if there is any worth in having cultivated the ancient faith and piety / and the arts of Pallas" (ll. 33-34), but "now daylight is present after the eleventh night" (l. 156). He has reached that point in time when he must "weep" for Diodati.[5] But this also suggests twelfth night after he has completed his poem; twelfth night thus becomes the epiphany, or manifestation of divinity, of Diodati. The poem itself becomes the epiphany.

The apotheosis involves "song and mingled lyre," which "rage [*furit*] with blessed dances," and "festal orgies," which "revel under the thyrsus of Sion." The Bacchic dance of ecstasy is a frenzied simulation of sexual intercourse: here there is harmony and yet also enfevered movement. The marriage is continually celebrated as this line imports. It is "festal," that is, sacred, and yet orgiastic; and capping the pagan-Christian collocation is the thyrsus of Sion. The thyrsus was a staff twined with ivy and vine shoots borne by Bacchantes, and Sion is the heavenly city of God, that is, God himself. The phallic image is clear; and the ivy and vine shoots symbolize immortality and generation. The vision of God with such human attributes is startling, yet to one like Milton it must have been further evidence of God's mysterious being which God tries to communicate to man through man's awareness of himself. But undoubtedly it has worked the other way: man in his attempt to galvanize himself against the void of death and nonbeing has fashioned a myth built on personal observation. Since life ensues for man only through coitus, with the implications of sexual differentiation before, during, and after the act, he can make "Death the Gate of Life" (*PL* XII, 571) only through a like act. Life emerges from intercourse; therefore, eternal life must ensue upon divine intercourse.

Even the metaphor of "gate" is dependent upon sexual meaning,[6] and the common meaning of "to die" is played on. The "gate" suggests the enclosed garden (Paradise) to be reached through entrance. The enclosed garden, or *hortus conclusus* of Song of Solomon 4:12, is a womb symbol,[7] and the womb as symbol of return brings the metaphor full circle. Exit through the "gate" of the enclosed garden-as-womb of generation is birth, from the secure, known world into the uncertain, unknown world of life; entrance through the "gate" of the enclosed garden-as-womb of return is death, from the trials and tribulations of this life to the bliss and serenity which are God. There is, of course, a reversal of

sexual relationship implied in this metaphor, from that of God as Father
to God as Mother figure, that aspect underlying the feminine attributes
of the Son (or the Holy Spirit).[8] That is, God as Father effects creation,
God as Mother bears, God as Mother admits man to return, and God as
Father unites man to himself.

The ending of "Epitaphium Damonis" thus places Diodati in
Heaven as the eternal bride of the Bridegroom; the marriage is accompanied by a dance of life, harmony, and "sexual" motion. This immortal
marriage receives particular significance because Diodati has "tasted not
at all" of "the delight of marriage" (l. 213). Indeed, he has "rejected the
rainbow with his foot" (l. 204). The imagery is involved: the rainbow is
the sign of God's covenant with Noah; it appears after the storms of life,
after "tears"; and Diodati is now in the pure air above the middle air in
which storms are generated. Implicitly, however, he has rejected a covenant involving water (a specifically female symbol), and he has rejected
it with his foot (a specifically phallic symbol).

The passage is thus seen to be underpinned by the worthiness of celibacy. The fire (a male image) in the festal orgies under the thyrsus of
Sion implies not only a balance to the destruction flood but also the sexual fulfillment that has come for Diodati through Death, his death becoming the gate (an explicitly female symbol). As Milton writes of
Diodati's death and his apotheosis, he views his dead friend as "female"
whose death is metaphorically a gate, who is united to God by the im-
mortalizing thyrsus of God, and who has assured himself of this position
by his actions in life, primarily his celibacy. Diodati has not been antiheroic in matters of faith; his life has shown "sweet and holy simplicity,"
"radiant virtue"; he is "Among the souls of heroes." But one wonders
why there has been so much emphasis on this mythic statement. Beneath the remarks are a sense of wrongness in human sexual activity
and a celebration of those who can conquer and control such human
bodily needs. "Blushing modesty" was dear to Diodati, according to Milton, but note the participle as well as the phrase "youth without blemish"
("sine labe juventus").

Although the metaphor is not unique, one is struck, I think, by the
imagery, which suggests psychodynamic signification. In addition to this
ending the reader recalls the prior statements of the poem which
present the poet's sense of loss (ll. 37-49, 83-86, 94-111). Implied is a homoerotic relationship, with Diodati as more dominantly "masculine" and
Milton more recessively "feminine." The poet surely reflects here the
tears and music and aesthetic leanings associated with the female. Such
an interpretation gives further meaning to lines like "with what *incessant* complaints he vexed the *caves* / and *rivers*, the wandering *streams*

and *recesses* of the woods" (ll. 5-6); "as the evil southwind / rattled all the *doors*, and whistles in the *elm above*" (ll. 48-49); "hidden in the *shade* of an *oak*, / and the nymphs return to their well-known haunts beneath the *waters*, / and the shepherds lie concealed, the farmer snores under a hedge, / who will bring back to me your flatteries, who then / your laughter and Attic salt, your cultured graces?" (ll. 52-56); "Alas, how entangled with insolvent weeds are my once cultivated / *fields*, and the *tall grain* itself is *drooping* with *neglect*, / the *unmarried grape withers* on its *slighted vine*, / nor do *myrtle groves* delight" (ll. 63-66); and "What is to become of you, Thyrsis? / What do you wish for yourself? that brow of youth is not wont to be / melancholy, nor its eyes grim, nor its countenance severe; / these things justly desire dances and nimble sports / and always love; twice miserable he who loved late" (ll. 82-86).

That Milton has purposefully used here female imagery of space, water, and enclosure, as well as phallic male imagery seems unavoidable once we observe the hint. Milton, we understand, is both consciously and unconsciously reporting his sense of loss of a dear companion who had supplied a need. Whether that need was recognized and/or satisfied is unclear from the remarks of this elegy, but that it was felt is apparent. The imagery suggests the female personality bereft of male being as well as sexual overtones by the darkness evoked and the flatteries given. Amaryllis and Neaera seem not to have joined the poet, ever, in those shades. Diodati is less certainly identifiable, for we cannot be sure that Milton's statements of his celibacy are in fact accurate. What is important is that Milton thought they were. This, of course, says more about Milton and his concept of his relationship with Diodati than about the dead friend. Although there is the possibility that these remarks concerning Diodati's sexual life refer only to heterosexual love, not homosexual love, Milton's insistence on Diodati's celibacy makes sense, really, only if Milton knew of or suspected nonheterosexual interests on Diodati's part. For even if Diodati professed virginity to Milton and if they had seen each other soon before Milton left for the Continent, Milton's statement could still, he must have realized, been in error.

Because the imagery of the poem points to this suggestion, we should not take the suggestion to reason why the imagery was used. That goes in circles. Yet we do ask ourselves why this imagery, and the answer seems to be Milton's "solitudinem" at age thirty. If there is any psychological validity in man's responses to given stimuli—in our language, in our way of thinking—then Milton's choice of certain images and allusions may have been governed by his (at least subconscious) relationship with Diodati. That it was conscious, however, will appear as we proceed through all the evidence. Sometime before, Milton had professed a desire for wife, family, and independent home,[9] and some-time well before that he seems to have been enamored of one Aemilia (see the Italian poems, mentioned before) and "bands of maidens, stars emitting seductive flames" ("Elegia prima," ll. 51-52) as well as "one sur-passing all others" ("Elegia septima," l. 61), the latter perhaps to be as-sociated with the background for Sonnet 1. But we know little of romance in Milton's life. Is perhaps this innocence of sexuality part of the difficulty that he encountered in his first marriage with Mary Powell some three years or so after he wrote "Epitaphium Damonis"?[10] We know nothing really of the circumstances of that marriage, though there have been speculations concerning financial matters and romanticizing about love-at-first-sight. And the reason for her almost immediate de-parture from his household—the differences in ages (33 and 16), the ages of her nephew-charges, Edward and John Phillips (12 and 11), the differences of background (social, religious, and political), and totally new surroundings—may have already been told. But a personality such as here hypothesized may hold part of the key to the abruptness of the marriage, the seeming familial and financial "arrangement," and the problems of those first two months.

Diodati was born in 1609, the son of a very important medical doctor, Theodore, and nephew of the well-known Swiss theologian, Jean. He lived with his family in the parish of St. Mary Magdalen, Castle Baynard Ward, London, from 1617 or 1618,[11] then in the parishes of Christ Church and St. Faith's, Castle Baynard Ward, by 1625, and finally in the parish of St. Anne's, Blackfriars, by 1638. His first home in London was only a few blocks from Milton's home, and both only a few blocks from Alexander Gill's St. Paul's School, where both were students. Milton en-tered the school around 1620, remaining through 1624; Diodati may have entered in 1617 or 1618 and left in 1622. He matriculated at Trinity College, Oxford, on February 7, 1623. He was admitted B. A. on De-cember 10, 1625, and proceeded through the M. A., awarded on July 8, 1628. Milton, though older, apparently went to St. Paul's later, left later, was only in his first year in college when Diodati was being graduated from college, and received his bachelor's degree nine months after Di-odati received his master's.

The extant writings connecting Milton and Diodati are two Greek letters to Milton, "Elegia prima" and "Elegia sexta" (both addressed to Diodati), Sonnet 4, addressed to Diodati, and two Latin letters to Diodati (plus "Epitaphium Damonis"). The two letters in Greek[12] from Diodati to Milton are undated; they have been assigned to 1625 and spring 1626, but the latter date is probably inaccurate, since the letter probably does not specifically relate to "Elegia prima." The first talks of the poor weather that seems to counter their plans to meet to "enjoy learned and philosophical discourse together." Diodati prophesies good weather will come and they will be able to proceed as planned. Like many letters of the time, it is written in the graceful style and is ornamented by classical allusion. It is thus unwise to impute deep significance to "so much do I long for your society," for such fulsomeness was expected. The second letter, however, contains some provocative language. After saying that he is enjoying himself in the country, missing only "some noble soul skilled in conversation" (that is, Milton), Diodati admonishes his correspondent for overstudiousness and for not enjoying his youth. Diodati is Milton's better in only one thing, "knowing the proper limit of labor," a point Milton was to make much later in his verse epistles to Edward Lawrence and Cyriack Skinner (Sonnets 20 and 21, written in autumn 1655). The differences in interests and activities and philosophy of life between Milton and his good friend are more fully explored in "Elegia sexta." But the differences implied in the letter smack of the commonplace attitudes toward "male" and "female" attributes (wrong though those attitudes may be): the one who plans and the one who follows; the one who is concerned with the here and now and the one who is concerned with lastingness; the one who is carefree and nonstudious and the one who is serious and overstudious; the one who is outgoing and the one who is withdrawn.

Then in the letter's "ornament" Diodati writes: "and be joyous—though not in the fashion of Sardanapalus in Cilicia [Soli]." Sardanapalus was an Assyrian king (seventh century B. C.) who was effeminate and voluptuous. While advising Milton to partake of lightness in life, Diodati warns also of moderation; but surely he had no fear that one of such "inexcusable perseverance" would move to a polar position. In fact, the allusion contrasts with an allusion just before, that if Milton were with Diodati, Diodati "would be happier than the King of Persia," meaning, apparently, one who enjoys complete abundance of all things.[13] The aura of this allusion is male; that to Sardanapalus is female. It is fraught with possibilities: such a joyous life as Milton would lead involves those things considered effeminate; a tendency toward the effeminate has already been observable; ironically, Milton has not previously shown a tendency toward voluptuousness (that is, Diodati pokes fun at Milton's not being voluptuous by warning him against being voluptuous); the general context of Milton's life and attitude had already been discussed between them. The allusions sound like an inside joke. Diodati as potential King of Persia must be one given to overeating, excessive drinking, leisure, and sexual fulfillment.

Diodati's two letters attest to their friendship, to the differences between them—differences of personality and thus of complementary personalities—and to Diodati's "male" role and Milton's "female" role in the commonplace separations of such role-playing. The reference to Sardanapalus suggests that these friends had discussed their personality differences—Milton's tendency toward the "female" life and his abstemiousness toward things of a sensual nature. The "joke" of this allusion—there are others in Milton's two Latin letters to Diodati later on—shows us the way in which meaningful things can be said obscurely, if one can be sure of the reader's understanding (in this case, Milton's), and the letters contribute to our awareness of a closer bond between the two than simply friendship.

"Elegia prima," written in April 1626, is concerned with Milton's rustication from Cambridge because of a disagreement with his tutor, William Chappell. This is almost the earliest extant writing we have of Milton's, only the paraphrases on Psalms 114 and 136, "Apologus de Rustico et Hero," the two fragments entitled "Carmina Elegiaca," and the prolusion "Mane citus lectum fuge" being datable in 1624-25. The first elegy is in response to a (nonextant) letter from Diodati, who was sojourning in Chester. Although Milton has been required to return to his home in London (probably that on Bread Street), he is not unhappy to be there and says that he does not even care to see the rushy Cam again. What his argument with Chappell was and what his relationship with fellow students was can only be surmised.[14] But in the first case the rigidity of Chappell as tutor, the nature of the program of study at Christ's College (criticized heavily some years later in *Of Education,* 1644), and Chappell's religious leanings (a clearly episcopal attitude which Milton, who was then studying for the ministry, might have disputed) probably supply the reasons. How "activist" Milton may have been in expressing his disagreement with the establishment of his day, we do not know, but at least he seems not to have been totally silent.

His relations with fellow students would also seem to have been strained, for two years later in the Sixth Prolusion, written in July 1628, he talks of there having been "disagreements over our studies" and of "an absolutely hostile and unfriendly spirit."[15] We know likewise that he was called the Lady of Christ's, an epithet deriving perhaps from his fine features (compare his portrait at age twenty-one, the "Onslow" portrait, and his remark in Sonnet 7 at age twenty-three that his "semblance might deceave the truth / That I to manhood am arriv'd so neer") and from his eschewing those activities of a frivolous, perhaps romantic, perhaps athletic nature common to the male college student. The circumstance is not much different from what today would evoke the term

"sissy"; our world's penchant for assigning certain attributes to the male
or to the female lies behind Milton's sobriquet. In the sixth prolusion he
discusses this nickname, working from the title of Father assigned to the
master of ceremonies at the exercises preceding the long vacation, since
Milton acted this role in 1628, through ribald puns. The omission of this
event the year before is explained as perhaps resulting from the fact that
"those who were about to become 'Fathers' conducted themselves so tur-
bulently in town that he, to whom this duty was assigned, taking pity on
their great exertions ['tantorum laborum'], of his own accord decreed
that they should be relieved of this anxiety." Sexual punning is clear. The
irony that he, Milton, the Lady of Christ's, should be "Father" is immediately seized upon: "But indeed how comes it that I have so suddenly
been made a 'Father'? Ye gods, grant me your protection! What prodigy
is this, surpassing the strange tales of Pliny! Have I by killing a snake
suffered the fate of Tiresias? Has some Thessalian witch smeared me
with magic ointment? Or finally, violated by some god, like Caeneus of
old, have I bargained for manhood as a reward for dishonor, so that suddenly I might be changed from a woman into a man?"[16]

The reference to Tiresias is particularly noteworthy. Seeing two ser-
pents in copulation, Tiresias killed the female of the pair with a stick and
so was changed into a female; seven years later he regained his sex by a
repetition of the act. The story allegorizes a man's rejection of maleness
(later femaleness) and subsequent "femaleness" (later "maleness")
through sexual inhibition. Within this passage of the Sixth Prolusion the
allusion indicates Milton's opposition to sexual licentiousness and his
subsequent "femaleness" in the eyes of his fellow students (now as "Father" regaining his sex). The reference to Caeneus also involves a change
of sex from woman to man, as Milton here changes from "Lady" to "Father" by the "dishonor" of having been "violated by some God" (as Caenis
was by Poseidon). The analogy suggests Apollo, god of poetry and song,
of moral and intellectual pursuits. Perhaps, too, there is a pun in the
term "Lady of Christ's" involving Milton's pursuit of these "female" interests controlled by Apollo, who is equated with the Sun (the Son) and
Christ, and thence the college. A similar pun on Phoebus-Sun-Son-
Christ's is employed in "Elegia prima," l. 14.

The term "Lady" suggests hauteur, and the term "Father" not only
indulges his "return" to maleness but requires sexual intercourse resulting in a pregnancy. His attitude toward his fellow students' philistinism
implies such hauteur; his children are those students who took part in
the Vacation Exercise. (Those who are known were all younger than he.)
He plays upon this in the verses called "At a Vacation Exercise," which
make clear the appropriateness of both terms. He continues, "From

some I have lately heard the epithet 'Lady.' But why do I seem to those fellows insufficiently masculine?" and then cites as answer his lack of "masculine" activities, such as wrestling, or plowing, or whoring.[17] The view of Milton that one sees is not quite what his biographers have tried to rationalize.[18] He was one who exhibited those qualities that the male-oriented world considered female: physical features, certain kinds of interests and activities, avoidance of and perhaps even objection to sexual behavior. But we should also recognize that he was aware of all this, and that he himself, as this occasion demanded, engaged in sexual punning. He may not have approved, but he did not totally avoid obscenities, and this is not uncommon in the sexually inhibited. Then, too, in order to understand a double entendre, as those who argue against censorship of the stand-up comic or the talk-show of television point out, one must already understand the joke before one hears it to recognize its off-color quality. Case in point: Milton next adds the line, "verum utinam illi possint tam facile exuere asinos, quam ego quicquid est foeminae" ("But would that they could as easily lay aside their asshood as I whatever belongs to womanhood"). The pun on "exuere [uncover or lay bare] asinos [asses]" is obvious—and obscene. And further, he obscenely implies, he could lay bare what is supposed to show his womanhood, but of course it would show his manhood.

In "Elegia prima" Milton remarks his joy at being able to read the classic drama (ll. 25-46) now that he is at home, and in contrast, in *An Apology Against a Pamphlet* (1642), he castigates his fellow students and the stage fare in the colleges: "when in the Colleges so many of the young Divines, and those in next aptitude to Divinity have bin seene so oft upon the Stage writhing and unboning their Clergie limmes to all the antick and dishonest gestures of Trinculo's, Buffons, and Bawds; prostituting the shame of that ministery which either they had, or were nigh having, to the eyes of Courtiers and Court-Ladies, with their Groomes and *Madamoisellaes*. There while they acted, and overacted, among other young scholars, I was a spectator; they thought themselves gallant men, and I thought them fools, they made sport, and I laught, they mispronounc't and I mislik't, and to make up the *atticisme*, they were out, and I hist" (14). ("Unboning" apparently means "loosening"; "dishonest," "unchaste" with strong sexual reference; "out," "finished," perhaps by exhaustion.) The picture of Milton that emerges is a youth so intellectually driven and so morally upright that he must have struck associates as their concept of the "female" personality. This is definitely not to say that Milton was overtly effeminate in attitude or had sexually exercised such personality traits. But it is to suggest that his orientation involved sexual inhibition and compensation in study, vicarious experience, and male attachment (the apparently singular close attachment to Diodati).

In "Elegia prima" he remarks that "the hours of spring do not hasten by without effect on me" (l. 48) and recounts the beauty of maidens whom he has observed beneath "the celebrated shade of a suburban spot" (l. 50). But it is only observance from afar; he has not communed with any of these young women of Britain. The lines seem to be trying to prove to Diodati that he is not exclusively studious, "bending over books and studies day and night," and that he has not totally despised "the gifts of nature," that he is living, laughing, enjoying his youth and the hours—these being phrases from Diodati's second extant letter. Indeed Cupid's indulgence permits Milton to prepare to return to Cambridge, much as he does not wish "to leave the favorable walled city" (l. 86). Curiously, and evidencing his sexual-moral attitudes and his inhibition, he is preparing "to escape from afar the infamous halls of faithless Circe, / preparing with the help of divine moly" (ll. 87-88). For Milton, here in 1626, sexual alliance implies "roul[ing] with pleasure in a sensual stie" ("Comus," l. 77), which is the way he expressed succumbing to bodily temptation in 1634. The "divine moly" which exists within him to resist the charms of Circe is his moral sense and his transmutation of such bodily urges to an aesthetic plane. The seductive maidens he has espied are likened to maidens of classic literature or history and to stars in the heavens. His maidens entice by shaking their hair, a symbol of sexuality ("hair") and thus of sexual activity ("shaking"; "tremulosque capillos"), and hair for Milton is that "by which deceitful Love extends his golden nets" (l. 60). Others, of course, frequently find themselves in "the tangles of *Neaera*'s hair."

"Elegia sexta," addressed "To Charles Diodati, sojourning in the country," pursues the differences in their personalities we have noted before. Diodati was one who apparently ate much, and Milton opens with an ironic contrast: "On an empty stomach I send you a wish for health, / which you, stuffed full, can perhaps do without." He also says that Ceres is favorable toward Diodati. His friend was one who imbibed noticeably; he talks of "the French wines consumed beside agreeable fires" and of Bacchus (in various guises) repeatedly. The nature of the poetry that Diodati might produce is Bacchian or Dionysian; his overeating and overdrinking should not inhibit his poetizing. That Diodati indulges himself is clear, and so is the fact that he is given to bodily satisfaction. The Bacchian reference in "Epitaphium Damonis" may thus have more personal meaning than has been noted. Apollo, as god of poetry and song, will have his effect on Diodati also, Milton contends, and one can hope for "gay Elegy" or amatory verse as in Ovidian elegy as the result. (Diodati had apparently been a medical student, and Apollo was associated with healing.) But for a poet such as Milton (in December 1629 when he was composing "On the Morning of *Christs* Nativity"), frugal life is the norm.

The work on which he was engaged—a birthday present for Christ—awaits Diodati's judgment.[19] The emphasis certainly is placed on Diodati's fleshly world and Milton's aesthetic one; the pair appear to Milton's way of thinking as complements to each other. Diodati is vacationing, feasting, and drinking; he is outgoing in manner and surrounded by people. Milton is at work, he is abstemious of food, he partakes of only "nonintoxicating potions from the pure spring [Castalia]," and he is alone. He is also embarrassed to talk of his work.

Two odd phrases appear in the poem that suggest something more for their relationship than the above dichotomy, which in itself has earmarks of a male-female relationship. "You would like to know by song," Milton writes, "how I return your love and revere you; / believe me, you can scarcely learn this from song, / for my love is not confined by brief measures, / nor does it itself proceed unimpaired on halting feet" (ll. 5-8). The apparent fact that Diodati has requested such a statement makes Milton's lines more than a commonplace avowal of friendship in a verse letter. Perhaps Milton had not written to Diodati in a while, or had not answered a letter prior to that of December 13, cited in the headnote. The possible anxiety on Diodati's part that such a question implies places an odd construction on their friendship. If we can read the implied question as a symptom of anxiety—that emotional state caused by anticipation of future failing of a present desire—then we recognize an attitude on Diodati's part suggestive of homoeroticism. It would seem that, by whatever actions would be usual—letters, meetings, exchanged avowals of friendship or love—Diodati has not recently been reassured of Milton's attitude toward him. It appears that Diodati does not think himself in the wrong for the disruption in their relationship but is anxious lest it be totally disrupted. On Milton's part is a tone that says, If friendship were confinable to song, it would not be very deep. There is also a tone suggesting that Milton is questioning Diodati's sincerity as friend. Diodati appears the insensitive one; Milton, the sensitive. Diodati appears the uncomprehending male; Milton, the long-suffering female of many a sentimental novel.

Secondly, an aside casts a curious light on Milton's attitude toward Diodati at this time: "But if you will know what I am doing (if only at least / you consider it to be important to know whether I am doing anything)" (ll. 79-80). Here the situation implied is that sometime in the not too distant past Diodati has seemed unconcerned, perhaps aloof and airy, has been less than seriously communicative about Milton's hopes and activities. The parentheses hint that there has been a strain in their relationship, just as lines 5-8 do, and that Milton has come to a kind of decisive stage in his view of that relationship by recognizing one who is less worthy of his intimate friendship than he had thought him in the past. The inference to be made, I think, is that Diodati was friendly with many people (perhaps specifically males) and that Milton was not, holding their relationship to be exclusive. The strain in their relationship arose from those contrasting attitudes, with Milton now in 1629 proceeding to a conscious assimilation of his subconscious drives. Evidence does not necessarily indicate homosexual activity. Later evidence, as we shall see, does suggest that some overt action may have emerged, and leads to the conclusion that Diodati was fickle and irresponsible in human relationships, while Milton was inhibited and guilt-ridden. Today it should not be shocking to recognize that amidst the student heterosexual amours were also, at times, homosexual acts; witness, for example, the burden of Julian Mitchell's play *Another Country* (1981), which explores the theme in a British college as backdrop to treasonous betrayal during World War II.[20]

At least after having received an M. A. at Oxford in July 1628, Diodati seems to have floundered in his career and in any kind of noticeable accomplishment. Whether or not we should assume that, like Milton, he retired to his father's home in London for medical study cannot be determined, but unlike Milton's situation his father was in good health and active in his medical practice, and there was a younger sister, Philadelphia, at home. (His brother John was at school, and we do not know whether his mother was then living, though it seems probable that she was, since his father did not remarry until sometime around 1637.) It is assumed that Diodati's studies in college had been to prepare him for medicine and that he then pursued further study or practice upon graduation. He may instead have been preparing for the ministry—but we just do not know. Not long after the sojourn referred to in "Elegia sexta," Diodati was abroad, enrolled as an English student of theology in the Academy of Geneva on April 16, 1630. His move to Geneva is explained by probable dissatisfaction with theological training in England and by his uncle's residence there. He remained at the Academy through at least September 15, 1631. When he returned to England we do not know. What he did thereafter we do not certainly know either, but he eventually began the practice of medicine before the end of 1637, outside London.

In other words, around the time of "Elegia sexta" the friendship of Milton and Diodati may have cooled, partially because they were following such different patterns of life—Diodati, as in the poem, given to the vacationing spirit and Milton to the compulsiveness observable throughout his life—and partially because of Diodati's seeming decline from what appears to have been a kind of precociousness in earlier life. The summary of Diodati's life in 1628-37 is not dissimilar to that of many others today: direction, indecision, abortive action, and return to the original direction. Milton's parentheses here hint that he has learned that he cannot trust Diodati's avowal of interest in his activities. The picture that arises from the total poem is a Diodati more or less pleased with himself and insensitive to Milton. The poem suggests that, though their friendship continued, it was to be less intense and less frequently reinforced by close associations than in the past.

Milton's own immediate activities after this time are less difficult to chart, for during the next year, from April 17, 1630, to around January 1631, Cambridge was closed because of the plague, and Milton was at his father's home (presumably Bread Street, since they seem to have moved to Hammersmith in 1631, although it is also possible that there was a suburban home in the parish of St. Martin's in the Fields from around 1623/24). The spate of poetizing that has sometimes been assigned to this period is corroborated by his freedom from required study and by its nature. "The Passion" attempts to recapture the mood of the Nativity ode, while he was still at Cambridge (March 1630), but "Elegia septima," the lines appended to that elegy, "Song: On *May* Morning," Sonnet 1, the Italian poems, and "On Shakespear" (all perhaps 1630 and some around May) suggest different and more leisurely concerns. There is an amatory veneer on "Elegia septima," on the lines, on "Song," and on Sonnet 1 that has seldom struck critics as very convincing. (These poems have sometimes been dated 1628 or 1629.) Perhaps their literary problem is that Milton was *trying* to write this kind of verse (and not succeeding very well) and their subject matter may be, at least partially, at fault. The Italian poems, however, are another matter.

Our first problem with the Italian poems is date. Since Milton purchased his volume of Giovanni della Casa's *Rime e Prose* in December 1629 and since the Italian poems reflect Casa's influence, the poems are often dated after that time. The freedom of being away from graduate study and the possible date of the other poems allows 1630 as their date, and there is no reason to place individual poems of the sequence at different times. But Sonnet 4 is addressed to Diodati, who was in Geneva by the middle of April. Of course, there is no requirement that Diodati be nearby when Milton wrote.

Next, why does Milton choose Italian as his vehicle? Most thinking has centered around the "Donna leggiarda," whose name, Aemilia, is given cryptically in Sonnet 2. It is suggested that she was one of the Italian colony in London, associated with the Diodatis, perhaps introduced to Milton by Charles, and so the address in Sonnet 4. In turn, this implies that Milton sent or intended to send the verses to her (he says that she reads Italian). In Sonnet 3 he writes that "Love on my alert tongue / awakens the new flower of foreign speech . . . by my good countrymen not understood." Pose is certainly involved, but is it pose in order not to be scoffed at? (According to "Canzone" he was.) Or is it simply experimentation in another language under the influence of having read Casa enthusiastically?

No situation has been discovered to back up the narrative of the sequence; no girl named Aemilia has been proposed; and the poems take on similarities to the near-succumbing to girls passing by that he relates in "Elegia prima" (1626) and "Elegia septima" (1630?). The canzone in which "Scoffing, amorous maidens and young men / mill about [him, saying], 'Why write, / why do you write in a language unknown and strange / versifying of love, and how do you dare?' " apparently refers to the preceding two sonnets, addressed to the girl. (This is an interesting device: the reader of the sequence is reading a poem about two poems that the reader has just read and is subtly being asked to compare the reaction to that of the scoffers.) The next sonnet is addressed to Diodati, and the last two again to "Donna mia." Were the sonnets sent to the girl? were they seen by the scoffers? were they sent to Diodati? The answer is almost surely, no.

Another problem is the substance and thus the sincerity of this little sonnet sequence. The enamoring seems to be only on Milton's part, unexpressed to the girl, although the "Canzone" implies that others have read these verses. I have previously suggested[21] that the sequence is concerned with love of heavenly being rather than human love, though working through human love and an actual experience (compare such lines as "grace alone from above enables him to withstand / the amorous desire which would lodge itself in his heart," Sonnet 2, ll. 13-14; "Oh! were my sluggish heart and hard breast / as good soil for him who plants from heaven," Sonnet 3, ll. 13-14), but there is no need to repeat that argument here. In any case, the sonnet in which Diodati is addressed says that Milton has been stubborn ("ritroso") about matters of love, that he used to contemn love ("amor spreggiar soléa") and frequently scoffed at its snares ("E de' suoi lacci spesso mi ridéa"), and that he has fallen where upright man (with physical pun) sometimes entangles himself ("Già caddi, ov' huom dabben talhor s'impiglia"). He has not been enticed by golden hair or vermeil cheeks (compare "Elegia prima") but by foreign beauty.[22]

The poem leads to a major, general realization: Diodati and Milton have discussed male-female love in the past, and Milton has resisted entanglement. He who falls is deceived, Milton believes, and is no longer upright; the moral stricture placed on love and the implication in the

pun of imminently ensuing physical sex are to be noted. Such sexual inhibition and the pall of "sinfulness" which lies over heterosexuality seem
never fully to have left Milton, even in the innocent love of Adam and
Eve depicted in Book IV of *Paradise Lost*. I would suggest that the Italian
poems related Milton's certain yet embarrassed reaction to a sexual
stimulus around the spring or summer of 1630 (?), one more emotional
than that described in "Elegia prima"; that Diodati would be surprised at
this reaction; that Milton assumes the role of Petrarchan lover through
the influence of such sonneteers as Casa, thus employing a pose, language, imagery, and "narrative" appropriate to that influence; that he
recognizes a parallel between sexual love and spiritual love and professes
(surely as pose) his lack of sufficient spiritual inspiration; and thus that
the sexual love of the sequence is basically vehicle.

Why does he address Sonnet 4 to Diodati? Probably because their
past discussions have little supported his reaction to his sexual stimulus
("I will say it to you with wonder," Milton admits). And probably because
shortly before, in "Elegia sexta," their strained relationship came to the
surface. It tells Diodati that he can be enticed by the siren's eyes and
voice, and since to fly himself he is in doubt (Sonnet 6, l. 2), he will de-
votedly render his heart to his lady and remain faithful. His heart is
above "chance and envy [and] the fears and hopes of common men."
While the sequence may be an honest statement of his attitude toward
Aemilia, it also serves to deny a continued relationship with Diodati as in
the past. For in distinction from their relationship of the past, these poems claim that Milton is capable of becoming a partner in a different
relationship with a different person. The question that we perhaps cannot answer with certainty is, Do the poems often assigned to 1630 ("Elegia septima," etc.) register a concerted effort to force heterosexual
attitudes? Their superficiality and the spiritual overtones in the Italian
poems as well as the break in relationship with Diodati suggested in "Elegia sexta" lead to an affirmative answer. The sequence may serve Diodati, therefore, fair warning that the kind of close relationship shared in
the past is at an end.[23]

The foregoing discussion of "Elegia sexta" and the Italian poems
points to an identity crisis for Milton in 1629-30, possibly extending
backward and forward. With the removal of Diodati from a close relationship with Milton, there were two specific compensatory reactions: a
superficial and ultimately ineffectual attempt to pursue male-female relationships, without concepts of sexual morality and inhibition being
overcome, and with the abandonment of the attempt thereafter, and a
deeper plunging into study and writing. The Nativity ode may represent

part of that reaction, as does the inept and overreaching "The Passion," and possibly we can add "On Shakespear." In 1631-32 he seems to have written two or three Hobson poems, "Epitaph on the Marchioness of Winchester," "L'Allegro," "Il Penseroso," and possibly the academic "Naturam non pati senium" and "De Idea Platonica." The seventh prolusion heralds his studious retirement to Hammersmith and Horton (1632-38). The retirement, however, may have been a result also, we note, of his father's and mother's advanced ages, since his sister Anne was married with children and his younger brother Christopher was at school. The sublimation that such removal from the mainstream of life effected is seen in the organized and systematic program of study that we can infer from his remarks in the seventh prolusion concerning the attainment of a full circle of knowledge of the past and from those in a letter to Diodati dated November 23, 1637. Additionally during this period he wrote "Comus" and other poems.[24]

The identity crisis, reflective of sexual repression, of a lack of familial individuation, and of uncertainty of career, would seem to have emerged because of the break in the complementary subconscious that Diodati provided for Milton. Perhaps Milton came to recognize at this time the need to alter his sexual indecision. The tightness of the view Milton presents of himself in "Elegia sexta," with its rejection of hunger (and thus sex) drives, not simply a control of such drives, and their replacement with spiritual justifications, leads eventually to the studious retirement. During most of 1630 he was ostensibly retired to his father's house, but the planned retirement of 1632-38 specifically avoids identity decision. The decision of career in the fall of 1637 came finally through familial individuation (provoked by the death of his mother in April 1637) and a subsequent acceptance of a male role in life. The death instinct to which this retirement points must be replaced by positivity and by matters of the future rather than of the past. The move to act positively to bring forward the future (not simply to prepare until such time as one is ready) can be seen, I believe, in the Letter to an Unknown Friend, in the writing during this period, in the letters to Diodati from November 1637, which indicate that Milton thought of taking residence in one of the Inns of Court, and in his trip to the Continent. While Milton seems not totally to reject the concept of continuing to try to be prepared (see remarks in *The Reason of Church-Government*, 1642), while he was preparing he was also doing: plans and subjects for creative works are recorded in the Trinity MS during 1639-42, what became *Paradise Lost* was begun during this time, and some of that writing remained in the completed poem more than twenty years hence. We do not see that "doing" during the years 1632-37, if my reading of this period and the works produced during it is correct, but we do see that "doing" in 1637-38.

In the Letter to an Unknown Friend,[25] Milton talks of his "tardie moving," which has not, however, been held back only by "the meere love of Learning." The fact is, he says, that he is now moving and thereby he is not one who "cutts himselfe off from all action and becomes the most helplesse, pusilanimous and unweapon'd creature in the world, the most unfit and unable to doe that which all mortals most aspire to either to be usefull to his freinds, or to offend his enimies." While the retirement may have been planned as a means to an end, according to this sentence, Milton seems only with this moving to recognize the significance of his having cut himself off from the world. The adjectives describing what has been his implied former helplessness, his pusillanimity, and his being "unweapon'd" suggest "female" attributes which the "tardie moving" will controvert into "male" attributes of independent action, courage, and active opposition. "Helplesse" and etymologically "pusilanimous" suggest Milton's awareness of his dependence upon his parents and his continued immaturity, and "unweapon'd" certainly points to the ideal of the soldier conquering by use of his sword, the "warfaring" Christian. (The sexual overtones are also interesting.) Indeed, as might be expected from someone who wrote the preceding letter, Milton had, to us, a curious concept of age, or at least of his age, as well as of "youth." For example, in the preface to *The Judgement of Martin Bucer* (1644), referring to the first edition of *The Doctrine and Discipline of Divorce* (1643), which he wrote when he was thirty-four, he said *"he knew not that what his youth then reason'd without a pattern, had bin heard already"* (B3v).

"Comus" too offers evidence of concerns during the period of the studious retirement and changes in attitude by 1637. The "Comus" we read today is not the masque presented at Ludlow Castle on September 29, 1634, as we shall note in Chapter 5. The Trinity MS and the dating of at least parts thereof (around fall 1637) on the basis of handwriting point to renewed creativity and inspired hopes for literature, but the changes in "Comus" have been insufficiently studied. Although the poem is offered as a commemoration of the Earl of Bridgewater's assumption of the Presidency of Wales and although a scandal in the family circle offers an intriguing backdrop for the work, as noted before,[26] it provides meaningful analysis of the attitudes of the 1634-37 Milton toward virginity, chastity, sex, and divine relationships. Briefly, the earlier "Comus" seems to have been less specific in its detailing of the Lady's resistance to Comus and in the Attendant Spirit's description of Heaven and the rewards for the virtuous. The masque is an elaboration of the temptation in the wilderness (see Matthew 4:1-11 and Luke 4:1-13) in mortal terms: in the dark forest of life (to use Dante's phrase) the Lady, en route to her father's house (with its obvious divine meaning), becomes victim of the hypocritical and sensual Comus, who has immobilized her body but who cannot control her mind. His offer of "all manner of deliciousness" and "his Glass" (the first temptation of need, *concupiscentia carnis*), his admonishment that one should partake of the bounties poured forth by nature "With such a full and unwithdrawing hand" (the second temptation of fraud, *concupiscentia ocularum*), and his *carpe diem* and *carpe rosam* argument against "that same vaunted name virginity" (the third temptation of violence, *superbia vitæ*) are rejected, for she discerns the "false rules pranckt in reasons garb." Yet to free her bodily the intervention of God is needed in the person of Sabrina, proving that "if Vertue feeble were, / Heav'n it self would stoop to her."[27] Here again, then, God's miracle aiding the true wayfaring Christian provides climax and resolution for the poem.

Comus's temptation was originally given in one long speech without interruption by the Lady (ll. 659-62, 666-71, 706-55, 672-78, 688-90, with some variations), the glass being unspecified in the stage direction and its specific offer being made only later (in ll. 811-13). The Lady then reacts with lines 662-65, 693-96, 701-3, 756-79; she counters Comus's arguments by pointing out his falseness and stressing that it cannot touch the freedom of her mind. But her remarks about the "Sun-clad power of Chastity" and Comus's inability "to apprehend / The sublime notion, and high mystery" which unfolds "the sage / And serious doctrine of Virginity" (ll. 782-87) are missing. These lines added in 1637 (or early 1638) just before the masque was published (our only source for them) pick up the Elder Brother's description of chastity and its "sun-clad power" in lines 381-82, 419-21, 425. In 1634 there seems to be a confounding of chastity and virginity; note the Elder Brother's "No goblin . . . has hurtfull power o're true virginity" (ll. 436-37) and ensuing reference to "the arms of chastity" (l. 440), the Spirit's request that Sabrina "undoe the charmed band / Of true virgin heer distrest" (ll. 904-5), and Sabrina's "'tis my office best / To help insnared chastity" (ll. 908-9). But chastity, by which is meant purity in conduct and intention, is not the same as virginity (with its implications of celibacy and the rewards of Revelation 14:4), and the Lady's added lines differentiate the two.

She attests a belief in the doctrine of virginity in contradiction to Comus's interpretation of meaning in the gift of beauty; yet she is basically speaking out against his "profane tongue" and "contemptuous [earlier, "reproachfull"] words" which have condemned "lean and sallow abstinence" (not total abstinence, but such as the abstemiousness discussed in

"Elegia sexta"). In lines 690-705, a passage that was reworked with new lines in 1637, the Lady indicts Comus's dishonesty and refuses his proffered drink since "that which is not good is not delicious / To a well-govern'd and wise appetite" (these lines were added in 1637). In question, of course, is not virginity but a general doctrine of chastity; the close relationship between food and drink and sex is fundamental in pre-Freudian literature, the interpretation of *concupiscentia carnis* being the most obvious evidence. The doctrine of virginity involves concepts of the sinfulness of sex and the rewards awaiting those not so "defiled"—basically a form of innocence supposedly approaching the prelapsarian world. Milton had not yet moved to all the implications in "Assuredly we bring not innocence into the world" (*Areopagitica,* p. 12), but he was presenting in "Comus" a picture of a nonfugitive and noncloistered virtue, one which was being exercised. The Lady is a clear prototype of the wayfaring Christian. Though a virgin, the real test is her chastity. Her lines do not make chastity the same as virginity; she recognizes that Comus has argued against chastity as well as virginity; but the "ideal" of virginity remains as a powerful force in Milton's thought.

A subtle change occurs between the seeming confusion of virginity and chastity in 1634 and their separation in 1637. The Milton of 1634 seems not to realize that the purifying trial he has plotted does not demand virginity. Untried, really, himself, surely virginal, Milton had seen opposition to the "cursed place" that is both Comus's palace and urban life coming only through inhibition and escape: this was his answer in "Elegia prima" and afterward. By 1634 there is recognition of the importance of trial and the control of chastity by freedom of the mind. Milton has changed since his pre-1629 days but he has not yet, in 1634, accepted sexual life. Comus's words are reasonable: the good of beauty "Consists in mutual and partak'n bliss, / Unsavoury in th' injoyment of it self,"[28] but since the intention of his words is unchaste, their concept is not developed in the "Comus" of 1634.

With the Spirit's revised epilogue, however, we have a reconsideration of the question.[29] The earlier epilogue (generally consisting of ll. 976-79, [1014-15], 980-83, 988-96, 998-99, 1012-23) describes heaven as a world of eternal summer and flowers, watered by Iris, goddess of the rainbow. The 1637 epilogue shows Milton's clear awareness that this is a mortal heaven "Where young *Adonis* oft reposes"—a heaven peopled by the "lovers" of this world, who, though they are "wounded" by sexuality, may still ascend to "Beds of hyacinth and roses." But such a heaven is not the preferred eternity, that which is available to the virgins. For "farr above in spangled sheen" is Psyche, the eternal bride of Cupid, that is, the soul that has undergone "wandring labours long" (trials such as the

Lady has overcome in the masque) and that has maintained its "fair un-spotted side."[30] Psyche becomes the bride of the God of Love (of Cupid mythologically, but of the Son anagogically). Chastity is acknowledged in 1637 as a wider concept than in 1634 and one that will be rewarded; but virginity, a more rarefied part of chastity, is the greater ideal and more clearly delineated than in 1634.

By the end of 1637 Milton's attitudes are more certain and less rigid than in 1629-30 or 1634. During the studious retirement, he avoided identity decision, familial individuation, and career decision. In career he was moving toward the world of the scholar and creative artist and more certainly away from the ministry. As late as 1641/42 in *The Reason of Church-Government*, he was to link the ministry and writing as parallel endeavors. The acceptance of creative art as career acknowledged his in-ability to function successfully as "father" surrogate through direct and personal action. His whole life had shown his withdrawn and anal-retentive personality, hardly the kind not to "deale worse with a whole congregation." The decision of a career is well entwined, I believe, with the resolution of identity, still unclear in 1634 but more certain in 1637. Subconscious psychological acknowledgment of his "femaleness" and ho-moeroticism had to occur before identity could be established. Probably the clarification of virginity and its rewards is a result of this identifica-tion of self as a justification of his past lack of heterosexual intercourse and the expected continuance of that life. Unfortunately the specter of celibacy seems to have hung over him through at least the period just before his marriage to Mary Powell. The break with Diodati in 1629-30 must have left Milton in a limbo of nondirection, such as underlies Son-net 7 (in 1631) as well as the 1634 "Comus." Only with a total rejection of forced sexuality (as seen in the poems of 1630) and of the relationship with Diodati (which had not sufficiently occurred even when Sonnet 4 was written) was Milton to conceive of himself as being able to move (as he says in the Letter to an Unknown Friend) and to think of family and home and to aspire to publishing the fruits of his attempted achievement.[31]

The letter presents one who has finally rejected escape and the sol-itary life and who is now ready to compete in the world of people. Mil-ton's identification with family and his implied immaturity aided in avoidance of decision and in maintenance of his sexual nonidentity. The death of his mother must have presented a crossroads. The psychologi-cal disruption which a mother's death can create for a son, particularly an unmarried son living at home, perhaps was the major catalyst to Mil-ton's "tardie moving." "Ad Patrem" suggests that there had been some question on the part of Milton's father as to what his son was going to do

with his life. And the letter to Diodati in November 1637 implies decision of a poetic career, but with a transferred continuance of his former
life to a world of men in London, only now with direction. The additions
and changes in "Comus" in 1637 reflect an acceptance of the world of
trial, of the chaste sexual life, and of the differentiations possible among
good human beings. Milton's seeming removal to London and then his
trip to the Continent place him in the middle of such life forces.

The ideas worked out in "Comus" seem to have stayed with Milton
through the writing of "Epitaphium Damonis," or perhaps they re-
emerged because they were subconsciously associated with Diodati and
Milton's identity crisis. The 1634 "Comus" ends (except for the Spirit's
epilogue) with songs and dances. The final (second) song presents the
Lady and her brothers to their parents as youths who have earned "a
crown of deathless praise" and who are thus enabled "To triumph in victorious dance / O're sensual folly, and intemperance" (ll. 974-75). The
dance is much less clearly defined than it is in "Epitaphium Damonis."
Here the dance caps the defeat of temptation, seen as assertion of chastity; but it does not emphasize the contrast with Comus's rout's dance
(ll. 144ff) since it seems to reject any kind of sensuousness (although
"dance" itself contains such an implication) and all thought of excess.
The allegory of the children's reaching their father's home after the trial
of the dark forest of life would suggest that the triumphal dance engages
all senses rightly used and without surfeit. The dialectic demands such
contrast, but it is not until "song and mingled lyre rage with blessed
dances, and festal orgies revel" for Diodati that Milton pushes the point
toward which he was heading in 1634 to its conclusion: sexuality is good
but it must be chaste. Still, virginity rather than successful trial remains
as an ideal; the wisdom of trial is not to be fully realized until the mid-
1640s, with the divorce tracts, *Areopagitica,* and the first attempts at *Paradise Lost.*

Whereas in 1634 heaven is seen as lying in the realms of Iris, the
goddess of the rainbow, with its lack of distinction between the chaste
lover and the virgin, in 1637 heaven is divided between the lower Elysium of Adonis and the celestial heaven of Cupid and Psyche. The latter,
lying above "the spheary chime," is the paradise which the followers of
the Lamb, the virgins, may aspire to. And in "Epitaphium Damonis," Diodati, as we have seen, has rejected the rainbow—the lower Elysium of
Adonis—to ascend to the higher heaven with God. Now, with our fuller
background in the "Comus" of 1634 and of 1637, we see the apotheosis
in the elegy more firmly as I suggested at the beginning of this chapter.
The poem becomes an excursion in nostalgia and in wish-fulfillment.
For example, remark the opening of the last verse paragraph, with its
questions concerning Diodati's disposition after death. Wishfully the an-

swer that he has ascended to the higher heaven comes through a continued belief in the rewards of virginity. If not, what is the worth of virginity? Is Milton in 1639 on the verge of realizing his assertion about good and evil (comprehension through opposites) that we find in *Areopagitica* in 1644?

The view of Diodati which the foregoing yields is of one who represented a dominant counterpart to Milton, one whose sexual life cannot be described but whose rough personality outlines—his excesses, his fickleness in friendship, his sensual nature, his drifting life—would not deny a rather promiscuous homosexuality. On the other hand, Milton would seem to be somewhere on the fringes of homosexuality through religious and ideological repressions of "natural" attitudes toward sex, high-mindedness, and "female" qualities of appearance, interests, and abilities. That there may have been homosexual experiences with Diodati does not demand a label of "homosexual" for Milton but rather a latent homosexualism that on occasion might possibly have emerged and a homoerotic personality that would seem to fit the total evidence of Milton's life.

Of significance in corroborating these statements are the epigraphs given on the title pages of *A Maske* (1637) and the *Poems* (1645). The first ("Eheu quid volui misero mihi! floribus austrum / Perditus" ["Alas! what have I brought on my miserable self? I have let the south wind ruin my flowers"]) is from Vergil's second eclogue, which tells of the shepherd Corydon's love for the beautiful Alexis. Alexis is aloof and cares nothing for Corydon's songs; the shepherd then laments his attempt to win Alexis by his poetic gifts. He concludes, "If Alexis treats you with contempt, you'll find another." The parallel with Milton and Diodati is unavoidable. The use of this epigraph has never before been adequately explained (cf. Parker, 142–43), but we can now see it as consciously reflective of Milton's firm farewell to his former liaison with Diodati. "Comus" by 1637 has exalted the virginal to a high estate, and in its Vergilian context the quotation shows that Milton realized that he had been neglecting (in his studious retirement, in the type of poetry he had written) his proper work. It is easy to understand why "Lycidas" begins with "Yet once more" and ends with "To morrow to fresh woods and pastures new."

Additionally, though, Eclogue 2 is a major source for "Epitaphium Damonis," not only in its statement of homosexual love but in its very language: from Corydon's seeking out lonely spots and the imagery of nature, to recalling their activities together, to the gifts (writing) he is saving for Alexis, to the changes in mood and employment of "disordered shreds of song." Milton rehearses within the elegy the "proper work" that he is planning, but with Diodati's death he berates himself for having turned to it and thus for having seemingly forsaken Diodati. Recognition of the epigraph and the significance of the eclogue for the elegy informs us that Milton, at least in 1637-39, understood the full implications of their relationship. Even possible past homosexual activity (I do not say that there was such action, please note) would not of necessity have forced upon Milton's consciousness all the implications that use of this epigraph indicates were now viable. Probably the relationship had to be repressed in some way before it could be recognized for what it was.

The second epigraph ("Baccare frontem / Cingite, ne vati noceat mala lingua futuro" ["Crown my brows with foxglove, lest a hostile tongue harm the destined poet"]) comes from Eclogue 7 and is spoken by Thyrsis in a singing match with Corydon. The point of the quotation is that excessive praise heaped upon the rising poet may bring envy from the gods; Thyrsis (Milton) asks to be bewreathed with foxglove to ward off such excessive (envious) praise. But the main point is that Corydon wins the match, and Corydon is the shepherd of she-goats while Thyrsis is the shepherd of sheep. "Goats" alludes to licentiousness and thus the kind of poetry so often popular and praised by the rabble, while "sheep" implies the followers of God and thus vatic poetry, such as Milton rightly considered his own. The quotation registers faith in his future accomplishments (he had already begun what became *Paradise Lost*). The dichotomy, however, suggests what appears in "Elegia sexta," and the sexual overtones of licentiousness (popular and rewarded in this life) and of high morality (rare and rewarded only by God) should be noted. Besides, Thyrsis recalls "Epitaphium Damonis," implying Milton's ultimate dedication and faith in himself in that poem. In the eclogue Thyrsis addresses the handsome Lycidas, asking him to spend more time with him in a passage whose imagery is trees—the ash, the pine, the poplar, and the fir. The tree, a male and phallic symbol, again images a submerged homosexual strain breaking through.

The homoerotic attitude toward Diodati can be seen to be dissipated, or at least repressed, by rupture in their relationship and by sublimation. Conscious effort would have little effect—and Milton's seems to have had little. Yet this psychological *Affekt* left its toll on Milton's life and work, matters too involved for attention in this chapter.[32] Certainly his marriages should be restudied, surely his attitude toward woman, undoubtedly the divorce tracts. Is not all this—his appearance, his "female" attributes, his high-mindedness concerning sex—responsible for Salmasius's calling him a catamite? I assume that any young man who rejected the available Italian ladies-of-the-night, whom he must have seen frequently enough, would have his manhood questioned. So Milton during his *wanderjahr*—one quite different from that of the typical wild oats sower. Was the anxiety potential in the married man with latent homoerotic tendencies contributory to the psychosomatic problems that seem to have advanced Milton's blindness?[33] And what of Milton's frequent young friends, of whom Parker wrote (473): "As he grew older, Milton was more and more attracted to the young, and he gathered about him a group of devoted disciples"? But these are matters for later chapters, and we must return now to the remaining evidence of Diodati's and Milton's relationship, two Latin letters of late 1637.

The two letters written to Diodati in November 1637[34] inform us that Milton had tried to communicate with him "in the beginning of autumn" (that is, apparently, late September) and to see him in London sometime around October, and that he has more to say about himself and his studies "but would rather in person." I interpret this to refer to his "tardie moving"—his decision about a career and his familial individuation. In the second letter (having received an answer to the first) he talks of his studies and the possibility that he will take up residence in one of the Inns. We learn too that Diodati is living somewhere in the north, though making trips to London, but not near Horton, where Milton's country residence was. Diodati was practicing medicine at the time, as the second letter remarks.

The letters establish the conclusions I have advanced in this chapter. Milton begins the first letter by saying that "Now at length I see plainly what you are doing: you are vanquishing me finally by obstinate silence." That there has been a falling out is evident;[35] that Milton has written or otherwise tried to communicate with Diodati is clear; and that Diodati has not only not answered or sought out Milton but has also not even kept his promises to visit Milton is explicitly stated. "Behold!" Milton says, "I write first," but if there may be any "contention" about this, "beware you think that I shall not be by many respects [*partibus*] the more excused." The word puns on the meaning "genitals," and Milton goes on to differentiate Diodati as one easily "drawn into literary correspondence" "by nature or by habit [*consuetudine*, meaning intercourse]" and himself as one whose nature is "slow and lazy to write [the Greek says that he is "cowardly" in the use of his "pencil"]"—and he adds, "as you properly [*probe*, with a moral implication] know." The puns without doubt point to a sexually active Diodati, thus an aggressive type ("male") who should not manifest this kind of silence, and to a sexually inhibited Milton, thus a recessive type ("female") who would be understandably slow to engage in any kind of "correspondence" [προσφωνήσεις, literally, and with sexual suggestion, speech sounds made face to face]. "I know your mode of studying [*studendi,* also "being zealous toward someone"] to be so arranged," Milton writes with hidden meaning, "that you repeatedly breathe in between [*orebro interspires*, implying breaths that come close on one another as in coition], visit your friends, write much, sometimes make a journey."

The puns simply do not let us imagine that Milton was ignorant of sexual activity and the physical actions accompanying climax. But Diodati apparently can be sexually diverted by other matters. Milton appears the serious and intense one, whose infrequent (if in fact actual at all) excursions into homosexual situations (there is no hint that there may have been any besides that possibly with Diodati) were guilt-ridden, and Diodati, the "stud," whose attitude was blasé. In contrast Milton says that he cannot delay "until I reach [*pervadum*, penetrate] where I am being driven, and complete, as it were, some great period of my studies." (*Conficiam*, "complete," likewise means "diminish," and *studiorum* implies also "desires" and "affection" and "zeal.") Because of this he "more slowly approach[es] discharging [his] offices spontaneously"; again there are easily recognizable puns, including *ultro* as "wantonly" or "gratuitously." He wonders whether in the area where Diodati now lives there are "any young learned people with whom [he] can associate with pleasure and chat, as [they] were accustomed." But *erudituli* are also "those experienced in love"; and *consuevimus* jokes that what they are accustomed to doing is "having sexual intercourse." (I do not make up these puns, as reference to a good Latin dictionary will attest.)

The obscene puns suggest prior relationships as frank and perhaps as sexually involved. But the tone of these puns does not suggest that Milton is emotionally upset by Diodati's manner and their lack of close relationship; rather, it points to a Milton who has accepted the situation, replaced whatever remains or could have developed into a "married" attitude on his part with resignation and humor, and recognized finally the uncomplementary differences between them. The break can be understood as Milton's demand—or Diodati's attitude toward what he considered Milton's demand—for a steady and exclusive relationship. The tone of the puns is in no way like that of the parenthesis "(if only at least you consider it to be important to know whether I am doing anything)" in "Elegia sexta." And he notes that when he heard that Diodati was visiting in London, he "hastened to [Diodati's] chamber [*cellam*, a room in a brothel]," a comment that, coupled with the remark concerning Diodati's repeated breathing in between, suggests that Milton suspected that Diodati's visits included carnal fulfillment. But did he mean that Diodati might have visited a brothel? The statements in "Epitaphium Damonis" hardly support that, if one thinks only of a female brothel (although male brothels also existed). Instead he seems to be joking—

though perhaps not seriously—that Diodati's room may have been the focus for homosexual assignation. The total view of Diodati seen from the extant evidence certainly points to a homosexual nature; of Milton, to a latent homosexualism that was probably repressed consciously (as well as subconsciously) from becoming overt, except *perhaps* with Diodati.

Such a view in turn suggests that Milton's father's opposition to his son's poetic career may have been kindled by the son's outward personality traits and by commonplace ideas of "male" and "female" roles. Milton, of course, argues that his father has likewise pursued certain aspects of the kind of role he is proposing for himself. Milton writes: "Now since it has fallen to me to have been born a poet" ("Ad Patrem," l. 61), a line susceptible of more meaning when we consider physical-emotional-psychological makeup and categoric role-playing. Further, the end of "Ad Patrem" clarifies the source of the argument: outsiders' gross aspersions about Milton. (Perhaps the Unknown Friend was only one of several who criticized Milton, though he kindly and nonslanderingly.) The poem reads:

> Begone, sleepless cares; begone complaints,
> and the twisted gaze of envy with oblique goatish leer.
> And do not open your serpentine jaws, fell Calumny;
> you can do nothing disagreeable to me, O most detestable band,
> nor am I under your authority, and with heart secure
> I shall walk, lifted high from your viperous stroke. [105-10]

We can only guess what the sleepless cares and complaints were, although the Latin connotations are suggestive of anxiety and self-hate. The gaze (*acies*), however, may also be a verbal contest, and the envy (*invidiæ*) may be ill-will, while the *transverso hirquo* implies a voluptuous person who has been misled. Does not the line therefore observe for the informed father that Milton is casting aside as defeated the false view of himself that has been given by some who are voluptuaries (rather than morally-minded) out of their ill-will and envy? Certainly calumny is this kind of false accusation and slander. Such people are detestable (*foedissima*), that is, dishonorable, filthy, but is not this the way the average person may view the unmarried and totally unattached man (less seldom woman) of thirty? With the publication of "Comus," if the suggested dating of "Ad Patrem" is accurate, Milton was able not only to show that his study and retired life have been meaningful, but also that questions of sexual morality have been answered. Suddenly the revised epilogue of "Comus," with its two-levelled Heaven and its emphasis on virginity, becomes powerfully psychological: it is a conscious effort to offset slander.

(And, too, we remember the epigraph on the title page.) Does the epilogue represent a truly believed or primarily a hopeful view? Does it resolve the sexual anxieties that Milton must have felt? Are indeed the *quereles* of "Ad Patrem" banished? And how does all this sit alongside the rape, sodomy, and general perversion lying in the Castlehaven background?

In April 1638 Milton went to the Continent, and a few months later Charles Diodati died (from the plague?) and was buried at St. Anne's, Blackfriars (August 27, 1638). From the headnote to "Epitaphium Damonis" we know that he heard of the death while abroad. Parker argues that he learned of the death when in Naples in December 1638, but this requires that mail would have been sent to him there, and in time for his receiving it. Since Naples may not have been on his original itinerary— certainly the aborted trip to Sicily and Greece was not—and since his times of arrival and departure at any point along the way, other than Venice, were and had to be uncertain, it is not cogent that mail would have been sent to him there.[36] Venice was, traditionally, the last port visited by English travelers before their return, primarily because of the important English embassy and thus colony there. One often returned to England from Venice by boat; Milton tells us in *Defensio secunda* that he spent a month there and sent back his books by boat.[37] Apparently Milton heard of Diodati's death in mail sent to him in Venice.[38] At least soon afterward he proceeded to Geneva to visit with Charles's uncle Jean (for about a month), with whom he spoke every day (*quotidianus versabar*). He returned to England toward the end of August 1639 and wrote the epitaph around October or so (see ll. 58-61).

"Epitaphium Damonis" may not tell us much about Diodati biographically, but it serves as a major clue to Milton's personality in his younger years and nostalgically provides evidence of its transcendence. The guilt and self-hate that the foregoing analysis predicates seem to have been sublimated in or around 1637, with a flaring up in 1639, when the reality of Diodati's death led Milton to deprecate his rejection of their relationship on Diodati's terms. Whether such guilt and self-hate and indeed such latent homosexuality did not flare up in later years must be left unconsidered here.

4

Decision to Become
a Poet

A number of years ago William Riley Parker noted the "legend" that "Milton's life was preternaturally consistent: that he knew early what he intended to do, set about it simply and directly, never swerved from his determined course, and died with every item on his mental list neatly ticked off as completed."[1] Unrealistic though this theory is, it has encompassed the basic commentary on Milton's decision to become a poet by occupation, as distinguished from the schoolboy writer of verse. Even the cautious statement of Merritt Y. Hughes is based on this theory: "Long before he took his degree, however, he must have resolved, at least subconsciously, to live the life of a man of letters."[2] Milton's determination to be a great poet, the date of such decision, and, reciprocally, the date of his rejection of a clerical career are clearly significant.

What was the probable point of inflection from which we may graph Milton's conscious activities to "imbreed and cherish in a great people the seeds of vertu, and publick civility" through literature?[3] The crux of the matter—which too many students of Milton, led by hindsight, have been incapable of confronting—is the difference between the casual poet who has a poem or two published in some literary journal and one who devotes his career experience to the writing of poetry. Milton, as a kind of seventeenth-century forerunner of our twentieth-century creative artist, moved to an academic attachment as he began tutoring in late 1639 and continued through 1647 and off-and-on thereafter. He did not, of course, have to follow a professional career to earn money for himself and his family, since his father's various investments and real estate ventures left him well enough off. His differences of circumstance from professional writers like Samuel Daniel or Ben Jonson or John Dryden emphasize that point and obviate the now popular consideration of patronage; career differences from poets like John Donne (who seems to have tried entering various fields and settled on the ministry) or Sir Henry Wotton (governmental personage and academic provost) define his life as a poetic career.

Fame, Milton concluded, is not achieved haphazardly but comes only after great sacrifice and labor. That he was eager for fame is seen in the letter to his friend Charles Diodati dated November 23, 1637,[4] in "Lycidas," and in remarks in *The Reason of Church-Government*. His hope for fame, explicit in the same writings, lay in literature, and it is manifestly poetic literature. Yet his calling as a poet is qualified by certain considerations: God must be glorified by the honor and instruction of his country, "For which cause," he wrote, "I apply'd my selfe to that resolution which *Ariosto* follow'd . . . to fix all the industry and art I could unite to the adorning of my native tongue . . . to be an interpreter & relater of the best and sagest things among mine own Citizens throughout this Iland in the mother dialect."[5] This resolution he had reached, according to these statements, about the time of the Italian sojourn of 1638-39; he recalled it here before February 1642. Within this two-and-a-half-year period, Milton had applied himself by reading extensively, by jotting down literary subjects, by drafting literary outlines, and by beginning what became *Paradise Lost*. Nevertheless, he was far from ready, for he tells us that *Reason* was written "out of mine own season, when I have neither yet completed to my minde the full circle of my private studies . . . " (36).

When did Milton decide to become a poet? In this same pamphlet he mentions the praise bestowed upon him by the "privat Academies of *Italy*," the urging of "divers of my friends . . . at home, and not lesse . . . an inward prompting which now grew daily upon me" to write (37). This would seem to place his decision to pursue poetry as a vocation not long before the Italian period. It is probable that he had previously written to his father to pardon his evident determination to be a poet, for, though undated, "Ad Patrem" seems to be placed before the Italian trip by the references (ll. 73-76) to removal from the noise of cities to the current high retreats of delightful leisure. In addition, the letter to Diodati and "Lycidas" both signify poetic aspirations and feelings of unpreparedness. He had, it would seem, resolved to follow a poetic life even before he left England—as has generally been taken for granted. His experience in Italy focused his intentions and gave them added fervor, his intimation in *Reason* that his experiences at this time begot his decision indicating its recency. Indeed, his sojourn aimed at seeing at first hand the culture of which he had read, and at making himself ready for the task of fame he envisioned.

In response to questions in the lost letter from Diodati of November 1637, answering his of November 2, Milton wrote that he was then thinking of immortality and that he was pluming his wings and meditating flight. These remarks to such a close friend are odd, even if they are read as an attempt at lightness: to Diodati's anxious questions Milton has supplied answers which, in essence certainly, should have been well known to his frequent confidant. Had they been known, some note of continuance would have been audible in his response. His adding, "seriously," that he planned to migrate to some Inn and that his studies had encompassed the Greeks to the late Hellenistic period and the Italians to the period of independencies does not alter the sound of revelation in his former remarks. He is self-consciously diverting attention to prosaic and tangible matters. There is nothing "unserious" about his earlier statements.

From the words "Listen, Theodotus, but let it be in your ear, lest I blush," it is evident that Milton's announcement of high endeavors was not generally known. It could be thought as smacking of conceit, as well. What follows is not explicitly a plan for the future, for a life's work; yet it implies what that life's work will be. It comes in answer to the anxious questions he had created by his vagueness in the silence-breaking letter of November 2: "I would say more about myself and my studies, but would rather in person." He is leading up to the next letter's information, not so much about the Inn and the studies as about his hopes. There is nothing in the comments about studies that would suggest a preference for private audience. Only in his modest revelation about himself and his life was there anything the self-conscious Milton would prefer not be circulated. The first letter explains his reserve, his obscurantism, and his attempt at lightness in the personal assertion of the second. A hint of what he means must suffice, for he would prefer discussing it in private, not in correspondence; if all this were known, he would blush.

Diodati was "curious," probably because of Milton's enigmatic remark: we can imagine his asking, "What can you be doing, or planning, or thinking that you prefer not to commit to paper?" He was not anxious over what literary fruits had proceeded from the "prolonged obscurity," for Milton's statement of caution ("listen but let it be in your ear") belies any idea that Diodati already knew of his desires for poetic fame and immortality. Clearly, Milton was not repeating himself. He says, "allow me for a little while to talk more loftily with you"; this "lofty language" could not have been spoken before. If Milton had retired to Hammersmith in 1632 to prepare for a poetic life or if he had reached such a decision shortly after "Comus" (1634), Diodati would have known. He knew of the "studious retirement" (as Milton's letters indicate), but he seems not to have been cognizant of any dedication to the poetic life. Milton, we can be sure, would not have desisted long in informing his friend of this all-engrossing aspiration, had it been crystallized much before November 1637. His obvious secretiveness, his lack of awareness about himself over some length of time, and his covert decision all manifest the anal-retentive personality.

Might not the remarks concerned with the tender-pinioned Pegasus come as a confession because Milton had only recently reached a verdict about his life? Aside from breaking silence, there is no specific reason for Milton's letter of November 2 except—the most provocative item in it—that he wished to tell Charles about himself privately. Why pen the letter just when his "return to that country-residence of ours . . . so presses" that he has "hardly thrown this together on the paper in haste," if something in it was not momentous; there had surely been other, more felicitous occasions to break silence. The death of Milton's mother on April 3, 1637, for instance, is not alluded to in his letters of November, although he speaks of taking residence at an Inn and of Diodati's "step-motherly war." Had the period of silence been at most only seven months? Milton now was writing to insure that he would see Diodati personally and soon, as he had tried to do "in the beginning of autumn" and "lately." The foregoing suggests that Milton's writing to Diodati was precipitated by his eagerness to inform him of his decision to become a poet, a decision he had reached only shortly before—in the early autumn of 1637.

But there were works written prior to this date that have been interpreted as indicating a poetic career for Milton, and his rejection of a clerical career must likewise be attended to. Much has been written about Milton's poetic leanings before this time; he tells us himself that "it was found that whether ought was impos'd me by them that had the overlooking, or betak'n to of mine own choise in English, or other tongue, prosing or versing, but chiefly this latter, the stile by certain vital signes it had, was likely to live" (*Reason*, 37). His reference is to things like the Latin elegies and the Gunpowder Plot poems, it would seem, as well as the companion poems. Yet this does not constitute anything but casual writing: it is not a declaration of a former poetic life, nor does re-examination of his early verse alter this conclusion. The difference lies in poetry as diversion and in dedication to poetry as lifework.

Milton's remarks in the academically required "Vacation Exercise" of 1628 indicate merely that he wishes to speak (or rather pun) in English and that he would prefer to write something serious, something not insipid and nugatory like the usual college prolusion:

> I have some naked thoughts that rove about
> And loudly knock to have their passage out;
> And wearie of their place do only stay

Till thou [native language] hast deck't them in thy best array;
. . . Yet I had rather, if I were to chuse,
Thy service in some graver subject use,
Such as may make thee search thy coffers round,
Before thou cloath my fancy in fit sound . . . [23-31]

The triviality of "Elegia quinta" (fine poem though it is) can be disregarded, for all it says is that he has not written a poem in a long while:

Am I mistaken? or are powers returning to my songs,
and is inspiration present in me by the favor of spring?
It is present by the favor of spring, and again begins to flourish from it
(who may suspect?) and even now demands some work for itself. [5-8]

"Elegia sexta," which discusses the differences in poetry wrought by environment and which notes the writing of the Nativity ode, asks, "But why does your Muse provoke mine, / and not permit it to be able to pursue its chosen obscurity?" Of course, Milton does not mean that he does not want to write at all, as the "Ode" shows; it is simply that he does not wish to poetize something casual and ephemeral, the point being that his Muse is privately engaged in other work.[6] Writing casual poetry (e.g., "Elegia quinta") must be distinguished from writing serious poetry occasionally (e.g., Nativity ode), and both from writing poetry as one's major bid to fame.

Recent criticism has pointed out the importance of the Seventh Prolusion, "Learning Makes Men Happier Than Ignorance," to Milton's biography. It preludes his "studious retirement" to Hammersmith, shortly after its probable delivery, better than any other evidence we have, but for what profession this "circular education" was effected he does not say. It will be noted that Milton is talking of the orator, who may include the clergyman, and that he divorces the poet from the orator.[7] A few months later, in Sonnet 7, he was again to talk in undefined terms of his life in reassurance of such beliefs as he had pronounced in the Prolusion.

Milton employs the sonnet, attached to the first draft of the letter to a friend in the Trinity MS, to show that he himself has wondered about his lack of accomplishment: "yet that you may see that I am something suspicious of my selfe, & doe take notice of a certaine belatednesse in me I am the bolder to send you some of my nightward thoughts some while since because they come . . . made up in a Petrachian stanza." Nothing here suggests that he intends this as an example of poetic activity preparatory to or indicative of a poetic career.

In contradiction to the usual interpretation of this poem as one dealing with Milton's later poetic career, analysis reveals that it has nothing to say on any specific activity, but that it is concerned with the central idea of the letter, his belatedness. It is a belatedness remarked when he compares the "timely-happy spirits"; it defines, to repeat, an anally retentive personality, the same one that finds his thirty-four years just before writing *The Judgement of Martin Bucer* to be a time of his "youth." The first four lines of the sonnet simply show that he had not achieved employment, position, profession, local recognition, or family—none of the "fond hopes that forward Youth & Vanitie are fledge with together wth Gaine, pride, & ambition." He has not ostensibly, as they say, "got anywhere." He goes on to conclude that, though he appears to be less mature than some other young men, all things that will occur to him are, and always will be, seen and allowed by God, his great taskmaster, just as long as he has the grace (the sum total of Christian virtues endowed by God) to undertake what is destined.[8] God's prescience, though certain, does not necessitate occurrence; that depends upon one's moral responsibility. No suggestion of hopes for a poetic career occurs in this sonnet; nowhere in it does Milton specify in what area his accomplishment will be. His immediate life will be what he has pursued in the past; his lot, that "Toward which Time leads [him], and the will of Heav'n." The only resolution here is one of continuance in order to be ready; the poem is one of reassurance.

None of the works before 1637 that have usually been adduced to indicate leanings toward a poetic career prove so under scrutiny. The writings before this date are all casual, or occasional, or done on commission.[9] Since none of them was a "bud or blossom" in 1631,[10] none can be considered the fruit of a poetic life in 1637. We may look back and descry tendencies toward a poetic life, but these are irrelevant if Milton did not realize where Time was leading him. It was not until 1637 that he recognized this calling and took steps to become more fit.

It would seem likely that Milton would have thoroughly repudiated a church career before coming to a decision in favor of another career. Had he by 1632 and the beginning of the period of studious retirement discarded a career in the church? There is nothing in the Seventh Prolusion or in Sonnet 7 that militates against his still having such expectation; on the other hand, only the emphasis in the former upon the needs of the orator, an obvious aspect of Milton's topic and situation, implies that it was not yet a closed issue. We must look elsewhere for an answer.

In an oft-quoted passage in *Reason,* Milton wrote of "the Church, to whose service by the intentions of my parents and friends I was destin'd of a child, and in mine own resolutions, till comming to some maturity of yeers and perceiving what tyranny had invaded the Church, that

he who would take Orders must subscribe slave, and take an oath with-
all, which unlesse he took with a conscience that would retch, he must
either strait perjure, or split his faith, I thought it better to preferre a
blamelesse silence before the sacred office of speaking bought, and begun with servitude and forswearing . . . thus [was I] Church-outed by
the Prelats" (41).

If we may believe what Milton tells us (and it is highly possible that
such a state of affairs was all that was needed to make the already wa-
vering Milton realize his alienation from the church and take stock of
himself), the tyranny that he accounts his catalyst must be that of
William Laud, who between 1633 and 1637 was conducting visitations to
the parishes to investigate the mode of worship. The slightest disagreement or noncompliance with his precepts, which constituted basically a
rigid conformity to the service prescribed in the prayer book as Laud's
group interpreted it, caused the discharge of the deviating local cleric.
By 1637—and notable then were the heavy fine and the mutilation of
the already famous William Prynne, John Bastwick, and Henry Burton
(June 14) for their antiepiscopal writings—Laud had set nearly the entire nation against the king in terms of religion, and no longer was there
a moderate group between the Puritans and the Laudians. In addition,
the July 11 decree of the Court of the Star Chamber concerning printing placed licensing authority in Laud's hands.

We can partially reconstruct what probably transpired for Milton
during 1637 and after his mother's death, when familial conditions were
being rethought. Isolated in study from the middle of 1632, he left only
"sometimes . . . for the purchase of books, or to learn something new in
mathematics, or in music."[11] That his interest in the church as a career
was waning had not impressed him until the despotic events of 1637 ob-
truded themselves upon his consciousness. Only then did he recognize
and admit his lack of aptitude and ardor. He clearly stated his equation
of preaching and writing: "These abilities [to create great literature] . . .
are of power beside the office of a pulpit, to imbreed and cherish in a
great people the seeds of vertu, and publick civility. . . . this may . . . be
not only in Pulpits, but after another persuasive method, at set and solemn Paneguries, in Theaters, porches, or what other place, or way may
win most upon the people to receiv at once both recreation, & instruction" (*Reason*, 39, 40). It would have been an easy step from a clerical
career to a poetic one.

Further analysis of his situation produced fresh, specific objectives;
and in one particular at least, he came to be like those public figures of
ancient Rome of whom he had written in the Seventh Prolusion, "They
once sought worldly honors, and now they sought immortality."[12] His

engrossment with the Greeks and Italians had shut him off from any real apprehension of civil events, but now, in the autumn of 1637, awake to his changed interests and endeavors, he began to make preparations for his altered future. Accordingly, one consequence of his enthusiasm was to get in touch with his good friend Diodati to inform him of his decision (finally by letter after not otherwise communicating with him); another was to apprise his unknown friend of the resolve mentioned in the letter to Diodati, an action he probably took during one of his trips to London in that autumn of 1637;[13] and still another was to explain himself to his father and uphold his decision—this would explain the dating of "Ad Patrem" during the spring of 1638, after he had achieved serious poetic publication. H.A. Barnett has shown that the poem was written in early spring—around March 5 or April 5. Since he would not have written the poem before this decision, and since it seems to date before the Italian trip, we may deduce a date of authorship in early March 1638, for in April he would have been busy making preparations for his sojourn.[14]

The best statement of Milton's thought during this period is found in "Lycidas." In many ways, of course, Lycidas is Milton more than Edward King, the one being commemorated. The equation of King and Milton is evident from lines 23-36, where their lives and experiences become parallels, and from their both having intended to follow clerical careers. But King's untimely death, coming at this time of transition and soul-searching, when little had been accomplished and much was hoped for, rudely awakens Milton, and he begins to wonder about himself.[15] He hopes, perhaps bathetically, that someone will mourn for him (ll. 19-22). In lines 73-76 he seems to question the use of his own high endeavors, when Atropos so quickly may cut off life before its prime, for surely King's few mediocre Latin poems are hardly sufficient bases for assuming that he meant King as strictly meditating the Muse. Rather, King and the similarities of their lives supplied Milton with a background for personal meditations, though his regret for King's fate was probably sincere enough.

We see Milton typically protesting his unpreparedness in lines 1-7 and 186; in fact, he tries to resist writing by "denial vain, and coy excuse." But he is compelled "yet once more" to poetry (not just elegiac verse),[16] though he had thought to forgo further new writing until the "mellowing year" (his circle not being completed). Is this perhaps the reason behind Milton's delay from August to November in writing "Lycidas"? He was then concerned only with experiment and revision—elements of his immediate enthusiasm for his new career—as recorded in the Trinity MS. Compulsion for "Lycidas," on the other hand, arose from contemplating the profit in pursuing a clerical life or a serious poetic life (ll. 64-66); it might be better to lead a carefree life—erotic, forgetful of one's charges—for the only guerdon seems untimely death (ll. 67-69, 73-76). The citation of Orpheus and his destruction, which even his mother Calliope, muse of epic poetry, could not subvert, raises the ineffectual worth that the poetic life provides (ll. 57-63).[17] King's death has finally sunk in: Milton's journey in life may very easily be cut short by Atropos before the quest has been fulfilled. Why not enjoy, why not *live*? Yet we know that this was not Milton's feeling: it represents not only that youthful and short-lived moment of despair and frustration summed up by a modern generation as "What's the use," but also the opposition he seems to have met from those around him—including his father, who, though he did not bid Milton "go where the way lies broad, where the field of wealth is easier and the golden hope of amassing money glitters sure," continued "to contemn the sacred Muses" and to think them "fruitless and contemptible."[18] Milton answers these doubts, if ever he seriously considered them, resoundingly: "Fame is the spur that the clear spirit doth raise / . . . To scorn delights, and live laborious dayes" (ll. 70-72), and though life go, praise remains. Fame mounts to Heaven, where it furnishes the basis for the final reward.

Milton's coupling of the clerical life ("the homely slighted shepherds trade") and the poetic life ("strictly meditate the thankless muse") reinforces remarks made earlier; and it shows that contemplation of a clerical life was not in the too-distant past. Indeed, a major concern of the poem lies in lines 108-31, the so-called digression on the corrupted clergy. Convention though it had become, "the rebuke administered to the corrupt clergy," as James Holly Hanford has remarked, "is an echo of his own determination not to go into the church."[19] His experience must have been recent to deserve such a shattering indictment when the ostensible subject of his poem, Edward King, right up to his death, had been contemplating a clergyman's life. And to subjoin the note "And by occasion foretells the ruin of our corrupted Clergy then in their height" to the 1645 edition, or to allow it to be subjoined, even though the antiprelatical controversy was recent, manifests the importance of the passage for Milton. In this passage he gives us good reason for his renunciation of the clerical life; those who "creep and intrude, and clime into the fold," the "blind mouths," "the grim wolf," and the lack of resistance to perversion ("little sed").[20] And as indicated ("then in their height"), it was in 1637 that this corruption became so palpable that the creeping prelatism (the subject of his first sallies into published argument in 1641-42) became so formidable.

In lines 186-93 Milton takes leave of his subject, and also of pastoralism (though he was to return briefly later). How metaphorical are these lines? I believe that it is not pushing interpretation too far to read this passage, and indeed the whole poem, as a metaphor of Milton's life, ambitions, and thought. "The uncouth swain" (that is, Milton, unprepared and unlearned, to his way of thinking) "sang" (wrote poetry) "to th'oaks and rills" (for a limited audience) "While the still morn went out with sandals gray" (while his early, unproductive life slipped imperceptibly away; he would be 29 within a month, with only one unattributed poem to his public credit). "He toucht the tender stops of various quills" (he composed various kinds of poetry), "With eager thought warbling his *Dorick* lay" (now writing this pastoral with enthusiastic and impatient thoughts for the future): "And now the Sun had stretcht out all the hills, / And now was dropt into the western bay" (but time has run out for continuing in his former stead, and for producing only additional *tenues sonos*). "At last he rose, and twitcht his mantle blew" (finally he roused himself from his "prolonged obscurity" and from his *juvenilia carmina, lusus*): "To morrow to fresh woods and pastures new" (in the future he will engage in new kinds of poetic expression for the wide and expansive world—the oaks have become woods, and the rills have been forgotten in favor of the pastures through which they run). "Woods" recalls the "sylvæ" of Statius or "The Forrest" of Ben Jonson, collections of occasional lyric poems, and "pastures," such pastoral poems as eclogues.

"Lycidas" is assuredly the best statement of Milton's thought during this period: in the words of Hanford again, it is "Milton's first great confession of faith—in himself and his earnest way of life, in God and immortality" (168). It is a farewell to the past, a heralding of the future. If this metaphoric reading of "Lycidas" is valid, it furnishes evidence that his "tardie moving" was just then taking place. The suggested date for "Ad Patrem" roughly concurs with the probable publication of *Comus*, as inferred by Helen Darbishire,[21] and later that of "Lycidas," explicating his then current estimate of himself more meaningfully than heretofore: "now that I am a part of the learned company, however humble, . . . I shall no longer mingle unknown with the indolent rabble."[22] Not only was he now "publishing & divulging conceaved merits," he was also preparing to take the grand tour—a tour that was to give him additional faith in his literary propensities and new directions for future performance.

5

Preparations

Upon deciding to emulate the great poets of all nations, Milton embarked upon a threefold program to be fit: he began a notebook of poetic writing, both improving some items of the past and recording "contemporary" poems; he set up a notebook of *topoi* drawn from his extensive reading with an eye to possible future use in the great literature envisioned; and he embarked on a sojourn abroad from around April 1638 to August 1639. The poetic notebook, the Trinity MS, was later also to record possible subjects for his writing—dramas in most cases—and some outlines, usually in prose, both brief and more extensive. The topical notebook, the Commonplace Book, was later to become a repository for materials useful in the prose of his left hand. The Commonplace Book deserves certain considerations it has not been given, particularly its place in Milton's growing ambitions and its reflection of personal attitudes and biographical concerns. The sojourn introduced him to foreign vistas at first hand, a world he had known only through his books.

The inception of the Trinity MS, also known as the Cambridge MS, has been dated by the inclusion of "Arcades," the omission of "L'Allegro" and "Il Penseroso," and the interpretation of a letter to an unknown friend, the first draft of which includes a copy of Sonnet 7. The omission of the companion poems has suggested a date after summer 1631, the time usually assigned to their composition. The letter, written probably not long after the notebook was begun, is limited by the date of the included Sonnet 7, that is, after December 1631. And "Arcades" would have been composed before "A Maske" (*Comus*), which was performed in September 1634. It is now dated May 1634.[1] The dates of the three English odes—"On Time," "Upon the Circumcision," and "At a Solemn Music"—have depended upon the dating of the aforementioned items. On these bases the notebook was certainly not begun before May 1634, although earlier dating has been uninformedly advanced by some commentators.

The letter talks of the sonnet as "my nightward thoughts some while since"; both are concerned with Milton's lack of accomplishment. "Some while since" could be taken to be two years (since early 1632, that is) or even five or six years. In the second draft of the letter is a further sentence that indicates appreciable time-lapse after graduation from Cambridge in July 1632: "whether it proceed from a principle bad, good, or naturall it could not have held out thus long against so strong opposition." Surely the years of formal study, ostensibly for the ministry, are not included here. The two years of 1632-34 seem insufficient to be construed as "held out thus long." Further in the letter he denies that "I have given up my selfe to dreame away my yeares in the armes of studious retirement." Again, those two years of studious retirement, his being with his parents at their Hammersmith home (until mid-1635 when they moved to Horton), seem insufficient for this statement. The point is iterated by his calling his studious retirement "prolonged obscurity." The previous chapter indicates decision for a poetic career in autumn 1637. Such a date—five years since his graduation—is more consonant with Milton's remarks in this letter: "some while since," "held out thus long," "yeares in the armes of studious retirement," "prolonged obscurity." And another phrase in the letter specifically refers to such decision and the action it would involve: "to give you account, as oft as occasion is, of *this* my tardie moving" (my emphasis).[2] A date of autumn 1637 for the inception of the Trinity MS is cogent.

The manuscript itself is largely transcription with numerous alterations; only "At a Solemn Music," the letter, and some of the Plans for Subjects show "original" inscription. Significant here, and pointing to autumn 1637 as the date of transcription, are the four appearances of Italian *e* in the basic transcription of "Comus": "plumes," 379 (19); "Goddesse" (first *e*?), 865 (26); and "scene" (second *e*) and "towne" in the stage direction between lines 957 and 958 (27). While one example of Italian *e* occurs in his handwriting of which we have examples from before autumn 1637,[3] it becomes frequent only at the end of 1637: "Lycidas," written in November 1637, has two Italian *e*'s in the basic transcription and three in reworked material; the pasted leaf of "Comus" (an additional rendering and development of ll. 672-706, written on a torn half-sheet and pasted in) shows eight such letter formations; the revised epilogue to "Comus" (29) has six; and the marginalia to his copies of Varchi and Aratus, where examples are numerous, are generally dated around 1638. He was abroad in April 1638-August 1639; thereafter the Italian *e* in his handwriting is almost consistent.

Dating the inception of the Trinity MS in autumn 1637[4] leads to this ordering of materials there recorded prior to the European trip: "Arcades" was transcribed; "At a Solemn Music" was composed; the letter was written; "On Time" and "Upon the Circumcision" were transcribed, as well as a clean copy of "At a Solemn Music"; "A Maske" was then entered (which transcription was begun probably about the same time as the three odes were entered); and "Lycidas" was transcribed. Revisions to "A Maske" were made both before and after the transcription of "Lycidas," and straight up through its publication (which occurred probably in early 1638—that is, prior to mid-March, although the title page reads 1637). Lines 779-806 of "A Maske" do not appear in the manuscript, and only a fragment of a second pasted leaf containing lines 350-65 remains. This dating, of course, obviates the illogical lack of use of the manuscript between 1634 ("A Maske") and 1637 ("Lycidas") created by earlier dating.

The date of composition of "At a Solemn Music" is that of the date of the manuscript, but the dating of the other two odes is not settled. They may have been composed any time before this, probably before the manuscript was actually begun. Their prosody, however, suggests the kind of experimentation that Milton is engaging in "At a Solemn Music" and "Lycidas." Perhaps they were early products of his decision and lie just before he began specifically to prepare for his lifework by starting the poetic repository, one in which he would first revamp items of a different medium (creating dramatic *poems* for reading rather than dramatic presentations) and items with which he was not entirely satisfied—because of limitations of occasion? commission? original time demands? "Upon the Circumcision" need not necessarily have been written around the Feast of the Circumcision, January 1, of course.[5]

This dating explains the exclusion of such poems as those written during the university years as well as the Greek version of Psalm 114 and "Philosophus ad regem," although no translations or foreign-language poems are recorded here at any time. Latin poems written during the European trip are not transcribed, nor is "Epitaphium Damonis," which we can understand as being worked on elsewhere and soon thereafter published. Nor do Latin poems, including "Ad Patrem" and "Ad Joannum Roüsium," and translations, including Psalms 80-88 and 1-8 and "The Fifth Ode of Horace," appear.[6]

After his return from the Continent, Milton used the manuscript to record (and at times revise) the remaining short poems, Sonnets 8-10, published in 1645 and usually dated 1642-44; Sonnets 11-17 and "On the Forcers of Conscience"; and Plans and Subjects for longer works (see Chapter 9). This takes us to the year 1652, when Sonnets 16 and 17 and the tailed sonnet were recorded, possibly by Milton's nephew John Phillips.[7] To the folio quire was added a quarto gathering, the inner leaves of which (3-6) are now lost. The quarto gathering records Sonnets

11-14, 21 (part), 22-23; presumably Sonnets 15-20, 21 (part), and "On the Forcers of Conscience" were transcribed on the missing leaves. After 1652 pages 10-12, 42, and 47-50 of the quire were still blank and could have been used to record Sonnets 18-23. Instead Milton chose to have sonnets from 11 onward recorded separately to follow the ten in the 1645 edition. An added headnote in the informal hand of Jeremy Picard on page 1 of the quarto gathering reads, "these sonnets follow ye 10. in ye printed booke." These are Sonnets 11-14 in the hand of a scribe employed by Milton in 1653 (he also made changes in poems in Milton's and in Phillips's hands in the folio manuscript); Sonnets 21-22 in the hand of Cyriack Skinner (?), to whom they are addressed, written and presumably penned in 1655;[8] and Sonnet 23 in the more formal hand of Picard.

The date of Sonnet 23 has been debated, largely because of the question of which wife was intended; the fact that Picard recorded it has suggested 1658 because he did other work for Milton in 1658-60. But, as I have indicated elsewhere,[9] there is reason to believe that he knew Milton in 1655, and it is possible that he was a former student. Thus the date of Sonnet 23 could be closer to 1655 if indeed the wife is Mary Powell, and it should be remarked that Picard's note and Sonnet 23 need not have been entered at the same time. Of the poems presumably recorded on the lost pages, the scribe of Sonnets 11-14 could have put down Sonnet 15-17 and "On the Forcers of Conscience" around 1653, if that were the only time he worked for Milton, and someone entered Sonnets 18-20 in 1655, the generally accepted date for those poems, although "When I consider how my light is spent" (Sonnet 19) has also been assigned earlier composition.

The only cogent reason for retranscribing Sonnets 11-14 (as well as 15-17 and "On the Forcers of Conscience") was to have a copy to send to a printer for a new edition of the shorter poems—presumably in 1653 when the scribe worked for Milton. But it is possible, surely, that this scribe continued to work for Milton through 1655 and that the quarto gathering was started then for a projected new edition. In a letter to me, Professor Maurice Kelley questions James Holly Hanford's[10] and my suggestions of 1653 for a new edition: "At that time Milton had on hand seven later sonnets and the 'New Forcers'—material requiring only four pages of the new, quarto gathering. Why, then, did Hand 5 [that is, the scribe of 1653] prepare an eight-page gathering when four would have sufficed and a second group of four blank pages would have served only to encumber the printer?" Further, the placement of "On the Forcers of Conscience" would, under a 1653 dating, put it on page 4 with four blank pages when it might then more logically have been placed on page 5.

Kelley's suggested dating of the quarto gathering as 1655 would yield the following arrangement: page 1, Sonnets 11-12; page 2, Sonnets 13-14; page 3, Sonnets 15-16; page 4, Sonnets 17-18; page 5, Sonnets 19-20; page 6, "On the Forcers of Conscience," leaving some blank space on page 6, and a blank leaf, pages 7-8.[11] Later Skinner (?) entered Sonnet 21 on pages 6-7 and Sonnet 22 on page 7, and Picard, Sonnet 23 on page 8. If this is what happened, then this unknown scribe did work for Milton in 1655 and would have entered Sonnets 11-20 and "On the Forcers of Conscience," as Kelley argues. Corroboration may lie in Sotheby's statement (95), as Professor Kelley has pointed out to me, "that the paper of the quarto gathering is of the same quality and size as that found in the latter part of the *De Doctrina* manuscript. . . . Milton resumed work on his theological treatise about that year." I thus revise my earlier thinking and conclude that it is more probable that in 1655, when Milton composed some additional shorter poems (Sonnets 18-20?), Sonnet 17 in 1652 being the next earlier one, he caused a transcription for a new edition to be made.[12]

This 1653-55? scribe may thus have produced the texts for *Defensio secunda* (1654) and *Defensio pro Se* (1655), as well as state papers, and Psalms 1-8 (1653) and personal letters to Oldenburg (1654), Philaras (1654), Aitzema (1655), and Spanheim (1655). This scribe, who makes a number of errors in his transcriptions of Sonnets 11-14 and who changes Milton's spelling and accidentals as recorded in the holograph versions in the Trinity MS, may thus be the cause for such seemingly un-Miltonic readings as "their" (three times), "so" and "wo" (for "sow" and "woe"), and inadequate commas in Sonnet 18; the indefensible punctuation of "ask; But", "gifts, who", and "best, his" in Sonnet 19; "Where" (rather than "Wher"), "sometimes" (rather than "somtimes"), and "*Tuskan*" in Sonnet 20.

We have been considering in the last few pages not Milton's preparation to further his decision to be a poet, honing his craft through poetic revisions and composition, but his continued poetic endeavors and the continued use of the two sections now joined and labelled as the Trinity MS. What should now first be noted is that the basic manuscript is not employed after 1652 with the entry of Sonnet 17 and "On the Forcers of Conscience." It suggests that during the years from mid-1652 through late 1655 Milton was not often actively pursuing his great purpose in poetic writing; only the experiments in prosodic form in Psalms 1-8 in August 1653 indicate such activity. As we now may look at 1655, if it be allowed that the unknown scribe prepared the quarto gathering then (and it would require his employment through November of that year, when Sonnet 20 was probably written), we can suggest that his corrections to the copies of the poems in the manuscript were made then, not in 1653, as has often been assumed, and, more importantly, that Milton was embarking anew toward achievement of his great purpose poetically.

This topic will be examined in Chapter 9, but suffice it to say here that 1655 can be seen as a kind of turning point in Milton's career. While he continued to produce state papers after May-July 1655 (when the spate of letters about the Piedmont massacre was written), they are quite few until April 1656. *Defensio pro Se,* of course, was published in August 1655, but the years until the return of the monarchy loomed and occurred in 1659-60 would seem to have engaged renewed poetic writing activity. In the midst of this period would seem to be reexamination of manuscript materials which he rediscovered (including Ralegh's *The Cabinet-Council,* published in May [?] 1658[13]). The only shorter poems we know of that were written just past the time when the unknown scribe may have transcribed the quarto gathering (November 1655) are Sonnets 21-23, which are also included in that gathering, as we have seen. Not only are no shorter poems produced after 1655 (other than Sonnet 23), but Milton had now turned his attention to the larger concerns of his great purpose by returning to what became *Paradise Lost.* Part of the impetus for a new edition of the shorter works at this time may have been a general lack of availability of the 1645 *Poems,* published by Humphrey Moseley. But Moseley's catalogue "Courteous Reader," in which the 1645 *Poems* continued to be listed, is found in versions dated 1656 or later in various volumes of later date.

Besides a "strong propensity of nature," achievement in great poetry requires "labour and intent study," according to Milton.[14] Milton's private studies at Hammersmith and Horton had progressed, by November 1637, through "the affairs of the Greeks as far as to the time when they ceased to be Greeks" and of the "Italians under the Longobards, the Franks, and the Germans, to that time when liberty was granted them by Rodolph, King of Germany."[15] These seem to describe two separate, though complementary, reading programs, not always chronologically parallel, but near completion at about the time he wrote his letter to Diodati. Shortly before this time, having decided upon the poetic life, I believe Milton commenced his repository of interesting, noteworthy, and literarily useful materials, the Commonplace Book (CPB).[16] Should this contention prove true, entries would have been made first around September 1637, and notes from some of the texts Milton had been perusing so that the plateau of studies mentioned above could be reached—a stage of reading best followed, he tells us, by separate study of the history of each state[17]—would probably be found there, entered during September-November. See the discussion of this reading in Appendix A.

With such seeming agreement as Appendix A suggests between the recorded reading and the comment in the letter to Diodati, a comment that sounds as if Milton had only just come to reach the chronological plateau he describes, the Commonplace Book could not have been begun very long before November 1637. As I have suggested for the Trinity MS as well, the Commonplace Book was probably begun at this time because of Milton's decision to pursue poetry as his major endeavor. He would have commenced this repository to acquire a source book for materials that would be useful to him in the future as he wrote literary works of worth. If so, the most likely date for the inception of the Commonplace Book is around September 1637. Such a conclusion implies that if any other commonplace books existed before this time, they were not kept with an eye toward use in poetic writing. But there is no evidence that another miscellany had been kept. The matter of "the other index," as Milton calls it (CPB, 221), the theological index noted by Edward Phillips (CPB, 197), has been discussed elsewhere[18] and need not divert us in the present study.

I have previously offered this same conclusion in slightly different terms: "A total view of the notebook and an analysis of contents does *not* lead me to wonder why certain things or authors are not included (a frequent enough speculation by others); it does lead me to recognize that the schematization of knowledge which Milton was achieving had a definite purpose for the future, one involved in asserting liberty and Christian virtue and in examining the sources of servitude and wrong reason. . . . If we can dispel the thought that Milton simply recorded material which struck him as potentially interesting as he read without a fairly clear though far-off view, we can realize that the Commonplace Book yields evidence of the preparation of a Milton to 'leave something so written to aftertimes, as they should not willingly let it die.' "[19] For the Commonplace Book is a collection of *topoi* or topics to be employed as proofs in Milton's envisioned championing of religious, domestic, and political freedoms. Nor does the dating that has been suggested for the entries in the Commonplace Book by Hanford and Mohl conflict with my suggested date: all dates include 1637 in their range of years, and only twenty-six are suggested as possibly ranging from before that date. It is illogical that twenty-six entries were made between 1635 and 1637 (twenty citations), or 1635 and 1638 (five citations), or 1635 and 1639 (one citation), when 1637-38 is concluded for twenty-nine other entries alone. Such incidental entry over a period of possibly two years as dating prior to 1637 allows cannot be squared with any meaningful intent on Milton's part.

The likely reason for late entries from books that Milton, in his chronological course of study, would have read before his Italian sojourn or soon after his return (Caesar, Frontinus, Codinus, Villani, Berni, Tasso) is that he read these with his students (ca. 1640-ca. 1647), and that as he reread, items for entry occurred to him. We know specifically that he studied "Frontinus his Stratagems" and "Giovan Villani" with them, for Edward Phillips tells us so in his life. Perhaps some of the other returns to earlier historical or literary materials, entered by amanuenses, are also due to this schoolteaching, the amanuenses being students. Cyriack Skinner in the earliest biography tells us, "The Youths that hee instructed from time to time servd him often as Amanuenses."[20]

After his return from the Continent, Milton continued his study of the early church, as we have seen. Also dealing specifically with the church, religion, or related matters is his later reading of Gilles (55), Bacon (65), Peter Martyr (73), Schickhard (82), and Rivet (98). The reappearance of Roman history (97) and Byzantine history (96) has already been mentioned; and there were a few other early authors or books on early materials entered after 1639: Aristotle (40), Justinian (71), Caesar (74), and Löwenklau (75). From the study of independent Italian states only one entry is found in the Commonplace Book in Milton's hand: that from Villani's *Croniche* of Florence (95) on 12, dated 1643-45 by Mohl. Besides the literary materials of the Italian Renaissance (Nos. 78-81, 94) recorded are one general history of Italy (Guiccardini, 93), two Italian Reformation works (Savonarola, 33, and Sarpi, 49), and Machiavelli's *Dell'Arte della Guerra* (43). General histories of Europe or the world are also found: Jovius (48); Thuanus (51-52); Cuspinian (61); and Ralegh (66). Soon after his return from Italy, but probably after having completed most of his reading of the early church, Milton seems to have progressed to a study of the history of Britain, along with a complementary study of the histories of Scotland and Ireland. Perhaps decisions about his poetic endeavors and the subject they were then expected to encounter lay at the base of this reading pattern. During or soon after his British study he was reading, besides the general histories cited above, the histories of the Holy Roman Empire (Sleidan, 46) and of France (Girard, 50 and 53; Commines, 54; and Sesellius, 60). As he moved into the controversy over divorce, he read and recorded arresting ideas from Cyprian (56), Sinibaldus (57), Selden (70 and 76), and Bodin (72).

Milton's calling as a poet, as already stated in Chapter 4, was qualified by the requisite glorifications of God through the honor and instruction of his country: "I apply'd my selfe to that resolution . . . [so] That what the greatest and choycest wits of *Athens, Rome,* or modern *Italy,* and those Hebrews of old did for their country, I in my proportion with this ever and above of being a Christian, might doe for mine" (*Reason,* 38). To this end, he began the study of the history of the British Isles (including Scotland and Ireland), as recorded in the Commonplace Book (34-39, 41-42, 44-45, 47, 58-59, 62-64, 83, all entered after 1639 and before ca. 1644). Likewise he was reading or rereading other British materials (67-69, 85-87) during these same years. The well-known passages of "Mansus" (78-84), "Epitaphium Damonis" (162-78), and *Reason,* Book II, and a few less than a third of the subjects in the Plans in the Trinity MS attest to Milton's preoccupation with British history. (Five other subjects in the Plans deal with items from Scotch history.) If his remarks in *Reason* are correct in the implication that his calling as a poet was closely related to British themes, just as their calling as poets was related to themes of their own countries for "the greatest and choycest wits of *Athens, Rome,* or modern *Italy,* and those Hebrews of old" (see his remark, "These thoughts at once possest me, and these other," 37), then his decision to be a poet could not have preceded his study of British materials (from 1639) by too great a length of time.

The studies of the Hammersmith and Horton periods, because they were not pursued with an eye to their use as literary background and because they did not cover British history, which became foremost at a later date, do not truly satisfy the "industrious and select reading" (41) avowed in *Reason* in order "to be an interpreter & relater of the best and sagest things among mine own Citizens throughout this Iland in the mother dialect" through poetic writing (38). But since his stress upon the British aspects of his accomplishment and the delimiting of his accomplishment to the area of poetic writing is actually part of his more comprehensive aim as stated in the Seventh Prolusion (to allow his mind to soar "through the histories and geographies of every country observing the condition and changes of kingdoms, nations, cities, and peoples in order to acquire practical wisdom and morals"), the studies of the Hammersmith and Horton period are as much part of the "industrious and select reading" as his continuing work in the history of philosophy, of Italy, of the Church, of France, of Russia, of law, of ethics, of marriage and divorce, and of war. The studies from 1637 onward attempt to complete the full circle Milton so often described, although some emphasis or material that might otherwise have been less or different probably proceeded from his new interests in a British poetic subject and from the issues in which he later found himself embroiled. At the same time, the studies of 1637, unlike those before that date of decision, are designed to prepare Milton for the "fresh Woods, and Pastures new," for those things which "the mind at home in the spacious circuits of her musing hath liberty to propose to her self, though of highest hope, and hardest attempting" (*Reason*, 38).

Once we consider that Milton's amanuenses in the Commonplace Book may have been his students we can reexamine entries for dating. We know that Amanuensis B, who entered two notes from Machiavelli's *Discorsi* (197) and the heading and index entry for 197, was Edward Phillips, Milton's nephew. The other notes from the *Discorsi* were apparently entered by his brother, John Phillips.[21] The usual dating of the Machiavelli entries, 1651-52, is derived from the fact that Edward's and the other scribe's hands are seen in letters to Hermann Mylius from November 1651 through February 1652. If, however, indeed both the Machiavelli scribes were not professional scribes but rather Milton's own nephews, there is no need to assume that the letters and the Commonplace Book entries were written down at the same time. According to the suggested dating for surrounding entries, the Machiavelli notes could have been entered any time after 1642-44. The uncertainly identified scribe's entries appear on 148, 185, 195 (2), 198 (2), 242 (3), 245, and 246; headings and index entries for 148 and 198 were also made by him. If these entries were made between 1644 and 1647, Edward would have been around fourteen to seventeen and John, a year younger. These ages are not odd: John, as I have argued elsewhere, wrote the "Ode to Rouse" manuscript, which was sent January 1647. Amanuensis A, who entered three quotations from Berni and Boiardo (71, 77, and 187), may thus also have been John Phillips. A date of entry after 1642 is all that is required for these quotations. Parker, incidentally, places Edward Phillips's leaving his uncle's home in the summer of 1646 (see 1:30 and 2:930 n. 40), although he may have returned thereafter and occasionally performed secretarial duties.

Amanuensis E, in the most poorly and erroneously penned note in the Commonplace Book, made a reference to Buchanan's *Rerum Scoticarum Historia* on 198 following two from the *Discorsi*. Such poor work on the part of a young student is more understandable than on the part of a professional scribe. Amanuensis F recorded material from Sigonius's *De occidentali Imperio* on 19 and 181 and two items from Costanzo's *Historia del regno di Napoli* on 5 and 248. He also wrote the heading for 248, the note at the head of 185, and the page number in the index. Probably the second page entitled "Tyrannus" (248) was not begun until most of the space on the first page (185) was used. The short Machiavelli item on 185 may have been squeezed in after the longer citation from Costanzo was made on 248. Milton's latest entries on 185 are tentatively dated 1644-47 by Mohl. The other three items by Amanuensis F need date only after 1639-41. Thus dates of entry between ca. 1644 and ca. 1647 for all these scribal notes satisfy requirements and allow that these scribes were students entering material from texts read early by Milton but reread during the period of his schoolteaching.

The preceding omits only Amanuensis C, Jeremy Picard, who worked on other materials from ca. 1658 to ca. 1660, and Amanuensis D, who scribed the manuscript of *Paradise Lost,* perhaps around 1665. Picard entered in the Commonplace Book a quotation from Rivet on 188 and a note from Augustine on 195. But he was working for the government in 1655 and may have worked for Milton before 1658 as well, as I have noted before.[22] Amanuensis D inserted between Edward Phillips's entries on 197 a note and two quotations from Dante, which Mohl dates without explanation as 1650-[67(?)], and noted on 249 material from Nicetas, published in 1647. He likewise wrote the heading for 249 and the index entry. My implication, of course, is that Picard and Amanuensis D were former students of Milton. Perhaps Picard became associated with the government as scribe by 1655 through Milton, having been his student before. Picard may have been the "Mr. Packer who was his Scholar," reported by John Aubrey,[23] as William R. Parker has suggested.[24] We do not know the names of a great many of Milton's students, but candidates for Amanuenses D, E, and F during the 1640s may be Richard Barry, Thomas Gardiner, and Richard Heath; Parker also conjectured William Brownlow and John Overton, as well as Edward Lawrence.

We must remember that Milton used a student to record Sonnet 8 in the Trinity MS,[25] apparently John Phillips to record Sonnets 16 and 17 and "New Forcers," and apparently Cyriack Skinner to record Sonnets 21 and 22.[26] Skinner's hand does not appear in the Commonplace Book, probably because he left Milton's tutelage before 1647.[27] Perhaps he left by ca. 1644 when Milton may have begun to use student-amanuenses to record in the Commonplace Book.

To summarize, then, the entries written by Amanuensis A, that is, John Phillips (?), are dated after 1641-42 by the surrounding entries. If the Machiavelli notes, which Phillips may also have written, were put down at about the same time, we may date them all after 1642-44 (see entries on 185, 193, 242). Probably the entries on 198 were put down after the work of Amanuensis B, that is, Edward Phillips. Milton's elder nephew would have made his entries perhaps after 1642-44, as well. The entries by Amanuensis C, Jeremy Picard, were made after 1642-44 and perhaps after those from the *Discorsi*. The edition of Rivet may have been that of 1651 or an earlier, uncollected volume. Amanuensis D made the entry from Nicetas Acominate in or after 1647, the date of the edition used; otherwise his work simply postdates Edward Phillips's entries. Amanuensis E's work was put down after the Machiavelli notes were made; the work of Amanuensis F was probably accomplished during 1644-47.

In all, the notes of the amanuenses in the Commonplace Book can be dated after 1642 and through 1647, dates coinciding with Milton's years as tutor, with only a possibility of one or two after that date. Milton's own entries are dated up to 1644-47. Perhaps the Commonplace Book was little supplemented after Milton suspended his tutoring around 1647, and more certainly not much supplemented after he began governmental duties in 1649. (See Appendix B for a discussion of languages employed in the Commonplace Book.)

Of his studious retirement Milton writes in his rebuttal of Peter Du Moulin's maliciously accusative remarks in *Regii sanguinis clamor ad coelum adversus parricidas Anglicanos*: "At my father's country place, whither he had retired to spend his declining years, I devoted myself entirely to the study of Greek and Latin writers, completely at leisure, not, however, without sometimes exchanging the country for the city, either to purchase books or to become acquainted with some new discovery in mathematics or music, in which I then took the keenest pleasure."[28] The nature of this studious retirement had been preluded in his remarks in the Seventh Prolusion, usually dated 1632, just before his graduation as a Master of Arts. The reasons for the retirement, aside from the desire to experience the "great joy . . . given to the mind that soars through the histories and geographies of every country observing the condition and changes of kingdoms, nations, cities, and peoples in order to acquire practical wisdom and morals," "to participate in every age as if one were living in it, as if he were born a contemporary of time itself," are conjectural. Milton did not receive a preferment at Cambridge or for any living (as a minister); he may have recognized his lack of ardent calling for the ministry, although we cannot call him "church-outed" at this time (see Chapter 4). But a more compelling reason may have been his parents, as has been suggested before. His father retired from his business in late 1631, moving to Hammersmith (by at least mid-1632), then appreciably to the suburban west of the city although now part of Greater London, and apparently giving up the Bread Street residence as a home.

Having been born in 1562, he was then about seventy. Milton's mother was about ten years younger. In late 1631 his sister Anne, a recent widow, had two young children, Edward Phillips, aged one, and John Phillips, newborn. She would seem to have married Thomas Agar in January 1632 and thus became step-mother to his infant daughter, and she gave birth again in October 1632. Agar—deputy clerk of the Crown in the Court of Chancery, succeeding Milton's brother-in-law, Edward Phillips—and his family came to live comparatively near the Miltons, it would seem, in Kensington, where Agar's brother John also resided. Anne could hardly be expected to take close care of her parents in 1631-32 or afterwards. (Another daughter was born a year or so later, perhaps in 1633.) Milton's brother Christopher, sixteen or seventeen in 1631-32, withdrew from Cambridge and entered the Inner Temple as a law student, perhaps in September 1632. Clearly, he too was in no position to care for his aging parents. It was only after the mother's death, any evidence shows, that Milton could contemplate maintaining his studiousness, but not in retirement. The move to Horton, Bucks, took place in 1635, and the so-called Horton period, which early biographers and (in error) some current commentators still date as 1632-37, is the second part of that studious retirement in 1635-37.

Milton continues in *Defensio secunda:* "When I had occupied five years in this fashion [mid-1637, that is], I became desirous, my mother having died, of seeing foreign parts, especially Italy, and with my father's consent I set forth, accompanied by a single attendant" (IV, i, 614). Compressed here is a year's time. His mother died on April 3, 1637, and he received a letter concerning his planned sojourn from Sir Henry Wotton, dated April 13, 1638. His departure is generally placed soon after that date. His letter to Diodati, November 23, 1637, is our only evidence of an intention to remove himself from where he was living "obscurely and cramped" and "to migrate into some inn of the lawyers where there is a pleasant and shady walk, because there there is a more convenient habitation among a number of companions, if I wish to remain at home, and a more suitable headquarters if I choose to make excursions to any place."[29] We do not know whether he actually carried out this plan or one similar to it. Parker describes the legal difficulties of the father just before and after the mother's death (153-55), with matters settling down by early 1638. Anne in 1637-38 had her family of husband and three children to tend (Agar's daughter by his first wife, Mary Rugeley, and his and Anne's first daughter, Mary, having died). Christopher, still a student at the Inner Temple until around January 26, 1640, when he was called to the bar, had married Thomasine Webber in 1637, well before

November. She seems to have gone to live with her father-in-law, perhaps in November 1637, while her husband concluded his studies and was living now again in the commons.[30]

Thus around November 1637 seems to be the first time that Milton would be freed of his immediate responsibilities and could contemplate the foreign vistas he had talked of vicariously in the Seventh Prolusion. Nothing here really suggests contemplation of the European trip until after November and the possible removal from Horton to London, whether to one of the law colleges or not. The activities of the months immediately before and after that date, as discussed in the foregoing considerations of the Trinity MS and the Commonplace Book, lead to a view of Milton at that time as one—though twenty-nine on December 9, 1637—akin to the "liberated" school or college graduate now finally on his own, with his own flat and only himself to account to.

In his mother's death there may be for Milton only the release of shifting familial relationships, but psychologically we can see more. Though his father was to live for another ten years, in November 1637 he was about seventy-five, and the critical question of Milton's future, which had apparently been submerged during his mother's lifetime, would have arisen with any realistic view of life and death. For Milton there was "about this tyme of a mans life . . . the desire of house & family of his owne . . . to wch nothing is esteemed more helpfull then the early entring into credible employment, & nothing more hindering then this affected solitarinesse" (Letter to an Unknown Friend, second version). Further, the death of Edward King in August, but which he may not have heard of until late September or so, may have crashed into his consciousness even more significantly because this turning point for the family had occurred. In the autumn of 1637 his "reciprocall contradiction" and "excuse . . . for not doing preach & not preach," plus his "tediousnesse," which would "spoyle all the patience of a Parish," and his lack of matter to haste "by the readiest ways of publishing & divulging conceived merits" were clear. With the rejection of a clerical life and with the acceptance of a literary one would come the realization that there was little of major importance to "publish and divulge": the "Nativity Ode," "Comus." Should we add the first seven sonnets? the companion poems? "Arcades"? Even so, a slim volume, nowhere like the ten-years-younger Abraham Cowley's *Poetical Blossoms* of 1633 and *Sylva* in the second edition of 1636, with a third edition in 1637, or the five-years-older Shakerley Marmion's *Cupid and Psyche* in 1637. Only "Comus" was something of a single balance, were it "divulged" through general performance and publication, to any one of William Davenant's works: "The Tragedy of Albovine" (1629), "The Cruell Brother" (1630), "The Just

Italian" (1630), "Temple of Love" (1635), "The Platonick Lovers" (1636), "The Witts" (1636), "Triumphs of the Prince d'Amour" (1636), or the masque "Luminalia" (1637) attributed to him. Davenant was only two years older than Milton. Surely the line about "som more timely-happy spirits" would have echoed often in his mind.

Out of such a psychological state of realization about the self and the need to reject "affected solitarinesse" and live in the world came the renewal of spirit seen in the workbook called the Trinity MS, in the repository for future employment, the Commonplace Book, and in the need to leave the chrysalis, first in an intermediary and local step and then in a full and more expansive flying forth. "Lycidas" begins "Yet once more," and one knows that literarily the line is setting up a comparison with the other poems of the past (which through revision the dramatic presentations "Arcades" and "Comus" were also becoming)—while he reprises that past. And it ends "Tomorrow to fresh Woods, and Pastures new," and one knows as well that literarily the line is setting up a comparison with envisioned longer, major poetry. It has now become commonplace to view "Lycidas" as counterpart to Vergil's *Eclogues* or Spenser's *The Shepheardes Calender,* but that commonplaceness does not make the parallel any the less significant or less accurate. Milton is *consciously,* I think, working up the pastoral elegy with its rejection of the past—the schoolboy life, the aborted career, the rejected frivolous life— in direct psychological parallel with his predecessors. To achieve what he now was envisioning as his bid to fame, his riding of Pegasus, he required such evidence of ability while closing the door (for the time being, at least) on anything that did not further his "conceived merits." But it also looked forward to Vergil's *Aeneid* and Spenser's *The Faerie Queene* as the fresh woods and new pastures to be emulated. We have already remarked the Arthuriad in Milton's mind in 1638-39, with its clearly paralleling hero, and the change in 1640 onward to the inchoate "more Heroic . . . argument" of the Trinity MS "Paradise Lost" / "Adam unparadiz'd." The parallel with Vergil does not break down, I have implicitly argued elsewhere by my suggested dating of Milton's brief epic, for the *Georgics* are there also as plateau toward reaching the epic *Paradise Lost* in the unfinished "Paradise Regain'd" of some date prior to 1655.[31] While there is no comparable work for Spenser, and any discussion would be too long and involved and diversionary, I believe that "Colin Clouts Come Home Againe," published after the publication of the first three books of *The Faerie Queene,* serves a similar function in leading Spenser to the next (last?) three books with renewed but different sights.

A mother's position in a home is usually the organizing principle of that home and its life, and the children, particularly, it would seem, the sons who have remained attached to that home even though they may reside at a distance, proceed to be freed of truly close ties with her loss. Milton's father remained in his home at Horton, and his daughter-in-law and her child(ren) joined him until such time as his son Christopher was finally on his own as a lawyer in 1640, at which time the father moved in with Christopher and Thomasine in their new home in Reading. The domiciles of father or of son, though the members in it be the same, are quite different in nature. We see a similar situation with Milton's father's joining his household in Aldersgate Street and then the Barbican from 1643 till his death in 1647. And, apparently in contrast, the conflict of "whose house" arose when his in-laws, the Powells, became part of that household in the summer of 1646 (after the fall of Oxford) through at least mid-1647 (until some time after the death of Richard Powell).

We can thus imagine that Milton may actually have left his father's home for a short time in November or December through the end of April; upon his return from the Continent he had lodgings in St. Bride's Churchyard for a few months without apparent return to Horton or Reading. We also realize that a question would have arisen over his decision to become a poet. There was the basic question of whether poetry was any kind of career at all. Milton's "I am going to be a poet" might easily have been greeted, as it probably would be still today, with "That's nice. But what are you going to do for a living?" Maybe even, "But what are you going to do with your time?" There were also the questions, "How do you know you can be?" and "How are you going to set about becoming a poet?"

"Ad Patrem" answers the basic question that his father seems to have asked. It has usually been given that kind of interpretation, but not necessarily in the time period 1637-38. Placing it in this time period—with mother gone, home somewhat disrupted, and a freer hand at pursuing his own poetic life at a distance from his father—yields a more contextually meaningful reading for "My Muse, her trifling songs forgotten," "I have reckoned up on this paper whatever I possess of abilities," "You should not despise the poet's task," "do not deem them [the sacred Muses] fruitless and contemptible," "Begone, sleepless cares; begone, complaints." The second question would be tested by reception to publication, and "Comus," published anonymously in early 1638 just prior to his writing "Ad Patrem," would seem to give meaning to "now that I am a part of the learned company, however humble," "now I shall no longer mingle unknown with the indolent rabble." By this time, too, "Lycidas" had perhaps been accepted for inclusion in *Justa Edovardo King naufrago* (1638), and Milton may have thought that he too, like Cowley, could bring forth a full volume of poems,[32] and not have to wait as Donne (1633) and Herbert (1633) had until after death:

> And you, O my juvenile songs and amusements,
> if only you dare to hope for immortality
> and to remain after your master's death,
> and to gaze upon the light,
> and if dark oblivion does not carry you beneath dense Orcus,
> perhaps you will preserve these praises and the name of the father
> sung again and again, as an example to a future generation.

So far as I am aware, no one has pointed out that these lines suggest a parallel with God the Father,[33] who in his manifestation through the Son is constant example to future generations. The Apollo figure of this poem and the Christ figure of religion had shortly before been united in "Lycidas" as Phoebus replies to "What boots it with incessant care . . . to strictly meditate the thankless muse?" that praise and fame live and spread aloft to all-judging Jove.[34] The author of "Ad Patrem" understands that "the fiery spirit that circles the swift planets" (l. 35) has enspirited him and serves as example in "his [Apollo's] immortal melody and indescribable song" (l. 37).[35] Milton's dismissal of "fell Calumny" through his secure heart "lifted high from [its] viperous stroke" (ll. 107-10) is the dismissal and nullification of such remarks as those made by the unknown friend: "that the howres of the night passe on," "that too much love of Learning is in fault."

Had the third question, how to become a poet, come up, Milton could point to the three subjects of this chapter. Much has been written about the European trip, the primary information deriving from Milton's own description of it in *Defensio secunda*. At times Edward Phillips's version in his *Life* of his uncle, which is taken from Milton's account and adds nothing to it in a translation that is not always exact and accurate, has been the source of later discussions. Milton tells us that his father approved his continental journey, a most different kind of *wanderjahr*, one more fitting for the older and more intellectually concerned person than for the college student or recent graduate. Wotton's letter, which talks only of France and Italy, probably reflects what itinerary Milton expected to pursue.[36] Indeed, Milton went only to France and Italy except that, once there, he contemplated going to Sicily and Greece and later, after having reached Venice, which was the usual last port of the English before returning home, he went to Geneva and visited with Jean Diodati, the well-known theologian and uncle of his friend Charles.

The mistranslation of Milton's remarks about forgoing a trip to Sicily and Greece, a mistranslation begun by Phillips, has led to a number

of antagonistic criticisms of Milton as falsely chauvinistic, as basically un-
trustworthy in his comments, since he did not immediately return to England to take first-hand action in the cause against monarchy, and as
terribly self-centered. But what Milton says in the *Latin* of *Defensio secunda* is that he forwent this extra, unplanned sojourn to Sicily and
Greece because it did not serve the purpose of his trip but was only for
personal enjoyment.[37] The purpose of his trip to the Continent was to
see the living Italy, to become acquainted at first hand with its antiquities, to meet and converse with "gentlemen eminent in rank and learning" (and he notes a number of them whom he did meet and whose
private academies he visited), and above all to fashion and cultivate a
mind that had, almost adolescently, just recently grasped literary
achievement as lifework. The burden of the intellectual life he encountered in Italy, according to the inferences from his remarks in *Defensio
secunda,* was both literary and religious. The Apollo of "Ad Patrem" continued to dominate, as it would in the major poetic works, once time allowed their advancement.

The literary significance which these foreign vistas supplied, aside
from the poems written during those months—"Ad Salsillam," "Mansus," and three epigrams to Leonora Baroni—and aside from such literary luminaries as Gianbattista Manso, Carlo Dati, Antonio Francini,
and Giovanni Salsilli, who supplied tributes printed in the 1645 *Poems,*[38]
was a reconcentration upon his own great purpose, an emboldening of
ability, and an intensified realization that God's Providence must be asserted, stripped of hoary ritualizations, that one must still defend "or-
thodoxam religionem" against unreformed thought. We find Milton
upon return home planning "Paradise Lost" and looking for other subjects to demonstrate the ways of God to men, such as "Sodom." But further, Pandemonium in *Paradise Lost* and the passage on Rome in *Paradise
Regain'd* seem to owe much to Milton's remembrance of his Italian trav-
els in these earlier years.

Most commentaries on this episode in Milton's life, including Parker's unfortunately, have not looked at the realities of that journey, which
would indicate the lack of a dated itinerary. Milton did not know exactly
where he would go and did not know exactly how long he would stay at
any specific place in his plan. He did "linger" in Florence for two
months; was "detained" in Rome for almost two months; went to Naples
without real preparation, being introduced to Manso "by a certain Ere-
mite Friar" whom he happened to meet in Rome; thought of passage to
Sicily and Greece—clearly unplanned and unstructured in time, and
thus implicitly an indication that further travel in Italy was not tied
down to time and generally not to place; and, according to his statement

in *Defensio secunda,* he rather casually in time returned to Rome and Florence and then "hastened to Venice" ("Venetias contendi"). Perhaps he reached Venice about a year after his departure from England, that is, May.

The reconstruction of his trip sustains that dating. Probably the planned sojourn was for a year or slightly more; in actuality it came to fifteen or sixteen months, for he spent a month in Venice and a month in Geneva, and traveling between those points and returning to England would have taken further time. What is to be underscored is that at no stop in his itinerary—except the last city, Venice, from which he sent home his books and from which, to repeat, an Englishman normally returned to England by ship—would relative or friend be certain of communicating with Milton, who could have left, say, Florence before letters for him would have arrived. His second lingering visit in Florence for about two months would not have been on his original itinerary, for example. Only in Venice before he sailed home might he be expected to receive letters. Here, it is most likely, not Rome or Florence and certainly not Naples, he would have picked up correspondence waiting at the English embassy, and we can conclude that such correspondence informed him of Diodati's death from plague in August 1638 and probably of his sister Anne's death.[39] He thus went to Geneva to see Diodati's uncle, having remained in Venice about a month, perhaps to observe the festival season at the very beginning of June (but he was in Geneva on June 10 and thus in all likelihood not in Venice on the actual feast day, June 2). Upon return to London he acquired lodgings for a few months in St. Bride's Churchyard, where his younger nephew, John Phillips, joined him, and then more spacious accommodations by 1640 in Aldersgate Street, where his older nephew, Edward Phillips, also joined him.

The tutoring he was then undertaking (partly for livelihood, since sons of other families came in on a day-school basis) would seem first to have been inaugurated to provide a good education for his nephews and, in view of the full situation, because financial circumstances would not have allowed his nephews to attend St. Paul's School or some other. In "Epitaphium Damonis," lines 14-15, he comments on his return "when his mind was full and the care of the flock / left behind called him home." We do not know when Anne died, but the boarding of his nephews certainly tells us of a disruption in her household. Without Anne's being alive in autumn 1639, Thomas Agar would have had the care of two step-sons, aged nine and eight, and a daughter, aged six or so. While we may like to think that he would want to care for his step-sons and provide an education, they were not his own children, and his salary as deputy clerk was not high. There is hereafter no mention of Anne in connection with her sons, who seem to have remained with Milton through the 1640s. Parker speculated that Edward left around 1646, and he was a student at Magdalen Hall, Oxford, briefly in 1650.[40] By the time of his majority (1651) he was working and residing in Shrewsbury. John, on the other hand, seems to have stayed with his uncle until about the time his majority was reached, in 1652. An argument against the preceding construction is Ralph Hone's belief that Anne Phillips's name on a Shropshire (Shrewsbury) deed dated December 29, 1639, means that she was then alive.[41] But of course it doesn't. Not only is she not Anne Phillips Agar on the deed, as she had been since 1632, showing the recorder's ignorance of her, but the entry is simply a *pro forma* copying from its earlier recording without adjustment of time. She was listed on the early form as part-owner, and that continued. It is not strange that the recorder of the deed in Shropshire did not know about the principals in the transactions.

The decade of the forties saw Milton furthering his hopes and dreams of great writing and discharging his great purpose in life, a seeming detour from them in prose controversy in a circumscribed world of people of conservative views, a return to and further delineation of those writing commitments to the self, and again a plunging into the demands of the world outside from which he did not fully emerge for over ten years. Interferences of the world were at hand.

Yet this episode in Milton's life has strong psychological and mythic parallels with constructs of such thinkers as Carl Jung and Erich Neumann. The need to separate from the negative mother archetype before the grounds for consciousness can be established[42] is discharged by his mother's death. With her death we see Milton asserting an independent ego consciousness to allow for an idealized identity associated with the father, which is the base of the concerns in "Ad Patrem." "Apollo, wishing to disperse himself between the two, / gave to me certain gifts, to my father others, / and father and son, we possess the divided God" (64-66). The poem likewise orchestrates the differences between what have been called the Two Heroes, the introverted figure and the extroverted figure, by making what exemplifies the powers of reflection become the accomplishment of great deeds, both in the publication of his achievement and in future envisioned "deeds." The dragon that Milton has conquered is "good" as seen through parental eyes (primarily a function of the mother archetype): established public and conventional career, settled family life, sexual apprehension; and the means has been self-examination and recognition, unleashed by his mother's death. The evidence of the Letter to an Unknown Friend, "Ad Patrem," "Lycidas," and his preparations for his new-found career defines Milton's individuation, before which time his directions and achievements were diverse and desultory. The parallel of the end of "Ad Patrem" suggested before implies a Father/Son relationship in religious terms, and again, as Jung has said, "self-realization—to put it in religious or metaphysical terms—amounts to god's incarnation."[43]

The basic "plot" of *Paradise Regain'd* is the experiences through which the incarnated Son comes to full self-realization as man/God, thereby individuating himself from the whole which is God by taking on, as example for man, the idealized identity associated with the Father. Such a Father/Son parallel as that observed in "Ad Patrem" would seem to lie behind some of the identity nexus in *Paradise Lost* as well: the Son functions for the Father over and over—the defeat of Satan and his cohorts in the War in Heaven, the Creation, the Judgment, and ultimately the incarnation to effect the defeat of Satan, Sin, and Death in the War on Earth. The Son first asserts independent ego consciousness in Book III of the epic—led, however, by the Father (as Milton by his)—in the speeches beginning, "O Father, gracious was that word which clos'd /Thy sovran sentence, that Man should find grace" (144-66) and "Father, thy word is past, man shall find grace" (227-65). Thereafter, in "filial obedience," "he attends the will / Of his great Father" (269-71). His assertion of ego would seem to oppose the impressions of the Father's speeches, and in his statements he shows his "meek aspect" and his "immortal love / To mortal men." But rather than oppose, his speeches use the Father's words concerning grace to push for mercy, whereby the Father's greatness will be shown, and his wholeness. The Son completes the Father.[44] The shift in emphasis on the Son, rather than on the Father, in the epic has been adumbrated in the ascendancy of the son over his father in "Ad Patrem."

For Milton the move toward idealized identity associated with the father can be seen first in his choice of career and second in a kind of rebelliousness.[45] His father, we will remember, had defied his father (who never directly enters anything we have from Milton's hand) over religion and left home. We will return to Milton's revolutionary tendencies later; for now we can observe that his career decision was a kind of opposition, though it is difficult to read any defiance or rebellion in his act or in his words related to that decision. Instead he argues in "Ad Patrem" that his father's greatness is shown by the creativeness of the son and that his father's being is made complete in his son. The Father/Son interplay in *Paradise Lost* may owe much to the workings of the doctrine of Subordinationism, but it would seem to owe much, as well, to Milton's perhaps conscious relationship with his father.[46] Independent ego asserted, he can now turn to what is ultimately filial obedience and in his cherished hopes for his creative talent to his "love To mortal man."

In 1637, but probably not fully until after 1655, Milton reached what James P. Driscoll calls a "metastance," that vantage point from which one is able to gain a fuller view of oneself, having previously assumed a seemingly valid stance. Through the metastance one establishes a qualifying context, a transcended context that enables the archetypal poet to "attain a vision compensatory to the tragic fragmentation of ordinary life, a comedic vision of the self and the universe in which both are whole."[47] The tragic dimensions of *Paradise Lost* would seem obvious to most readers, but it is the comedic overview that prevails.[48] While *Paradise Regain'd* is comedic, any man for whom the Son is example but who is not "one greater Man"[49] will find only the tragic. Its companion poem, *Samson Agonistes,* is tragic as presented, but any man who will be "With inward eyes illuminated" will know the comic reward of life.

The subject of this section has been Milton's European trip, a part of his preparation for his envisioned career. It becomes a watershed for the son and for the poet. He has removed himself more firmly from the parental home than even the possible move to London would have done. He has had etched more firmly his resolve and, according to his remarks in *The Reason of Church-Government,* had its validity confirmed by Italian friends, poets, and literati. And beneath his experiences we see the context for his great work arising—religion, the true (Protestant) God, both the ontology of God's world and its epistemology. Mythically his sojourn is a night sea-journey, that movement from west to east whereby one who lacks full drive to accomplish his task is reborn to assume his responsibilities. Neumann calls the slaying of the dragon the first period of centroversion, ending with the birth of the ego; the night sea-journey is the second part, ending with the birth of the self.[50] Important always in this latter birth is the stabilizing of the conscious and the social identities (the ruling conceptions of one's self and the attitudes of one's social context toward one's social roles and their performance). For the time being, at least, Milton in 1639 has stabilized these identities. There would be interferences to disrupt or tend to disrupt this "union," but finally Milton was able to move to full ideal identity through a better understanding of the conscious identity—as we shall see in Chapter 6—and through acceptance of and willingness to live his real identity.

6

The Left Hand and the Great Purpose

Since at least the publication in 1895 of the little piece by A.W. Verity on "Milton's Great Purpose," appended to his edition of the sonnets,[1] it has been commonplace to consider the writing of a great poem John Milton's major objective in life. Increasingly, however, the prose works have been looked upon as a fulfillment of urges to write great literature and to educate men in the ways of God. E.M.W. Tillyard stated the attitude most directly: "It is usually thought that Milton's early ambition was to be a poet; that the prose works were undertaken entirely against his will, and that without the special occasions that evoked them they would not have been written. . . . He wished to sway men, to be a great teacher. Now at the end of the autobiographical passage in the *Defensio Secunda* he speaks of his earlier pamphlets as if they were a systematic exposition of the idea of liberty in the various spheres of life. And though actually these pamphlets were occasioned by specific political or domestic events, there is no reason to doubt Milton's statement that they embody a coherent mass of teaching on which he had pondered long before he committed it to print."[2]

Before the end of the nineteenth century the prose, as a corpus, was little attended to and often the source of antagonism on political, religious, or moral grounds. Only *Areopagitica* and *Of Education* were widely read and published,[3] and in certain ways misread. The writing of the prose was felt to be an interlude that would have had lasting and disastrous effects on his reputation had not Milton, because of the changes in his political world, returned to complete *Paradise Lost*. Milton himself helped create this dichotomy by his frequent reference to being "snatched . . . unwilling from studies far different and altogether more delightful."[4] One of the byproducts of this critical attitude has been the former disregard of *Paradise Regain'd* and *Samson Agonistes*, and in certain ways their misreading. We can infer a treatment of the prose in the twentieth century as "lesser and cruder contributions to the lofty design that culminated in the universalized teaching and high argument of the epics,"[5] to quote Ida Langdon. But the question to be asked is where an emphasis should be placed when we look at these works: on their universal message, as the autobiographical section of *Defensio secunda* suggests? or on their temporality? or on their individual worth as literary objects?[6] We will answer this question as we look at Milton as prose writer, but we must also attend to his great purpose in life and a definition of his talent.

Was Milton's great purpose in life to write a great poem, at first a nationalistic and historical epic, and was his talent the writing of significant poetry? Prior to autumn 1637, when "Lycidas" was composed, with its clear dedication to the thankless muse, Milton had written little that aftertimes would not willingly let die: a contemporaneous public was appreciative of "A Mask" (that is, *Comus*) if we fully credit Henry Lawes's prefatory letter to the first edition of 1637 (or rather early 1638),[7] but that is all. A modern public today would probably add "On the Morning of *Christs* Nativity," "L'Allegro" and "Il Penseroso," and Sonnet 7, but nothing else. Had it been Milton rather than Edward King who drowned in August 1637, even the scholarly public would not know his name, for there would undoubtedly not be even a footnote of reference to him in a fairly detailed history of seventeenth-century British literature.[8] The quantity, success, and nature of the writing prior to autumn 1637 offer no evidence of one with particularly literary ambitions, let alone unswerving belief in literary talent.

In Chapter 4 I reviewed what internal evidence has been alleged from "At a Vacation Exercise" (which should not be read out of its context as part of the sixth prolusion) and Sonnet 7 (whose "bud" or "blossom" is in no way limited to literary production) and found it wanting. Quite uncritically the myth of Milton the poet during his college days persists: he is epic poet in search of a subject, dedicated Apollonian, denying self for his art. The attitude crops up over and over again. We must, apparently, keep reminding ourselves of the difference between poetry as a life-work and bid for fame and poetry as product of a time and place. We must also keep reminding ourselves that the poem we read today as *Comus* was not the same masque that was presented at Ludlow in September 1634. Unfortunately much discussion continues to ignore this point. For the difference between "masque" and "poem" may thus be noteworthy, and surely the Castlehaven scandal and the Margery Evans affair would have been differently greeted in 1634 and three years later by the *reading* public. No matter when one wants to date the Trinity MS workbook in which appears a transcription of the text of *Comus*, in turn much revised and augmented, part of the final text is not found therein, and revised parts must be dated during autumn 1637 at the earliest.[9] What we read today is what Milton created as a poem to be read; what was presented at Ludlow—whatever that specific and different text was—was what he created for dramatic performance. The two texts are not the same.

The usual view of Milton as poet—since, aside from his tutoring and secretarial post with the Cromwellian government, he had no other work experience—is that poetry had always been his intended occupation, and the earlier poetry has been read from that slanted angle. Read not in that way, poems like "L'Allegro" and "Il Penseroso" may be allowed to join their rightful confrères as ludic pieces rather than as "serious," "biographical," or "psychological" statements. Read not in that way we can experience the humor of something like "In Obitum Eliensis," with its satiric use of indecorous meter, and comprehend the contrast of personalities that informs the sixth elegy as dominant structural principle in this informative verse letter, one showing the demonstrative mode in both halves of that contrast. The question that "Elegia sexta" should raise for us is: What is poetry as occupation and what is simply writing poetry? In this poem Milton discusses his current poetry writing, the Nativity ode; he does not lay out some kind of statement of occupational expectation. Hindsight does not (rather, should not) change our perception of this.

Autumn 1637 was the turning point in Milton's career, as I have already argued—that is, that time when he admitted to himself his incapacities as well as his abilities, discovering his inadequacy for the pulpit and admitting the drift of his recent years—a set of circumstances, the counters appropriately changed, that hardly seems to require documentation for today's analogous baccalaureate and post-baccalaureate generation. There is no evidence adducible prior to this time of *any* great purpose in life unless we accept the ministry for which he was being trained, and no evidence prior to this time that he had articulated any sense of a talent. The seventh prolusion, which argues for learning over ignorance, affords the raw stuff on which a sense of talent could be based—his intellectual excitement, the lack of confinement felt for anything that might engage the mind, the ability to learn and to analyze and to reify knowledge. But no such "talent" is verbalized by Milton, though I state it here as what could be the basis of his talent, needing only a direction and empirical opportunities.

While building upon the tenor of my argument,[10] John Spencer Hill goes on to dissociate, he says, Milton's decision to become a poet and his decision to abandon a career in the church. "The decision to become a minister of the Word, was taken early; and the vocational streams issuing from these twin resolves run parallel and are of equal strength until at least 1637 when he composed *Lycidas*."[11] Hill, however, finds the rejection of the clerical career as occurring with the Laudian *Canons* of June 1640 and Milton's becoming a schoolmaster. And while he still reads "At a Vacation Exercise" as showing poetic vocation, he links the rejection of the clerical career to Milton's decision for a poetic vocation by placing it after the Italian journey and having it concluded with the writing of *The Reason of Church-Government* in 1641/42. Hill has not taken into account Milton's actions during 1637-41 or their implied reasons— the plans for a dramatic work called *Paradise Lost* in 1640-41 offer a clear example, as do the revision of *Comus*, for reading rather than dramatic performance in 1637, or the keeping of the Trinity MS and of the Commonplace Book, or the European trip itself in 1638-39.

Whatever view we accept of the date of Milton's decision to follow a poetic life and his subsequent activity to effect that career, we can turn to examine his great purpose in more detail.[12] First, Milton's statement of one facet of his purpose was that "by labour and intent study . . . joyn'd with the strong propensity of nature, I might perhaps leave something so written to aftertimes, as they should not willingly let it die."[13] He realized that relatively little could be left of overpowering worth even during the inspiratory period around 1639 when he declared in "Epitaphium Damonis," lines 171-72: "omnia non licet uni / No sperasse uni licet omnis." His reward, he wrote in the same poem (ll. 172-78), would be ample and his glory great if, though unknown to the outside world, men of the British Isles read his work; in *The Reason of Church-Government* he professed not to be concerned with being "once nam'd abroad, though perhaps I could attaine to that, but content with these British Ilands as my world" (38). But this parochialism died at least with the far-reaching of his *Defensio prima*, "Of which all *Europe* talks from side to side."

Second, bestowal of the poetic gift by God was acknowledged by promise through this immortal literature "to celebrate in glorious and lofty Hymns the throne and equipage of Gods Almightinesse, and what he works, and what he suffers to be wrought with high providence in his Church" (*Reason*, 39). Third, what he would leave to aftertimes must honor and instruct his country, as shown in previous quotations from *The Reason of Church-Government* and the belief that the gift of God can "imbreed and cherish in a great people the seeds of vertu, and publick civility . . . allay the perturbations of the mind, and set the affections in right tune" (*Reason*, 39). Aims two and three were of course interwoven:

"These abilities . . . are of power . . . to sing . . . the deeds and triumphs of just and pious Nations doing valiantly through faith against the enemies of Christ, to deplore the general relapses of Kingdoms and States from justice and God's true worship" (*Reason*, 39).

This great purpose of instruction—for that was the goal of his life in its simplest terms—was iterated often.[14] The second of his pamphlets, *Of Prelatical Episcopacy*, indicates clearly why he forwent studies and poetic writings for diatribe:

Seeing therefore some men, deeply conversant in Bookes, have had so little care of late to give the world a better account of their reading, then by divulging needlesse tractats stuff't with specious names of *Ignatius*, and *Polycarpus*, with fragments of old *Martyrologies*, and *legends*, to distract, and stagger the multitude of credulous readers, & mislead them from their strong guards, and places of safety under the tuition of holy writ, it came into my thoughts to perswade my selfe, setting all distances, and nice respects aside, that I could do Religion, and my Country no better service for the time then doing my utmost endeavour to recall the people of GOD from this vaine forraging after straw, and to reduce them to their firme stations under the standard of the Gospell: by making appeare to them, first the insufficiency, next the inconvenience, and lastly the impiety of these gay testimonies, that their great Doctors would bring them to dote on.[15]

Not only does he show positively that the aim of that present writing was educative, but also he implies negatively that he had desisted from active participation in civil affairs before this time because he felt that he would do religion and his country service through some other means (that is, through his poetic writing).[16]

An excerpt from *Reason* attests to the same conviction:

Teaching over the whole book of sanctity and vertu through all the instances of example with such delight to those especially of soft and delicious temper who will not so much as look upon Truth herselfe, unless they see her elegantly drest, that whereas the paths of honesty and good life appear now rugged and difficult, though they be indeed easy and pleasant, they would then appeare to all men both easy and pleasant though they were rugged and difficult indeed, [39] . . . but this I foresee, that should the Church be brought under heavy oppression, and God have given me ability the while to reason against that man that should be the author of so foul a deed, or should she by blessing from above on the industry and courage of faithfull men change this her distracted estate into better daies without the lest furtherance of contribution of those few talents which God at that present had lent me, I foresee what stories I should heare within my selfe, all my life after, of discourage and reproach. [35]

Indeed, Milton makes it quite clear that *Paradise Lost* also was to be, among other things, didactic and spiritually uplifting.

Education was the great purpose of Milton's life even when he contemplated a clerical life. It is from 1637 onward that a course of action for its accomplishment in great poetic writings is envisioned. Once assured of his path, all else was deterrent, and so we see him longing to pursue poetic writing during his early pamphleteering (1641-45) and through his middle prose period and civil duties (1649-51). In *Animadversions* he attested to his hope of accomplishing the first two facets of his purpose: "And he that now for haste snatches up a plain ungarnish't present as a thanke-offering to thee, which could not bee deferr'd in regard of thy so many late deliverances wrought for us one upon another, may then perhaps take up a Harp, and sing thee an elaborate Song to Generations."[17] In *Reason,* he indicated belief in a schism between current and desired activities: "Lastly, I should not chuse this manner of writing wherin knowing my self inferior to my self, led by the genial power of nature to another task, I have the use, as I may account it, but of my left hand" (37).

The equation of strength with the right hand and of weakness, or at least less proficiency, with the left is commonplace. The difference for Milton, I believe, lies in the methods or paths that prose was taking at this time and that poetry was expected to take in the future. Sonnet 8 (November 1642) reveals his classification of himself as a poet, though little was yet written to justify his remarks fully. And the epilogue to *Defensio prima,* written in 1658, records his continued thought of achieving a great work (clearly referring to his return to what became *Paradise Lost*): "I am earnestly seeking how best I may show not only my own country, to which I devoted all I have, but men of every land and particularly, all Christian men, that for their sake I am at this time hoping and planning still greater things, if these be possible to me, as with God's help they will."[18]

The preparation at which he hints in this last reference was an old subject with Milton, whether the means of accomplishment of his purpose be clerical or literary. Besides such statements in the Seventh Prolusion, Sonnet 7, the Letter to an Unknown Friend, "Lycidas," and *Reason,* he remarked in *Apology for Smectymnuus* "that he who would not be frustrate of his hope to write well hereafter in laudable things, ought him selfe to bee a true Poem, that is, a composition, and patterne of the best and honourablest things; not presuming to sing high praises of heroick men, or famous Cities, unless he have in himselfe the experience and the practice of all that which is praise-worthy."[19] This echo of the thought of the sixth elegy indicates Milton's high ideal of preparation for his great purpose in personal qualities, the former references emphasizing intellectual preparedness. Milton thought of himself as trying his utmost to attain this goal of preparation, both in the past and in the future: "but that none hath by more studious ways endeavour'd, and with more unwearied spirit that none shall, that I dare almost averre of my self, as farre as life and free leasure will extend" (*Reason*, 40).

We can, then, see Milton's great purpose as contributing to people's spiritual and personal freedom through what can be labelled a "negative" path of nullifying actions and thinking that would inhibit such freedom—for example, as a result of political or governmental action—or through a "positive" path of inducing humankind to seek, achieve, and maintain its individual, internal, spiritual, and personal freedom—for example, as a result of one's esteem for the self, galvanized against those idols of the theater, marketplace, and cave that Sir Francis Bacon wrote of. And we can recognize that the prose (much of it at least) followed this negative path to the achievement of his purpose, as he himself in *Defensio secunda* came to realize. This is not to say, of course, that each prose work was written with such purpose in mind or in some sense of grand pattern and interrelationship. David Loewenstein also argues that "there was no divorce at all in his imagination between literary and political discourse—political discourse *was* aesthetic. Revolution was thus less an interruption of Milton's poetic development than a series of occasions for Milton to rechannel his creative energies directly into polemic, to employ his literary and imaginative writing in the service of political activity."[20]

The divorce tracts—which brought such opprobrium to Milton in his own time—provide example of that. While *The Doctrine and Discipline of Divorce* argued against one let on personal freedom, resulting from a combination of religious and legal statute and of human attitude developed through religious and sociological pressures rather than through thought, Milton felt compelled to offer further ideas on the subject from a well-esteemed theologian, Martin Bucer, to try to break down resistance—for people do succumb to testimonial—and then to offer his own interpretation of "The foure chief places in Scripture, which treat of Mariage, or nullities in Mariage" to counter the belief that divorce is sacrilegious. *Tetrachordon* provided major argument from the Bible, the word of God, equating itself with the light of the sun (or Apollo) in the metaphor of light as knowledge. But in addition *Colasterion* was needed to argue through ridicule of an opponent to divorce that the cold light of the moon (or Diana), reflected light, also illuminated the path for the pilgrim through life's night (or darkness as ignorance). These three divorce tracts do not fall into any preplanned pattern of attack but are a consequence of the times: *The Judgement of Martin Bucer* provides a further avenue of persuasion; *Tetrachordon* and *Colasterion* develop into a coeval whole (not unlike, in a way, the coeval whole that Sir Thomas Browne's *Hydriotaphia* and *The Garden of Cyrus* are) to counter people's penchant for acceptance of those idols, particularly in this case the, for Milton, "false" interpretation of the Bible and teachings of God.

Related, perhaps, to my separation of the great purpose into two paths, we might note that philosophy frequently divides into two basic lemmata: the practical and immediate, and the projective and idealistic. Scholars concerned with the practical changes in government and society during the seventeenth century—for example, in terms of constitutionalism—have been little drawn to Milton as thinker. He certainly is not Thomas Hobbes or John Locke, or even Sir Henry Vane or Sir Robert Filmer. We shall return a little later to the seemingly practical path; let it suffice here to note that the immediate path for Milton was most often through prose in terms of attack, what I have called a negative path. We may classify under this rubric the antiprelatical tracts (although *The Reason of Church-Government* is much more than that by its setting forth of positive vistas), the divorce tracts, *Areopagitica, Observations on the Articles of Peace, Eikonoklastes, Character of the Long Parliament*, the three *Defenses, A Treatise of Civil Power, Considerations Touching the Likeliest Means to Remove Hirelings Out of the Church, Brief Notes Upon a Late Sermon*, and *Of True Religion, Hæresie, Schism, Toleration*. Educational in intent, and thus somewhere between the negative and the positive, are *The History of Britain, Accedence Commenc't Grammar, Artis Logicæ Plenior Institutio*, and, yes, *De doctrina christiana*, which, as William B. Hunter has argued,[21] aimed at compounding the theories of the Reformed scholastics, the school of Saumur, and the Arminians into a single system of theology.

The few prose works unnamed—bypassing the letters, prolusions, state papers, and *Declaration, or Letters Patents*—all arise from similar concerns as fountainheads. A few offer practical ideas as well: *Of Education, Letter to a Friend, Concerning the Ruptures of the Commonwealth*, "Proposalls of Certaine Expedients for the Preventing of a Civil War Now Feard, and the Settling of a Firme Government," *The Ready and Easy Way to Establish a Free Commonwealth*, and *The Present Means, and Brief Delineation of a Free Commonwealth, Easy to Be Put into Practice, and Without Delay*. One prose work moves into the only positive way to achieve the great purpose, that is, its underlying philosophy of the need for people to be themselves "a true Poem"—*The Tenure of Kings and Magistrates*. Here is the projective and the idealistic. In other words, Milton in his prose little pursues the projective and the idealistic and for this reason has not attracted study alongside Filmer, Hobbes, and Locke.

What was Milton's talent? Part of the question is, of course, what was Milton's conception of his talent, and part is what can we discern as his talent with the hindsight of history? Milton refers to his talent or talents through the biblical allusion to Matthew 25:14-30 in five places. In the first draft of the Letter to an Unknown Friend in the Trinity MS he remarks "the long knowledge of a contrarie comand from above, & the terrible seasure of him that hid his talent" (6).[22] In *Reason* (35) he said, as quoted before: "but this I foresee, that should the Church be brought under heavy oppression, and God have given me ability the while to reason against that man that should be the author of so foul a deed, or should she by blessing from above on the industry and courage of faithfull men change this her distracted estate into better daies without the lest furtherance or contribution of those few talents which God at that present had lent me, I foresee what stories I should heare within my selfe, all my life after, of discourage and reproach." The sonnet "When I consider how my light is spent" speaks of "that one Talent which is death to hide." In *Apology* the biblical text emerges without use of the specific word: "that it be lawfull to attribute somewhat to guifts of Gods imparting, which I boast not, but thankfully acknowledge, and feare also lest at my certain account they be reckon'd to me many rather then few" (2). And in *Defensio secunda* the inception of his antiprelatical work comes from his decision "huc omne ingenium, omnes industriæ vores transferre" (89). The Yale Prose translates "omne ingenium" as "all my talents" (IV, i, 622), a normal and certainly defensible rendering, although the singular "all my talent" is also apt.

Michael Lieb in his examination of *Talents* in *A Milton Encyclopedia*[23] discusses the relationship between the biblical parable and Milton's use of the concept, and shows Milton's fear, as in the sonnet, of being outcast, of "punishment incurred when the talent is not properly used: death." This view of the parable accords with the Old Dispensation of the Mosaic Law rather than the New Dispensation achieved through Christ. Whether singular or plural, whatever gifts Milton had through God's grace are to be used, and in all five instances of Milton's direct reference to the parable that use is to dispel ignorance, as I suggested some time ago in examining the sonnet.[24] The opening lines—"When I consider how my light is spent, / E're half my days in this dark world and wide"—metaphorically indicate this same point: his light (eyesight) has been extinguished, and around him is only a dark world, which to the blind man has no point of reference or closure; the ignorance which is in this vast world could be dispelled—or partially dispelled—by wisdom (God's light within humankind), but Milton's means of extending his light is spent, and darkness becomes everduring. His fear, of course, is that, like the unprofitable servant of the parable, he has been cast into outer darkness already, as his everduring night would seem to evidence. (In *Paradise Lost* III, 45-46, he speaks of the clouds and "ever-during dark" which surrounds him, and we should relate the great purpose of the epic to the resolution of this sonnet.)

He continues in the sonnet to say that his talent is lodged with him useless, with the implication that his light (wisdom) has been spent. The word *spent* has usually not been given the weighty meaning it should: not only is the eyesight "extinguished" but it has been "used up" "In liberties defence, my noble task, / Of which all *Europe* talks from side to side," as he consoled Cyriack Skinner in another sonnet. Yet, further, it has been "exchanged" as currency for the purchase of liberty, which constitutes a large part of the "true account" he will offer his Maker. Part of his consolation in the sonnet recalls John 12:35, "Yet a little while is the light with you. Walk while ye have the light, lest darkness come upon you," for he has used his light though darkness is now upon him. Part of the consolation, the more meaningful consolation of the sestet, as Lieb has shown, lies in the move from justification by works by which his light (wisdom) has been spent to justification by faith. The light of God's gift is not spent and useless, he must learn: God surely does not need anything, neither man's work nor his own gifts repaid.

Thus Milton's "talent" is not spent and is not useless, as long as he does not conceive of it only as producing some kind of works, artifacts. A letter to Henry Oldenburg on July 6, 1654, manifests Milton's change of mind that Tillyard spoke of in the quotation given earlier. It was a necessary step for Milton to recognize that the prose works did embody a coherent mass of teaching and that they did indeed fulfill at least one branch of his great purpose. He wrote: "To prepare myself for other labors, whether noble or more useful I do not really know (for what among human endeavors can be nobler or more useful than the protection of liberty)" (YP, IV, ii, 866). A paper by Dayton Haskin, "Milton's Sonnet, 'When I Consider . . .' and the Perkins Tradition,"[25] makes the point that what we have in the sonnet is "the representation of a particular state of mind, and not a definitive representation of self." Milton, rather, is "wrestling with a fundamental problem that faced ordinary people within a tradition of experimental predestinarianism," and the sonnet "shows how one may get beyond an overwhelming feeling of despair." As Haskin says, Milton is here both model and teacher. His ensuing action, once he had become less psychologically driven, could now follow the fully positive path as occasion allowed.

The defining characteristics of Milton's talent are his intellectual excitement as a youth, the lack of confinement felt for anything that might engage the mind, the ability to learn and to analyze and to reify knowledge, as suggested before. In *Reason* he recognized his "labour and intent study (which I take to be my portion in this life)" (37). The prose works provide clear evidence that Milton's talent encompassed an ability to communicate meaningfully and memorably, a great capacity to learn and remember and thus to know many things and interrelate them, and an ability to comprehend others' ideas, incisively to recognize not only their invalidity and irrationality but also their truth and competency. His talent was to bring these abilities to a focus to argue against enemies of liberty and brawlers (his word) like Peter Du Moulin and Alexander More; his talent was to marshall arguments for his polemical position. Milton as prose writer was not an "original" thinker, but this should not denigrate his achievement for us.

The term "originality" is, of course, wrong in this context: Milton is polemical rather than theoretical. Yet there have been those who have shown disregard, even disparagement, because of that lack of the theoretical in his prose, and who have, I believe, misplaced his achievement in the poetry because they have sought and presumably found ideological concepts in it. His originality lay in what he did with what he received, how he revamped it for its own intrinsic worth or effect, the profit he saw in acceptance, revision, or rejection of others' ways of doing or thinking. And replacing "prose writer" by "poet" does not diminish the greatness—not simply the worth or masterfulness, but the greatness—of his poetic accomplishment. Here the "originality" lies in the materials chosen, the way in which they are interwoven into a cohesive experience, causing us to ponder the concepts and their implications, and putting ourselves in the center of this poetic stage to determine who is, indeed, the greater man who will restore us. The "originality" lies as well in the stuff of poetry employed and how it is employed: the prosody, the structures, the metaphoric world, the language, the characterizations and events, and the tropic construct, using antithesis, metonomy, and the like.[26]

The nature of Milton's originality can be seen in those prose works that offer practicalities: *Of Education*, in William Riley Parker's words, "is still remarkable" because of "its high degree of integration and progression, its tight texture and firm efficiency." Though it is built on existing educational practices—or on opposition to such practices—Milton's educational scheme advocates "motivation and reinforcement, attention to character development, discovery of individual aptitudes, periodical review, and progression from easy to hard."[27] *The Ready and Easy Way*, with its proposals for elections limited to the well-affected in order to augment the Rump and for a perpetual legislature as a supreme council, may be looked at as typical of the 1659-60 tracts, whose primary aim was to influence the settlement of the inevitable Restoration. There is haste and expediency here. A republican cast for that settlement is supported through Milton's reviewing the deleterious effects of a monarchical restoration (the negative path still). The so-called utopian plan of Milton's tract derives from classical and modern theories and governmental models; but its force is fully of the present: it is a *ready* and *easy* way, a free commonwealth, *easy to be put into practice,* and *without delay.*[28] As Barbara K. Lewalski concludes: "It proposes no new institutions or complicated machinery, only the stabilization of the status quo as a ready and easy way to settle the government."[29]

On the other hand, *The Tenure of Kings and Magistrates,* which Milton remarked was "written to reconcile men's minds, rather than to deter-mine anything about Charles" (YP, IV, i, 627), develops far beyond its contemporary origins and moves thus into a more "original" plane. Its projectivism and idealism lie in the "deeds in substance" it urges from all people, which deeds alone will lead to justice for humankind. The pos-itive path that leads to spiritual and personal freedom is internal and developed within rather than imposed from without as by law and in-stitution. I have previously suggested eight points that I find in this tract as Milton's contribution to political theory. Among them are the educa-tion of humankind in discrimination of ideas and action and in self-discipline, and the removal of the fears of the future by developing a proper regard for self in each person.[30]

My view of Milton as prose writer stresses his ability with words, his ability to adapt his style to the style demanded (most evident in the at-tacks on specific people or works), and his ability to make cogent the ideas and substance of others (extending as well into those educational materials noted before, such as the *Art of Logic,* which owes so much to the work of George Downham on Ramus). Surely these abilities are an important aspect of creativity; they demand a sharp mind, an intelli-gence, a facility at communication. They add up to "good writer" at least; their success—and surely Milton's writings were frequently suc-cessful, both infamously and positively—will alter that to "master writer" or "great writer." For his times Milton in his prose was a "good writer" and often a "master writer," for those items we have listed before as tem-porally significant, drawn as they were from temporal concerns, were telling documents for the English people. The use to which Continental advocates for divorce put Milton's work, as Leo Miller has docu-mented[31]; the importance of *Areopagitica* in the licensing controversy of 1679 and William Denton's and Charles Blount's plagiaristic arguments, as well as its entry into the copyright legalities of the eighteenth century (see, for example, the various suits of the publisher Andrew Millar and the work of Catherine Macauley [later Graham] in *A Modest Plea for the Property of Copy Right* in 1774); the fundamental influence in the Whig settlement which George F. Sensabaugh has manifested[32] and which is made specific by Samuel Johnson's and Thomas Hunt's plagiarisms in the 1680s—all these attest to "master writer."

The influence has continued as a substratum in our own day, although few read any of these prose works of Milton or have even heard of them except for *Areopagitica*, the constant allusion every time a reactionary group wants to pull *Huckleberry Finn* or "To His Coy Mistress" from library shelves or teachers' syllabi. As William Haller remarked, "The truth could be made known to men by the power of words. Whatsoever talent a man might find within himself—and it was his duty to know and esteem his own gifts—was, he held, a command to serve God thereby. . . . But the talent Milton discovered within himself was this same power to use words. This discovery and the shaping into act of the resolution to render back his talent enriched by great accomplishment was the decisive experience of his youth."[33]

The collectivity of Milton's prose in his own century, which perhaps we can define generally as his milieu, might be represented by notice of *The Tenure of Kings and Magistrates*. These statistics bear out some of my previous remarks about the substratum of Milton's influence to be observed in later years, and perhaps suggest that in this tract at least Milton deserves the epithet "great writer." The tract received five issues in two editions in 1649-50 and was reprinted in *The Works* (1697) and *A Complete Collection* (1698). But it also was cleverly altered in 1689 (perhaps by Sir James Tyrrell) for the controversy over the succession of William III. It was given the title *Pro Populo Adversus Tyrannos: Or The Sovereign Right and Power of the People over Tyrants, Clearly Stated, and Plainly Proved*. The first edition of *Tenure* immediately influenced Bulstrode Whitelocke's *Parliamenti Angliæ Declaratio* (1648/49), which was translated as *A Declaration of the Parlament of England, Concerning Their Late Endeavors in a Peaceable Waie, To Remove All Misunderstandings, and Differences Between the Common-wealth of England, and the Kingdom of Scotland* (1649, in two editions); it was reissued in 1650. John Canne's *The Golden Rule. Or, Justice Advanced* (1649), John Lilburne's *An Outcry of the Youngmen and Apprentices of London* (1649), and the anonymous *Tyranny No Magistracy, or a Modest and Compendious Enquirie Into the Nature, and Boundaries of That Ordinance of Magistracy* (1687) show influence throughout, as does John Twyn's *A Treatise of the Execution of Justice, Wherein Is Clearly Proved, That the Execution of Judgement and Justice, Is As Well the Peoples as the Magistrates Duty; and That If Magistrates Pervert Judgement, the People Are Bound By the Law of God to Execute Judgement Without Them, and Upon Them* (1663), which title, we recognize, is Milton's thesis in a nutshell.

This influence is found in ideas and arguments from the tract, an influence that cannot be doubted since these authors generally use Milton's own language. One of the most interesting examples, however, of the significance of *Tenure* for this late seventeenth-century world is Algernon Sidney's three-page *The Very Copy of the Paper Delivered to the Sheriffs, Upon the Scaffold on Tower-Hill. On Friday, Decem. 7. 1683 . . . Before His Execution There.* Sentences are directly drawn from Milton's tract and presented as Sidney's political beliefs. *The Very Copy* was reissued in London and published in Dublin. But there were ten further documents that either reprint the paper or reprint portions of it or, like Elkanah Settle's *Remarks on Algernon Sidney's Paper,* reproduce these same sentences of Milton. None of these documents, however, would seem to be aware of the source. Sidney's *Discourses Concerning Government,* published posthumously in 1698 and very important politically in the later eighteenth century, when it was often reprinted, not only has a quotation from *Paradise Lost* but is thoroughly influenced throughout by Milton's *Defensio prima* and *The Tenure of Kings and Magistrates.*

John Goodwin in *Hubristodikai. The Obstructours of Justice* (1649) examines the tract at various places and quotes from it often. Sir Roger L'Estrange discusses the tract in *Le Non-Confirmiste Anglois dans ses ecris, dans ses sentiments, & dans sa pratique* (1683), and Pierre Bayle talks of it in *Nouvelles de la republique de lettres* (1684), reprinted in 1686. Quotations are found in L'Estrange's *The Dissenters Sayings and in Requital for L'Estrange's Sayings* (1681), a different book from another of similar title (there were two more editions in 1681 and others in 1683 and 1685). Thomas Long quotes from *Tenure* in *The Original of War: Or, the Causes of Rebellion* (1684), and there is a paraphrased quotation in J.P.'s (John Prince's?) *Tyrants and Protectors Set Forth in Their Colours* (1654). Manuel Schoenhorn has pointed out to me that a sentence from the altered version, *Pro Populo Adversus Tyrannos,* was adapted by Edmund Bohun in *An Answer to the Desertion Discuss'd* (1689). Milton's work is alluded to in numerous volumes: Canne's *The Discoverer* (1649); John Hakluyt's *Metropolitan Nuncio* (1649); N.W.'s *A Discourse Concerning the Engagement: Or, the Northern Subscribers Plea* (1650); G.W.'s *Republica Anglicana or the Historie of the Parliament in Their Late Proceedings* (1650); Ephraim Elcock's *Animadversions on a Book, Called A Plea for Non-Scribers* (1651), which also has a quotation from Milton's tract; and L'Estrange's *Considerations and Proposals in Order to the Regulation of the Press Together with Diverse Instances of Treasonous, and Seditious Pamphlets, Proving the Necessity Thereof* (1663), which incidentally does not refer to *Areopagitica.* Allusions are found likewise in L'Estrange's *Toleration Discuss'd* (1663), the revised version of which in 1670 and 1673 also includes quotations; it was reissued at least twice in 1681 in *A Collection* of L'Estrange's works and given a third edition that same year.

Further allusions occur in Edward Pelling's *A Sermon Preached on the Thirtieth of January, 1678/9. Being the Anniversary of the Martyrdom of King Charles the First* (1679), another sermon preached in 1682, and yet another sermon preached in 1685, as well as his *The Good Old Way or, A Discourse Offer'd to All True-Hearted Protestants Concerning the Ancient Way of the Church, and the Conformity of the Church of England Thereunto* (1680) with a quotation also. And we can note still more allusions in Matthew Rider's *The Power of Parliaments in the Case of Succession* (1680); Thomas Wilson's *A Sermon on the Martyrdom of King Charles I. Preached January 30. 1681* (1682) with several quotations and reedited the same year; and George Hickes's *A Sermon Preached Before the Lord Mayor, Aldermen, and Citizens of London, at Bow Church, on the 30th. of January 1681/2* (1682), with some paraphrasing from *Tenure* (this was reissued in 1683). Milton's work also appears in various book catalogues, British and Continental, before 1701.

Undoubtedly I have weighed the reader down with statistics, but to do so for *Defensio prima* would be much worse. This summary demonstrates, certainly, that Milton as prose writer may have been vilified by many—one thinks easily of Dr. Samuel Johnson—but there were others who found truth in his views. As prose writer he may not have been very "original," but we need teachers too.

7
Education as Means

The prose works of John Milton have often been dismissed or vilified because of his argument against monarchy, his defense of the Cromwellian government, his championing of divorce, and his rebuttal of Charles I (or rather, of *Eikon Basilike,* supposedly written by Charles). In the seventeenth century itself we have Joseph Addison (1694) advancing praise of Milton's poetry and dismay at some of the prose:

> But when, with eager step, from hence I rise,
> And view the first gay scenes of *Paradise;*
> What tongue, what words of rapture can express
> A vision so profuse of pleasantness.
> Oh had the Poet ne'er profan'd his pen,
> To vernish o'er the guilt of faithless men;
> His other works might have deserv'd applause!
> But now the language can't support the cause;
> While the clean current, tho' serene and bright,
> Betrays a bottom odious to the sight.[1]

In 1698 Thomas Yalden, a minor poet of the period, echoed those sentiments:

> These sacred lines with wonder we peruse,
> And praise the flights of a seraphic muse,
> Till thy seditious prose provokes our rage,
> And soils the beauties of the brightest page . . .
> We own the poet worthy to rehearse
> Heavn's lasting triumphs in immortal verse:
> But when thy impious mercenary pen
> Insults the best of princes, best of men,
> Our admiration turns to just disdain,
> And we revoke the fond applause again.[2]

The catalyst for Yalden's reactions at this time was the appearance of the three-volume *A Complete Collection of the Prose Works of John Milton,* often mislabeled John Toland's edition because of the "Life" printed in the first volume. The praise and the contempt continue for much of the eighteenth century—Samuel Johnson's remarks are only the most note-worthy, not exceptional. But attention was paid during the century and a half, though not popularly, to Milton's historical writing and his con-tribution to historiography, a field as we understand it only then emerg-ing in England. The prose was before the reading public through an edition of many of the prose works in 1697; through the aforemen-tioned *Complete Collection* of 1698, which omitted only *Mr. Milton's Char-acter of the Long Parliament;* through Thomas Birch's two-volume *Complete Collection* in 1738, which inserted *Character of the Long Parliament* into *The History of Britain,* from which it had been excised in 1670; and again through Richard Baron's revision of Birch in 1753. There were also some reprintings of individual titles during the latter years of the sev-enteenth century and throughout the eighteenth.

Among his works exhibiting educational purpose directly, being ba-sically expository rather than argumentative, are the histories; at times, however, they imply a positive way and at times a negative way as a means to his great purpose. A review of the historical works in terms of their presentation of the past and in terms of their validation of "truth" provides a statement of mundane teachings that can set the mental stage needed to apprehend the "high mystery" of life: the "magick structures" of this world, "rear'd so high," must needs be "shatter'd into heaps."

Milton's works of historical substance are *The History of Britain, The Character of the Long Parliament,* and *A Brief History of Moscovia.* Yet such tracts as *Of Reformation* and the life of Ramus in *Artis Logicæ Plenior In-stitutio* also have their historical dimension. The concept of historiogra-phy under which I proceed involves a judgment of evidence used and/or reported, from all known sources, weighed and examined as to validity, and the adjudged results presented in a coherent account, one as factual as possible.[3] Most of us are well aware of the kind of history that, say, Raphael Holinshed (and others) wrote in 1577, and we recognize the changes that were being wrought twenty-five years later through anti-quarian groups, who caused emphasis to be placed on documents rather than on legend or hearsay and who began the extension of the substance of history beyond events of politics, governments, and wars into social and cultural history. We think of William Camden's *Annales Rerum An-glicarum et Hibernicarum, Regnante Elizabetha ad Annum Salutis 1589* (1615) as well as his chorographic *Britannia* (1586) and his *Remaines of a Greater Worke Concerning Britaine* (1605); and of John Speed's *History of Great Britain* (1611), which uses Camden and the manuscript collection of Sir Robert Cotton. Cotton's collections were available to various scholars at his home in Westminster near Old Palace Yard until a short time before his death in 1631, and then later, after governmental restrictions had subsided, through his son Sir Thomas and his grandson Sir John. The library was deposited in Essex House in 1712 and in Ashburnham House in 1730; it has been in the British Museum only from 1753 on. Further we should remember that lectureships in history, with an emphasis on civil rather than ecclesiastical history, were established at Oxford by Camden in 1621 and at Cambridge, finally, by Fulke Greville in 1628, a time when Milton was still an undergraduate there.

An example of the kind of historical material presented by Holinshed (in this case derived from Robert Fabyan's *The Concordance of Histories* [1516], according to a marginal note) is the following:

Edmund, who reigned as king in that season ouer the Eastangles, being aduertised, raised an armie of men, and went foorth to giue battell vnto this armie of the Danes. But he with his people was chased out of the field, and fled to the castell of Framingham, where bying enuironed with a siege by his enimies, he yéelded himselfe vnto them. And because he would not renounce the christian faith, they bound him to a trée, and shot arrowes at him till he died: and afterwards cut off his head from his bodie, and threw the same into a thicke groue of bushes.[4]

Milton, indicating his source from Ingulf (that is, the pseudo-Ingulf as published in Sir Henry Savile's *Rerum Anglocarum Scriptores post Bedam* [reprinted and revised, Frankfort, 1601]) gives only this: "The *Danes* thence passing on into the Country of *East-Angles,* rifl'd and burnt the Monastery of *Elie,* overthrew Earl *Wulketul* with his whole Army, and lodg'd out the Winter at *Thetford;* where King *Edmund* assailing them, was with his whole Army put to flight, himself tak'n, bound to a stake, and shot to Death with Arrows, his whole Country subdu'd."[5]

Now, Milton knew his Holinshed well, although we have no indication that he used or even knew Fabyan. Matthew of Westminster (in his *Flores Historiarum* [Frankfort, 1601], 164-65), Henry of Huntingdon (in his *Historia Anglorum,* V [in Savile], 349), and Asser (in his *Ælfredi Regis Res Gestæ* [1574], reprinted in William Camden's *Anglica, Normannica, Hibernica, Cambrica, a Veteribus Scripta* [Frankfort, 1603]) present accounts similar to Holinshed's, and Milton frequently used and quoted from Matthew, Henry, and Asser in other sections of his *History.* In the subjects taken from British history entered in the Trinity MS as possible themes for dramas, Milton had entered "Edmond last k. of ye East angles martyr'd by Hinguar ye Dane." He references Speed, Book VIII, Chapter 2, but immediately before this he had entered the subject of "Osbert of Northumberland slain for ravishing the wife of Bernbocard and the Dans brought in," with citations of Stow, Holinshed (Book VI, Chapter

12, the same place from which I have quoted the account of Edmund), and Speed. He thus knew Holinshed's account and undoubtedly he knew Matthew's, Henry's, and Asser's; yet he omits the extravagances of the story, particularly the kind of inflated or nonobjective language we find so frequently in Holinshed, such as "cut off his head from his bodie" and "thicke" grove. Milton, in other words, reduces the historical statement to the direct account, in language that does not create any kind of fictionalized feeling.

It is interesting to see what happens to this episode in two other histories, both by authors who knew and used Milton's *History*, although I do not imply that either went directly to this specific account in Milton. What is important, I think, is that Milton's rendering of such material does involve a judgment of the evidence and an objective presentation; he is not the only writer of history who does this, of course, and his is not the only history that would have created this historiographic influence, but he is nonetheless important in the development of such influence and indeed was directly used by some chronologically close writers. Sir James Tyrrell, to whom we shall return in a moment, in his *The General History of England as Well Ecclesiastical as Civil* (London, 1696), writes:

In the mean time the *Britains* spoiling the Country as far as *Grant-bridge* (now *Cambridge,*) they then fell upon, and burnt the famous Nunnery of *Ely* killing all that were therin both Men and women, and carrying away a great deal of Riches, which had been brought thither from all parts for their better security; from whence they passed over into the Country of the *East-Angles,* where they slew Earl *Wulketule* coming against them, and making a stout resistance with his small Forces, from whence they marched against King *Edmund* himself, of whose Life and Martyrdom, I shall out of *Asser*'s Annals, give you a particular account and tho I will not pass any word for the truth of all his Relation, being written after the manner of the Legends of those times, yet the substance of it is no doubt true, and the rest may serve, if not to instruct yet at least to divert the Readers.[6]

The similarity of the report so far to Milton's is owing to Ingulf, whom Tyrrell cites in the immediately preceding sentence. But note his disclaimer of the truth of the story from Asser that he will relate two pages later. It is a disclaimer akin to a few in Milton's *History*, although Milton is given to simply omitting such "manner of the Legends." But Tyrrell seems to have suffered from the pedantic affliction of "detailed completeness," which has stuffed many a book with unnecessary data. We have Edmund "cruelly beaten," "bound to a Neighboring Tree," "inhumanly whipped," "shot . . . so full of Arrows, that it [his body] seemed capable of receiving no more," but not having died from this treatment, Edmund's head is cut off, which Asser "describes with a great deal of

Monkish Eloquence." Edmund's head is carried off and flung into a wood. While the substantive extravagances appear, Tyrrell's language (even aside from his skeptical comments) is not colored in the way Holinshed's and Asser's are. He completes his account with the legend that the people of the area sought to retrieve the head, finding it only after the head answered, "Here, here," to their "Where are you?" Tyrrell remarks: "As for this part of the Story, it sounds so like a Legend, that I shall leave it to be swallowed by those who are apt to be taken with such Things." While Tyrrell's history does not really answer the stringent demands of a major history, it is important to note that it appeared in the year following Sir William Temple's charge in *Introduction to the History of England* (1695) that no adequate full history existed. Toland, in his *Life of John Milton*, quoted the passage from Temple in full and remarked Tyrrell's then-current *General History*. Tyrrell's work was reprinted in 1697, 1698, and 1700.

On the other hand, one who was not given to the inclusion of all available material and who, like Milton, simply omitted what his judgment would not credit, was David Hume. In *The History of England, From the Invasion of Julius Caesar, to the Revolution in 1688* (London, 1761) all he presents is: "[The Mercians] broke into East-Anglia; defeated and took prisoner Edmund, the king of the country, whom they afterwards murdered in cool blood: and, committing the most barbarous ravages on the people, particularly on the monasteries, they gave the East-Angles cause to regret the temporary relief which they had obtained, by assisting the common enemy."[7] Both Tyrrell and Hume show influence from the kind of historiographic approach that had been developing in the latter seventeenth century, an approach that Milton's *History of Britain* represents well and seems to have aided. Milton built his narrative on sources that he generally makes explicit. For example, in Book IV, 174, he writes: "But two years after, while *Eadbert* was busied in War against the *Picts, Ethelbald* the *Mercian,* by foul fraud, assaulted part of *Northumberland* in his absence, as the supplement of *Beda*'s Epitome records. . . . *Huntingdon* doubts not to give them a great Victory. And *Simeon* reports, another Battel fought between *Britans* and *Picts* the year ensueing." He gives marginal notation here to William of Malmesbury, the Saxon Chronicle, and Simeon of Durham. But he also often specifically questions his sources and the historical content they present, a necessary point for the historian, as Camden had previously admonished. For example, "saith *Mat. West.* annexing thereto a long unlikely Tale" (Book V, 180-81); and "[It] is a long story, told . . . by *Malmsbury;* and under the year 821. by *Mat. West.* where I leave it to be sought by such as are more credulous then I wish my Readers" (Book IV, 186); and "Hard it is, through the bad expression of these Writers, to define this fight, whether by Sea or Land; *Hoveden* terms it a Sea fight. Nevertheless with 50 Ships (Asser and others add 300) they enterd the mouth of *Thames*" (Book V, 194). Reference here is to Roger of Hoveden (or Howden)'s *Chronica*, edited by Savile in 1601.

The use of one source against another is also frequent; for example, after having cited Asser, Malmesbury, Simeon, and the Saxon Chronicle, he says, "*Huntingdon* on the other side much praises *Ethelbald*, and writes him buried in *Serburn*, with great sorrow of the people, who miss'd him long after. *Mat. West.* saith, that he repented of his incest with *Judith*, and dismiss'd her: but *Asser* an Eye witness of those times, mentions no such thing" (Book V, 198). The fabulousness of some of the early accounts is also indicated, as here:

Notwithstanding all these unlikelyhoods of *Artur*'s Reign and great acheivments, in a narration crept in I know not how among the Laws of *Edward* the *Confessor*, *Artur* the famous king of *Britans*, is said not only to have expell'd hence the *Saracens*, who were not then known in *Europe*, but to have conquer'd *Freesland*, and all the North East Iles as far as *Russia*, to have made *Lapland* the Eastern bound of his Empire, and *Norway* the chamber of *Britain*. When should this be done? . . . *Buchanan* our Neighbour Historian reprehends him of *Monmouth* and others for fabling in the deeds of *Artur*, yet what he writes thereof himself, as of better credit, shews not whence he had but from those Fables; which he seems content to believe in part, on condition that the *Scots* and *Picts* may be thought to have assisted *Artur* in all his Wars, and atchievments; whereof appears as little grownd by an credible story, as of that which he most counts Fabulous. [Book III, 125-26]

It should be observed that Milton at no point refers to Holinshed. On page 118 of Book III, for example, in relating the story of Ambrosius, he cites Geoffrey of Monmouth, Gildas, Bede, and Nennius, but Holinshed, who gives his account in Book V, Chapter 1, is passed over because Milton is concerned with original sources, not a compendium of authors. Similarly Speed and Stow are not included in Milton's *History*, although we know, from the subjects for dramas in the Trinity MS and from the Commonplace Book, that he read them well.

At times, however, modern research has indicated that certain matters or details come from specific but unnamed sources. An example appears in Book VI, 367: "*Elfred* was sent for by the King there at *London;* but in his way met at *Guilford* by Earl *Godwin*, who with all seeming friendship entertain'd him, was in the night surpris'd and made Prisner, most of his Company put to various sorts of cruel Death, decimated twice over, then brought to *London,* was by the King sent bound to *Eely,* has his Eyes put out by the way, and deliverd to the Monks there, dy'd soon after in thir Custody. *Malmsbury* gives little credit to this story of *Elfred,* as not Chronicl'd in his time, but rumour'd only." Milton gives his source as Simeon of Durham, *De Gestis Regum Anglorum* (*Historia Regum Anglorum et Dacorum*) in Sir Roger Twysden's *Historiæ Anglicanæ Scriptores X* (1652). French Fogle in his edition of Milton's *History* (YP, V, i, 367, n. 90) indicates that details also derive from Matthew of Westminster (210) and Henry of Huntingdon (VI, in Savile, 365). The reference from Malmesbury comes from *Gesta Regnum* (II, xii, printed by Savile, 77). Comparison of Milton's account with Holinshed's (Book VII, Chapter 14) indicates Milton's weighing of the matter and rejection of a sensational style.

Coherence and content are also important to Milton:

I am sensible [he writes, 177-78] how wearisom it may likely be to read of so many base and reasonless Actions, so many names of Kings one after another, acting little more then mute persons in a Scene: what would it be to have inserted the long Bead-roll of Archbishops, Bishops, Abbots, Abbesses, and thir doeings, neither to Religion profitable nor to morality, swelling my Authors each to a voluminous body, by me studiously omitted; and left as their propriety, who have a mind to write the Ecclesiastical matters of those Ages; neither do I care to wrincle the smoothness of History with rugged names of places unknown, better harp'd at in *Camden,* and other Chorographers.

After having noted a number of slayings and changes of rulers, he comments (183-84): "no reason of thir Quarrel writ'n; such bickerings to recount, met oft'n in these our Writers, what more worth is it then to Chronicle the Wars of Kites, or Crows, flocking and fighting in the Air?" His dismissal of wars and popular concepts of the heroic as subject for his epic poem may be echoing in our minds.

The History of Britain was first published in November 1670; a new issue appeared in 1671; a second edition is dated 1677, and a second issue, 1678; its third edition is 1695, again with two issues. For *A Complete History of England, With the Lives of All the Kings and Queens Thereof; From the Earliest Account of Time, to the Death of His Late Majesty King William III,* 1706, but first advertised in *The Post-Boy* in May 1697, three volumes, John Hughes chose Milton's work for reprinting. To this, which is in the first volume, he added Samuel Daniel's history from the Norman Conquest through Edward III, new histories of Richard II and Henry IV, V, and VI, John Habington's life of Edward IV, Sir Thomas More's lives of Edward V and Richard III in translation, George Cuk's life of Richard III, and Sir Francis Bacon's life of Henry VII. The third volume covering more recent times was written by White Kennett, and thus the edition has incorrectly been referred to as his. The second edition, corrected, was published in 1719. Milton's *History*, we can see, was easily enough available during the period of 1670-1753. The copy in the 1698 *Complete Collection* is advertised as "Publish'd from a Copy corrected by the Author himself," and has most of the errata corrected and other revisions of the individual printings. Hughes did not give this text, but he does correct some of the errata. Birch, followed by Baron, gives this text but omits the table or index, incorporating it into his own general index. The treatment of the table in modern editions is an egregious example of bad editorial practice: the Columbia Edition prints it separately in a different volume, and the Yale Prose omits it completely. It is thought to have been compiled under Milton's direction; it certainly is a useful and, for those times, "modern" aid not usually appearing in histories, since their chronological ordering seems to obviate the need for an index. But Milton's table stresses ideas, not merely events: "Learning and Arts when began to flourish among the Saxons"; "Sleda erects the Kingdom of the East-Saxons"; "Edilwaele the South-Saxon perswaded to Christianity by Wulfer."

The History was used with approbation of its content and style, those aspects that go to the heart of the developing historiography, by John Aubrey in his *Natural History of Wiltshire* and his topographical study of Wiltshire (both around 1670); by Thomas Blount in 1672 in *Animadversions upon S*^r *Richard Baker's Chronicle, and It's Continuation*, who uses it to charge Baker and Edward Phillips, Milton's nephew and the continuer of the *Chronicle*, with misuse of history and downright errors as well as "stuffing" the account in a marginal citation of Milton's statement that he will relate only "things worth the noting"; by Aylett Sammes in 1676 as authoritative source in his discussion of the antiquities of ancient Britain as well as for a paraphrase of Gildas; and by Edmund Bohun in his addition to Degory Wheare's *The Method and Order of Reading Both Civil and Ecclesiastical Histories* (1685, 1st ed.; 1694, 2d ed.; 1698, 3d ed.); Bohun had commented most favorably on the work in his diary under date of August 4, 1677. The influence from Milton's *History* is so obvious throughout *The State of Church-Affairs in This Island of Great Britain under the Government of the Romans, and British Kings* (1687) that it has been attributed to Milton himself and most frequently to his brother Sir Christopher; it is so listed in most library catalogues. Hermann Conring, the very important religious, political, and philosophical writer, used it in his *Examen rervmpvblicarvm potiorvm totivs orbis* in chapters XXII ("De Regno Angliæ") and XXIII ("De Regno Scotiæ"), published in his *Opera* in 1730.

Tyrrell, mentioned before, not only gives long quotations from Milton's work on 17 and 116 (second pagination) but has pertinent comments elsewhere. In reviewing British histories up to his own time, he remarks (vi):

But since the Restoration of K. *Charles* the *Second,* there are several who have undertaken this Province, the first of whom was Mr. *Milton;* and it must be acknowledged, that he wrote this *English Saxon* History with Judgment, though not with that Diligence and Exactness as we may see he did his other Works of a different Nature; since either through want of Opportunity to consult Antient Manuscripts, (several of which have been published since he wrote) or else by not making use of those Authors he might have had, and by confining himself too much to the relating of Military Matters, and almost wholly neglecting Ecclesiastical Affairs, or looking into those things which he by way of Contempt called *Cathedral Registers;* as also by omitting the giving us any Account of the Antient *Saxon* Laws, and Original Constitutions of this Kingdom; he has thereby rendred that Work much more dry and imperfect than otherwise no doubt it would have been from such a Pen as his. [reverse italics]

The dates of composition of Milton's *History* are not entirely certain. Perhaps he produced Books I and II before fall 1648, Book III during 1648, Book IV before mid-March 1649, with an addition sometime after 1652, perhaps when Books V-VI were written. A range of years from 1653 or 1655 through 1659 is not unlikely.[8] It seems clear that Milton did not research the manuscripts that could have been available to him personally around 1648, and he explicitly neglects ecclesiastical affairs as being diverting from his purpose of writing history. But attention should be called to his use of such material as the forged letter from Emma in *Encomium Emmæ Reginæ,* which he translated into his history from its edition by André Du Chesne in *Historiæ Normannorum Scriptores Antiqui* (1619). Further, the years when the later books were produced were years when Milton was totally blind and, it would seem, generally house-ridden. He apparently did not know Anglo-Saxon and, we would have to conclude, did not feel that it behooved him to learn it in order to examine at first hand various documents. Not our ideal historian, yet one who did advance the cause of historiography. Milton is not, indeed, a historian engaged in historical research but an author intending an account as factual as possible of a history that had been given numerous treatments by often nonobjective and conflicting writers. He is not aiming at determining the so-called "Original Constitutions," for instance, but he is determined to get rid of the absurdities, and in a style that, though dry to some, would not be appropriate to epic.

Tyrrell, following the concepts of historiography that we have been discussing, says that he has culled material from previous writers, Greek and Roman as well as British, and has compared original documents in the Cottonian library whereby he has been able to add remarks to prior statements. And he continues, "tho I do not pretend to have added much to what Mr. *Camden* and Mr. *Milton* have already collected from those Writers relating to the History of *Britain;* yet I hope I have from . . . [various people] not only illustrated, but settled divers things relating to that part of our Ecclesiastical, as well as Civil Affairs, not commonly taken notice of before." [viii; reverse italics]

It is curious, I think, that Fogle, in his essay on historiography in *A Milton Encyclopedia* and in his edition of *The History,* totally omits even an allusion to Tyrrell. His only reference to him, an identification as "a minor historian mentioned by Toland in his life of Milton" (YP, V, i, 411 n.), is the allegation that Tyrrell may have caused *The Character of the Long Parliament* to be published. I should therefore call attention to the suggestion, not noted anywhere in the Yale Prose, that Tyrrell was the editor who revised Milton's *A Tenure of Kings and Magistrates* in 1689 in the midst of the succession controversy as *Pro Populo Adversus Tyrannos: Or the Sovereign Right and Power of the People Over Tyrants.* Parker's discussion in 1942[9] was aware that the publisher Randal Taylor had advertised it in 1691 as Milton's and that Anthony Wood, also in 1691, included it in his list of Milton's works. But it has not been noted that John Locke, in a manuscript in the Bodleian Library dated 1689-91, also called it Milton's.[10]

On p. 20 of his *History,* Tyrrell, sounding somewhat like Milton at first, admonishes the reader that

since I intend to confine myself only to write of such Actions as were perform'd within the compass of this Isle . . . I shall rather chuse sometimes to leave a gap in the Story it self, than to write Things foreign and impertinent to the Subject I am to treat of: And indeed I could willingly have forborn Writing this Part of the History at all, since it hath been done already by Mr. *Camden* in Latin, and Mr. *Milton* in English, who have scarce omitted any thing which is worth the Collecting out of the *Greek* and *Latin* Historians, that was necessary to compleat this Period. Therfore, were it not for leaving too great a Chasm in our intended Work, I could very willingly have excused my self from so ungrateful a Task, in which I confess it is hard to equal, and much more to exceed such great Authors.

And on page 136 we read a discussion of King Arthur in which Tyrrell remarks, "yet since Mr. *Milton,* as well as others, have been pleased to question, whether there was ever any such King who Reigned in *Britain,* it were not amiss if we did a little clear [sic] and establish that Point before we proceed any further, since so great and remarkable a part of the History of the *British* Kings depends upon it."

It seems manifest that Milton's work is considered authoritarian, if not definitive, and, if one makes comparison between Tyrrell, such other historical writers of the period as Robert Brady, William Howell, and Robert Sheringham,[11] and people like Holinshed and Speed, one sees immediately the development of a historiographic sense and language in the same concise, plain, and sometimes unprejudiced style that Milton exhibits.

During the eighteenth century the reviewer of Hughes's compendium in *Acta Eruditorum* for 1709 pulled out Milton's *History* for special commendation. Aaron Thompson, in *The British History. Translated Into English from the Latin of Jeffrey of Monmouth. With a Large Preface Concerning the Authority of the History* (1718), calls upon Milton's authority four times, particularly in regard to names; Milton's influence is clear in the preface. Laurence Echard, in *The History of England* (1707-18), alludes to him and includes a brief biography. Despite their opposed positions on history and historians, John Oldmixon in *The Critical History of England* (1724-26) and Zachary Grey in *A Defense of Our Ancient and Modern Historians* (1725) both agreed on Milton's position of authority and his scholarship, discussed further by Grey in *An Appendix to the Defense of Our Antient and Modern Historians* (1725). Oldmixon's counterattack, *Clarendon and Whitlock Compar'd* (1727), iterates his assessment in references on pages xiv-xv. Even the American poet Richard Lewis in notes to his English translation of Edward Holdsworth's "Muscipula," called *The Mouse-Trap, or the Battle of the Cambrians and Mice* (1728), cites *History of Britain* as authority. Later in the century William Dodd, the imprisoned and executed prelate and forger, wrote an extensive discussion of *The History* with quotations in *The Christian's Magazine* (December 1760), and in 1760 Lewis Morris, the literary critic, saw the Welsh attitude toward the work as laudatory, a not common attitude toward British writers on Welsh history. The historiographic view of Milton as one who reexamined the past without the weight of traditional theory can be seen in the nineteenth century's attitude, "but at the same time," as I have noted elsewhere, "as an imperfect historian, one whose attention to the demands of history and to details was at best temporary."[12] The problem is that Milton has been read as if he were a historian, which he is not.

The "profit" in Milton's work is always educationally oriented, and in that orientation always moral and corrective. As he says in *Of Education*, "the end of learning is to repair the ruins of our first parents" (2). *The History of Britain* is a guide to lay bare the workings of providence, Milton's aim as well in *Paradise Lost*: to "assert Eternal Providence, / And [thereby] justifie the wayes of God to men." Adam and Eve leave Paradise to begin human history with "Providence thir guide." Fogle writes,

"He drew the notion that the prime end of history was instruction, whether in statecraft, in a knowledge of human motives in action, or in morality" (*ME* 3:192). Surely Milton was in agreement with Howell's statement in the preface to *An Institution of General History* (1661): "by the knowledge of History we are taught wisdom, and led to vertue" (A3). Milton's *History* is one of the academically corrective works written, or begun, during his schoolteaching years in the 1640s, even though they were not published until later: *Accedence Commenc't Grammar, Artis Logicæ, The Character of the Long Parliament,*[13] *A Brief History of Moscovia,* the lost Greek thesaurus, and the lost Latin thesaurus. *Paradise Lost* (and *Paradise Regain'd* and *Samson Agonistes,* if one will entertain the notion that these poems were also begun in this period) supplies the other kind of corrective work needed to ravage the heart and soul (the *dolce,* as it were) in order to influence the mind (the *utile*). These provide the "positive" way; the *History* and the others, a combination of the "positive" and the "negative" ways. Milton's and Howell's (and others') attitude toward history has not been lost on people like Hume with his Tory biases and James Anthony Froude with his aristocratic conservatism. It is clear how his work on *The History of Britain* fits exactly into the concept I laid out in Chapter 6.

In reference to style, we should also set forth William Warburton's epitome in a letter to Thomas Birch, dated November 24, 1737: "It is best suited to his 'English History;' his air of antique giving a good grace to it. It is wrote with great simplicity, contrary to his custom in his prose works, and is the better for it. But he sometimes rises to a surprising grandeur in the sentiment and expression, as at the conclusion of the Second Book: 'Henceforth we are to steer', &c. I never saw any thing equal to this, but the conclusion of Sir Walter Raleigh's *History of the World.*" And further we must cite James Burnet, Lord Monboddo, from Volume V of *Of the Origin and Progress of Language* (1789): "As I have mentioned modern historians, it would be improper to omit the greater writer in English, both in verse and prose, and who has also merit as an historian; I mean Milton, who has given us a history of England from the earliest times down to the conquest. . . . The stile of his history is altogether classical, such as might be expected from so great a scholar as Milton. But it is not so much composed in periods, as I am persuaded it would have been, if it [had] been a formal history at full length. . . . There is nothing however in Milton like what I call the short cut of stile; and he has distinguished his language from common speech by all the variety of arrangement, and all the abbreviations, which the language could admit of." Indeed, although Monboddo did not recognize it, Milton's stylistic and formalistic influences were Sallust and Polybius.

Milton's *A Brief History of Moscovia* is primarily a chorographic history praised for its accuracy of report and names and for describing an important world entity rather than for inditing the military as did so many of the other works on Russia flooding the surely small market in the 1650s through 1670s. Why it took so long for Brabazon Aylmer to publish it (in 1682) after Milton's death is not clear, except that it is not long (109 pages, including a two-page bibliography) and that he probably did not recognize its worth. He perhaps finally published it only because it was written by Milton. Its fourth and fifth chapters recite the succession of dukes and emperors and the discovery of Russia by the English. In 1698 Jodocus Crull without proper acknowledgment adapted Milton's Chapter IV as his Chapter XII in *The Ancient and Present State of Muscovy*. He does refer to Milton's work in the preface.

Milton's *A Brief History of Moscovia* represents that other side of historiographic writing, description of the geographic land, but it too should involve, and does, a judgment of evidence, weighed and examined as to validity, and presented in a coherent and factual account. The ignorant attitude of its most recent editor, the late George B. Parks, in the Yale Prose, is deplorable: for him it is inadequate because of its "scanty coverage of Russia and its ignoring of much necessary material." He thus sees it as fragmentary and unfinished. It is these things only if one expects a chronological state history; Milton in his preface makes crystal clear what he is doing: "The study of Geography is both profitable and delightfull . . . [One can] assay something in the description of one or two Countreys, which might be as a Pattern or Example. . . . What was scatter'd in many volumes, and observ'd at several times by Eye-witnesses, with no cursory pain I laid together, to save the Reader a far longer travaile of wandring through so many desert Authours" (A2-A3v).

Of *The Character of the Long Parliament* Sarah and Rowland Collins in their entry on *The History* in *A Milton Encyclopedia* (3:194) remark, "Milton's reason for omitting the digression is cloaked in ambiguity. Whether the decision was reached solely to strengthen the narrative line of Book 3 or to avoid trouble in getting by the Licenser has been a matter for speculation." Fogle suggests that its arguments were already sufficiently used in other writings before 1670. Woolrych removes it from *The History* as written prior to 1660 and casts it as a kind of afterthought to Book III in 1660, with its removal being charged to the political scene of 1670. The rather simple reason for deletion, I think, is obvious when one thinks in terms of the historiographic, as Milton did, whenever he wrote it. *The Character*—whether written in late 1648, when Milton may have been completing Book III of *The History*, or in April 1660 (but for what reasons he would have returned to *The History* Woolrych does not make clear)—anachronistically discusses a contemporary situation as an analogy or parallel to the situation in Britain after Roman controls had ended. In the *History* he invites the reader to compare the "confused Anarchy" then with the "interreign" of that period when Charles was not in full control and when Parliament was hardly consolidated as a government. But the "Digression," as it is called in the surviving scribal manuscript, simply opposed the "plain, and lightsom brevity, to relate well and orderly things worth the noting, so as may best instruct and benefit them that read" (3), as he expressed his intention in the *History*. It also opposed the objectivity requisite for good historiography. Its inclusion would have suborned his statement in the first paragraph of the *History:* "Certainly oft-times we see that wise men, and of best abilitie have forborn to write the Acts of thir own daies, while they beheld with a just loathing and disdain, not only how unworthy, how pervers, how corrupt, but often how ignoble, how petty, how below all History the persons and thir actions were" (2). It is obvious that I can assign the deletion of this work to Milton's own perspicacity, not to Tyrrell or to Arthur Annesley, Earl of Anglesey.

Milton's contribution to British historiography is not singular and may have had any direct effect for only about a century after publication of *The History of Britain*, but there is contribution not in the researching but in the *writing* of history and that I think is "worth the noting."

Milton was undoubtedly one of the best-read authors in all of English literature; indeed, he may have been the most learned Englishman of his time. Classicists, Hebraists, specialists in the Neo-Latin and national literatures of the Renaissance, historians of science and philosophy—all find ample evidence that Milton was well-read in their respective areas. Yet Milton seems to have had but a nodding acquaintance with Anglo-Saxon and medieval authors, as we have noted, a surprising lapse in a man with such a firm control over other areas of western thought. Looking at his relative unfamiliarity with the writings of the period may shed some light on Milton as a student of the past, on his own historical context, and on the biases toward the period—his own and his age's. We will see reflected both sources of knowledge and criticisms of the state of culture and education that inform the historical studies we have just looked at. At the same time we can reach some conclusions about the student/writer Milton and come to understand that we may know less about that student than we would like. While education may be a means to prepare one for the comprehension of the "high mystery" of life, that education demands broad and full study, unfortunately not always possible, as it was not for Milton in British pre-Renaissance history or in his pregraduation study of astronomy, we might note.

Where does the Anglo-Saxon period end and the medieval begin? If we take the usual and convenient eleventh century as the turning point, we find that Milton's knowledge of Anglo-Saxon materials is largely an acquaintance with histories. This knowledge was derived from reprints of Bede, Alfred, Asser, Gildas and others by seventeenth-century scholars such as Abraham Wheloc, first encountered during 1639-41 when Milton was reading British history. He employed these materials in his own *History of Britain* as we have seen. Francis Junius's edition of the Caedmon MS in 1655, the first Anglo-Saxon "literary" text to appear, has been linked with *Paradise Lost* and repeatedly rejected as source, and of course *Beowulf* was still unknown. What this indicates is that one of the reasons for the paucity of Milton's knowledge of Anglo-Saxon life and literature accounts for his apparent paucity of knowledge of medieval literature: much of it simply was not available.

Non-British authors of the medieval period (that is, those prior to the mid-fifteenth century) that Milton did seem to know include St. Thomas Aquinas, Boccaccio, Dante, John Hus, and Petrarch. Historians known through more recent and often compendium editions include probably Johannes Cinnamus, Georgius Codinus, Florence of Worcester, Geoffrey of Monmouth, Henry of Huntingdon, Ingulf, Matthew Paris, Roger of Hoveden, Simeon of Durham, and William of Malmesbury. Most of this reading emerges in *History of Britain,* written for the most part shortly after the seventeenth-century edition of these medieval texts. And, of course, some of this reading is also recorded in the Commonplace Book in entries dated 1639-41; these entries often coincide with references in the earlier prose, such as the antiprelatical tracts. What should also be evident, however, and what needs constant underscoring, is that the universities were not studying any of these historical or, one should add, philosophical, scientific, or literary works of medieval or Renaissance vintage. Milton's contribution to the historiography of his era was what the late seventeenth- and early eighteenth-century historiographers praised him for: his skepticism over the extravagancies of the received "histories"—a generally "modern" view, that is—and his chronological revision of the confusions of the reported past. Of the British authors of the medieval period, Milton would seem to have known Chaucer, Gower, Langland, Malory, and Wyclif. Jackson C. Boswell[14] has compiled a listing of works unquestionably in Milton's ken, possible inclusions, and doubtful items offered speculatively by some modern scholars. Among possibilities are St. Bonaventure, John Lydgate, and medieval drama. But those I have noted are the only certain or fairly certain authors.

One important study is Ernest E. Kellett's "Milton as Medievalist."[15] Kellett is almost totally concerned with *Paradise Lost*, in which he sees similes and metaphors, cosmography, perhaps even blank verse and elisions, resulting from a medieval cast of mind. The sources of Milton's thought, such as Seneca, are the sources of medieval views. "In fact," Kellett writes, "Milton is simply saturated with medievalism, . . . he read the Scriptures in a medieval light, and . . . his study of the classics, while profound and wide, was touched at every turn by medieval influence" (105). For Kellett a sure sign of the medieval cast of mind is the mingling of scripture with classics, romance, and tradition. We can argue with these restrictive characteristics and definitions, and words like "saturated" and "touched at every turn" strike us as overstatements.[16] But the fact is that the end of the sixteenth century still showed vestiges of "medievalism," as in Marlowe's "Dr. Faustus" and Shakespeare's "Richard III," despite the Renaissance cast of mind of the hundred or so years immediately preceding. The seventeenth century not only obliterated such "medievalism" but by its end had moved out of a simplistically Renaissance world to the threshold of a modern era. By medievalism here I mean the reliance upon a man-centered universe, a vertical sociopolitical structure sanctioned by God, a scholastic way of thinking, an allegoric way of presentation of ideas, and the like: a fairly closed system, as opposed to the opening up of all these attitudes characteristic of the Renaissance cast of mind. Milton is far from Donne in reflecting medieval stances: the world of thought and its expression are multileveled, each level interpenetrated by others, but it is not a scholastic world. Rather it is a world not delimited by boundaries, though codified Ramistically because of its immensity. The evidence does not yield Milton a medievalist.

Two reasons have been offered for the apparent paucity of Milton's knowledge of medieval authors: the unavailability of texts and the educational emphasis on the classics, and, even so, only certain classics. We should remember that Milton, as was normal then, did not read Plato until after he had become a graduate student in 1629. He did not come upon Copernicus and his heliocentric theory directly until well after graduation.[17] But with the advent of some texts and a growing awareness of the numerous pasts, Milton like others moved into an investigation of at least some formerly disregarded subject areas. The apparent paucity may be only that: apparent. Through November 1637 we know from the letter to Diodati and from the Commonplace Book that his organized reading had proceeded in theological studies to the late Latin fathers and in history to the pre-"Italian" states: he was filling in those periods not covered in his formal schooling (which ended in 1632). The years 1639-41, prior to the interventions of Civil Wars, domestic matters, and public concerns, saw the expansion of his studies into later national histories (not only British), with their intertwined matter of religious, sociological, governmental, and educational problems. The years after 1641 had not the leisure to allow compulsively organized reading, but reading did continue, and there may have been more study falling into the medieval period than we have evidence for. The Commonplace Book was little used after 1647-48, and the prose written after Milton became Secretary for Foreign Tongues to the Council of State reflects usually contemporary books. Perhaps some of the speculations on Milton's reading that Boswell records were actual.

In any case, Milton's knowledge of medieval authors would seem not to have been less than that of others, excepting only such antiquarians as Sir Robert Cotton and Francis Junius. Milton as a student of the past seems to understand the persistence of history, its amalgamation and assimilation into any present, and its influence on what worlds lie ahead. And his prose arguments, regardless of subject, are always anchored in the explanation that what is is an outgrowth of the past and that at times radical action is needed to cut those roots for the good of the present and future. Again the view is a modern one; it is not really the Renaissance concept of use of the past for its own sake. Rather, it is the study of the past to understand the present and to alter the future. I do not see Milton in this channel of thought until after 1639; before that his goal, as in the Seventh Prolusion, emphasizes acquisition of knowledge only. His intellectual change is not to be common until the Enlightenment and the rejection of the conservative neoclassicism of those fifty or so years and of the medieval chains of being that Pope lamented.

Most of our knowledge of Milton's reading of the aforementioned medieval authors comes from citations in the Commonplace Book and in the prose. It seems likely that he, like all of us, read works that he did not quote or reference, and influences can easily be subliminal. We need two studies: one of the works available to him, both in print and in manuscript; and one of tentative influential works and authors. He owned two different editions of Boccaccio's *Vita di Dante Poeta Florentino,* and it is difficult to discount acquaintance at least with the *Decameron* and the *Filocolo.* He owned and used Bernardino Daniello's edition of Dante, and his copy of the *Convivio* is in the New York Public Library. Citations and translations in *Of Reformation* and *The Reason of Church-Government* along with seeming parallels in *Paradise Lost* attest to Dante's significance for him. Petrarch's *Opera* has often been alleged, although the sonnet tradition into which Milton falls was intervened by Giovanni della Casa and Cardinal Bembo. (We should note that all of Milton's sonnets are "Petrarchan," even that to Cromwell where the last two lines rhyme, and even in spite of the frequent displacement of the volta, as in the Piedmont sonnet. He is never in the English tradition.) In *Apology for Smectymnuus* Milton adds Petrarch's *Apology Contra Gallum* to our book list. St. Thomas's *Summa* and his *Opuscula* complete Milton's attested reading of non-British works. Generally the use to which these authors are put is for authority, for ideas that are thus indicated as being established, even conventional, and not individualistic and newfangled. But St. Thomas has not been seen as a deeply pervasive force as has Augustine or Irenaeus.

That literary aspects of the works of Dante, Boccaccio, and Petrarch—language and metaphor, form and structure, style—also obtain is not difficult to accept, though evidence is internal and interpretive. We should remember that there is only the same kind of evidence, and not much more of it, for Milton's reading of Spenser and Shakespeare. Whether he was aware of French romances, of Chrétien or Jean de Meun (other than through Chaucer), or German Arthurian literature or the minnesingers, we can only infer. Such inferences from scholars are still generally forthcoming, although we assume—quite rightly—that allusions to *La Chanson de Roland* mean that Milton knew that poem.

One of my speculations, thus, is that our study of Milton's works, particularly of the poems, and particularly after about 1639, may suggest, tentatively to be sure, that he read or was otherwise aware of more medieval non-British authors than our limited sources of evidence provide. Surely there was a great stress on Italian and Italian authors. We know from "Ad Patrem" that Milton had studied French, and it is not unlikely that he would have been reading important French texts, literary and otherwise, for which we have no record today. (The Commonplace Book has entries from Renaissance French authors—largely historians—dated 1640 or later.) Perhaps that earlier study and continued reading brought some medieval Italian and French texts into his purview. Of the German and other literatures, who knows? We have, I think, been misled by assuming that the Commonplace Book records his reading program fairly well, when it clearly is only a notebook of interesting historical occurrences and ideas on various subjects, that, from probably 1637 onward, struck him as potentially usable in whatever path his writing regimen might take. There is no attempt at creating some kind of ledger; there are certain kinds of works and certain authors that do not get entered; and the entries come in somewhat limited chronological spurts.

Among the works of British authors owned were Speght's edition of Chaucer, Gower's *Confessio Amantis,* and Langland's *Piers Plowman.* There are entries from the first two in the Commonplace Book and allusions from all three in the prose. References to Arthur imply Malory's *Morte*

Darthur. Milton's citation of Duns Scotus in *Areopagitica* strongly urges another addition to our list. But literary uses must be inferred: Milton left no statements of literary theory that involved these authors—not even in the preface to Book 2 of *The Reason of Church-Government*—and no literary criticism of any discursive nature. The Commonplace Book entries involve ideas, and allusions in such works as *Of Reformation, Apology, Areopagitica, Defensio secunda,* and the prolusions are geared to evoke images or attitudes. They are truly allusive, gauged to recall the original context and accumulated responses to those contexts. The simile of the plowman in Book IV of *Paradise Lost,* for instance, if it does allude to Piers (as well as accumulated sociological meanings), recalls an overply of the allegorical and politically-charged man behind the plow that Langland's *Vision* and Luke 9:62 conjure up.

The reference to the Squire's Tale in "Il Penseroso" is like most of Milton's allusions to classical literature in, say, "At a Vacation Exercise"— an evocation of a story or image with little real texture of meaning. And this seems generally to be the case in the poetry written before "Lycidas" (including at least part of "Comus"). During 1639-48 Milton is concerned with history and traditional ideological foundations, and citations establish these while offering up what thoughts he wishes to implant. It is, of course, the period of much prose and relatively little poetry, at least published poetry. After 1648 whatever medieval literature has effect upon him would seem to be those things read in the past (except that there are entries from Dante in the Commonplace Book dated thereafter, but the dating of these late items is dependent on factors that are perhaps questionable). References in the prose written after 1648 (other than the completion of *The History of Britain*) are very few. The medieval literary influence instead emerges in the poetry of *Paradise Lost*—not the other works—by inference, and is the result, I would speculate, of reading prior to his blindness in 1650-52. Action in *Paradise Regain'd* is controlled not to allude to anything historically placed after Jesus' temptation, although simile may; and *Samson Agonistes* is likewise limited basically to a historical period before Samson's death, with only an occasional image postdating it (for example, the "snowy *Alp*" of line 628). The extent of the reading before his blindness may be more than we have evidence for but was certainly hampered, as I have said, by the unavailability of texts.

The one author I have not yet specified further is John Wyclif. What Milton read was his own copy of Arnisæus of Halberstad's rendition of Wyclif's *Dialogus* ("Speculum Ecclesiæ Militantis"), a text in turn taken from Corasius of Tolouse. Milton refers to Wyclif in various works, including *Tetrachordon*, complaining in the latter about the poverty of English libraries. He is annoyed that he has been unable to read Wyclif in a complete and original text, only in one twice removed. It is not surprising, then, that medieval authors so relatively seldom find their way into his work. Yet, as has been said, there may have been more extensive use of medieval authors than we have evidence for, and careful study on our part may unearth some tentative conclusions of additional titles or of more and deeper understanding of those works we know he did read.

8

Covenant:
Sacred and Profaned

The first seven chapters of this different biography have proceeded somewhat chronologically from Milton's earlier life to the time when his great purpose was being enacted. But they have also shot ahead to consider that purpose through an overview of his accomplishments and thus to suggest a readjustment in fact of that purpose. Ahead will be considerations, on the one hand, of his thinking, his beliefs, his personal self, and, on the other, his further achievements, again taken up somewhat chronologically. When dealing with a creative artist, a biographer—or even a kind of biographer—should probably stress certain works, for it is through important productions that the creative artist continues to be of interest to the public, and it is in such productions that much of the person and the factual action of the life appear. One aspect of Milton's thinking lies in religious belief, and such belief will emerge in, will indeed control, what he wrote. Humankind's relationship with its godhead is a manifest element in his works, and it is to that subject as seen in his concepts of covenant that we now move. It is basic to his three major poems, but also to his social and political arguments. It may at first appear to be "nonbiographical," but it is perhaps the most basic of biographical substructs for Milton.

Covenant implies three concepts: unilateral covenant (God toward man), mutual covenant (God and man), and federal covenant (the group in allegiance to God). Extending these concepts, the metaphor of covenant is employed for human relationships: for example, political covenant (a fusion of mutual and federal), which describes compacts of men and men, generally of groups for mutual protection or achievement. Another metaphor of mutual covenant (man and woman) was marriage, as in Milton's divorce tracts. "The Covenant" and "Covenanters," during the mid-seventeenth century, however, always meant the political covenant of the National Covenant of Scotland, concluded at Greyfriars

Kirkyard, Edinburgh, on February 28, 1638, and developed by the Presbyterian General Assembly in Glasgow in November 1638. The Covenant was an outgrowth of reactions against the Service Book of 1637 as Popish and of English compilation, leading to the Confession of Faith after the English Westminster movement joined with the Scots.[1] The Solemn League and Covenant between the Covenanters and the English Parliamentarians, August 17, 1643, was an extension of the National Covenant, more strongly in the sphere of politics, and referenced frequently by Milton in prose and poetry. Milton, it would seem, took the Covenant, by which is meant that he subscribed to the Solemn League and Covenant, but he came to repudiate Presbyterian coercive policy.[2]

I am concerned here, first, with Milton's attitudes toward the Old Covenant, that of the Old Testament as cited between God and Moses on Mount Sinai, and the New Covenant, that of the New Testament as exemplified through the Son. One view of Milton and covenant has been that expressed by B. Eugene McCarthy: referring to a statement in *De doctrina christiana* (I, xii),[3] he writes: "Such a covenant was to Milton not Old Testament in nature, for there God imposed his will on people, but distinctly Christian, a new covenant of grace, a true covenant that allowed voluntary acceptance by man."[4] Working out of the metaphor of mutual covenant applied to men and men, as in *The Tenure of Kings and Magistrates* (1649)[5] or *A Treatise of Civil Power* (1659),[6] Milton scholars have talked of the need for faith on both sides of covenant and of benefit for both parties, but they have little examined the concept in Milton's theology.[7] Before looking at Milton and covenant, we should review covenant theology, for it is not a clear-cut philosophy nor a simple set of scriptural readings.

Two covenants are involved: that of works and that of grace. John Cocceius (1603-69) is often credited with the division of the covenant of works as existent before the Fall and of the covenant of grace as existent thereafter, and in this latter concept he is considered a founder of federal theology and soteriology. This kind of division posited a first covenant of works between God and man (unilateral covenant), broken as Adam and Eve abrogated natural law within each of them. Prior to the seventeenth century, however, the ideas and divisions lay in numerous writings. In contrast William Perkins (1558-1602) talked of a covenant of grace for the elect before Creation, because of God's prescience, and of a covenant of works only after the Fall.[8] Obedience can be related to a covenant of works, and thus Mosaic Law has been seen as part of that covenant. Such a view posited a second covenant of works in reaffirming natural law in the Ten Commandments (the Law), and led to assignment of Old Testament covenant as an imposition of God's will on the people, such as that to which McCarthy refers. Implied in the Law is God's healing of man's depravity through their trust in a future Messiah.[9] *The Dutch Annotations upon the Whole Bible* contrasted a Covenant of the Law with a Covenant of Grace.[10] But since perfect obedience for man after the Fall is impossible, further thinking concluded, the covenant of grace came to subsume works.

For the strict Calvinist the covenant meant an absolute grace for the elect. But for other believers, the Arminian, for example, it was a conditional grace for the faithful and repentant. Previously Heinrich Bullinger (1504-75) had argued that the Mosaic law was not part of the covenant of works and that only a covenant of grace existed for man. Zacharias Ursinus (1534-83) viewed the covenant of grace as informing both the Old and the New Testament, and it was out of Ursinus's arguments that covenant theology arose. Thus, the protevangelium is the first statement of the covenant of grace, which is seen as mutual covenant, man's action being true faith and true obedience. The Confession of Faith, deriving from the mainstream of beliefs in the sixteenth and seventeenth centuries, assigned Adam as federal head, acknowledged both covenants, but saw the covenant of grace as that of the Law and the gospel.[11]

Ideological problems exist in the treatment of the Tree of Knowledge and the Tree of Life. The Tree of Knowledge represented the covenant of works, and it thus, for some, came to represent the Law. The sun in the Heavens represented Justice, and shadow represented the dispensation of mercy or God's grace. While Adam and Eve were able to partake freely of the Tree of Life, the Tree of Knowledge after the Fall became the source of the material of the Cross, the Crucifixion occurring upon the same spot as the disobedience. Through Christ's mediation, the Tree of Knowledge was abrogated for man, who through his acceptance and maintenance of the covenant of grace could hope for a future partaking of the Tree of Life. It was a rather easy equation for some to see the Tree of Knowledge as the covenant of works and the Tree of Life as the covenant of grace. To William Ames (1576-1633), the Tree of Knowledge was a sacrament of death; the Tree of Life, a sacrament of life.[12] Was therefore the covenant of grace existent before the Fall? and was there then no true covenant of works?

While the Old and the New Covenant were repeatedly contrasted— one written on stone, the other on human hearts; one a written code, the other the spirit of the living God; one condemnatory, transient, and veiled of glory, the other righteous, permanent, and directly manifesting God's glory[13]—Christian concepts of the sixteenth and seventeenth centuries saw both as covenants of grace, although as Delbert R. Hillers remarks, "The Christian had something new, but it was not a covenant."[14] Covenant, of course, implies something agreed upon whereby one party does this if and when the other party does that. Covenant required parties to the agreement, stipulations, and ritual enactments (for which an exchange of commodity, a handshake, or the like, could replace blood sacrifice). The Hebrew word for covenant, *b'rît* (from Akkadian *brt*, to bind), was used in the Old Testament to express federal covenant. It could be achieved metaphorically through stones (Job 5:23), eyes (Job 31:1: "I made a covenant with mine eyes"), death (Isaiah 28:15), or day and night (Jeremiah 33:20-21: "Thus saith the Lord; If ye can break my covenant of the day, and my covenant of the night, . . . then may also my covenant be broken with David my servant, that he should not have a son to reign upon his throne"). It was related frequently to marriage (e.g., Proverbs 2:17), and it became equivalent with the Law (e.g., 1 Kings 8:21) and true religion (e.g., Jeremiah 9:13).

The Christian theologians satisfied the terminology of *covenant* and *binding* by making man's faith and obedience his part of the agreement, although they split on man's ability to fulfill his conditions and thus elicited postulations of absolute or of conditional grace. Accordingly the Ten Commandments of Moses were read in terms of the "new commandment" of Jesus (John 13:34), "That ye love one another; as I have loved you, that ye also love one another." "The person of Jesus has, so to speak, taken over the original notion: the saving event is *his* death, the new commandment is to love in imitation of *his* example, the guilt of abusing communion is that one has profaned *his* body and blood."[15] Blood sacrifice, Mosaic or Christological, transfers guilt to the people who will suffer the fate of the sacrificed, should they fall into disobedience and a lack of faith. Blood sacrifice always invokes curse. The blood of Christ is seen as inaugurating the New Covenant.[16]

Christian thinking on covenant of grace thus retained certain conceptions of *b'rît*, namely, its connotation of the mysteries of God's salvific acts, its divinely guaranteed promise, and its expectation of man's obedience. It implied promises for obedience and penalties for disobedience. Covenant is likewise perpetual; see Genesis 17:13. Among the ritual enactments is circumcision (see Genesis 17:10-11 and Acts 3:25, 7:8); among the signs of the covenant is the rainbow (see Genesis 9:13 and Isaiah 54:9-10, where it is called the *b'rît* of peace). While the God of the Old Testament had been viewed by some theologians as a man of war and a taskmaster and the God of the New Testament as a god of love, others, such as William Ames, a student of Perkins, saw the Old and New Covenants somewhat reversed: "1. In the kind, for that [the Old] was as it were a covenant of friendship betweene the Creator and the creature: but this [the New] is a covenant of reconciliation between enemies. / 14.2. In the efficient: for in that [the Old] there was an agreement of two parties, namely God and man: but in this [the New] God onely doth covenant."[17]

Milton's position can be outlined as follows:

1. The prohibition of eating of the Tree of Knowledge does not constitute a covenant of works: it is not a covenant and it does not involve works (*CD* I, x; CM XV, 113).

2. No command is properly a covenant (*CD* I, x; CM XV, 115). The Tree of Knowledge does not, therefore, represent a covenant of works, and Mosaic law, though it involves works, is not a covenant of works since it involves commandments. It is, rather, a covenant of grace (*CD* I, xxvi; CM XVI, 99).

3. The Tree of Knowledge does not constitute a sacrament (*CD* I, x; CM XV, 115). The Tree of Life should probably not be considered a sacrament but a symbol (or the nutriment) of eternal life (ibid.).

4. "Every covenant, when originally concluded, is intended to be perpetual and indissoluble, however soon it may be broken by the bad faith of one of the parties" (*CD* I, x; CM XV, 173, 175).[18]

5. Covenant requires mutual action and independence (*CD* I, xii; CM XV, 215, quoted in part in note 3).[19]

6. Covenant implies certain conditions to be performed by both parties (*CD* I, xxv; CM XVI, 79).

7. The covenant of grace always implies the stipulation that man follow God's commandments and seek Him in faith (*CD* I, iv; CM XIV, 113, 115). Therefore, there could be no covenant of grace existent before the Fall because Adam was filled with natural law.

8. Predestinated humankind are those who maintain the covenant of grace (ibid.). Likewise God extends sufficient grace for salvation to all; he "excludes no one from the pale of repentance and eternal salvation, till he has despised and rejected the propositions of sufficient grace, offered even to a late hour" (*CD* I, iv; CM XIV, 153).[20]

9. The covenant of grace is first declared in Genesis 3:15 in God's prophecy of the efficacy of Eve's seed, the protevangelium (*CD* I, xxvi; CM XVI, 99).[21] Its manifestation consists in its exhibition and ratification, and both existed under the Law and continue under the gospel (ibid.).

10. The covenant of grace gave promise of Messiah, and thus the law's imperfection was manifested in the person of Moses himself (*CD* I, xxvi; CM XVI, 109, 111). "But what neither the law itself nor the observers of the law could attain, faith in God through Christ has attained, and that even to eternal life" (*CD* I, xxvi; CM XVI, 111).

11. "The gospel is the new dispensation of the covenant of grace, far more excellent and perfect than the law" (*CD* I, xxvii; CM XVI, 113). The gospel (the New Covenant) abolished Mosaic law (the Old Covenant) (*CD* I, xxvii; CM XVI, 125).

12. The representation of the covenant of grace was circumcision and the passover under the Old Covenant and baptism and the lord's supper (which is metaphoric) under the New; these latter two are sacraments (*CD* I, xxviii; CM XVI, 165, 193).

13. Church-discipline implies federal covenant (*CD* I, xxxii; CM XVI, 321, 323).[22]

Clearly Milton is not in agreement with William Perkins, Johann Wollebius (d. 1629),[23] or William Ames on many of these issues. But aside from No. 8 above, alongside No. 10, his views are not exceptional: he sees the Old Covenant fully supplanted by the New Covenant, although its signs (such as circumcision and the rainbow) are still significant as signs; he understands the Law both as a representation of the covenant of grace and as works by which man can manifest his obedience to God; he views the covenant of grace as being made in the protevangelium and continuing to the present time; the covenant is prophetic,[24] promising Messiah and salvation in return for faith and obedience, that is, in return for love.

Milton's passage in *De doctrina christiana* on free will and divine decrees has been badly translated by Sumner, leading to confusion of what he asserts later in the treatise and what Adam says in *Paradise Lost*. Milton wrote (*CD* I, iii; CM XIV, 80): "Qualis itaque materia sive obiectum divini consilii erat, nempe angelus vel homo libera voluntate impertiendus, qui posset labi, vel non labi, tale procul dubio decretum ipsum erat, ut omnia quæ exinde consecuta sunt mala, potuissent sequi, vel non sequi: si steteris, manebis; non steteris, eiicere: si non comederis, vives; comederis, moriere." Sumner's translation is: "Seeing, therefore, that in assigning the gift of free will God suffered both men and angels to stand or fall at their own uncontrolled choice, there can be no doubt that the decree itself bore a strict analogy to the object which the divine counsel regarded, not necessitating the evil consequences which ensued, but leaving them contingent; hence the covenant was of this kind: If thou stand, thou shalt abide in Paradise: if thou fall, thou shalt be cast out; if thou eat not the forbidden fruit, thou shalt live: if thou eat, thou shalt die." There is no mention of covenant in the original, nor could there be in Milton's way of thinking; the other extrapolations may be excused because they are implied in the relationship here between free will and the event which *comederis* particularly alludes to.

Carey's translation in the Yale Prose (VI, 163) is a great improvement, though not without fault: "The matter or object of the divine plan was that angels and men alike should be endowed with free will, so that they could either fall or not fall. Doubtless God's actual decree bore a close resemblance to this, so that all the evils which have since happened as a result of the fall could either happen or not: if you stand firm, you still stay; if you do not, you will be thrown out: if you do not eat it, you will live; if you do, you will die." What Milton presents in the last part of this passage is a paraphrase of Genesis 2:16-17, 3:2-3. Not to eat the fruit of the Tree is a prohibition, involving commandment, and therefore no covenant is made. The exercise of free will in connection with this prohibition will bring a corresponding enactment of God's decree, which is that, through exercise of free will, angels and men may fall or not fall. The eating of the fruit is clearly symbolic: it symbolizes whether Adam and Eve will *stand firm* (*steteris*), that is, show faith by not eating, or will not stand firm, that is, show a lack of faith by eating. The significance is not in the eating or not eating except as it evinces faith or nonfaith. One eats to live, but this eating brings death; not to eat can lead to death, but this not eating brings life. The prohibition has *not* involved a contractual arrangement, although there is a reward or a punishment attached to the observance of that prohibition.

Michael Lieb has shown that Milton's view of the first prohibition is not only extralegal but also dispensational; it is reflective of ceremonial law and harkens backward to the concept of taboo. Accordingly the first prohibition is associated culturally, not doctrinally, with ceremonial law and had no basis in reason, which is the foundation of moral and natural law.[25]

The confusion in some minds—such as Sumner's—comes from an equation of prohibition with covenant and both with decree. Each is a separate concept, however interrelated they may be. Prohibition exists for specific acts (or nonacts), though it may be symbolic of many, and is expressed by a superior or authority figure (e.g., parent, teacher, law enforcer) only; clearly, reward or punishment is implied. Covenant may exist for specific acts or for a range of acts and entails acceptance from both parties to the contract; clearly forfeiture for *either party* is implied should covenant be broken. In the matter of God, breaking of covenant is rejection of that God who does not uphold his part in the covenant; Milton's concern in *Paradise Lost* is to explain God's actions to men and thus to argue against man's interpretation that God has not upheld his part in the covenant, a concept one finds at the base of modern revisionist theology. Decree may apply to a specific act or a range of acts whereby a superior or authority figure has declared future action which he has power to enforce; whether that future action takes place and the nature of that future action may involve prohibition but it *never* involves covenant. Compare the Father's remarks on prohibition in *Paradise Lost* III, 94-99, on decree in *PL* III, 100-28, and X, 43-47, and on covenant (which word appears in *Paradise Lost* only in Books XI and XII after the Fall and the annunciation of the protevangelium) in *PL* XI, 113-16, in comparison with the Judgment (not yet covenant) of *PL* X, 179-81, and Eve and Adam's acceptance in *PL* X, 930-36, 952-65, and 1086-92, repeated as 1098-1104. Immediately thereafter, as Book XI begins and Provenient Grace descends, the Judgment with its protevengelium has become covenant.

Adam's words in *PL* X, 752-59, in the midst of his soliloquy which, as often observed, reflects a human wallowing in blame-placing and ego-aggrandizement, indicate a lack of understanding of prohibition and a kind of equation of it with covenant, an equation that has persisted in the minds of commentators on the Bible and on Milton:

> To the loss of that,
> Sufficient penalties, why hast thou added
> The sense of endless woes? inexplicable
> Thy Justice seems; yet to say truth, too late,
> I thus contest; then should have been refus'd
> Those terms whatever, when they were propos'd:
> Thou didst accept them; wilt thou enjoy the good,
> Then cavil the conditions?

Adam talks of "terms," of their being "propos'd," and of his acceptance of them; but the prohibition has not involved and does not involve "terms" (only reward or punishment), was not "propos'd" to him but imposed (as he himself has just argued, his will did not concur to his being), and has not therefore brought in any question of acceptance or nonacceptance. When the teacher says to the student, "You will not cheat," there are no terms, no proposal for the student to accept or not accept. Adam's reading of the prohibition, *now, after the Fall,* as covenant is in a way, Milton implies, at the base of Satan's and man's lack of understanding of God's ways: certainly no one thinks that God made a covenant with the angels, including Satan. He made a decree, that is all: through the exercise of free will angels may "fall" or not "fall." No prohibition was expounded for the angels because none was deemed necessary; for man, prohibition as symbolic of faith or nonfaith was deemed necessary. Since prohibition was broken through guile rather than through *totally free* will, mercy is granted by means of covenant. The teacher says to the cheating student who admits his act, If you in all further tests and papers do not cheat, you will receive a passing grade and your first infraction will be ignored; if you do cheat in any way, you will be immediately failed without further recourse.

Another case of inaccurate translation that causes major difficulty on this issue is found in *CD* I, xi, "On the Fall of Our First Parents, and Of Sin": "Adamus enim communis omnium parens et caput sicut in foedere, sive mandata accipiendo, ita etiam in defectione pro universa gente humana stetit aut lapsus est" (CM XV, 182). Sumner has: "For Adam being the common parent and head of all, it follows that, as in the covenant, that is, in receiving the commandment of God, so also in the defection from God, he either stood or fell for the whole human race" (CM XV, 183). Carey reads: "For Adam, the parent and head of all men, either stood or fell as a representative of the whole human race: this was true both when the covenant was made, that is, when he received God's commands, and also when he sinned" (YP, VI, 384-85). Kelley adds a note for *covenant:* " 'foedere.' For Milton's earlier denial of any covenant on this matter, see above, p. 351." Neither translator has rendered *accipiendo* or the words around it correctly, and so Kelley's note to the *translation* is beside the point: the word is a gerund in the ablative case and means "in receiving" (which Sumner does give). But the phrase is parallel with *in foedere*, and the two parts are separated by *sive*, "or," thus removing them from apposition. The fairly literal translation should be: "Indeed, Adam, the universal parent and head of all, just as in the covenant, or in receiving commands, so likewise in his defection stood or fell for the whole human race." Milton's concern in this passage is to explain "AND IN THEM ALL THEIR POSTERITY." Milton says that all Adam's posterity partake of all his actions: just as in Adam's covenant with God (that described at the end of *PL* X and the beginning of *PL* XI, as we have seen) and in the *commands* he received (it is plural, not simply the singular prohibition against eating of the Tree of Knowledge), so in his rebellion.

Thus, for the Milton of *De doctrina christiana*, a covenant between God and man did not exist until the Fall. Indeed, there was no need, Adam and Eve being filled with natural law.[26] Covenant is a covenant of grace, first stated in the protevangelium and continued in perpetuity despite some men's failures; it is the Old Covenant when it posits a future Messiah and it is the New Covenant when the Son of God has been incarnated as Jesus to become the Christ. The Old Covenant of grace is dispensed through God's promise of Messiah and salvation in return for faith and obedience, which are within man's control as gifted with free will.

The mediatorial office of the prophet (such as Moses) is to instruct the people in profitable things; this is seen in the Law. Such instruction will help man achieve works by which he will manifest his obedience to God. The New Covenant of grace is dispensed through the example of the Son's humiliation and exaltation (that is, as shown in the gospel). The mediatorial office of the Son as prophet "IS TO INSTRUCT HIS CHURCH IN HEAVENLY TRUTH, AND TO DECLARE THE WHOLE WILL OF HIS FATHER " (CM XV, 287, 289). Providence includes the begetting of the Son before man's time began because God's prescience foresaw the need for the atonement and the example of the Son, whose "prophetical function began with the creation of the world" (CM XV, 291).[27]

The mediatorial office of the priest (such as Melchizedek) was to act as mediator between God and man, to perform sacrifice, and to enact sacred rites in order to aid in the salvation of man. The Son's priestly role is as redeemer of sinners through his sacrifice and as intercessor with the Father (CM XV, 291). Again God has provided for man "from the foundation of the world" (CM XV, 293). The mediatorial office of the king (such as David) is to unite and lead his people, protecting them and subduing their enemies. A federal covenant is involved.

The Son's kingly function is to govern and preserve the Church by an inward law and spiritual power, having purchased it, and to conquer and subdue its enemies (CM XV, 297). The inward law, the gift of the spirit, is the covenant written on men's hearts, "given at Jerusalem on the fiftieth day from the crucifixion, as the Mosaic law was given on the fiftieth day from the passover in Mount Sinai" (CM XV, 299), that is, on Pentecost, the feast of the descent of the Holy Spirit. The Church, of course, is "THE ASSEMBLY OF THOSE WHO ARE CALLED . . . whether actually regenerate or otherwise" (CM XVI, 219).[28] In all, Christ's mediatorial office is "that whereby . . . HE VOLUNTARILY PERFORMED, AND CONTINUES TO PERFORM, ON BEHALF OF MAN, WHATEVER IS REQUISITE FOR OBTAINING RECONCILIATION WITH GOD, AND ETERNAL SALVATION" (*CD* I, xv; CM XV, 285).

The covenant of grace is a mutual covenant between God and humankind: God will shine His grace—that is, his free and unmerited favor—on that person (potentially a sinner) who follows the stipulation of God's commandment and who thereby seeks him in faith. The person who by an act of will breaks obedience and thus implies a lack of faith in God's covenant causes God to withdraw his grace. God's grace withdrawn, the human being falls into sin, having given vent to so-called original sin, that is, the innate propensity to sin (evil concupiscence), as well as personal sin. While humankind can never rid itself of "the sin which is common to all men," as Milton calls it (CM XV, 181), it can reject the act of sin and thereby reject personal sin, both its evil concupiscence and its act. Though the covenant has been abrogated by the person who sins, however, the covenant continues in perpetuity, and God will shine His grace on him who abides by his part in the covenant thereafter. For

the sinner may be renovated. The covenant is sealed by sacraments, but
for Milton and Protestantism in general these include only baptism and
the Lord's supper.[29] Man as part of Christ's church, the invisible church,
is engaged in federal covenant as well as mutual covenant. Christ's kingdom governs not only the bodies of men and man, but their and his
minds and consciences. Governance is achieved through inward law and
spiritual power, not through external force.

It should be clear, I think, that Milton did not consider Old Testament theology one in which God imposed his will on the people; that he
looked upon the Old Covenant as one of grace, not one involving a reconciliation between enemies; and that the difference of Old and New
was the difference between following a set of rules and being of such inward spirit (essence) that righteousness (insofar as humankind is capable) would lead inevitably to obedience.[30] The Old Testament was
looked upon typologically, even in such matters as covenant; the fulfillment came with the antitype of the New Testament. The nonexistence
of covenant prior to the protevangelium (for Milton and others) obviates
any typological dimension before that time. Its creation at the protevangelium, which points to Christ for the Christian, brings into being the
antitype, and thence types which preceded the antitype. The new commandment was not, indeed, a commandment at all but a sure sign of the
shift from law to spirit. It is also clear, I think, that Milton's attitude toward predestinated mankind has tendencies toward what is called
Arminianism, but it has only tendencies. It is not the same thing, although most have used the term Arminian as if all Reformed Protestants
of the early seventeenth century were to be categorized as Calvinist or
Arminian only.[31] That is, there seems to be an attitude that if one is not
a strict "Calvinist," he is an "Arminian," and further that no other Protestant group could carry the label "reformed."

While some Calvinists seem to have believed in a strict doctrine of
election and thus of absolute grace, others in varying ways and degrees
held that grace was not confined to the elect and that election included
both those elect from the beginning of time and those who gained salvation through obedience and faith. Milton specifically dissociates God's
prescience from predestination as meaningless of concern. The problem
basically lay in Calvin's division of all men into the elect and the repro-
bate, which leads to supralapsarianism, the belief that God decreed the
Fall of man.[32] The Calvinist emphasized the covenant of grace[33] for an
elect and was also concerned with freedom of will.[34] The Church of England and others emphasized man's freedom of will by which he could
satisfy or not satisfy his part in the mutual pact. While Arminian views
had their effect upon the Church of England during the 1620s and

1630s, Church of England dogma is not coincident with Arminianism. The umbrella of a basic Reformed dogma covers both: "The elect are introduced into the covenant of grace by two means:—(1) by the *meritum Christi,* since Christ merits for believers not merely righteousness and eternal life, but has also secured that they should be reborn to faith; and (2) by the 'effectual regeneration of the Spirit of life in Christ, which is also called conversion.' "[35]

The standard interpretation of Milton's theology seems to be that he was opposed to Arminianism at least through the 1640s (see remarks in *The Doctrine and Discipline of Divorce,* 39, and *Areopagitica,* 14). Kelley writes, "Just when Milton took his leave of Calvin and orthodoxy is not certain" (82). But the discussion in *Areopagitica* of purifying by trial suggests to him that "if Milton had not consciously and openly accepted Remonstrant doctrines by the time of *Areopagitica,* he had at least taken a position that would logically develop into the Arminianism advanced in the *Christian Doctrine*" (ibid.). Milton's Arminianism rests for Kelley in Milton's belief in man's freedom of choice and denial that predestination was an absolute decree.[36] Yet he notes differences from Arminian dogma: predestination "not *to* belief, but *on condition of* belief and continuation in faith"; and Milton's rejection of reprobation.

The point is that Milton's thinking agreed with certain ideas set forth by Arminius and accepted by others, but did not agree with other ideas. To call Milton an Arminian is thus invalid, despite agreement with certain ideas. Further, there is no evidence that Milton changed his ideas on the matters raised in this chapter, whether around 1644 or during the late 1650s. This all leads Kelley into two strange statements: first, he writes, "Milton's second doctrinal errancy is Arminianism" (74; the first for Kelley is antitrinitarianism, which issue I shall not engage here), and second, "For his beliefs on decrees and predestination Milton's sources have yet to be determined" (85). Surely antitrinitarianism is of a totally different realm of "errancy," since it goes to the heart of Christian theology from that of Arminianism, since that differs only with (basically) one theologian's concepts. Certainly Arminianism is not doctrinally errant except to him who advances Calvinist thought as doctrine, a position Milton would never allow. Further, of course, Arminius staunchly argued his Calvinist orthodoxy.

Kelley's second strange statement implies that Milton, of necessity, must have derived his ideas from some source, not allowing for the possibility that the ideas are independent and resultant from thinking about such issues, provoked by the writings of various people—Perkins, Wollebius, Ames, Episcopius, et al. It is, I think, time we stopped calling Milton an Arminian and acknowledge instead his agreement with only certain Arminian ideas.[37] And it should be pointed out that this in no way means that he took those ideas from Arminius, though I would not deny the possibility of influence.

James Dale, in the entry on "Arminianism" in *A Milton Encyclopedia* (1:83-84), falls into the trap: "*CD* and *PL* are both Arminian," and after *Areopagitica* Milton "never attacked the Remonstrants in any way. Rather, it is clear that he turned again to their position, sympathizing with them in *Way* (6:366; 1st ed. only) and expressly defending their position as scriptural in *TR* (6:168)." In *The Ready and Easy Way* Milton wrote: "in summ, I verily suppose ther would be then no more pretending to a fifth monarchie of the saints: but much peace and tranquillitie would follow; as the United Netherlands have found by experience: who while they persecuted the *Arminians*, were in much disquiet among themselves, and in danger to have broke asunder into a civil war; since they have left off persecuting, they have livd in much more concord and prosperitie" (p. 15 of Ed. 1). In no way is this a positive statement or a negative statement toward the Arminians: Milton is citing an example of the good results of toleration. In *Of True Religion, Hæresie, Schism, Toleration* Milton wrote: "But here the Papist will angrily demand, what! Are Lutherans, Calvinists, Anabaptists, Socinians, Arminians, no Hereticks? I answer, all these may have some errors, but are no Hereticks" (6); and "The *Arminian* lastly is condemn'd for setting up free will against free grace; but that Imputation he disclaims in all his writings, and grounds himself largely upon Scripture only" (7-8). Milton is concerned with the accurate use of the word *heresy,* as his discussion following indicates, and with an accurate understanding of what Arminians have written. It is not a defense of the Arminian position, by any means. His words *cannot* be interpreted to mean that he was an Arminian.

De doctrina christiana is not Arminian: its theological position agrees in some points with that of Arminianism—that is all. Had commentators addressed themselves to the audience of Milton's work they would not have been led into such unfounded categorizing.[38] The audience for the work, as William B. Hunter has shown, is three groups: "the Reformed scholastics on the continent, with their unmentionable brethren in Scotland and England, the school of Saumur, and the Arminians. Representative opinions from all three are cited, and authorities from the former two are named. Milton, however, does not commit himself to identification with any single point of view."[39]

Milton says of predestination (by which he refers to election only, not reprobation) that "GOD IN PITY TO MANKIND, THOUGH FORESEEING THAT THEY WOULD FALL OF THEIR OWN ACCORD, PREDESTINATED TO ETER-

NAL SALVATION BEFORE THE FOUNDATION OF THE WORLD THOSE WHO
SHOULD BELIEVE AND CONTINUE IN THE FAITH" (CM XIV, 91). "Election . . . is not a part of predestination. . . . For, speaking accurately, the
ultimate purpose of predestination is salvation of believers" (CM XIV,
99); "predestination was not an absolute decree before the fall of man"
(ibid., 103). That is, God elected before time began those who were to be
saved, but he predestinated those who would be saved through Christ.
The Father says in *Paradise Lost* III, 183-97:

> Some I have chosen of peculiar grace
> Elect above the rest; so is my will:
> The rest shall hear me call, and oft be warnd
> This sinful state, and to appease betimes
> Th'incensed Deitie, while offerd grace
> Invites; for I will cleer thir senses dark,
> What may suffice, and soft'n stonie hearts
> To pray, repent, and bring obedience due . . .
> And I will place within them as a guide
> My Umpire *Conscience*, whom if they will hear,
> Light after light well us'd they shall attain,
> And to the end persisting, safe arrive.

While election "is nearly synonymous with eternal predestination," they
are not the same: predestination purposes the salvation of believers;
election elects those who are saved. Prescience, in the sense of foreknowledge of who would and who would not be saved, is inapplicable
both to predestination, which did not exist until after the Fall, and to
election, which is the act of saving, through Christ, those who believe
and continue in the faith (CM XIV, 125).

The profanation of covenant lies in two areas: the personal and the community. Milton's personal covenant had not been profaned, as we have
seen, in the area of prose, whether through the negative path or in the
worlds of politics and government, religious institution, domestic life, or
social contracts. The extension of the concepts of covenant into human
relationships could be seen particularly in "The Covenant" of mid-seventeenth century Scotch and English history, where it was found
wanting, and in marriage, where it was frequently found abrogated. Milton's reactions to these temporal issues can be viewed—should be
viewed—as recognition of humankind's profanation of covenant. My
discussions in Chapters 6 and 7 are enhanced, I trust it is agreed, by
an understanding of the nature and meaning of theological covenant
for Milton.

But what of the positive path, and what of the poetry? While *The Tenure of Kings and Magistrates* does address the nullification of covenantal profanation in government, it does so through the positive path, and this ultimately is always in the realm of the personal. While concern may receive impetus from community failures and failings, and while answer may emerge from the community action, ultimately it is only personal action that supplies answer and maintains whatever achievement is reached. We do not change the world by changing its institutions: we change it by changing its people. And so remaining for the right hand is the positive way, the assertion of covenant in one's personal and individual world. Thereby—and only thereby—will profanation of covenant with God be renovated into faith and love. The great purpose thus conceived will be discharged only through the writing of great poetry, great poetry that will engage his talent, great poetry in which the self appears as both driving force and commentator and human representative of the power and effect of covenantal thought as it happens—the self that will be in the world though not of the world. Man profanes the covenant with each deed or thought that diminishes his loving of God, Milton believed, each deed or thought that exhibits faithlessness in God, now and in the future—disobedience, personal aggrandizement, uncreation. The next chapter will consider the three major poems, each in its way a realization of Milton's great purpose and each an example of the positive way to the elemental existence of covenant in every human. Without them Milton would not have fully acquitted himself of his covenant with his God.

9

Moves toward the
Great Purpose

The form that Milton's writing would take during 1639-40 was a historical poem, one, for the most part, involving materials of an Arthuriad. In "Mansus," written while abroad in 1639, Milton contemplated such a poem, and in "Epitaphium Damonis," written probably toward the end of 1639,[1] he talks of having made an attempt at it. In fact this contemplated poem may constitute his life work (line 168), or once finished, he may be able to compose a quite different work on British themes. Perhaps the discouragement he felt in not being able to produce worthwhile poetry at this time caused Milton to change, from around middle 1640, not only the subject but also the form of his great work, for the drafts of a drama on "Paradise Lost" and many biblical topics precede the British subjects in the Plans, which Masson dated 1640-42.[2] But since the historical subjects of page 38 would have to be written before the description of "Sodom" on page 39, as it contains a note that was to be inserted four lines up on page 39, and since the Scotch subjects were put down after "Abram," "Baptistes," "Sodom," and "Adam unparadiz'd," we know that he vacillated further between historical and biblical and again historical subjects late in this period. The discarding of Arthurian and related themes during the seventeenth century has been discussed by R. Florence Brinkley;[3] it was a process Milton must have gone through before the beginning of 1642, for his discussion in *Reason* (38-39) not only does not mention Arthur but exhibits perplexity over what king or knight before the conquest could be chosen, Arthur apparently already having been discarded.

Simply, then, in 1640-42 Milton was searching for a theme to satisfy his great purpose, and this admitted of both nationalistic and religious subjects and apparently of both dramatic and poetic forms.[4] His activities were interrupted though not necessarily stopped in 1641, from around May to at least July, for the writing of *Of Reformation, Of Prelatical Episcopacy,* and *Animadversions,* and in late 1641 to early 1642, from

around November through March, for the writing of *Reason* and *Apology*.
The vestiges of his literary outlining were probably set down, therefore,
in 1640, in 1641 (January-April, July-November), and in 1642 (April-
December). His comments in *Reason* that "Time servs not now" (38) and
that he trusts "to make it manifest with what small willingnesse I endure
to interrupt the pursuit of no lesse hopes then these, and leave a calme
and pleasing solitarynes, fed with cheerful and confident thoughts" (41)
indicate a cessation of such literary pursuits during his pamphleteering.

Dating of the Plans in the Trinity MS can be based on a textual examination and on spelling practices.[5] Since the mature autograph of the
Plans employs the Italian "e," the earliest date is the fall of 1639; 1642
has usually been considered the *terminus ad quem*. The application of
spelling principles to the Plans rests on the conclusion that early (1639
to mid-1640) Milton retained "e" on pertinent words (as in archaic or
present-day practice, where he later omitted it as redundant), that from
about mid-1640 he began to delete the "e," that through mid-1641 he
mixed both forms, increasing omission of the "e," and that from the latter half of 1641 on, except for errors and lapses of practice, he was fairly
consistent in maintaining this principle.[6]

Appendix C discusses and details the evidence for dating the Plans.
There is a period in mid-1640 when page 35 and part of page 36 were
entered; late 1640 through early 1641 when parts of pages 36, 37, and
38 were penned; early through mid-1641 when Milton wrote page 39
with some overflow to page 40; mid- through late 1641 when entries
were added to page 36 and pages 40-41 were employed; and finally late
1641 through early 1642 when additions were made on pages 38, 39, 40,
and 41. The evidence suggests a development of thoughts on his subjects for poetic work over a period of about two years, during which time
he was also engaged in antiepiscopal polemics and in reading extensively, particularly in British history.

From 1643 it is difficult to assign even such loose bounds of time as
the foregoing to Milton's activities. For some time before August 1643,
when *The Doctrine and Discipline of Divorce* was published, Milton must
have been working on that book, and much time after that date must
have been given to its revision and augmentation, published February 1,
1644. With *Of Education* (June 5), *The Judgement of Martin Bucer* (July 15),
and *Areopagitica* (November 23), being published in 1644, and *Tetrachordon* and *Colasterion* on March 4, 1645, little time could have been available for sustained poetic writing during 1644 and the early part of 1645.
Likewise the times available for extensive poetic work after 1645 must
have been limited to April 1645 through December 1648, March 1651
through April 1654 (though total blindness, the death of Mary Powell

Milton, and secretarial duties would have reduced "free" time and emotional disposition greatly during this period), June 1654 through June 1655 (but again blindness, emotional disturbances, and duties would reduce productivity), September 1655 through December 1658, May through September 1660, and January 1661 through 1671. Sometime during the foregoing periods from 1640 Milton was planning, writing, and revising *Paradise Lost, Paradise Regain'd,* and *Samson Agonistes.*

The continued hope of producing "greater things" (the prime reference is to *Paradise Lost,* expressed in the epilogue to *Defensio prima,* 1658) indicates that what time had been devoted to poetic writing before this date had proved abortive. All three poetic works may have been begun by this time and even well worked out, as Gilbert and Parker suggest for *Samson Agonistes.*[7] And Milton's remark to Henry Oldenburg on July 6, 1654—"To prepare myself, as you suggest, for other labours . . . I shall be induced to *that* easily enough"—implies that as yet Milton had not begun completion and revision of the major poems (as also reasonably by his preoccupations between 1651 and September 1655), thus seeming to limit major poetically productive periods to the greater part of 1640-43, 1645-48, 1655-71. In addition to other poetic attempts and occasional poems he was also writing during these times *The History of Britain, De doctrina christiana, A Brief History of Moscovia, Accedence Commenc't Grammar,* and *Artis Logicæ Plenior Institutio,* and editing his shorter poems and Ralegh's *Cabinet Council.*

My *guess* as to Milton's poetic writing during these seemingly possible times is that *Paradise Lost* was begun, as we have seen it was, in 1640-41, worked on from time to time in 1642-43, perhaps slightly thereafter until 1655, then in 1655-58, and pursued more uninterruptedly from 1661 through 1665, when, according to the dating of Thomas Ellwood's testimony,[8] it was complete. Certainly something like the proem to Book VII indicates a time of composition after the fall of the Interregnum and Restoration of Charles II and Milton's imprisonment (October?-December 15, 1660). But further, Book VI, the War in Heaven, yields prosodic evidence of being latest in composition;[9] and it is colored in its sense of the futility of war, which emerges as a comic treatment of Satan, gunpowder, and militarism,[10] by a perspective possible for the militaristic Milton only after the rubble of the fall of the Interregnum had settled. I would think that the earlier dramas out of which the full epic poem evolved came into being in those early years before 1655, that during the later 1650s the chronological form (perhaps still drama, perhaps poem) posited by Gilbert[11] was produced, and that in 1661-65 the transition was made to epic with revisions of past writing and new sections added. Too frequently, I suppose, critics have assumed a thorough revision of the poem so that all ideas, all religious and political attitudes, and all artistic elements were made into a piece. Rather, the poem shows strata for all of these matters, ranging over time.

Among the poetic writings of the pre-1655 period were the inauguration of what became *Samson Agonistes* and *Paradise Regain'd*. The poems were published as "Paradise Regain'd. A Poem. In IV Books. To which is added *Samson Agonistes*." in 1671; the separate title page for the latter work reads, "Samson Agonistes, A Dramatic Poem." and again the date is 1671. The volume is an octavo. Thomas Tomkyns licensed it on July 2, 1670, as the endorsement opposite the volume's title page records. Term Catalogue, No. 3, for Michaelmas Term 1670, lists both poems (see Edward Arber's edition, 1:56); the catalogue was licensed on November 22, 1670, and Milton's work is advertised as an octavo. Clearly the poems were at least ready for publication in mid-1670. "A Catalogue of Books. Printed for John Starkey," a separately printed gathering of A[4], added to the end of Christopher Wasse's translation of Benjamin Priolo's *The History of France under the Ministery of Cardinal Mazarine* (London, 1671), lists the volume on A3v; two other books at the end of the list are said to be "In the Press 29th. *May*, 1670." As J. Milton French remarks, "This note seems to indicate that the whole list was made up at that time. If it was, then Milton's poems must then already have been in print or at least well enough along toward publication so that its publisher could plan to advertise it."[12] There are numerous versions of Starkey's catalogue. Interesting is one that is given in Sir Francis Bacon's *History Natural and Experimental of Life & Death* (London, 1669), printed on signatures Hhhh1-2, which are not, however, continuous with signatures in the rest of the volume. Milton's works are included on Hhhh2v as Number 61. Curious, also, is the entering of *Paradise Regain'd* dated 1670 in *Catalogue Impressorum Librorum Bibliothecæ Bodlejanæ in Academia Oxoniensi. Cura & Opera Thomæ Hyde è Coll. Reginæ Oxon. Protobibliothecarii* (Oxonii, 1674), 457.

John Aubrey lists *Paradise Regain'd* as a quarto, as does Anthony Wood, who also gives 1670 as the date.[13] Wood may have received information on the size of the volume from Aubrey (who had collected biographical information for Wood), but the date is a problem because one would think that Wood should have referred to a volume in and around the Bodleian himself. Cyriack Skinner wrote that *Paradise Regain'd* and *Samson Agonistes* were "finish'd after the Restoration";[14] Edward Phillips lists it as octavo and says, "It cannot certainly be concluded when he wrote his excellent Tragedy entitled *Samson Agonistes,* but sure enough it is that it came forth after his publication of *Paradise Lost*, together with his other Poem called *Paradice regain'd*, which doubtless was begun and finisht and Printed after the other was publisht, and that in a wonderful short space considering the sublimeness of it."[15] John Toland, wherever he derived his information, perhaps from Wood, unequivocally wrote, "In the year 1670 he publish'd his *Paradise Regain'd*, consisting of four Books."[16] Logic suggests that there was a concatenation of misinformation about the size of the volume and its date of publication rather than a number of separate errors, or that it was indeed published in 1670. Parker, following Fletcher and French,[17] indicates what may lie behind the confusion of date: "The date 'MDCLXXI' is badly centered in both title pages; this fact, and the placing of the signature letter 'I' below and between the 'C' and 'L' of the date on the *Samson Agonistes* title page, suggest that the 'I' was carelessly added after the type had originally been set to indicate publication in 1670."[18] Parker does not specifically articulate the possible solution to the problem of the recorded date that his remarks point to: copies of a 1670 issue may have been run off before revisions (suggested by textual variations, the cancel of signature N3, and the *omissa* of *Samson Agonistes*) were made, including that of the date, although no such copies are now known.

Concern with but one year's difference in publication is understandable when we remember what Phillips said about the time between *Paradise Lost* (completed by around July 1665, perhaps earlier, and published apparently in August 1667) and *Paradise Regain'd* and *Samson Agonistes*. According to the usual dating of these works, Milton would have written both *Paradise Regain'd* and *Samson Agonistes*, completely, between July 1665 and early in 1671, although this latter date is inaccurate, as we have seen. The end-date should rather be at latest June 1670. A period of five years for the composing of both poems is not impossible, yet it does not sit well with Milton's otherwise observable practices. Other activities during this period, as far as we know, include return to London in February 1666, after the plague, publication of *Paradise Lost* and its further issues, publication of the earlier *Accedence Commenc't Grammar*, a residential move to Artillery Walk, Bunhill Fields, and the publication of the earlier *The History of Britain*. Further, Milton's three daughters seem to have left his home in 1669, perhaps precipitating the move from Jewin Street and family difficulties.

The most important piece of evidence for dating *Paradise Regain'd* for most people is his former pupil Thomas Ellwood's statement:

> Som little time before I went to *Alesbury* Prison, I was desired by my quondam Master *Milton* to take an House for him, in the Neighborhood where I dwelt, that he might get out of the City, for the Safety of himself and his Family, the *Pestilence* then growing hot in *London*. I took a pretty Box for him in *Giles-Chalfont*, a Mile from me; of which I gave him notice: and intended to have waited on him, and seen him well settled in it; but was prevented by that Imprisonment.

But now being released, and returned Home, I soon made a Visit to him, to welcome him into the Country.

After some common Discourses had passed between us, he called for a Manuscript of his; which being brought he delivered to me, bidding me take it home with me, and read it at my Leisure: and when I had so done, return it to him, with my Judgment thereupon.

When I cam home, and had set my self to read it, I found it was that Excellent POEM, which he entituled PARADISE LOST. After I had, with the best Attention, read it through, I made him another Visit, and returned him his Book, with due Acknowledgement of the Favour he had done me, in Communicating it to me. He asked me how I liked it, and what I thought of it; which I modestly, but freely told him: and after some further Discourse about it, I pleasantly said to him, Thou hast said much here of *Paradise lost;* but what hast thou to say of *Paradise found?* He made me no Answer, but sate some time in a Muse: then brake of that Discourse, and fell upon another Subject.

After the Sickness was over, and the City well cleansed and become safely habitable again, he returned thither. And when afterwards I went to wait on him there (which I seldom failed of doing, whenever my Occasions drew me to *London*) he shewed me his Second POEM, called PARADISE REGAINED: and in a pleasant Tone said to me, *This is owing to you: for you put it into my Head, by the Question you put to me at* Chalfont; *which before I had not thought of.*[19]

Since Ellwood was arrested on July 1, 1665, and released about a month later, the general interpretation of his words has been that *Paradise Lost* was finished by mid-1665 (how soon before has not been speculated[20]) and that *Paradise Regain'd* was first conceived as a result of Ellwood's question, thus dating it later (?) in 1665 through the next year or so (1667?). Ellwood was briefly imprisoned again in early 1666 (March 13 through June 25), and Milton had returned to London in February 1666. From what he says, his attendance on Milton in London would have been frequent earlier than 1667, but a date before 1667 would seem to be much too soon for the writing of the poem. Nonetheless Walter MacKellar writes, "According to Ellwood's account *Paradise Regained* was composed between August 1665 and, at the latest, the summer of 1666," noting that on the basis of the dates of imprisonment, Ellwood "received the manuscript of *Paradise Regained* before 13 March or soon after 25 June."[21] Again, though possible, less than a year for composition of the poem strikes one as improbable. It is particularly improbable when one remembers what else was occurring in terms of residence and Milton's methods of composition and revision. Parker, not fully attentive to Ellwood's "And when afterwards I went to wait on him there," speculates that Milton dictated part of *Paradise Regain'd* (the "narrative" additions to and revisions of some earlier dramatic version) up through July 1670,[22] by which date the manuscript of both poems seems to have been in the printer's hands.

The honest and naive Ellwood was surely honest in what he wrote, but his asking Milton, "what hast thou to say of *Paradise found*?" implies something other than what the usual interpretation admits: he really did not understand the moral and didactic statement of *Paradise Lost*. The opposition of lost/found rather than lost/regained indicates a misapprehension: for Paradise to be lost in any sense that would allow it to be found implies a kind of tangibility, mislaying or giving up of what constitutes Paradise and rediscovering it by search or accident. Ellwood's words imply that Paradise on earth was still existent but in need of being rediscovered or recognized; this describes James Russell Lowell's "The Vision of Sir Launfal," not Milton's *Paradise Lost*. Rather, a different Paradise, one within, happier far, is possible, Milton teaches us, but not one just lying about awaiting recognition. Paradise was lost by action (disobedience); it can be regained only by action (obedience). But since Man is born into the world no longer innocent, more is required than just obedience: it requires heroic action, the heroic action that the Son exhibits in *Paradise Regain'd*.

"Regained" represents the epistemological issue of *Paradise Lost*: Paradise must be regained, achieved, and striven for, and the means to achievement is true heroism. Michael says that, through such heroism, Adam and Eve will *possess* a Paradise within, not discover or recognize or even create a Paradise. As Fletcher has argued,[23] the source for that achievement lies unobscured in *Paradise Lost*, although Ellwood did not discern it. But then it has taken a long time for scholars to recognize (as some still do not) that *Paradise Lost* is not, as a total poem, simply a narrative of the Genesis story of Adam and Eve's succumbing to temptation and being expelled from Eden. Such readers, of course, find Books V and VI indecorous excrescences, and Books XI and XII unnecessary and dull. What Ellwood's question made clear to Milton was that his philosophic statement concerning the Paradise that is available to fallen mankind had not been communicated. It is an uncontrovertible fact, in Milton's view, that mankind is fallen; *Areopagitica* is firm on this point, and so is *Of Education*. The subject of *Paradise Lost* is the disobedience of humankind to God and the subsequent loss of Paradise (Argument to Book I); determining the causes of that disobedience and loss—which begin with Satan's envy and rebellion—is required to be able to nullify their effect, and the Son is th exemplar for rejection of the potential causes within oneself:

> Henceforth I learne, that to obey is best,
> And love with fear the onely God, to walk
> As in his presence, ever to observe

His providence, and on him sole depend,
Mercifull over all his works, with good
Still overcoming evil, and by small
Accomplishing great things, by things deemd weak
Subverting worldly strong, and worldly wise
By simply meek; that suffering for Truths sake
Is fortitude to highest victorie,
And to the faithful Death the Gate of life;
Taught this by his example whom I now
Acknowledge my Redeemer ever blest. [XII, 561-73]

Michael, remarking that Adam "This having learnt, . . . hast attained the sum / Of wisdom" (XII, 575-76), amplifies the means to reverse human-kind's fallen condition from the example of the Son: "onely add / Deeds to thy knowledge answerable, add Faith, / Add Vertue, Patience, Tem-perance, add Love, / By name to come call'd Charitie, the soul / Of all the rest" (XII, 581-85). The Son "The Law of God exact . . . shall fulfill / Both by obedience and by love, though love / Alone fulfill the Law" (XII, 402-4). Mankind is fallen, and to regain Paradise one must reverse that fallen condition through trial and active love (which implies faith and thus obedience), as does the Son as Man, not through merely discover-ing what constitutes Paradise, as if it were a commodity.

The thought that Ellwood's remark was necessary for Milton to con-ceive of what became the substance of *Paradise Regain'd* is incomprehen-sible to me. "*This is owing to you: for you put it into my Head, by the Question you put to me at* Chalfont; *which before I had not thought of*" does not require that construction. The "*it*" is not the thought of the poem but the need for the poem, two very different matters. "It" is not a poem on how to regain Paradise, for surely Milton had not only long contemplated the message of the eventual poem but had included its substance already in *Paradise Lost*. "It" was the need for a more explicit statement to belay questions about *Paradise found*. "It" is the physical, separate work itself and its need, *which before* he *had not thought of* and which thought Ellwood *put into* his *Head*. Surely "which" cannot refer to "question."

A preceding sentence is significant here: "He made me no Answer, but sate some time in a Muse." The wheels of Milton's mind were turn-ing. Was the "Muse" a contemplation of the validity of the suggestion in terms of *Paradise Lost,* which had not achieved his intentions with at least one reader, and thus in terms of that "unfit" audience he had often en-countered in other areas of his work? Was the "Muse" a contemplation of what he might compose to delineate a *Paradise found* or what he might resurrect from the past and reconstruct? We see Milton in the Trinity MS constructing *A Mask* from some former draft, with sections and lines rearranged and reused, the whole augmented and unified, with additions right up to publication and change after publication.[24] We see the beginnings of *Paradise Lost* there as not dissimilar, and we remember the argument of Allen Gilbert's study of the epic as a compositorial structure of seemingly disparate parts. At least we should acknowledge that Ellwood's report is subject to more than one interpretation, and thus it may mean (unbeknown to Ellwood himself) that Milton sat contemplating what material he had at hand to fashion a poem that would more explicitly carry his message for the regaining of Paradise, since that need was apparently real.[25]

While the full question of the date(s) of composition of *Paradise Regain'd* cannot be explored here, we should recognize that the external evidence allows for revision of earlier materials by changes, rearrangements, additions, deletion, and unification into a whole as companion to *Paradise Lost* during 1665 (after August?)-1667(?). Indeed, that is more probable than the production of the poem *ab ovo* during that brief time. Cyriack Skinner's "finish'd after the Restoration" may be meaningful, and Edward Phillips's "doubtless" in talking of its having been "begun and finisht and Printed after the other was publisht" manifests his lack of knowledge. In fact that statement says it was not begun until 1667 (except that Phillips, notoriously in error concerning dates, placed the publication of *Paradise Lost* in 1666), and that does not square with Ellwood's story.

Publication of *Paradise Lost* may have been delayed because of the plague and then the Great Fire (September 2-5, 1666). (The contract is dated April 27, 1667, however; the entry in the Stationers' Register is August 20.[26]) And since it sold so poorly—witness its double issues in 1667, 1668, and 1669, with the addition of outdated arguments in the second issue of 1668 to aid the reader (and increase sales)—we can little expect a publisher to have taken *Paradise Regain'd* during those years. By 1670 there may have been some talk of a second edition of *Paradise Lost*,[27] and at least a move did occur to print *Paradise Regain'd*. This poem may have been published separately, with the addition of *Samson Agonistes* a slightly later thought, though I firmly believe that the *received* texts exhibit purposeful intertextuality.[28] *Paradise Regain'd* was perhaps a result of further cogitation about a drama on Christ as first suggested for different "plots" in the Trinity MS, page 41, dated in early 1642. Work may have occurred in the pre-1649 period. The first, basically the second, and the third temptations may then have been amplified by a fuller development of the second temptation (primarily Book III).[29] Whether any further work occurred on the drama before 1665, I cannot conjecture, but it was not revised into the brief epic—that is, some "narrative" sections were not developed from former "dramatic" sections or newly created, and the prosody revamped—until after 1665.

There is no corresponding statement to Ellwood's for *Samson Agonistes*. Skinner includes it as "finish'd after the Restoration," and Phillips says, "It cannot certainly be concluded when he wrote" it. Arguments have attempted to place its composition well before 1665 (1667?)-1670, but little attention has been paid to the dates of composition for the two poems in relation to each other, despite the acceptance of their complementary nature. The most recent survey of the state of *Samson Agonistes* is by Mary Ann Radzinowicz.[30] One side in the argument seems to say that the other side must prove its case, and whichever argument is advanced usually chooses what it wants to bolster its position, often with statements that are simply not logical or objective. For example, Radzinowicz concludes her discussion by remarking that

1. "objective evidence is not lacking for the late date"; but the only objective evidence is publication in 1671.

2. "artistic practices and theories do not militate against it"; but this depends on what practice and theory is advanced and what one is side-stepped.

3. "thematic links between *Paradise Regain'd* and *Samson Agonistes* confirm it"; but these same links would exist if both poems were early or if one were written expressly to be complementary to the other.

4. "and the existence of allusions from autobiography and current affairs points so strongly to the late date that early daters have to expend heroic effort to discredit intentional and biographical readings in general before mounting their own claim that in *Samson Agonistes* Milton was anticipating in dread what late daters abundantly see him as already having undergone"[31]; studies disabusing *Samson Agonistes* of such reductionism have been numerous, and no "intentional and biographical readings" have had general acceptance except by those, like Christopher Hill,[32] who wish to maintain traditional dating.

The possibilities for the composition of *Samson Agonistes* as we have received it as a text are: 1) total composition shortly before mid-1670, perhaps between 1667(?) and mid-1670; or 2) final revised composition shortly before mid-1670 (between 1667 and mid-1670), revised from an earlier version a) written perhaps in the later 1640s or b) written perhaps in the later 1640s and first revised and further developed later, perhaps in the earlier 1650s.[33] All of the "perhapses," of course, indicate the uncertainty of date. Acceptance or nonacceptance of any dating not only depends on one's evaluation of arguments presented, but rests on whether or not the dramatic poem is viewed as evidencing strata of composition. It is likely that *Samson Agonistes* as we know it was finalized after

Paradise Regain'd was considered completed, although it is possible that they were worked on together. Thus if work were done on *Paradise Regain'd* in 1665-1667, we could conclude that work was pursued on *Samson Agonistes* in 1667 to mid-1670. There could, of course, be an overlapping of years, and probably as publication loomed final touches were given to both poems. The prose statement preceding *Samson Agonistes,* "Of the Dramatick Poem," was probably written as a result of Milton's realization that a prose statement on the verse of *Paradise Lost* was necessary in 1668, after the publication of John Dryden's *Essay on Dramatick Poesy.* Perhaps it thus is dated 1669-70. The preface attempts to justify the nature of Milton's Greek drama, which is a dramatic poem rather than a play, and the fact that it flies in the face of Eugenius's argument may link it as reaction more than "literary criticism." The move from Jewin Street (to which he had moved in early 1661) during 1669 may have been particularly significant in regard to *Paradise Regain'd* and *Samson Agonistes.* Did it delay publication? Did it disrupt writing or the final printer's text? Did it discover a near-completed work that needed only a year's further writing to develop as finished dramatic poem and companion piece?

While the great purpose was amply served by *Paradise Lost,* Ellwood's question made it clear that even those one might have numbered among the fit audience were not. The great purpose had to be spelled out more directly, more barely. The artistry of the diffuse epic has over the years obscured much for its readers who think it a story about Adam and Eve or who read it as a document setting forth Milton's not-so-hidden doubts about God's worthiness. Unfortunately, many modern Miltonists have not allowed themselves even to go objectively very much past where their teachers took them, who didn't go objectively very much past where their teachers took them. And so we still have querulous complaints about the Father and about Books XI and XII, or revival of dead issues (if only the critic would do just a little research!) like Milton's spelling in the poem or the possibility of his authorship of the translation of George Buchanan's *Baptistes.*

Paradise Regain'd prints in bold letters the positive way to spiritual and personal freedom by seeking, achieving, and maintaining it within one's self. It is esteem for the self—a *good* narcissistic attitude when temperized and opposite to self-hate—that leads to this freedom. God the Father and God the Son represent a good narcissistic attitude; Adam exhibits an untemperized attitude; Satan, of course, is the prime example of the opposite, or one whose narcissism is directed toward the emanations of that opposition, Beelzebub first and Sin next. Humankind's emulation of the Son of *Paradise Regain'd,* who exercises his freedom of will but without improper regard for his abilities and inabilities, with proper understanding of his limitations, is Milton's counsel as the means to such spiritual and personal freedom. Samson comes to be in the received text of *Samson Agonistes* one whose overweening narcissism must be thoroughly replaced by a proper understanding of his abilities and limitations and by a realization of the distinction between works and faith. Just as all humans may be, he is renovated. Part of that renovation, as *De doctrina christiana* (I, xvii) discusses it, is "submission, itself natural, to the divine call. It is accompanied by a confidence also natural." The great purpose is realized in three complementary pieces of literature, each in its own way a contribution to the world and its people, each offering a self that will conquer the world and rise above it.

The significance of covenant as Milton conceived it, detailed in Chapter 8 above, overlies the great purpose and goes to the heart of it. These covenantal beliefs inform the poetry, the three major poems, yes, but also the earlier ones, which ideologically are steps toward his later journey to realize his great purpose. "Upon the Circumcision" talks of "that great Cov'nant which we still transgress" and its full satisfaction by Christ. Reference is to Genesis 17:7, 10, the everlasting covenant made with Abraham that every man child be circumcised as a sign of the covenant. While the poem is dedicated to the Feast of the Circumcision of Jesus, January 1, eight days after his birth, Milton's double vision superimposes the rite on the passion of Christ, whereby Jesus as man has given example of the entire satisfaction of God's covenant of salvation for man's faith and obedience, that is, love. The circumcision becomes a seal of obedience (just as the sacraments are seals of obedience), intended as a constant reminder to man of the covenant. Jesus has united the Old and New Covenants through his following of the Law and his love: "O more exceeding love or law more just? / Just law indeed, but more exceeding love!" That man is potentially sinful and needs the example of Christ to fulfill his part in the covenant is clear throughout the poem. The relationship of the two epics of later date, and particularly the need for the explicitness of the brief epic, is manifest in this English ode. The blood sacrifices of circumcision and of crucifixion are detailed: as the "wounding smart" moves to become "Huge pangs and strong" that "Will peirce more neer his heart," the bodily has proceeded to the spiritual. Without the incarnation of the Son "we by rightful doom remediles / Were lost in death" because of "our excess." This poem, written sometime in the 1630s, illustrates well the attitude toward covenant that underlies *De doctrina christiana*.

Sometime earlier, perhaps in December 1631, Milton had talked of his lot in life, whether mean or low: "All is, if I have grace to use it so, /

As ever in my great task-maisters eye" (Sonnet 7, ll. 13-14). Read against the covenant of grace, the lines indicate the prescience of God, but not any ordination from Him, the expectation of predestination, and the grace extended to humankind through the inward law (his "inward ripenes"). The inward ripeness is, first, a maturity of mind and self (as opposed to external physicality), but second, in context of covenant, it implies that he has not been faced with circumstances demanding his obedience in such theological terms: his virtue has been, so to speak, cloistered, it has not been sufficiently exercised and breathed, it has not sallied out to see the adversary (see *Areopagitica,* 12). His inward ripeness much less appears, but the gift of the spirit differs for men, "according as God hath dealt to every man the measure of faith" (Romans 12:3).

The rainbow as sign of God's covenant has significance for "On the Morning of *Christs* Nativity," *Comus,* and "Epitaphium Damonis." In stanza XV of the "Nativity Ode" Truth, Justice, and Mercy, the collocation drawn from Psalm 85, are viewed as "Orb'd in a Rain-bow." These are also the three daughters of God representing the three persons of the Trinity—the Father, the Holy Spirit, and the Son—and who, combined as indivisible, are Peace, the fourth daughter. The stanza comments upon the immediately preceding stanza, the central stanza of "The Hymne," which contemplates salvation for the person who is "long" enwrapped in "holy Song." The "speckl'd vanity / Will sicken soon and die, / And leprous sin will melt from earthly mould," and "Heav'n . . . Will open wide the Gates of her high Palace Hall." "Long" implies one's lifetime of "holy Song" rather than only spasmodic singing, and the "holy Song" implies praise of God through the only real means of praise, emulation of the Christ whose birth is being celebrated in the poem. Again Milton presents a double vision, one the start of humankind's redemption and the other the result of the maintenance of an individual's part in the covenant of grace. The rainbow that descends reminds one of one's sinfulness, of the punishment that such truth demands, but of the mercy that will intercede ("Mercy will sit between") for the singer enwrapped in holy song.

Milton's reference to Christ's College in "Elegia prima" is interesting in this connection. "Its bare fields are unwelcome, so unyielding are they of mild shadows," he writes; "how improperly that place assembles the followers of Phoebus!" (ll. 13-14). While the landscape reflects the fen-country of Cambridge and while the reference to Phoebus puns on the students' being at *Christ*'s College (as well perhaps on the lack of receptivity of poetry), Milton has engaged the Tree-Sun-Shadow (Truth-Justice-Mercy) image cited before. There is no Law (the Tree) in the Christian sense here (no covenant of grace, that is), only "the threats of a stern tutor"; and ironically at Christ's, there is no mercy (the shadow) for infractions of or disagreements with those threats. Suggested is rigidity in idea and conduct (apparently devolving for Milton from William Chappell), allowing the presence only of the Sun ("justice"), not of the Son. Here is unilateral covenant descending from authority only, a concept consistently rejected by Milton. It does not involve prohibition.

As *Comus* begins, the Attendant Spirit, whose world lies "Before the starry threshold of *Joves* court," is garbed in "sky robes spun out of *Iris* woof." As it ends he returns to his "Ocean" where "*Iris*...with humid bow / Waters the odorous banks that blow." The sign of the covenant frames this poem/drama of the need for chastity, which may be bodily assailed without spiritual succumbing. The sign reminds the auditors and readers that humankind, whose virtue may be feeble in countering force, will still be saved when one upholds one's part of the covenant. Heaven itself will stoop by sending a redeemer, a Sabrina, for those who have successfully resisted the temptations of the wilderness of the dark forest of life. The scriptural content of lines 1003-11—for example, out of Matthew 25:1-13, Luke 15:3-7, Matthew 19:28-29—should be manifest: the Son, Celestial Cupid, will be the bridegroom of the unspotted soul, Psyche, the soul that has wandered in labors long, and the result of the union will be eternal life and bliss. It is an intricate passage of classical and Christian imagery, but one turning on the covenant of grace. Man—the Lady or Psyche—after "wandring labours long" which leave him "unspotted" (Man's part in the covenant as faithful and obedient) will be rewarded "so *Jove* hath sworn," through the doctrine of predestination. Comus's use of "rainbow" in his deceptive and false account of the passage of the Lady's two brothers only emphasizes its significance in covenantal terms for the poem. He says,

> I took it for a faery vision
> Of som gay creatures of the element
> That in the colours of the rainbow live
> And play i'th plighted clouds. I was aw-strook,
> And as I past, I worshipt; if those you seek
> It were a journey like the path to Heav'n,
> To help you find them. [298-304]

The virtuous, though untried, brothers do live in the rainbow of the covenant of grace; seeking and indeed finding them will, metaphorically, lead to the path to heaven. To find such a path takes "the best landpilot's art," Christ's art.

As Milton completes "Epitaphium Damonis" with Damon's apotheosis, he records that "Damon lives in the pure air, / the air he so pure possesses: he rejected the rainbow with his foot" (ll. 203-4). The Latin is: "purum colit æthera Damon, / Æthera purus habet, pluvium pede reppulit arcum." That is, Damon saved, as befits one of "blushing modesty and youth without blemish," one unmarried and deserving the "rewards of virginity," has ascended above the middle air of the heavens into the pure air of Heaven. His foot, as it were, treads the rainbow lying beneath him in that middle air; for Damon the covenant has been satisfied, its signs are no longer viable for him. We have here, of course, another example of Milton's earlier orthodox belief that the soul does not die and descend into the grave with the body (as also in "Lycidas," written some few years before). Later Milton espouses mortalism, specifically thnetopsychism. Damon or rather Damon's soul has joined in the immortal marriage in heaven.

Paradise Regain'd is a concentrated study of the means by which one can experience faith and obedience, fulfilling the covenant with God, who will save humankind as He has the Son as Man in the literal removal of the Son by "a fiery Globe / Of Angels" "From his uneasie station." Psalm 91:11-12 reads, "For he shall give his angels charge over thee, to keep thee in all thy ways. / They shall bear thee up in their hands, lest thou dash thy foot against a stone." This covenant, incompletely recited by Satan in Matthew 4:6-7 and thus in *Paradise Regain'd* IV, 556-59, has been fulfilled by the Son's faith in standing on the tower and not being tempted to force God to prove His word, despite the potential danger of falling, and by God's salvation. Metaphorically, man is always in danger of destruction when Satan tempts, whether he resist or not; but the faithful will learn that destruction will not come to pass, for God's power is limitless and His covenant will be fulfilled. The simile of Satan's fall and the Sphinx's suicide when the answer to her riddle, "Man," was pronounced, reinforces the point that Man as Son will always defeat Satan. Herakles, the man-god, always can defeat Antaeus, the child of Earth.

The Son likens his reign on David's throne to "a tree / Spreading and over-shadowing all the Earth, / Or as a stone that shall to pieces dash / All Monarchies besides throughout the world, / And of my Kingdom there shall be no end" (IV, 147-51). This tree is the Law (Truth), and yet because of it there will be shadow (Mercy). The stone meting Justice is that in Jesus' parable to the Temple priests (Matthew 21:42-44): "Did ye never read in the Scriptures, the stone which the builders rejected, the same is become the head of the corner: this is the Lord's doing, and it is marvelous in our eyes? / Therefore say I unto you, the kingdom of God shall be taken from you, and given to a nation bringing forth the fruits thereof. / And whosoever shall fall on this stone shall be broken: but on whomsoever it shall fall, it will grind him to powder." And it is "Jesus

Christ himself [who is] the chief corner stone" (Ephesians 2:20). The
Son's words particularly recall the vision in Daniel of the great image of
gold, silver, brass, iron, and clay, which the "stone . . . cut out without
hands . . . smote . . . upon his feet that were of iron and clay, and brake
them to pieces" (Daniel 3:31-34). The stone "became a great mountain,
and filled the whole earth" (verse 35).

But the covenant of grace existent during the time period of the
poem is undergoing change into the New Covenant: the tension of the
poem is that between the Old Covenant, which was represented by
the Law and which gave promise of Messiah, and the New Covenant,
which is presented by inward law and which is in the process of being
created by the Messiah who has come. Milton's poetic character is the
Son, Jesus, the Savior, or the Messiah. The poem does not depict the
literal blood sacrifice of the Christ, but it is with the blood of Christ that
the New Covenant is inaugurated for humankind. His sacrifice transfers
guilt to the people who will suffer death, should they fall into a lack of
faith and disobedience. This is futural. Satan, of course, cannot know of
or understand the New Covenant being formed; his temptations try to
get the Son to abrogate the Law; he tries to ascertain whether this is indeed the Messiah prophesied. But he is not capable of discerning how
the Messiah's acts will come to free the people from his bondage. The
Son is aware of his being Messiah, as his first soliloquy makes clear, although he does not presume upon that knowledge, drawn from his
mother's words, John the Baptist's address, and the Spirit descended.
The assertion of his Messianic acts is the burden of the poem, only after
which is he ready to "Now enter, and begin to save mankind." His Messianic acts all rest upon an inward law, asserted and reasserted as its
maintenance becomes increasingly difficult. His glorious work in life will
be to instruct humankind in heavenly truth and to declare the will of his
Father, the mediatorial office of prophet. Such glorious work will instill
an inward law in the faithful who follow him, confirmed by his death
and resurrection, from which time the New Covenant will exist, and en-
graved on their hearts with the descent of the Holy Spirit. The poem,
however, is concerned with the development of that New Covenant of
grace, and with cogent example of the means to salvation. It is the clear-
est, most direct statement of the great purpose, of course, thereby Milton's own favorite of his poems, as Edward Phillips reported.

Samson Agonistes is likewise a concentrated study but of the man who
through pride (and uxoriousness) has not held faith and obedience and
who through humiliation has been renovated. The prophecy of the
Great Deliverer, like all covenants, has not been voided by God, only by
Samson, who must regain his inward spirit (the "inward eyes" by which

the blind man is illuminated), for God extends "sufficient grace, offered even to a late hour." The delivery from bondage does not mean, Samson must learn, by force and by works. His recapitulation of the temptations conquered by the Son allows him to reject ease, worldly position, and pride through the development of inward being. Although he is an Old Testament figure, Samson develops under a New Testament concept of grace. The presentation, however, has not created an anachronistic text. For the changes within him have been seen as regeneration, although renovation is more accurate.

Objections to Samson's "regeneration" may have some foundation; instead of this term, with its questionable connotations for the dramatic poem, we should probably view the changes in his inner self as a development of the effect of God's grace upon him. One problem for Samson in the past, and that finds negative and positive reprises in the interviews with Manoa, Dalila, and Harapha, is that works were conceived of as covenant. Samson consistently argues for his fulfilling God's purposes by works—the slaying of the men at Ashkelon, the hundred foxes, the ass's jawbone—but it is not until inward spirit has wiped away pride that he can achieve one great act of deliverance (l. 1389) that represents faith and obedience. He is not constrained to the Temple of Dagon (l. 1370); he goes in some important cause, he knows not what (l. 1379); and he concludes: "Happ'n what may, of me expect to hear / Nothing dishonourable, impure, unworthy / Our God, our Law, my Nation, or my self, / The last of me or no I cannot warrant" (1423-26). In complement to *Paradise Regain'd*, where the New Covenant is developed and contrasted with the Old, *Samson Agonistes* shows how the covenant of grace was operative in Old Testament history and how the concept of the covenant as one of works is false.

It is *Paradise Lost* that most reflects covenant theology, particularly in Book XII, as Adam learns "a better Cov'nant, disciplin'd / From shadowie Types to Truth, from Flesh to Spirit, / From imposition of strict Laws, to free / Acceptance of large Grace, from servil fear / To filial, works of Law to works of Faith" (XII, 302-6). Kelley presents extensive parallels between the epic and *De doctrina christiana* in the notes to his edition of the treatise. Duncan specifically relates the ideas we have looked at to the epic, pointing out Adam's erroneous view of his relation to God as covenant of works (X, 754-59) and explaining the dialogue between Father and Son in Book III as the basis for the covenant of grace. The first use of "Mediator" in the poem, in conjunction with "Redeemer voluntarie," occurs in X, 60-61, just before the statement of the protevangelium in X, 179-81. Repentance and prayer end this book of the epic, dramatizing, as has been remarked, the change in Adam and Eve at the beginning of the book and their selves as they leave Paradise and the epic ends. "Prevenient grace" has descended simultaneously with this repentance and prayer (X, 1086-92, which because of its monumental importance, is repeated in ll. 1098-1104, the final lines of the book). Its descent is stated in the third line of Book XI, confirming the covenant that now exists. It has removed "The stonie from thir hearts" and made them "new flesh," detailed in line 4, perhaps with a glance to the mysticism of numbers. The rainbow as sign ends Book XI and will have such force "till fire purge all things new, / Both Heav'n and Earth, wherein the just shall dwell," referring to 2 Peter 3:12-13 ("Looking for and hasting unto the coming of the day of God, wherein the heavens being on fire shall be dissolved, and the elements shall melt with fervent heat? / Nevertheless we, according to his promise, look for new heavens and a new earth, wherein dwelleth righteousness").

As Book XII and the poem draw to a close, Michael reprises the protevangelium and the conclusion of the world in a great conflagration, out of which will come "New Heav'ns, new Earth, Ages of endless date / Founded in righteousness and peace and love, / To bring forth fruits Joy and Eternal Bliss" (XII, 549-51). The parallel with the ending of *Comus* should be noted, and its further source in Revelation 21:1. Adam accepts this covenant of grace, having learned "that to Obey is best, / And love with fear the onely God" (ll. 561-62) for himself and his posterity. The poem will end with allusion to the further lines of Revelation 21:4: "And God shall wipe away all tears from their eyes; and there shall be no more death, neither sorrow, nor crying, neither shall there be any more pain: for the former things are passed away." The covenant of grace has clearly had its efficient beginning in the brief "now" of the narrative related from the end of Book X to the end of the poem, and its actual beginning for humankind as Adam and Eve proceed "down the Cliff as fast / To the subjected Plain." The Plain of Earth is, of course, to be contrasted with the Plain of Heaven at the center of the poem, above which only the Son acting for the Father has "Ascended" (VI, 762). Movement in life will be from one plain to the other (Eden having existed in some middle realm, appropriately), depending on where one chooses one's place of rest. The covenant of grace that informs the total poem is the absolute assertion of Eternal Providence and thus the absolute means whereby the ways of God are justified to men (I, 25-26).

Perhaps insufficiently remarked, however, is the importance of recognizing that up to the Fall, God has not covenanted with Adam and Eve, in Milton's way of thinking.[34] They are filled with natural law and have freedom of will. While the Old Testament saw, for instance, covenant in night and day, Adam and Eve's apostrophes (IV, 724-29; V, 160-79) praise what is simply nature. The promise of "from us two a

Race / To fill the Earth, who shall with us extoll / Thy goodness infinite"
(IV, 732-34) is one only of natural begetting, as the things of Eden reproduce and grow. It is not covenant. This progeny has no commitment,
yet, to "Light after light well us'd." No human progeny is produced in
Eden,[35] and the telescoped time would not so allow, but Milton does not
have to face that issue of what might have been had Adam not been
"fondly overcome with Femal charm" (IX, 999), since such matters are
not biblical.[36]

What we have in Books IV, V, VII, VIII, and the first part of IX, the
prelapsarian books, is a view of humankind in whom "the whole law of
nature [has been] so implanted and innate . . . that he needed no precept to enforce its observance" (CM XV, 115). The prohibition against
the doing of one act does not establish covenant, is not involved in precept. "Man being formed after the image of God, it followed as a necessary consequence that he should be endued with natural wisdom,
holiness, and righteousness" (CM XV, 53). One aspect of that natural
wisdom permits Eve to counsel division of their labors, Adam tending
the woodbine (with its connotations of symbiotic nature) and ivy (with its
connotations of immortality) and Eve tending the roses (with their symbolic associations and beauty) and myrtle (with its connotations of immortality) *till Noon* (IX, 214-19); Adam says she has "well . . . motion'd,
well thy thoughts imployd" (IX, 229). Freedom of will enters to weigh
warning, not covenant, when Adam considers that "harm / [may] Befall
thee sever'd from me" (IX, 251-52). Another aspect of that natural wisdom concludes that her firmness to God and Adam should not be in
doubt, though she is seduced (IX, 279-81). There is no breaking of covenant, no loss of grace, no defiance of God, no bad faith, and no
disobedience.

With Eve's seduction and the partaking of the fruit of the Tree of
Knowledge, there still is no breaking of covenant, no loss of grace, nor
even defiance of God, but there is disobedience which at least unconsciously exacts a lack of faith. Eve's argument that they are forbidden
good and thus wisdom turns on the difference between knowing good by
its being total (which would seem an impossibility) and knowing it
through contrast with its opposite, and on the difference between innate
wisdom and acquired wisdom through experience. There is only prohibition to be broached, and "Such prohibitions bind not" (IX, 760). After
the Fall, humankind cannot in this life experience total good or achieve
wisdom except through experience.

The grievous fall for humankind is Adam's fall, for he is not seduced
directly by Satan but by a narcissistic view of Eve as "Flesh of my Flesh, /
Bone of my Bone": "Our State cannot be severd, we are one, / One
Flesh; to loose thee were to loose my self" (IX, 914-15, 958-59). "Against

his better knowledge, not deceav'd" he eats of the fruit, "fondly over-come with Femal charm" (IX, 998-99).[37] (Perhaps we should remark that Adam by his action keeps what we would consider his marriage cov-enant with Eve, to be discussed later, and contrast Samson's attitude and Dalila's actions.) Eve's is an act of disobedience and lack of faith through seduction; Adam's is an act of disobedience and a lack of consideration of faith. Milton is clear to state this: "Man falls deceiv'd / By the other *first*" (III, 130-31, my emphasis), where *first* may relate to humankind's continued fall in the mortal world but may also stress that the first stage of the Fall is by deception (and thus it is through Eve that redemption must come) but implies that the second stage, which is continued through humankind's life, will be "Against man's better knowledge, not deceived." The reversal of the Fall must therefore be through obedience and faith potentially perverted by will.

Satan and his cohorts fall "by thir own suggestion . . . Self-tempted, self-deprav'd" (III, 129-30). Again there is no covenant involved, and there is not even prohibition, but there is obedience and thus ultimately faith. The Father at the begetting of the Son says, "him who disobeys / Mee disobeys, breaks union, and that day / Cast out from God and blessed vision, falls / Into utter darkness, deep ingulft, his place / Ordaind without redemption, without end" (V, 611-15). Satan, through pride, "Thought himself impaird" (V, 665) and moves to disobedience, largely because of a lack of faith in God, who sees all his angels as "United as one individual Soul" (V, 610). (After the defeat of the rebel-lious angels, Michael, it will be remembered, reduces his army "Under thir Head imbodied all in one.") Satan's sense of individuation has set him apart from the Son, but also, it should be recognized, from the other angels, a more clearly observed fact after their fall at the begin-ning of the great consult in Book II. But that individuation has begun with the "begetting" of the Son; it does not scrutinize and grasp the distinct *essentiæ* which are all of one *substantia*. It does not allow for the acceptance of subordination that underlies both *Paradise Lost* and *De doc-trina christiana*. It has caused hierarchy in heaven, even among the an-gels, to become levels of superiority rather than of administration. What Milton is paralleling here is the need for mutual covenant for all being—human and otherwise, since only God is capable of understanding nat-ural law, oneness, oneness which has many parts, and existence which unrelentingly manifests love. The realization of the great purpose lies there in his readers' understanding of that need—those "that by due steps aspire / To lay thir just hands on that golden key / That opes the palace of Eternity" (*Comus*, ll. 12-14), those who are "fit audience . . . though [unfortunately] few" (*PL* VII, 31).

10

A Biographical and Literary Overview to 1674

The years immediately after 1645 saw Milton immersed in his own study and writing, partially as a reaction against the hurt and anger felt over being cast as a "divorcer" with that label's moral and irreligious connotations. The public figure involved in controversy receded to the private world of tutoring and poetry and "educational" writing. From all accounts he had progressed somewhat in composing what became *Paradise Lost,* whether as a single dramatic work along the lines of a morality or as a number of dramatic works, as Allan Gilbert argued, to be combined later into a major creation, at first still dramatic and at some point epic. While he may have continued to revise this drama during the period of 1645 to 1649, it seems likely that his creative time was also being spent on other poems and prose. We know that he had begun his *History of Britain,* four books of which had been completed by the time of the Interregnum, 1649; that he had worked on the *Brief History of Moscovia* around 1648; that he had apparently produced *Accedence Commenc't Grammar* and *Artis Logicæ Plenior Institutio* in these or the immediately preceding years. It has been argued, as well, that his two other major poems, *Paradise Regain'd* and *Samson Agonistes,* were begun prior to the ascent of the Cromwellian government.

The dramatic poem, particularly, can be read to reflect the contemporary political scene, both in the figure of Samson as champion against the oppressive overlord and in the need for active participation to bring about God's expected millennium, even if through military means. Though Samson is a rallying symbol to assert the hoped-for new nation under God (*Areopagitica,* 34), he is also one in need of renovation for his uxoriousness, his violence, and his conceit.[1] Milton's further reference to the biblical figure in the *First Defence* makes explicit the symbol and the needed renovation, as well as the discouragement that the people of Dan, equated with Milton's fellow sufferers under Charles I, engendered in him: "Even the heroic Samson, though his countrymen reproached him . . . still made war single-handed on his masters, and, whether prompted by God or by his own valor, slew at one stroke not one but a host of his country's tyrants, having first made prayer to God for his aid. Samson therefore thought it not impious but pious to kill those masters who were tyrants over his country, even though most of her citizens did not balk at slavery" (YP, IV, i, 402).

The translations of Psalms 80-88, written in April 1648 in the midst of the Civil Wars, reflect the same kind of dejection caused by his pusillanimous fellow countrymen and the same kind of hope for enlightened leadership. It is an attitude toward the mass who should, in Milton's judgment, recognize the need for such liberty as divorce (rather than license) in 1645 and for the removal of the king, but who draw back in 1649.[2] Milton, who reputedly carried a sword, was not the pacifist some readers of the War in Heaven in *Paradise Lost* would make him.[3]

The date of composition and the nature of that composition of the three major poems are clearly paramount in any biographical/psychological reading of the author. Those who would place the total writing of the brief epic and the dramatic poem in the period of 1665-71 must read a different Milton from the one I read. The political contemporaneity of the dramatic poem could not have had much meaning in those later years, certainly not the same meaning. The author writing in the later period only would have to be one nostalgically looking back, one not acknowledging either the errors of the Interregnum or its advances, one not recognizing the bifurcation in monarchic rule that was occurring and that was to lead to the 1688 settlement and the ascent of William and Mary. Such dating denies the chiliastic underpinnings of the poem, a substruct that informs *Tenure*[4] as well as Sonnet 18, written in 1655, two years before the prognosticated millennium. Charles I as antichrist seems clear; the theocracy idealized (at least before 1653 and the promulgation of the Instrument of Government establishing the Protectorate) in the hopes of nonmonarchic government and the renovation of the people fleeing the Triple tyrant and Babylonian woe—all underlie the action of Samson and the dismay at the drawing back by the people (of Dan, of England) from like action to effect change and be ready for the millennium envisioned by, among others, the Fifth Monarchists. But in 1665-71 there have been "republican" advances on government, there are no continued thoughts of imminent millennium, there has been the recognized need for compromise, as in *The Ready and Easy Way* and *Present Means,* and there has been the full realization that "a nobler task awaits" a leader's hand than "Warrs" that "endless warr still breed, / Till Truth, and Right from Violence be freed" (Sonnet 15, written in August 1648).

If *Samson Agonistes* does date for initial composition in the later 1640s, its completion (as well, surely, as the prefatory statement about the dramatic poem) in 1667-70 (more realistic dates, the poem being ready for publication in mid-1670) would involve revision and tightening of language, prosody, and development—literary matters rather than ideological ones. The rhythms and rhymes and language of some of the choruses have appeared particularly problematic, even "unfinished," to scholars; the somewhat loose and perhaps overly extended *kommos* and *exodos* between the messenger and Manoa (and chorus) hits my ear as less perfected than the opening *prologos, parados,* and first episode. And the treatment of Dalila may provide some thought concerning dating as well. Though she is a biblical figure and popular example of the treachery of woman and her seduction of man, Milton's Dalila offers substance that makes her more than just stereotype; for some few critics she is to be seen as sincere, once we look at the narrative from her point of view, thus offering a psychological dramatic character rather than a mere agent of patriarchal aggrandizement.

This sincere and psychological reading suggests a view of woman not dissimilar to that in the divorce tracts: one who may have her own integrity and superiority but is also a helpmate to the husband, who generally functions in a more commanding role. Dalila in the poem, unlike other renditions of the story, is wife to Samson, a circumstance that is stressed over and over and that becomes the nub of Samson's argument. As wife, she should have been faithful to her husband, regardless of her origin and past life in a different nation: as the Bible says of Adam and Eve (but from the male view only), "Therefore shall a man leave his father and his mother, and shall cleave unto his wife: and they shall be one flesh" (Genesis 2:24). Samson is, of course, being self-serving and sublimating guilt in putting much of the blame on Dalila. After the Fall, Adam tries a similar rationalization. The Samson of the narrative before the poem opens is not admirable (in Milton's terms), but the poem is concerned with the renovation possible to him (and all others) to become truly the Great Deliverer. While Dalila may be supported in her political action for her people against even the vows of wedlock, she is presented as one who backslides into a kind of sour grapes attitude and a boasting of what her reputation will be among *her* countrymen. Thus she does appear as popular stereotype of enticing woman, potential repenter and acknowledger of "wrong" doing, but not a true repentant and not the force that woman may be in helping man overcome himself. This reading of Dalila represents attention to the man/woman question beyond that examined in the divorce pamphlets, but not to the philosophic attitudes and exemplars seen in the Eve of *Paradise Lost.* If there is any validity in this reading, it suggests that the character of Dalila as woman could not have been newly imagined after the conception of Eve to which Milton came.

The above comments imply that *Samson Agonistes* was first composed in the later 1640s and left unfinished, that it was not returned to in ensuing years until around 1667-70, and that it was not thoroughly revised literarily. The case of *Paradise Regain'd* is conditioned by its prosody and form, and its need for explicit statement for such imperceptive readers of *Paradise Lost* as Thomas Ellwood. The substance of the brief epic lies within the longer one, as has been pointed out before. If it too dates from the later 1640s for inception, it would not have been reworked until Ellwood's question put its need into Milton's mind as he sat in a "Muse" in Chalfont St. Giles (in 1665-66), where he had gone through the good offices of Ellwood to escape the plague.[5]

Milton's return to London after the visitation of the plague and the Great Fire seems to have brought a reexamination of older manuscripts lying about, with their publication in the years 1669-72, and to these may then be added the unfinished poems that became *Paradise Regain'd* and *Samson Agonistes*. The epic poem would, under this hypothesis, have been expanded somewhat, particularly to relate it to the longer epic, would have been revised as to prosody and epic form (from what might have been Milton's kind of dramatic poem probably), would have been altered into a more complex treatment of the temptation motif with its accompanying reordering of Book I (the first temptation) against a sweeping flow of Books II-IV (the second temptation), with the latter part of Book IV presenting the third temptation, and would have been articulated with its companion piece. Though the prosody takes on a quality more appropriate to the calmness of the story and the nonbaroque or late baroque of the Restoration period, it is not the more experimental prosody of *Paradise Lost,* lying instead closer to that of *Comus.* Critics have not always praised the prosody when they compare it to *Paradise Lost,* although it has always been for me literarily correct for this poem. And though Satan is Adversary (as in Job) rather than dramatic personage, he has been seen as an uninteresting (less successful) character by critics wanting him to be the Other. While again the presentation may be quite right (although I feel differences in this regard between the Satan of the temptations and the Satan of the Councils in Hell in Books I and II, written after *Paradise Lost*), the Satan of *Paradise Regain'd* may owe something to his earlier development in the late 1640s.

Aside from the major poems and whatever other writing, not extant, that may have gone into them, the poems written after 1645 are not numerous. These were published in the second edition of the shorter poems in 1673, with the exception of Sonnets 15, 16, 17, and 22, which because of their political nature were excised. They appear in the Trinity MS (the last three in scribes' hands) and in garbled versions in Edward Phillips's edition of the *Letters of State* in 1694. The sonnets of this period, Numbers 11–23, show an increasing development of enjambment, and often a clear demarcation between the octave and the sestet in the volta (or turn) is lacking. The sonnets are occasional: Numbers 11, 12, 15, 16, 17, 18, 19, 22, and "On the Forcers of Conscience" have political or public associations along with personal meditation. Numbers 13, 14, 20, 21, and 23 are commendatory or private. We observe the anger against his antagonists for his divorce position in 11 (1645?) altering to amused sarcasm at the ignorant public's inconsistent attitudes to true liberty and war in 12 (1647?). There is praise for asserters of freedoms and (as in the Cromwell sonnet, Number 16, 1652) some suspicion of leaders, along with a recognition that respite from constant thought and anxiety at all the changes being wrought in the mid-century world was necessary (as in Numbers 20 and 21, 1655).

Sonnet 19 ("When I consider how my light is spent"), like Sonnet 7, records a self-evaluation, denying what seems to be a lack of achievement through a reestablishing of self-esteem and a restated belief in God's grace that we have seen in his first extant poem, "A Paraphrase on Psalm 114." We can see Milton's transformation, after the losses of wife and child, the advent of blindness, the uncertainty of the governmental experience, and the obloquy that his own efforts to achieve civil liberty (an echoing of the opprobrium that greeted his earlier efforts in 1645), here in 1655 in terms that Kohut and Wolf have set out. As they write, "Failures in the responses of the mirroring and the idealized selfobjects . . . lead to the gradual replacement of the selfobjects and their functions by a self and its functions."[6] There has been a "redistribution" and an "integration of the primitive psychological structures into the mature personality."[7] The ego that Milton has now achieved, with adjustments of his relation with the world and his acceptance of his lot in 1655, has been transformed by narcissism (becoming attitudes and achievements of the personality): 1) a clearer sense of one' creativity; 2) an ability to be emphatic; 3) a capacity to contemplate one's own impermanence; 4) a sense of humor; and 5) wisdom.[8] The humor that the *Tetrachordon* sonnet showed finally in 1647 and the kind of "humor" and wisdom that Sonnets 20 and 21 show soon after Sonnet 19 in 1655 attest to these adjustments of the self.

Wisdom "rests on acceptance of limitations of physical, intellectual, and emotional powers," according to Kohut.[9] In 1645/1647 Milton had not yet reached the kind of wisdom he found by 1655, being reactive to outside influences only for adjustment rather than transformation and replacement of the idealized selfobjects. What has occurred is a kind of "night-sea journey" whereby the personality has delved into its dark side, experienced a fusion of noble (or idealized) and baser (here, realistic) elements, and has emerged with the past behind and the future as an understanding of that personality's beginning, a somewhat circular movement ultimately. Milton is able in Sonnet 22 to accept his blindness and to "bear up and steer/ Right onward," his ego assured that the loss of sight (and we may add Milton's other losses and failures here) has been brought on by a "noble task," "liberties defence." The world and its "vain mask" have been encountered by a self assured that "All is . . . As ever in [his] great task-maisters eye." His "better guide" is the God who shines forth "To give light to them that sit in darkness and in the shadow of death, to guide our feet into the way of peace" (Luke 1:79).

The dating of Sonnet 19 is crucial to an understanding of Milton. Reading "E're half my days in this dark world and wide" as an allusion to the biblical three score years and ten (a lifetime of seventy years, that is) and ignorantly influenced by Bishop Newton's title for the poem, "On His Blindness," critics have placed the poem in 1652, just after his blindness became complete, even though he turned thirty-five in 1643. (It has even been argued that the poem should therefore date in 1642.) Of course the poem in *not* on his blindness, which is only a background to it, but on the resolution for himself (and for others as well) that we have indicated above. Psychologically it is impossible to view Milton's having reached such resolution in 1652 or before a letter to his friend Leonard Philaras, dated September 28, 1654, describing his blindness for consultation with the French doctor François Thévenin. "And so, whatever ray of hope also there may be now shine forth from this physician, still as in a case incurable, I prepare and compose myself thus; and I often think this, that since many be the days of darkness, as the Wise Man warns [Ecclesiastes, the Preacher; Eccelesiastes 12:9], destined for everyone, my darkness hitherto, by the singular kindness of the Divine Will, amid rest and studies, and the voices and greetings of friends, has been much milder than that deathly one.[10] But . . . [I am] capable of seeing, not by [my] eyes alone, but sufficiently by God's leading and providence[.] Verily, while He looks out for me, He provides for me; because He does, he guides me and leads me forth as with His hand through my whole life; truly I shall have willingly bid my eyes rest from work, since it has seemed best to Him" (619).[11]

The reference to metaphoric lifespan is, rather, to Isaiah 65:20: "There shall be no more thence an infant of days, nor an old man that hath not filled his days; for the child shall die an hundred years old but the sinner being a hundred years old shall be accursed." In 1655 (the date to which such externals as numbering and what would have been manuscript position point[12]) Milton would have become forty-seven in December; and the poem may have been written in October of that year (truly ere half his metaphoric days in the world) when much was occurring governmentally and politically with the appointment of the ten major-generals controlling ten divisions of England and imposing various "blue laws" as the Cromwellian Protectorate deemed appropriate to its theocratic rule. This "New Jerusalem" envisioned (as in Isaiah) was to have come into full existence shortly before the forecast millennium of 1657, whether Milton truly joined others in believing this prophecy or not. Isaiah's words (65:17 and 66:22) are the words of Revelation (21:1) and their eschatology. Against this background of activity Milton is not providing "day labour": rather than being some emissary or member of a major-general's staff, he learns through patience that God also needs retainers awaiting whatever bidding will arise. Such retainers must "stand," a verb (as opposed to "sit") that, for Milton, implies activity and alertness.[13]

As I have previously noted, "On August 9, [1655] ten Major-Generals were named to command the militia in ten districts of England, and on August 22, seven instructions of a political nature for all to follow were drawn up in an effort to establish the democratic ideal. Seven additional instructions, first entered by Lambert on October 4, were adopted on October 9 with amendments. The last five of these fourteen instructions, which were distributed to the Major-Generals to enforce on October 11, dealt almost entirely with moral or social orders—orders aimed at obliterating vice, drunkenness, corruption, and violation of the Sabbath. While all this was afoot, Milton could only stand and wait."[14] John Lambert had served as general in the Parliamentary army and as a member of Cromwell's various Councils of State. He was opposed to various moves to recall Charles II and was even known as "Lord Lambert." In Sonnet 19 is a Milton who has transcended the seeking of the ego-ideal (*Ichideal*) of the past to an ideal ego (*Idealich*) through a sublimation involving object libido. The idealization deals, instead, with an object which has been ennobled and elevated, the "real" (as opposed to the "true") self. By 1655, with the earlier years of his governmental service behind him and some recognition of the inadequacies of that government for which he has served, Milton has been able to replace such representatives of ego-ideal as Lambert with his "real" self that does not need to force "day-labour," that can recognize in his "noble task" "In liberties defence" an ideal ego, and that has come to understand achievement of his great purpose in certain ways in the past and in certain ways to be further pursued in the future. The patience of being able to stand and wait—or to spare time to interpose proper delights, as he counseled Edward Lawrence in Sonnet 20, or to measure life in ways for which mild Heaven ordains a time, as he admonished Cyriack Skinner in Sonnet 21—displaces the ego-ideal imposed from without; that is, a narcissistic captation has occurred.[15]

Milton's apparent renewal of activity to achieve his great purpose in his great poem, interrupted only by occasional public duty as Latin secretary and familial concerns—raising his three daughters, his marriage to Katherine Woodcock (1656), and her and her daughter's deaths (1658)—maintained itself even through hiatus in 1659-60, with the advent of the Restoration and its immediate aftermath to 1665.

In Milton's personal life from 1645 on, much had occurred that has already been alluded to. In 1645 his first wife Mary returned, perhaps during the summer, a period in which adherents of James Graham, Marquis of Montrose, Alexander MacDonnell (known also as MacColkitto and MacGillespie, the "Asp" of Milton's *Tetrachordon* sonnet), and James Gordon, Lord Aboyne (the "toad" of the sonnet) were achieving victories over the Parliamentarians and being well talked of favorably for such victories, even by those on Parliament's side. Mary's family came to live with the Miltons for a while and until her father's death sometime in the autumn; their daughter Anne was born on 29 July 1646; his father died around 13 March 1647; their daughter Mary was born on 25 October 1648, and Milton was appointed Secretary for Foreign Tongues to the Council of State on 15 March 1649. His daughter Anne was impaired in some way; she may have been somewhat retarded or possibly spastic and lame. During these years, as has been said, Milton returned to private concerns and writing, with the publication particularly of the shorter poems at the end of 1645 and the production of *The Tenure of Kings and Magistrates* at the end of January and beginning of February 1649, which, along with (apparently) testimonial from friends, brought him the governmental appointment.

Among his duties were producing correspondence in Latin, the diplomatic language of the time, for the Council and specifically for Oliver Cromwell; writing "official" works for the government; and for a short while, ironically, licensing periodicals and books for them. The first "official" works were *Observations upon the Articles of Peace* (May 1649), to counter the effect of the Royalist-Irish "treaty"; *Eikonoklastes* (October 1649), to counter the sympathetic effects of *Eikon Basilike* (around February 1649), allegedly written by Charles I while in prison; and *Pro populo Anglicano Defensio* (February 1651), to counter the popular view and justification of Charles given by Claude Saumaise (Salmasius) in *Defensio regia pro Carolo I* (available in England around November 1649). Rather than counter such positive reactions of the people toward Charles, these works came to vilify Milton and cast him as a regicide, which to this day has made him anathema for many people.

The *First Defense*, as it is called, being in Latin, was read on the Continent and discussed; but this "noble task, / Of which all *Europe* talks from side to side" (Sonnet 22) may reveal ego enhancement rather than truth. Milton's position against prepublication censorship argued in *Areopagitica* led to his dismissal from licensing duties when he allowed William Dugard to publish the Racovian Catechism, a Socinian document denying the Trinity, in March 1651. This action of approval gives good example of the basically impractical Milton, led by "ideal" beliefs and not really capable of understanding the ordinary person and what impresses such people. Even though *Eikonoklastes* and the *First Defense* were assigned works, there is much of Milton the person in them (some of the representations that Goldberg talks of) and they show an author who is oblivious to the verity that logic and fact are not persuasive arguments for those given to prejudgment and emotional concerns or for those of lesser intellectual abilities.

In the disastrous year 1652 Milton lost full eyesight (around February, having lost the sight in the left eye in 1650); his son John, having been born on March 16, 1651, died on June 16; his daughter Deborah was born on May 2, but his wife died a few days later as a result of childbirth; and he was frequently attacked vituperatively in print for the two aforementioned prose works. These works were to be burned publicly in France, again in England by order of King Charles II in 1660, and yet once more in Oxford on July 21, 1683. An earlier attack was addressed by his nephew John Phillips's *Responsio Ad Apologiam Anonymi* (October? 1651), apparently with much help from Milton, and later ones were defended in *Pro populo Anglicano defensio secunda* (the *Second Defense*) and *Pro Se Defensio* in May 1654 and August 1655 respectively. (The humor of the latter work should be noted in regard to former remarks made here.)

The psychological adjustments discussed above led to Milton's second marriage, to Katherine Woodcock on November 12, 1656, and to renewed writing activity, by all accounts, on *Paradise Lost*. His daughter Katherine was born on October 19, 1657, but on February 3 and March 17, 1658, wife and then daughter died. The clearly impending return of Charles II during 1659 and its occurrence in early 1660, ushering in the Restoration monarchy and reactions against those involved in the Interregnum government, evoked various tracts aiming at revision of the theocracy, or at avoiding clashes between the two sides, or at influencing that approaching settlement. *A Treatise of Civil Power* (February 1659) is quite straightforward in its arguments for tolerance and separation of church and state, being addressed to Richard Cromwell's new Parliament. Intolerance and Erastian positions characterized the Interregnum government and were to become major concerns in the ensuing Stuart years, with Milton restating some of his ideas in *Of True Religion, Hæresie, Schism, Toleration* (May? 1673). A promised second part of his 1659 tract (one on tithing) came forth in August as *Considerations Touching the likeliest means to remove Hirelings from the Church*, but it seems to have been written in 1652 and only touched up for this later publication. Around October *A Letter to a Friend, Concerning the Ruptures of the Commonwealth* and "Proposalls of certaine expedients for the preventing of a civill war now feard, & the settling of a firme government" were produced (the former not published until 1698 and the latter not until 1938). March and April of 1660, just before the arrival of Charles in London, saw *The Ready and Easy Way to Establish A Free Commonwealth* published, *The Present Means, and Brief Delineation of a Free Commonwealth* written but not published until 1698, and *Brief Notes Upon a Late Sermon* answering Matthew Griffith's sermon entitled *The Fear of God and the King* (March 25, 1660). *The Ready and Easy Way* emphasized the two adjectives, as has been noted by others, and offered a commonwealth that was not really utopian (it has even been labelled "antiutopian") and that implied a superiority of some people over others, not an egalitarian position in a modern sense. *Brief Notes* works on theological issues, as had the 1659 tracts, rather than political ones, but perhaps the intention was to discredit all like Griffith (he attacked both Presbyterians and Independents) who seemed to see the restoration of monarchy as the means to assure a dominance of Anglicanism and a reduction, if not obliteration, of sectarian groups.

The Act of Oblivion enacted on August 29, exacting the death penalty for some, omitted Milton, but an order for his arrest seems to have stayed on someone's agenda, and he was imprisoned in October, remaining there until December 15, when friends paid his fine. He had, apparently, not wanted the fine paid through a sense of indignation and of rightness for his political ideas and works. (As noted, *Eikonoklastes* and the *First Defense* were called in and publicly burned by proclamation of the king in August.) The remainder of his life was to be a period of general retirement and writing, primarily on his major poems. He married Elizabeth Minshull on February 24, 1663, and they and his three daughters stayed in the extant cottage in Chalfont St. Giles, Bucks, from about

June 1665 through possibly February 1666, to avoid the devastating plague and the Great Fire of London.

While *Paradise Lost* was conceived in 1640-42, as the Trinity MS shows, and written in part, we cannot be absolutely sure when it received further development, except that among the more likely times were the period through 1645, around 1653 and later 1655 through 1658, and then again most continuously from 1661 through 1665. Among the few shorter poems other than sonnets that Milton wrote after 1645 are translations of Psalms 1-8 in August 1653. Each translation is in a different verse form or meter, and, though rhymed, the lines are not end-stopped but rather seem to be experimenting with what comes to be the verse paragraph employed in the verse of the epic. We have already glanced at the period of 1655-58, with the postscript to the *First Defense,* and we might note the publication in May? 1658 of "Sir Walter Ralegh's" *The Cabinet-Council,* the manuscript of which Milton may have come across as he was looking through various unpublished materials, including the 'Paradise Lost' "originals" and the sonnets that were transcribed into the quarto sheets now bound with the Trinity MS, perhaps transcribed in expectation of a new edition. (A note that they are to follow the ones in "the printed booke" was entered by Jeremy Picard after the first transcriptions by a different amanuensis.) The epic seems to have been complete by 1665, when Milton was at Chalfont St. Giles, from the testimony of Ellwood in his autobiography. Ellwood was the amanuensis who wrote out the extant receipt for payment from the printer in 1669, as well. Publication would have been held up in 1665-66 because of the plague and fire. Whether or not a second edition was hoped for in 1670, as has been speculated, it did not appear until 1674, having not sold well in prior years. There are two issues of the first edition in each of the years 1667, 1668, and 1669. In the second issue of 1668 the prefatory material was added: "The Verse" in rebuttal of John Dryden's position in *An Essay on Dramatick Poesy,* the printer to the reader, and the arguments. It was not until the second issue of 1669 that parts of the poem had to be reset (because sheets had now been used up?).

The years following 1665 and up to 1670 included the writing or finishing of the two other major poems, as discussed earlier in this chapter. If indeed they were rewritten during this period, prompted by Ellwood's question, upon returning the "Paradise Lost" manuscript, concerning "what hast thou to say of *Paradise found,*" we may owe other works to Milton's search of materials formerly produced, as listed before: in 1669, *Accedence Commenc't Grammar;* in 1670, *The History of Britain;* in 1672, *Artis Logicæ Plenior Institutio;* and further, the additional shorter poems in

1673 (a volume that also printed the second edition of *Of Education*); and in 1674, *Epistolarum Familiarium Liber Unus* with the seven prolusions. Remaining for posthumous publication were the State Papers (1676), the *Character of the Long Parliament* (1681), *A Brief History of Moscovia* (1682), and *De doctrina christiana* (1825).

We know little of the day-to-day world of Milton after 1660, other than the inferences we can take from the previous two paragraphs. His household consisted of his wife, Betty, his three daughters, Anne, Mary, and Deborah, and at least one servant, Elizabeth Fisher. His other relatives and his friends and acquaintances visited from time to time, but it would seem to have been a generally retired life, the ego-ideals of the past being transcended. His final year of life will be the focus of Chapter 17. As for an overview of his writing and publication, there seems good evidence of the ideal ego being put forth and a reliance on these works as defining "that same lot, however mean or high, / Toward which Time [led him], / and the will of Heav'n." These post-Restoration works are the "fresh woods, and pastures new"; and though some may be poorly received by biased breasts, "a rational posterity will know if [he] deserve any merit." They will be proof whether he has borne God's mild yoke and served him best; they will record in God's book that he was one of God's sheep. They will offer various representations of "John Milton," but compositively they are the talent that he was.

11
Interferences of the Self

One of the interferences between Milton's self and his world—and I do not imply anything negative by the word "interference"—lies in the influence of his mother, an almost nonexistent figure in his biographies except for the question of her name before marriage and except for slight mention of her relatives—such as William Blackborough, who would have been part of Milton's extended family. Indeed, little has been investigated about Milton's extended family, even by Parker. The reader's own experience will suggest the importance of Milton's extended family to him and his life. His extended family, for example, included his sister's second husband's first wife's family—the Rugeleys, including Luke Rugeley, an important medical doctor, and Simon Rugeley, a significant colonel in the New Model Army—as well as his connections with the Bolles and Fleetwood families through his brother-in-law's nephew's marriage to Mary, daughter of Sir Richard Bolles, and through his brother's son's marriage to Martha, daughter of the prominent Sir William Fleetwood, brother of the Charles Fleetwood, a member of the Council of State. Thus we need to consider the importance of his mother in Milton's development and personality, in his relationship with others, including relatives through the maternal side, and particularly in the relationship with his wives and daughters, and in his career.

Not only is John Milton's mother a very minor figure in biographies of the poet and champion of liberties, she is not even minor in criticism of his works. Yet one salient fact looms decisively as we take perspective on the biography: with his mother's death on April 3, 1637, Milton was able to begin to stir out of his long obscurity and studious retirement. In the following fall he talks of being in London at least for visits and of contemplating taking up residence at one of the Inns of Court. Soon he had proceeded to plans for that often acknowledged watershed of his life, his trip to the Continent in April 1638. Important as that trip was, a clearer watershed was the alteration in his family's household caused by his mother's death and the release of certain familial duties. It becomes the break in his pattern of life that allows for the *wanderjahr,* which begins a year later.

Milton refers parenthetically to the sad event of his mother's death in his autobiographical statement in *Defensio secunda,* a work aimed at countering slanderous statements and innuendos in Peter Du Moulin's *Regii sanguinis clamor.*[1] This personal account of his life, recalled in May 1654, begins with remarks that include a very brief panegyric of his mother: "Who I am, then, and whence I come, I shall now disclose. I was born in London, of an honorable family. My father was a man of supreme integrity, my mother a woman of purest reputation, celebrated throughout the neighborhood for her acts of charity." He discusses his father and the country place to which he had returned upon graduation from Cambridge in 1632, and then writes: "When I had occupied five years in this fashion, I became desirous, my mother having died, of seeing foreign parts."[2] The Latin is "post matris obitum," not quite the same as the translation: either, however, indicates that the possibility of seeing foreign parts was not thinkable while his mother was alive.

The reasons given for his return to his father's home after graduation, rather than entering the ministry for which he had been schooled or some other lifework and rather than taking up residence in London on his own, have over the years usually been tainted by antagonisms toward Milton: he did not receive the fellowship given Edward King or any other university preferment or any ministerial post, and so he retreated to the parental chrysalis. Or, he is seen as already church-outed, even though in July 1632 he signed the Subscriptions Book, which required allegiance to three significant Articles of Religion, set out in the thirty-sixth ecclesiastical canon of 1604. That is, he acknowledged the liturgy and doctrines of the Church of England, and royal supremacy in all ecclesiastical matters. It must be pointed out that there is no evidence that Milton sought either an academic or a parochial preferment, and indeed no evidence that none was offered him. And unless one wants to argue hypocrisy and opportunism on his part in signing the supplicat, he expected for all intents and purposes to pursue ministerial work at some time, ministerial work that was not in opposition to the Anglican establishment, although there may have been disagreements with some practices. During the 1630s, of course, Archbishop William Laud exerted so many interpretations of parochial duties and enforcements that many ministers came to oppose him, as noted in Chapter 4. The church-outing could not have been *in esse* in 1632, but it apparently was after April 1637. Jung's analysis of the church as mother figure and mother substitute suggests in the case of Milton in 1637 that the loss of his mother defused the need for "a higher spiritual substitute for the purely natural, or 'carnal,' tie to the parents. Consequently it forces the individual from an unconscious natural relationship which, strictly speaking, is not a relationship at all but simply a condition of inchoate, unconscious identity."[3]

I have already discussed the "country place" and the reason for his removal to it, as well as the more extended family situation at the time. What can be inferred from his statement in *Defensio secunda* is that Milton went to his family's home because of the infirmity of his father, although patently he should have said something about his *parents*. With the death of his mother and the apparent change in his father's household when Thomasin Webber Milton came to live with the father, Milton was free to assert himself.

William Kerrigan, the only critic to include Milton's mother in a reading of the work, writes, "The death of Sarah Milton was the first step in lifting the spell that bound him to his home,"[4] using a word calculated to build an impression. Milton's mother's death did free him to prepare a future world, but he was under no spell—unless superego is always so cast. Kerrigan's juxtaposition of lines 1018-24 of "Comus," written in 1634, although other lines in the full epilogue were not written until 1637, as E.M.W. Tillyard showed years ago,[5] with Milton's mother's death in 1637 leads to and is built upon specious ideas about virginity and chastity in the poem. While Milton was surely virginal when he married in 1642 (and, to repeat some of the substance of Chapter 2, the sobriquet "the Lady of Christ's" probably devolved upon him because he did not partake in male college student activities such as drinking, engaging in sexual intercourse when one could—or at least boasting that one had—or playing sports), and while he seems to hope that Charles Diodati would find salvation because he was not one defiled with women and therefore was a virgin (alluding to Revelation 14:4), Milton is praising virginity in the poem only to the point when that condition will morally be altered, that is, through marriage, and is arguing that chastity, before and after marriage, is an ideal to be maintained. The sage and serious doctrine of virginity is, and need be, nothing more than that. We may cast moral injunctions against premarital, extramarital, and frequent sex as old-fashioned and fatuous, but such morality is still commonplace. The Lady says that since Comus dares even the sun-clad power of chastity, he surely could not understand why virginity should exist.

The attachment to the mother is seen in psychological studies influenced by Freud in terms of love that creates repression, for the self is put into her place and a narcissistic relationship develops. Thus concepts of morality, particularly those treating sexual matters, are associated with the other figure. These statements are always focused on the male and given by male-oriented writers, but since our subject is male, we do not here have to consider their inappropriateness for the female, who is usually discussed in seemingly opposite, rather than separate, terms. If we accept this as a beginning concept, recognizing that it is a simplistically stated complex answer to a very complex question, we see Milton's high ideals of conduct between the sexes as deriving from the mother and his relationship with her. From negative evidence we would assume that Milton's mother was a "typical" housewife and mother of the seventeenth century: one who bore children (at least six), who took care of the home as needed for the father and the children, who was guided by her husband, who was the focus around which domestic and extended family life existed. Milton's father had rebelled against the Roman Catholicism of his father and left home to make his fortune, soon after being in London, and soon after that marrying Sara Jeffrey. (This paternal self has been little explored in considering Milton's rustication, his rejection of the church and the nature of his ultimate "religion," his ideas and rebellion against monarchical precepts, and even his constant literary innovation. He, indeed, is his father's son: "Ad Patrem" talks of their division of the gifts of Apollo; it could have talked as well of their division of Jonathan against the falsity of Saul.) Accordingly, ties with paternal relatives are unknown except for Richard Milton, who was apprenticed to Milton's father and who may have been a distant relative (he was the son of Thomas of Cheltenham). But, though they are not many, a few relatives from the mother's side do enter Milton's biography and are particularly significant because it is through two of them, Hester Jeffrey Blackborough and her husband, William, that the reconciliation with his wife Mary took place in 1645. Milton was still living on Aldersgate Street, and the Blackboroughs, whom report has it he visited often, lived on St. Martin's-le-Grand, within Aldersgate, a very short distance away.

It is best at this point to take a moment to elaborate upon the male/female role-playing implied in the previous paragraph. Concepts of masculine and feminine, glanced at in Chapter 3 and to be examined further in Chapter 12, have been with us a long time. These gender concepts derive largely from anatomical, endocrinological, and birth-function differences, and thence from the sociological and environmental differences that developed around them. Gender stereotyping occurred and expanded to nonsexual matters; we may deplore stereotyping, but it occurs, and gender stereotyping has been particularly insidious. Yet the point in any "opposite" pairing such as black/white or good/bad is that those ideas or artifacts to which the terms may apply generally fall somewhere along the spectrum between those absolute extremes, with even absolute colors being only scientifically producible.

Still, we voice concepts or associations or characteristics that we unhesitatingly place in the "good" box or in the "bad" box, and the main point of separation, as Milton remarked in *Areopagitica*, is the contrast with the Other. The contrast has to be made in the same arena or the alleged distinction is specious. And with such categorizations as "good" and "bad" a point of view enters on the part of the person doing the categorizing: the category may depend on efficacy, on morality, on sense of aesthetics, or on many things. Nonetheless the terms are useful, and so with "masculine" and "feminine," terms having connotations, contrastive concepts, or associations or characteristics, which are probably in some way always wrong. A user's employment of the terms may tell us something about that person's values or morality or aesthetics. The problem in using these terms and their supposed attributes occurs when we think they are absolute and isolatable, when they become stereotypes, when we expect or demand "masculine" things from men and "feminine" things from women, and when we condemn men for "feminine" matters and women for "masculine" matters. The philosophy of the androgyne (not the hermaphrodite as some writers have it) from Plato's Symposium onward has been the fusion of "masculine" and "feminine" into an integrated self that will obviate the need to contrast gender except as far as anatomical differences and any other differences arising from anatomical differences are concerned.

Interesting thus for our consideration is the recent analysis of *Paradise Lost* by Stevie Davies: "The bisexual poet receiving inspiration from a bisexual deity is, throughout the poem, seen to create a bisexual world. . . . Man and woman in Milton's Eden are only just different: Eve tells over Adam's words in calling her 'Part of my soul . . . My other half' (IV. 487, 488). . . . Self dissolves into self, and in that dissolution the two sexes become one another. This is the secret of sexual and spiritual joy, which are not in Milton's epic distinguished: the containing of self in the solitary confinement of individual identity is a painful consequence of the Fall."[6]

If then we see Milton in his advocacy of chastity as one exhibiting some repression of otherwise "natural" feelings and desires for an active life, sexually or ideationally, we can find the effects of his early personality-development in his lack of attachment to friends, in his disclaiming of certain schoolboy antics (as he does disclaim them in the Sixth Prolusion), in the subjects of poetry prior to 1637—the father-oriented paraphrase of Psalm 114, the emphasis on the virgin birth of the Christ child and its accompanying imagery of the naked shame of the earth, pollute with sinful blame, and the saintly veil of maiden white, in the abstemiousness of the Apollonian poet described in "Elegia sexta," and in "Comus." If we see further the "sage and serious doctrine of virginity" as a specific part of that attitude toward chastity, we are better able to understand his vision of Damon as one of blushing modesty, as one without "blemish," as a virgin who will therefore achieve salvation, even so late in Milton's life as 1639 or 40, when he was thirty-two. These virgins of Revelation (and they seem to be only male, and they are so construed by Jung) are ones, according to Jung, "who, following in the footsteps of the young dying god [that is, Jesus as the Christ], have never become complete human beings, but have voluntarily renounced their share in the human lot."[7]

Diodati's mother died sometime well before 1637, we might note, and he did not get along with his step-mother, Abigail. Diodati's apparent virginity may also be seen as reflecting the importance of the mother figure; the absence of the mother by death, if it occurred at the end of the 1620s, may account for what has seemed a confusion of professional activities: after having been graduated from Oxford on July 8, 1628, instead of following his father in medicine, Charles went to Geneva during 1630-31, studying theology. Jung's concept of the church as mother substitute may be apt here. Charles returned to England in September 1631 and did study medicine, his well-known physician father, Theodore, being his tutor.

In "Comus" Milton explores the concepts of virginity and chastity—but we must keep in mind the Castlehaven scandal as we read; for example, as we read such lines as "beauty . . . had need the guard / Of dragon watch . . . / To save her blossoms and defend her fruit / From the rash hand of bold incontinence" or "defilement to the inward parts" of the soul, whose body has "link't it self by carnal sensualty / To a degenerate and degraded state," or "victorious dance / O're sensual folly, and intemperance."[8] The Elder Brother's view—and note its underlying sexual and eating image—is that evil will recoil on itself "and mix no more with goodness, when at last / Gather'd like a scum, and setl'd to it self / It shall be in eternal restless change / Self-fed, and self-consum'd." These high moral ideals and hope in their ultimate power in the world may derive from the influence of the mother and may take the form of repression, as Freud postulated. The devouring uroborus, a female archetype, takes on a regressive symbol (the snake eating its own tail), and such regression in the male has a psychic castrating effect, killing feminine relatedness. A symptom of such regression is obsessiveness and the damming up of psychic energy. The biographical facts of Milton's life during his studious retirement can certainly be read as corroboration. The archetypal devouring uroborus demands perfection and permanence (the circular symbol connotes both), and in the high moral ideas that Milton puts into the Elder Brother's mouth (the Lady's also) we have clear statement of such perfection and permanence, both derived from sexual repression. The recoiling and self-consumption of evil equate the being of the uroborus; its permanence is seen as "eternal restless change."

Jung linked the saved virgins of Revelation to those of the cult of the Great Mother, corresponding to the emasculated Galli, and equated them with the eunuchs in Matthew 19:12 "who have made themselves eunuchs for the sake of the kingdom of heaven" and with the priests of Cybele who used to castrate themselves in honor of her son Attis. Repression thus may be viewed as psychic castration, occurring physically as virginity, backed up by concepts of ultimate achievement and salvation. The blossom, as it were (to use the image in "Comus") must be allowed to develop into the fruit, and the fruit, to reach maturity. Erich Neumann writes of Medusa as a Terrible Mother figure whose shield rigidifies her victims, creating an opposition to the mobility of life.[9] Deliberate baldness, which can be seen as a form of repression, is a characteristic of the initiates of the Great Mother; in contrast, the shield of Medusa consists of snake hair. For the one there is repression of a sexual and phallic symbol; for the other, an overwhelming presence, for snakes are phallic symbols, too. This cult of the Great Mother revolves around beliefs in the efficacy of celibacy and repression, with appropriate symbols, while the cult of the Terrible Mother revolves around beliefs in sexual freedom and activity and their appropriate symbols. But the religious mind of the past, and the present, has seen reverse values in these opposing forces: repression and psychic castration were seen as good, while the Terrible Mother was viewed as one with teeth in her vagina (the upper mouth thus becoming surrogate for the vagina), which would dismember the male who consorted with her. The inactive life brings ultimate life; the active life brings death.

It is thus pertinent that the Elder Brother employs a variant of the Medusa myth in his lesson to the Second Brother:

> What was that snaky-headed *Gorgon* shield
> The wise *Minerva* wore, unconquer'd virgin,
> Wherwith she freez'd her foes to congeal'd stone?
> But rigid looks of chast austerity,
> And noble grace that dash't brute violence
> With sudden adoration, and blank aw. [ll. 447-52]

The wise Minerva, symbol of the mind, fused the protective shield of her father Jove with the shield of Medusa that turned its viewers to stone. (The image appears earlier in "Elegia quarta," ll. 108-11.) For the Elder

Brother—for Milton?—the means to stave off the death that "carnal sensualty" would bring is to emasculate assault by outward look (chaste austerity) and inward grace (adoration and awe of the godhead). The outward look, like the shield of Medusa, would offer sexual performance only to castrate, and the inward grace would protect against any "hurt-full power."

I can thus only partially agree with Kerrigan's statement (51) that "The virtue of maternal love disappears from the text of *Comus,* replaced by the form of its sterile and unblemished opposite. Virginity is the response to a mother's love that, suspending his maleness, makes a lady of a son." Maternal love is not part of the masque, nor should it be. But that is not at issue. Kerrigan seems to be using the inappropriate term "maternal love" to mean oepidal sexual intercourse (actual or psychological)—the only way in which virginity is its opposite. The concepts of virginity and of chastity (which I insist are presented by Milton under both pre- and post-marital circumstances) are at issue. We may not consider premarital sex a "blemish," but Milton did, whether because of moral values inculcated by his mother, by his church, or by society itself in its holy moments. While nonsexual activity will not bring birth, Milton and those who disavow premarital sex are not advocating sterility, and Kerrigan's phraseology again becomes part of a rhetorical strategy suggesting inappropriate attitudes for Milton's. The question of the maleness or femaleness of a person is one of degree, and the influence of either parent will in various ways at various times seem to emerge for most people, with repressions or lack of repressions of those influences occurring as one views oneself and society's expectations, sometimes consciously, more often not. In Milton's case, we do see a feminine side, as Kerrigan explores it in his study, but this brings us into archetypes of male and female, the masculine and the feminine, and their applicability to personality, to action, even to artifacts. (I assume that for most people building a bridge is somehow more masculine than writing a musical composition, though the bridge be an aesthetic achievement and the composition the kind of mathematical wonder that a Bach invention is, wrong as such gendering is.)

Gender characteristics are at the heart, for example, of those two often debated lines in Book IV of *Paradise Lost:* "For contemplation hee and valour formd, / For softness shee and sweet attractive Grace" (ll. 297-98). The male prototype emphasizes man's mind and his heroic use of his strength; the female prototype, woman's gentleness (with a suggestion of the soft nonmuscularity of her body) and beauty, charm, refinement, ease of movement. A stress is man as mind, woman as body. Allegedly these are stereotypes of the male and the female, and in today's world at least they are far from accurate, though past cultures may yield a superficial acceptance. In the full passage Milton is trying to delineate the prototype of all males and all females beyond their genital and mammary parts: he has hair to his shoulders, for example; she, to her waist. Adam is the first man and Eve is the first woman, and Milton assigns them gender characteristics that are hardly unique with him. But note—one cannot say this strongly enough—that the passage gives us the scene and couple through Satan's eyes: they "seemd Lords of all," "And worthier seemd," "though both not equal, as thir sex not equal seemd." The words are those of the narrative voice but filtered through the consciousness of the viewer, Satan, where comparison of the couple with himself is clear in the words "nobler Shape" (288) and later Satan's own "Little inferior" (362). The narrative voice is as much that of a character as Satan's words are those of a character: Milton, the would-be dramatist, presents characters in this drama of life, not spokespeople. The narrative persona is conditioned here in what he sees and reports by Satan, the viewer whose verbal responses are given immediately before and after the "narrative" section; the imagery of the narration is defined by that conditioning and stresses the sexual and envious reactions of Satan as voyeur.

The gender stereotypes of the two lines follow immediately upon "though both / Not equal, as thir sex not equal seemd": the first "not equal" does not demand anything more than "not the same," just as they are in sexual parts not the same. But the second "not equal" then picks up, because of the word "seemd," connotations of nonsameness in sexual ability, activity, and gratification. After all, their "sex" is not the same physically; there is no question of seeming or not seeming "equal" in their physicality. In "as thir sex not equal seemd" the narrator is saying that the voyeur Satan thought them not equal in the same way that they seem not to be equal sexually: they are not equal physically, but the implication that their sexual ability and activity (in the commonplace view the man "acts" and the woman "receives") only *seem* unequal is false. Sexual gratification, if indeed the reader acknowledges gratification as a result of sexual ability and activity, only "seemd" not equal, implying that it is or could be equal, and by like implication "both" beings only "seemed" "Not equal," but were or could be. (Milton *is* describing sex before the Fall and its resultant physical and emotional effects.)

The differentiations of male and female in lines 297-98, offered as example of that "nonequality," are only seemingly "not equal." The differentiations of their physicality (like their sexual parts) may stress the man's physical strength (valour) and the woman's physical beauty (sweet attractive Grace), but these are "not equal" only as "not the same." Adam gets it right when describing the creation of Eve, a point in the narrative that is significantly the focal point of the full poem (see Chapter 12, n. 10): "under his forming hands a Creature grew, / Manlike, but different sex" (VIII, 470-71). Adam continues with what for him (man?) makes Eve (woman?) the desired Other: "so lovely fair, / That what seemd fair in all the World, seemd now / Mean, or in her summ'd up" (VIII, 471-73). The "seemd" here says that what is fair in all the world is *not* mean, only comparison with Eve for him makes it possibly so. Eve, having also succumbed to the adoration of the Other, contrastingly remarks, just a little after the debated lines of Book IV, "see / How beauty is excelled by manly grace / And wisdom" (489-91). (The "manly grace" picks up the second item in the second line, "sweet attractive Grace," and "wisdom" picks up the first item in the first line, "contemplation.") This is Eve the character speaking in a specific situation, not Milton making a philosophic axiom. At most Milton has observed that the Other (man toward woman and woman toward man) is often exalted in comparison, with a corresponding reduction in Self: he is talking about prototypical male and prototypical female. If we approach lines 288-355 of Book IV as lines written by Milton the poet to be the words of a narrative persona in order to relate a scene observed by Satan, with elements and stresses that would have impressed Satan and with interpretations therefrom that he would have concluded, we should desist from assigning to Milton's philosophic and sociological beliefs the images and assumptions of the passage. We dismiss otherwise the writer writing. The views of Adam (and Satan) toward Eve are the views of the "average" male toward woman, and the views of Eve toward Adam are the views of the "average" female toward man. Neither view is "correct": certainly "grace" is "grace," whether "sweet attractive" or "manly"! They are not the same, but they are "equal."

Satan has, of course, lost grace (94) but observes it in the human pair: "such grace / The hand that formd them on thir shape hath pourd" (364-65). Grace has been given to both male and female; it lies observable in their bodily forms; more significantly, however, it has, for Satan, been poured on "thir shape," the singular suggesting their bodily form as one shape, one being: their humaneness. Satan's perversion of love, his psychological character, seems to be advancing for the astute reader, stresses sexuality and envy of sexuality (physical and emotional), which perversion would seem to be turned inward into both self-love and thence self-hate. The narrative emphasis on the couple's nakedness (290, 319), their sex (296), the mysterious parts (312), love's embraces (322), their being "linkt in happie nuptial League" (339), even the "supper Fruits" and the "Nectarine Fruits" on "compliant boughs" (331-32), the "Lithe Proboscis" of the elephant (347) with their sexual figuring, and those "Bedward ruminating" (352), make clear the reaction of Satan, who is viewing this scene. That reaction is first imaged as "the Serpent [with its phallic figuring] sly / Insinuating, wove with Gordian twine / His breaded train" [with its coitional picture, as well as the pun on "breaded" as "braided" and food]—a foreview of the wile/guile ("train") that Satan will employ in his seduction. In other words, the reaction is: "League with you I seek," recalling the "happie nuptial League" of Adam and Eve alone. The sexuality of the whole passage is manifest; Satan's psychological makeup and influences govern the narrator's images. Or rather, the poet's intent in figuring Satan is made clear through the words given to the persona of the narrative voice, who represents an attitude and valorizing that are moral and ideal. These may have affinities with Milton's own attitude and values, but they are pointedly employed to create in the reader valorization of that gendering that only *seems* accurately descriptive.

What is it that is objected to in lines 297-98? I suppose it is mainly that the word "formd," being executed by God, implies that men are expected to use their minds and women are not; it implies that she was formed for her beauty, but that involves the beholder of that beauty, the man. Milton's strategy—which has backfired for a lot of people—was: 1) to set up descriptions identified with the male and the female, 2) to make those descriptions opposite, just as the two people were sexually opposite, 3) to indicate how in role-playing and in expected role-playing they were not "equal" despite their seeming equality, including the seemingly balanced descriptions, and 4) to indicate how they only *seemed* not equal, anatomy aside. Ultimately the objection is to that ubiquitous idea that the male is superior, an idea that Milton subscribed to in general circumstances, at least, earlier in his life. But Milton's further strategy is to make the two beings two parts of a whole that together contained everything—that idea of the androgyne that goes through the whole poem. This point is made in their symbolization *together* as Christ through the chiasmus of the two lines: contemplation is to attractive grace as softness is to valour. The chiasmus, chi (X), a sign of Christ, underscores the belief that only man/woman as one, hand in hand, separate of essence but joined in being, can achieve the meaning of the Christ.

Following his investigation of oedipal influence on and patterns in Milton, Kerrigan summarizes: "The stasis of *Comus* derived from the fusion of the two fundamental anxieties of man in psychoanalysis: separation from the mother and castration by the father. Their opposites are reunion with the mother and the giving of a phallus by the father, and these are precisely the symbols of power that nourish the easy flow of the creation of *Paradise Lost*" (189). Kerrigan argues reunion with the mother through the inspiring muse of the patroness of the epic; the phallus of the father will generate the child, that is the poem.

For the period before 1637, however, we should also recall one of the Latin elegies. In the first to Diodati, Milton writes of walking in a park in London during his rustication:

Here you may often see bands of maidens, stars
emitting seductive flames, go dancing by.
Ah, how many times have I been stunned by the wonders of a becoming figure
which might refresh even the old age of Jove;
Ah, how many times have I seen eyes surpassing jewels
and even all the flaming stars which either pole rolls round;
and necks which excel the arms of twice-living Pelops;
and in which flows the vein dyed with pure nectar,
and uncommon grace of brow, and shaking hair,
by which deceitful Love extends his golden nets,
and seductive cheeks against which the purple of the hyacinth seems
of small account, and the blush of your flower, Adonis, as well.

Despite the intended hyperbole—and notice the gender characteristics—we observe an emphasis on seduction and understand that it is fully in the mind of the beholder: a sexually ready but repressed, naive kid. It is not that virginity has to be maintained: it is that succumbing to the urge beneath, he knows, would lead to other thoughts, if not actions, and that, he believes, would bring the morally upright boy grievously close to sinfulness. If we have not seen that, the ending of the elegy makes it all very clear, particularly with its use of an image to reemerge in "Comus": "But I, while the blind boy's indulgence permits, / am preparing to leave the favorable walled city most quickly; / and to escape from afar the infamous halls of faithless Circe, / preparing with the help of divine moly." Even stressing the poetic imagination, we must be amazed at the psychological being who, seeing some girls walking along, experiences such lustfulness that London is equated with Circe's sensual sty. The seventeen-year-old male, we know through modern research, is at what will be the peak of his sexual drive: to repress his urge Milton "most quickly" returns to the world of men at Christ's College!

A female archetype has also appeared in the elegy: mother as city (metropolis) as well as enclosure, "the favorable walled city," an urban *hortus conclusus*. He represses the mother figure (some undertones of incest rear up) and returns gladly to the male environment where the sun (male archetype) beats down and the Phoebicoli—students of Christ's and poets (who seem to write rather than experience)—assemble. We should be remembering the fourth sonnet, that addressed also to Diodati, in which Milton says "With wonder" that "I who used to contemn love and frequently scoffed at his snares, now have fallen where upright man sometimes entangles himself." The blind boy's snares have caught him, but note the word *dabben;* it means well-behaved, respectable, upright. The moral pressures show. The very weak "Elegia septima" reprises the subject and makes one feel that Milton is only playing writing games, but "Elegia quinta" is a tour-de-force of the Ovidian style, showing what he can achieve poetically when he is not the fictional center.

Before looking at Milton's divorce tracts, taken up in the next chapter, and some of his other poetry, briefly in this, I should make clear what I mean by "interferences." I use the term to indicate what can be viewed as interrupting or diverting or changing some expected action from taking place. And in this book I am often concerned with aspects of Milton's own self which interfered with intended action. The most obvious interference has been talked about for a long time, Milton's forgoing work on his great masterpiece to spend time in governmental service. But love of country and conviction of the evil of monarchy and its religious underpinnings may not be sufficient, I think, to explain either the positive action of doing or the negative nonaction of tabling when we consider the self. The influence of the mother supplies some of the answer in terms of morality, orderly and retentive anality, the sense of high justice, as well as anxieties over not completing what has been planned at the level hoped for. A man, says Jung,

may have a finely differentiated Eros.[10] He may have good taste and an aesthetic sense which are fostered by the presence of a feminine streak. He may be supremely gifted as teacher because of his almost feminine insight and tact. He is likely to have a feeling for history, and to be conservative in the best sense and cherish the values of the past. Often he is endowed with a wealth of religious feelings. . . . In the same way, what in its negative aspect is Don Juanism can appear positively as bold and resolute manliness, ambitious striving after the highest goals; opposition to all stupidity, narrow-mindedness, injustice, and laziness, willingness to make sacrifices for what is regarded as right, sometimes bordering on heroism; perseverance, inflexibility and toughness of will; a curiosity that does not shrink even from the riddles of the universe; and finally a revolutionary spirit which strives to put a new face upon the world.[11]

There has also been an interference by Milton's values, and one's sense of value is certainly an index of self. The orderliness of anality that won out with his finally publishing such prose works as *Accedence Commenc't Grammar* may have been overcome by the fastidiousness of getting things just right that seems to have kept *De doctrina christiana* in revision up to his death (assuming his authorship). We see this fastidiousness, in fact, often: observe the total rewriting of *The Doctrine and Discipline of Divorce* to double its first length (Kerrigan sees the four divorce tracts as an example of the stubbornness of anality), the revisions of *The Tenure of Kings and Magistrates* and of *Eikonoklastes* within a year of first publication, the alterations in the 1658 *Defensio prima,* in the 1660 *The Ready and Easy Way,* in lines in the printed *Comus,* "Lycidas," and "Nativity Ode," even perhaps in the second edition of *Paradise Lost,* let alone the changes in the poetry recorded in the Trinity MS.

The foregoing discussion has been moving toward a concept of "mother fixation" for Milton. I use "fixation" to mean the failure of one instinctual component to accompany other components along the anticipated path of development. We see mother fixation in Milton, I believe, in the ways we have glanced at above: repression, morality, anality. As we move into 1637 we have, for Milton, an individuation that consciously sublimates that mother complex, but it has also subconsciously become part of Milton and determines much in his future life. Neumann (25-26) talks of the elementary character of the Feminine as holding fast to everything that springs from it: "Everything born of it belongs to it and remains subject to it; and even if the individual becomes independent, the Archetypal Feminine relativizes this independence into a nonessential variant of her own perpetual being." It is the foundation of the conservative and unchanging part of man. Symbols this character yields include form and enclosures. The transformative character of the Feminine accents a dynamic element of the psyche, according to Neumann (28-29), driving toward transformation and bringing unrest. It is through such transformative character that creativity is identified with the feminine. And it is clear that we have here a coordinate for Milton's "tardie moving," as he called it in the letter to an unknown friend in the Trinity MS. But further there is the uroborus as dragon, and we see in 1637, as I argue in Chapter 4, the inflation that the dragon predicates. Here finally is ego freed: hope and action for creative recognition so that the *"serpentine jaws"* of Calumny and its *"viperous stroke"* will do nothing disagreeable to him, no longer to be unknown. The death of the mother has released a further uroboric effect with the undamming of psychic energy.

One of the first creative results of this transformation was "Lycidas," written in November 1637. The image of Orpheus and the inability of his mother Calliope, Muse of epic poetry, to save him are central to our understanding of Milton's newly conceived future and his perseverance, his rejection of Calliope as his muse in *Paradise Lost,* and his hope and faith in himself, for "O ye *Dolphins*" will "waft the hapless youth," be he Arion or Melicartes or the uncouth swain, or the nonspecific hope in salvation that "dolphin" as a symbol of Christ suggests. The assertion of ego for Milton in 1637 derives from the narcissistic identification with external Imagos. One of those was the father as Milton passed into Lacan's third stage of transference.

The female mana-personality has an occult and bewitching quality, endowed with magical knowledge and power. When the anima—that is, for Milton, his mother—loses her mana, the man who has mastered that anima acquires her mana.[12] And it is the ego that takes over the mana. The circumstances for Milton in 1637 corroborate Jung's analysis: His mother has died; the transforming character that has now been released in him is satisfying or is about to satisfy his unrest; he is creatively active again; and his ego has asserted itself, as it will also in publishing *A Maske* and in writing "Ad Patrem." This poem is not only a calm acceptance of the father, it is a rejection too. It ushers in a new world for its author, as much as the fresh woods and pastures new. And it plays upon the feminine within the father, who too had pursued the arts.[13] The decision to be a poet and the tardy moving, not into the ministry, not into the world of business or government, and not into family life, but into that uncertain poetic world, must have been a blow to Milton Senior. Jung's analysis of the mana-personality is exactly apt, however, for Milton's situation in 1637, and emphasizes the significance of the publication of *A Maske* at this time, as well as the poem "To My Father," which shows his exultation from his moving at last: "Therefore, now that I am a part of the learned company, however humble, / I shall sit among the ivy and the laurels of the victor. / And now I shall no longer mingle unknown with the indolent rabble / and my steps shall shun profane eyes" (ll. 101-4). "In differentiating the ego from the archetype of the mana-personality," Jung writes, "one is . . . forced . . . to make conscious those contents which are specific of the mana-personality. . . . Conscious realization of the contents comprising it means, for the man, the second and real liberation from the father."[14]

The force behind this sublimation of demands of the Logos and thus behind rebirth is the magical efficacy of the Feminine, according to Neumann (291). "Not only does the night [we might read *prolonged obscurity*], leading through death and sleep to healing and birth, renew the cycle of life; but, transcending earthly darkness, it sublimates the very essence of life through the eruption from the depths of those powers that, in drunkenness and ecstasy, poetry and illumination, manticism and wisdom, enable man to achieve a new dimension of spirit and light" (291). He continues (and we should think of Milton's life as well as the broad outlines of *Paradise Lost*), "Renewal is possible only through the death of the old personality, such as through sleep in the nocturnal cave, through a descent to the underworld realm of the spirits and ancestors, through a journey over the night sea" (292). We are bombarded in our minds by the narrative voice's descent to hell, his journey through Chaos and Old Night with Satan, who can proceed only to the created universe while the poet continues to ascend to Heaven.

The feminine part of the poet Milton, sustaining the mother fixation within, is examined by Kerrigan, who notes that Milton is even reported to have talked about being "milked" by his amanuensis each morning. He has the image confused, however, when he says that Milton is the child and the Muse the mother. "To be milked" means to have milk taken from one, such as a cow; surely it does not mean "to be given milk." The image rather suggests Milton as woman and the poem as food. The feminine principle, deriving from the anima (the life-giving principle) of the mother, controls inspiration, intuition, and narcissistic ego. One need look only at such poems as "Ad Patrem," "Mansus," and "Epitaphium Damonis," all from 1638-40, to observe Milton's ego at work—justified as he was. The ego and disdain for the riffraff in "I did but prompt" became ego and facetiousness in "A Book was writ" a few years later. They continue in the "Ode to Rous" (1647), when he talks of "the insolent speech of the multitude and . . . the vicious throng of readers," and in his exultation of his 1645 *Poems'* being placed in the Bodleian Library amidst the "august names" of Greek and Latin authors. He continues:

> But our distant descendants,
> and a more prudent age
> will perhaps exercise a fairer judgment
> of things from its unbiassed breast.
> Then with envy entombed,
> a rational posterity will know if I deserve any merit.

The poet in his three major poems produces characters that share a female principle; perhaps his own mother-influence attuned him to these matters, that without strong maternal influence might have been different. The Son in *Paradise Regain'd* shows archetypal behavior assigned (rightly or wrongly) to the female. He is tempted as one person (that is, as both male and female). He is to become the Christ, with his likeness to Eve, who offers redemptive action, for the Son and Eve share various parallels in *Paradise Lost* (see Kerrigan, 186, for some specific instances). I have elsewhere discussed the play of father/mother roles and constructs in the brief epic: "*Paradise Regain'd* presents the transcendence of the man Jesus into the man-God Jesus; it is a blending of the conscious with the unconscious, of the animus with the anima, of the male principle with the female principle. Jesus combines in his ministry the strength of the eagle and the gentleness of the dove, the power of the lion and the meekness of the lamb. He represents the oneness of Man and Woman, and *Paradise Regain'd* proclaims that Mankind's place of rest will be attained only by the symbolic Adam and Eve within us all going forth hand in hand."[15]

Jackie Di Salvo has looked at "Samson's Struggle with the Woman Within," recognizing Samson's early "feminine" archetypes, his emasculation before the dramatic poem begins, and his compensatory, exaggerated masculinity. She notes the repression of the past that has kept him virile and the castration that has occurred because of his breaking silence. Samson is, of course, blind, psychologically a symbol of castration.[16] Indeed, the dramatic poem would best be explored as man's struggle between the God-Mother, whose "nursling once" Samson was, "destin'd from the womb," and under whose "special eie / Abstemious . . . grew up," and for whom he did "mightiest deeds . . . Against th' uncircumcis'd," and, on the other hand, Dalila, who exhibits many characteristics of the Terrible Mother for Samson but should not for us (see Chapter 12).

Adam after the fall, in his attempt to avoid blame, exhibits those supposed feminine identifications, dependence, relational needs, and emotions; he finally cries, allowing the feminine to surface and accepting the contents of his self, but here he is joined with his wife, who has just shown her masculinity by strength of character, through admitting her "wilful crime." The two great sexes walk off hand in hand as one. For Milton it is that mental unity that must exist along with the sexual unity of coition that will finally let humankind choose its place of rest as the blissful seat. Adam takes on femininity with his masculinity; Eve, masculinity with her femininity. For Jung, "The later blending . . . of the sentimental, cultured man with nature is, looked at retrospectively, a reblending with the mother, who was our primary object, and with whom we truly were once wholly one."[17]

In looking at Milton's treatment of Eve there is so much to remember: John Phillips stressed the way in which religions founded on the Bible have cast Eve "not quite as much in the image of God as he," and her becoming the instrument of evil, since hers is the "weaker nature." The "feminine character in general, is regarded as less rational and less firmly in control of the passions, more gullible, more gifted in the arts of deception and persuasion, and more easily flattered into disloyalty." His assessment should be shouted and echoed: "Eve is guilty of wishing to be in control of her own sexual life. Some very deep, partially unarticulated fears are behind the male insistence that she be denied the freedom to make her own decisions about her bodily life."[18] Milton, of course, believed the Bible, and the Bible forces this idea of woman's inferiority to man. The Pauline accounts particularly might serve a therapist with interesting material. The male-oriented biblical accounts ultimately belie man's assurance of self and point to such unarticulated fears of maleness that are the Other to Freud's concept of female "penis envy." Such fears imply a sense of inferiority and inadequacy in those supposed male domains of strength, mental ability, and particularly sexual prowess. *Male* "penis envy" is real enough, and may most tellingly annotate Dalila's defensive taunt that her name "may stand defam'd . . . for falshood most *conjugal* traduc't" "among the Circumcis'd," but she will "be nam'd among the famousest / Of Women" among the uncircumcised (975-83, emphasis added). Milton comes in for antagonistic feminist criticism because *Paradise Lost* is such a major and influential work that some readers seem to confuse what is in the Bible with what is in the poem. The influence contributes to the maintenance of the subservient position of woman in people's minds. But I find the attack on the person Milton for not having shucked off this early teaching misplaced—misplaced particularly because it does not recognize that the status of woman through Milton's Eve is much higher than in comparable works. Nor does it understand the indictment of Adam, who falls undeceived.

The mother fixation, Kerrigan cogently maintains, emerges in Milton's Muse, specifically in the Patroness of Book IX. Further, as he points out, it would seem from a report by John Aubrey that Milton may have inherited his weak eyes from his mother. Is there, then, an involvement of attitudes toward her as he becomes blind, with its castrating symbolization? The images and similes of blind people in his works may reveal deep concern about going blind and then about being blind. I find totally insubstantial a reading of *Samson Agonistes* on a biographical level as usually advanced, but surely the blindness or the possibility of blindness had its effect on his presentation of the hero, and the Terrible Mother that Dalila purportedly resembles may reach back to recesses of woman as seducer that we have seen in other works. The repression of Milton's early years, one supposes, never fully left him.

12

The Personal World:
Man and Woman

The motif of Adam and Eve hand in hand is a major one in *Paradise Lost*, as we all know. They are introduced into the poem in Book IV at line 288: "Two of far nobler shape erect and tall, / Godlike erect, with native Honour clad / In naked Majestie seemd Lords of all" (288-90). Thirty-three lines later—and we remember the significance of that number in Gunnar Qvarnström's investigation of the poem[1]—we read: "So hand in hand they pass'd, the loveliest pair / That ever since in loves imbraces met" (321-22). The phrase indicates both their individuality and their union, their oneness. It is not to be unlikened to the "two great Sexes [which] animate the World" (VIII, 151): each sex, male and female, is a separate, individual being, but in coition they are one, one flesh and one being, and they are to be affectively one at all other times as well, as the hand-in-hand motif states. When Adam and Eve are about to retire for the night, the image is repeated: "Thus talking hand in hand alone they pass'd / On to thir blissful Bower" (689-90), with its overtones of forthcoming sexual activity.

The lines frame a presentation of the pair in the Garden, Satan's envious dismay and move to observe them close, and their remembrance of God's admonition and their first meeting, when Adam with his gentle hand seized Eve's (488-89)—a balancing of two hundred lines between the first and second and the second and third occurrences of the image. Between the second and the third citations Milton ranges Satan's soliloquy of scorn, the introduction of Gabriel and Uriel's arrival to report Satan's escape from Hell, and Adam and Eve's dialogue preluding their retirement. Satan plots the way in which he will abrogate their relationship of being "Imparadis't in one anothers arms" (506) through knowledge gained by tasting of the fatal tree: "They taste and die," he says (527). There is no mention of fruit in this passage. He leaves them a happy connubial pair: "enjoy, till I return, / Short pleasures, for long woes are to succeed" (534-35).

The sexual imagery should be clear: in the *hortus conclusus* which is the Garden stands a forbidden tree; there are other trees, of course, particularly the Tree of Life planted by "that onely Tree / Of knowledge." The womb with its phallic tree of life allows Eve and Adam to enjoy their short pleasures, to live on rejuvenated and, it is implied for the future, as begetters of life. Uncertainties have been raised by critics as to whether Milton's Adam and Eve partook of sex prior to the Fall. Even a casual reading of the poem insures us that this was wedded bliss with its short pleasures. The Tree of Life may be construed as a symbol of Christ. What Satan will do is make their embracement "unparadis't"; that is, by partaking of the other tree, another phallic symbol but different in kind, they will find death. Allegoric overtones are clear. Partaking of that other tree will demystify physical love, yield knowledge, cause them to *die* in the common parlance of that word, in sharp contrast to the (nonexhausting) sexual activity implied when they partake of the Tree of Life. The Tree of Knowledge may be construed as a symbol of Satan; that is, of the Adversary (not of the Devil).

The tree is a signifier in Jacques Lacan's sense: it "lifts the veil . . . from the function it performed"; it becomes what is signified by designating as a whole the effects of the signified. The signifier works through metonymy and metaphor. The Tree of Life as phallus and signifier, but not in gender terms, functions as all that is positive in sexual activity: pleasure principle and progenitor, uniting desire and need. The Tree of Knowledge as phallus and signifier functions as what is negative since it replaces desire with demand and need with gratification; that is, it represents the Other, the unconscious, the emergence of the nongender-oriented castration complex. The Tree of Knowledge in Milton's presentation of it, even more clearly than the mythic substruct of the story, unties the mysterious knot—and interestingly in *The Doctrine and Discipline of Divorce* he calls the helpmeet an amiable knot—that Lacan defines as "that element in the proof of love that is resistant to the satisfaction of a need." Further, he comments unwittingly on the fusion we can see for Milton's image of hand-in-hand for God and Adam and for Adam and Eve when he says, "The phallus is the privileged signifier of that mark in which the role of the logos is joined with the advent of desire." That is, the taking of Adam's hand by God the logos and Adam's desire for companionship, ultimately to be cast as a sexual privileging, set up the phallus as signifier in the mysterious knot, maintaining "proof of love"; Adam and Eve's joining hands images the mysterious knot, uniting the sense of logos, or "love," and the advent of desire, through the joining agency of the phallus. But then what occurs in the Fall is a *Spaltung* (a splitting), a subtraction, as it were, of satisfaction from love:

the *Spaltung* takes place on a human level for Adam and Eve, but also on a divine level.[2]

Adam's taking of Eve's hand when they first meet is of course a reprise of God's taking Adam's hand at his creation: "One came, methought, of shape Divine, / And said, thy Mansion wants thee, *Adam*, rise, / . . . So saying, by the hand he took me rais'd" (VIII, 295-300). The latter is also signified when Michael, "the gentle Angel," takes Adam "by the hand / Soon rais'd" from his enforced sleep to view biblical history from the Hill of Speculation (XI, 417-22). The motif, so interrelated, emblemizes "Hee for God only, shee for God in him" (IV, 299). For in Milton's account of this asexual creation, Adam takes on the image of his "sire," God (*creatio ex deo*); Eve takes on the image of her "sire," Adam (creation from part of Adam's being). (Both creations are from *substantia*, not from nothing.) God (and later Michael) gives his hand to Adam; Adam gives his hand to Eve. The bliss of Adam and Eve as one being is reaffirmed symbolically when Raphael in Book V greets Eve: "Hail Mother of Mankind whose fruitful Womb / Shall fill the World more numerous with thy Sons / Then with these various fruits the Trees of God / Have heap'd this Table," and the narrative voice continues, "Rais'd of grassie terf / Thir Table was, and mossie seats had round, / And on her ample Square from side to side / All *Autumn* pil'd, though *Spring* and *Autumn* here / Danc'd hand in hand" (V, 388-95).

The symbol of the square with seats encircling it implies the quadrature of Heaven, encircled; this supposed impossibility of squaring the circle is, of course, a symbol of their miraculously idyllic world and contrasts with Sin's false boast later that Satan has divided God's "Quadrature, from thy Orbicular World" (X, 381). The produce of autumn harvested is likened to Eve's numerous sons, begotten in springtime, the inception and the result, as it were, going hand-in-hand—*dancing*. While the image here seems to equate spring and male (rather than Primavera) and autumn and female (rather than Vertumnus), they are in this idyllic world indistinguishable, dancing together, with sexual overtones in the word "danc'd." And indeed the implications of confusions of sex (Adam/Primavera, Eve/Vertumnus) underscores the fusion in generation, since the sons are begotten in spring and born nine months later in autumn.

The image and symbol are prepared for in lines 15-17 of this book as Adam wakens Eve: "Then with voice / Mild, as when *Zephyrus* on *Flora* breathes, / Her soft hand touching whispered thus." As the plot proceeds in Book IX, the motif is iterated as: "from her Husbands hand her hand / Soft she withdrew," and similes of male/female potential seduction ensue: "To *Pales*, or *Pomona* thus adornd, / Likest she seemd, *Pomona* when she fled / *Vertumnus*, or to *Ceres* in her Prime, / Yet Virgin of *Proserpina* from *Jove*" (IX, 385-96). Yet sinless, that is, Eve has set the stage for sexual assault and non-oneness with Adam by withdrawal of her hand.[3] But Adam is also culpable in that he does not maintain a "hand-in-hand" symbolization: he accepts Eve's withdrawal of her hand though he should have desisted. It is not the literal non-hand-in-handness, but the symbolism of their not being together working side by side that allows Satan to perpetrate his fraud. "Hand in hand" and sexuality in *Paradise Lost* should be "considered a symbol for or a sublimation of the more primary human desire for union with God," as Joseph H. Summers has written.[4] A breaking of that image or an aberration of such sexual union is a breach in one's union with God. And so we know that the Fall from God's command is about to occur, a breach in union with Him to fissure all people's lives thereafter. To reinforce these interpretations by contrast, Milton has Adam and Eve next join hands lustfully just after the Fall, when Adam seizes Eve's hand with "amorous intent, well understood / Of *Eve,* whose Eye darted contagious Fire" (IX, 1035-37). They disport themselves in the shade (amorously playing out the swain's rejection of sporting with Amaryllis in "Lycidas"), hidden, furtive, in mutual guilt. And only as they leave Paradise do we see them again truly one as Michael catches their hands so that "They hand in hand with wandring steps and slow, / Through *Eden* [can take] thir solitarie way" (XII, 637, 647-48).

I examine the poetic rendition of Milton's concept of ideal marriage because *Paradise Lost* has so frequently been the source of commentary on Milton's views, particularly on his views of woman, and because this motif does emphasize what I think is of prime importance: the individuality that husband and wife can maintain while one in being—bodily and spiritually.[5] Milton is certainly and emphatically not a misogynist, a term that indicates not only that the user has not read Milton with even a modicum of perception, but that the user does not know the meaning of the word. Milton is not, of course, the twentieth-century person whom one finds in short commodity: the firm believer in total equality of the sexes. Some today would have us believe that all women and some men believe in emotional, sociological, political, religious, vocational, financial equality of and for the sexes, when in truth such persons are surely very few; and all should admit that there is wide range in those matters arising from one's womanness or manness, with their anatomical and endocrinological differences. There are modal possibilities of "female" and "male," but the great cluster of people lies somewhere between, with only tendency toward one or the other mode. Perhaps one problem is that some who vociferate this question substitute "equality" for "equivalency," although "equivalency" is hardly possible because the physical substances are different. Certainly another problem is that stereotyping has led not only to a "male" view of woman but also to a countering feminist attack on that male view by seeing all women (and all men) as the same, which they are not.

In comparison with others of his time Milton was liberal on this issue, arguing for a high degree of position for women. Katherine M. Rogers, while recognizing that a combination of "sensuality and misogyny . . . was not unusual" in the seventeenth century, inaccurately casts Milton as using a "traditional interpretation of Adam's motivation, which gilds his sin with amiable weakness while aggravating Eve's."[6] "Gilds," "amiable weakness," and "aggravating" are invalid concepts here and are calculated to influence the reader to condemn Milton as somehow akin to those who called woman responsible for the Fall and Death and the litany of ills Adam recites in Book X. Adam in his denunciation of Eve becomes, postlapsarian as the time then was, the prototype of those of the human world who vent their antiheroic self-hate on some scapegoat—so often for the male, the female. Much of the writing on this issue adverse to Milton is a result of inadequate reading of Milton's words and of some kind of belief that Milton should have thrown off all the shackles of tradition and myth as we few enlightened ones today have. This latter difficulty is the basis for Virginia Woolf's formulation of "Milton's bogey," which Sandra Gilbert has explored largely in the meaning of Milton's "inferior and Satanically inspired Eve, who has . . . intimidated women and blocked their view of possibilities both real and literary."[7] A study of Woolf's self-hate would have been more apt. Milton is a much studied author and the texts read, whether accurately or inaccurately, have influenced many people. One thinks of the story of the Fall, and though there may be some who will think first and perhaps only of the Bible, a most usual picture is Milton's.

Were such readings as Rogers's and Gilbert's not so deleterious toward an appreciation of Milton, one might simply dismiss, say, Jean-Jacques Rousseau's "Woman was formed to yield to man, and even to bear with his injustice," in his educationally-oriented *Emile*. But such readings of Milton are misreadings and suggest a general ignorance of other authors, influential and not, who are examples of what such readings would make of Milton. Milton is forced to take the brunt of the prejudices that still exist against women, not only in the prejudicial male mind but in some female minds as well. Gilbert is unfortunately correct, however, in pointing out that readers have been influenced by Milton's acceptance of the assumption of male superiority through its subtext in *Paradise Lost*. Perhaps, though, some of the blame in casting *Paradise Lost* in such a dominant influential role should be put on those who misread, who would find like gender-attitudes elsewhere, and who were probably raised with the same unconscionable belief.

Critics like Rogers and Gilbert wrench substance in whatever way they can to castigate Milton: their attack is rhetorical rather than substantive. The language and images employed furnish examples of the colored language of propaganda. Milton has not proceeded to a rejection of such unacceptable notions as man's superiority over woman or as gender-oriented abilities and interests. But neither does he sustain a comment like Gilbert's "Despite Milton's well-known misogyny, however, and the highly developed philosophical tradition in which it can be placed, all these connections, parallels, and doublings among Satan, Eve, and Sin are shadowy messages, embedded in the text of *Paradise Lost,* rather than carefully illuminated overt statements. Still, for sensitive female readers brought up in the bosom of a 'masculinist,' patristic, neo-Manichean church, the latent as well as the manifest content of such a powerful work as *Paradise Lost* was (and is) bruisingly real." She goes on to talk of "the unholy trinity of Satan, Sin, and Eve, diabolically mimicking the holy trinity God, Christ, and Adam." Gilbert has a footnote here that does not negate her illogical understanding of trinity or of Christ or of sex and birthing or of the text she has supposedly read. Her rhetorical statement and lack of knowledge appear in such typical sentences as "Milton, who offers at least *lip service* to the institution of matrimony, is never so *intensely misogynistic* as the *fanatically celibate Essenes*" (374; emphasis added). And so even though much has been written on this matter, before one can set down what seem to be Milton's ideas of marriage and divorce, one must deal with Virginia Woolf's bogey.[8]

The question of Milton's treatment of the Fall has often been inadequately and even inaccurately treated. God the Father, comparing Satan and his cohorts' act with Man's, says, "Man falls deceiv'd / By the other first: Man therefore shall find grace, / The other none" (III, 130-32). The prohibition which will be abrogated by that deception Adam expresses thus:

> for well thou knowst
> God hath pronounc't it death to tast that Tree,
> The only sign of our obedience left
> Among so many signes of power and rule
> Conferrd upon us, . . . Then let us not think hard
> One easie prohibition, who enjoy
> Free leave so large to all things else, and choice
> Unlimited of manifold delights. [IV, 426-35]

The Fall is a two-stage action that does not yet constitute the Fall by the first stage alone. Satan deceives Eve; he does not deceive Adam.[9] "Man" in God's words just quoted emphasizes three things: "Man" does not mean "male being," Eve is included in the generic word "Man," and Eve and Adam are as one in the deception wrought by Satan. It is thus clear that any redemption from the results of that Fall can be possible only through the one first deceived, that is, through woman as represented by Eve. But that Fall will not be fully reversed until a renovation contrary to the action of the second stage is realized. Insufficiently is Milton's amelioration of Eve's "guilt" in her act observed. In Book III Uriel, the Regent in the Sun, is deceived by the hypocrisy that is Satan, by his outward appearance and by his false statements, just as Eve will be in Book IX. If Uriel can be taken in, it is not unlikely that Eve or Adam could be taken in. The second stage is Adam's deliberate and undeceived decision to disobey. Full reversal is possible, therefore, only through display of obedience, initiated through those mythic concepts that "woman" defines. Indeed, Eve is central to the myth and to the poem, and the idea of Eve is central to redemption and to the theme of love.[10]

The description of the first stage is: "So saying, her rash hand in evil hour / Forth reaching to the Fruit, she pluck'd, she eat: / Earth felt the wound, and Nature from her seat / Sighing through all her Works gave signs of woe / That all was lost" (IX, 780-84). We should stress the word (and concept) *hand* in this passage; it is one hand of the "hand-in-hand" motif, separated from the other. The weakness comes not from its being Eve's hand but from its not being the joined oneness of man and woman. The rhyme (eye-rhyme at least, since the word would have been pronounced "et") likewise implies a weakening at this point. Though "all" may be lost—and since part is lost, "all" cannot now be whole—Earth is only wounded and Nature gives only signs. In contrast and also comparison is the description of the second stage:

> So saying . . . from the bough
> She gave him of that fair enticing Fruit
> With liberal hand: he scrupl'd not to eat
> Against his better knowledge, not deceav'd,
> But fondly overcome with Femal charm.
> Earth trembl'd from her entrails, as again
> In pangs, and Nature gave a second groan,
> Skie lowr'd, and muttering Thunder, som sad drops
> Wept at compleating of the mortal Sin
> Original. [IX, 990-1004]

Milton is explicit that original sin is not completed until Adam's action, an action that is mortal by bringing Death (*mors, mortis*) into the world and mortal by connoting future humankind who will inherit that sin.

Eve's hand is now liberal (from *libera*, free): not only does she liberally present much fruit, but her hand is no longer restricted by the prohibition or by the concept of "hand-in-hand." The reference to Eve's liberal hand (singular) is an ironic reminder of Adam's praise of God and discontent with being alone, thus setting up the creation of Eve (the focal point of the poem, as we have noted), in Book VIII:

> how may I
> Adore thee, Author of this Universe,
> And all this good to man, for whose well being
> So amply, and with hands so liberal
> Thou hast provided all things: but with mee
> I see not who partakes. In solitude
> What happiness, who can enjoy alone,
> Or all enjoying, what contentment find? [VIII, 359-66]

God has *liberal hands* (plural), and that word *all* echoes again. Only at the end of time (since the Fall has occurred) will there be "All in All" again. Eve, who has become "like" a god, gives liberally of only one thing, not of "all." Adam's words here, remembered at his fall, ironize that "contentment" which partaking of the fruit will bring.

Milton is also explicit that Adam does not fall deceived by Satan or by Eve; surely his is the true act of disobedience, the subject of the poem, his more grievous action. While Eve is disobedient, she is so through fraud; not so Adam. Further, he acts against "his better knowledge," the action bringing "forbidden knowledge" of carnal desire, intoxication, lasciviousness, burning lust (1008-15). In *The Sacred Complex* William Kerrigan discusses knowledge as food, including "the progressive dilation of nourishment through Books 5-8" in preparation for the Fall, and goes on to point out that the penis is a symbol of hunger.[11] Adam is "fondly," both lovingly and foolishly, overcome by female charm. But we are to remember the frequent reference, iterated just shortly before, that Eve is "Flesh of my Flesh, / Bone of my Bone." Indeed, it is narcissism by which Adam is overcome, a less contemptuous narcissism than that displayed by Satan when he saw Sin,[12] but a more sexual narcissism than that between the Father and the Son whose love begets the Holy Spirit. It can be seen as *projection* in Jungian terms. Eve has succumbed to hunger at noon and symbolically to the signifier phallus, but Adam has succumbed to the signifier phallus through partaking of the fruit, though hunger is not specifically noted. Milton has emphatically not gilded Adam's sin; Adam has emphatically not shown amiable weakness; and most emphatically Eve's sin is not aggravated.

The two-stage Fall corresponds symbolically to the two beasts of Revelation, the account of which Milton had used to introduce Sin and

Death in Book II. Many people have in error talked of the beast in Revelation; rather, Chapter 13 presents a beast rising out of the sea, with seven heads and ten horns, whose name is Blasphemy, and "another beast comming vp out of the earth" with two horns, and its number is 666. This second beast "had power to giue life vnto the Image of the beast, that the Image of the beast should both speake, and cause that as many as would not worship the Image of the beast, should be killed." Milton translated this into Sin and Death (II, 648-73):

> Before the Gates there sat
> On either side a formidable shape;
> The one seem'd Woman to the waste, and fair,
> But ended foul in many a scaly fould
> Voluminous and vast, a Serpent arm'd
> With mortal sting . . .
> Farr less abhorr'd then these [the Hell Hounds]
> Vex'd *Scylla* bathing in the Sea that parts
> *Calabria* from the hoarce *Trinacrian* shore . . .
> Nor uglier follow the Night-Hag, when . . . she comes
> Lur'd with the smell of infant blood, to dance
> With *Lapland* witches, while the labouring Moon
> Eclipses at thir charms. The other shape,
> If shape it might be call'd that shape had none
> Distinguishable in member, joynt, or limb,
> Or substance might be call'd that shadow seem'd,
> For each seem'd either . . .

The first beast and Sin, whose femaleness is underscored by reference to sea and moon as well as the simile involving infants, are in the background of Eve's action and suggest a relationship of woman and sin through sexuality. Sin, like Scylla and Spenser's Error, is attractive and enticing above the waist but ugly in the nether region. (The nonidyllic, nonchaste sexual alliance is meant, not sexual intercourse itself. Both ways of meaning—from the female view as well as from the male view—*should* be meant, but since these myths and images are graphed by men, it is woman who has provided concepts of a nonchaste sexual alliance.) A womb kennelling gnawing, barking dogs proclaims a womb in contrast to the dark abyss from which dovelike creatures may emerge. The myth of woman's beauty that Chambers talks of is its subtext. The partaking of the Tree of Life (as phallic signifier) will beget dovelike creatures, and sex is thus seen as potentially beautiful and productive of good; the partaking of the Tree of Knowledge (also as phallic signifier), on the other hand, will beget only monstrous beasts, and sex is thus seen as potentially lustful, ugly, and productive of evil.[13] The infant blood associated with Sin juxtaposes the inheritance of sin that the Fall will bring, and we note the sexual imagery of "to dance," the "labouring" moon, and the witches' "charms." Adam will be seen as being overcome by female charms, a kind of witchcraft now that the first stage of the Fall has occurred. But in actuality Adam falls enamored of his projection of himself in Eve; the sexual double entendre is intended, for the phallicism of the serpent at Eve's fall suggests another kind of penis envy underlying Adam's fall. (Freud's "penis envy" is female because of Freud's own psychological negativity toward woman; Lacan makes clear that such sexual concept may be male-directed toward the female, as well. We can read the scene as connoting Adam's "penis envy" of the phallic serpent, and his eating of the fruit, which signifies the womb, as peremptory to his continued phallic projection in Eve.)

The second beast and Death, with maleness suggested by the warlike image and the "Kingly Crown," are in the background of Adam's action. Death, "the other shape," is introduced at line 666, and in literal numerological reversal Adam falls at line 999: "But fondly overcome with Femal charm." Adam thus relates to the Great Beast, to Death, to the mortality that his act brings to their progeny, and to detumescence.

The narcissistic undercurrent is highlighted in *Paradise Lost* by Eve's remembrance of her image in the smooth lake. The female imagery of water, cave, expansive plain, and flowers portrays the universal anima, but the image she sees is a projection of her animus. The voice that leads her says it will bring her to him whose image she is and where there is no shadow from flowers. Eve's "vain desire" is indeed the reflection of Adam that she is: seemingly enamored of herself, she is really enamored of what she sees of the shadow within herself. What Milton presents, therefore, is primary narcissism, not in any way a negative concept: it releases the imago (or idealized self, with its various sexual overtones) as identification, freeing the alienating function of the ego, as Freud, Erikson, and Lacan have argued. Satan, of course, is able to determine this as "organ" of her fancy when he visits her, squat like a toad (IV, 799-802). He is close at her ear, a womb symbol emphasizing the underlying sexuality of the full story. But at this point of trying to determine means to build their ruin he is a toad, that is, amphibian, and thus effectual in water (with its implications of the female) and on earth (with implications of the habitat of the second beast); he is indeterminate, that is, of what approach to take. (The question of Satan's real "toadness"— as well as the other creatures he is likened to—has often been raised. Here, rather than seeing implications in the specific form of the image, readers may assign it to only a devolution to lower form. Yet for Milton's writing I think that such uninvolved, nonmetaphoric reading is insuffi-

cient: his images constantly provide layers of meaning.) Playing upon
Eve's femaleness he later, through a false kenosis, will become serpentine, and phallic.

We learn in Book V when Eve tells her dream that when he sat squat
at her ear he learned her predilection to music, beauty, smell, and taste,
and the power that his future remarks on forbidden knowledge and men
as gods will have. The sense of touch is missing, but of course in a dream
touch brings in such reality that a dream may be dispersed. Reality enters, and the dream ends, both through Ithuriel's spear touching Satan
and through Adam's soft touching of her hand (ll. 15-17). The hand-in-
hand motif is again iterated, as is its significance for the rejection of the
Other from their paradisiacal world. The dream is a flying dream, as
well, posing an anxiety on Eve arising from the prohibition and the Tree
of Knowledge (the Tree of Life is not mentioned) of which she and
Adam had talked shortly before they retired. Her transport to "out-
stretcht immense" and then her sinking down suggest the sexual content
of the shadow that has emerged in her dream: the sexuality that has
been latent. Thinking of the signifier Tree of Knowledge (the Other), of
which they have just talked, releases both questions of what the tree is
(what it signifies) and her animus: the "One shap'd and wing'd like one
of those from Heav'n" puts forth a "ventrous Arm" (with its phallic correspondence) to pluck the fruit (with its vaginal overtones), so that Eve
is chilled by damp horror. The sexual import is strong, and it is "more
sweet thus cropt." Satan has determined that she is the weaker of the two
and more likely to succumb to his blandishments. Milton repeatedly indicates that he accepted the theory of female weakness, and this, coupled with the biblical account, leads him to have Satan pursue Eve. But
we should not just stop at this to castigate Milton: he does proceed to
have Adam fall through breaking faith and rejecting reason, through
succumbing to his inner self projected to the female.

Ultimately Milton could not have given rise to any speculation about
what might have happened had Adam not partaken of the fruit,[14] nor
could he have altered the action related in Genesis 3:6: "And when the
woman saw, that the tree was good for food, and that it was pleasant to
the eyes, and a tree to be desired to make one wise, she tooke of the fruit
thereof, and did eate, and gaue also vnto her husband with her, and hee
did eate." But the account Milton presents shifts the blame away from
Eve and makes Adam culpable and more certainly the disobedient one.
Actually, this is another indication of male "superiority": the fate of humankind would not rest on woman alone. For Milton it rests on woman
and man, and man is the more grievous cause; for other men, woman
becomes simply the scapegoat to deflect guilt from man's desire. The

Fall recounted for Eve in the Bible plays only on the senses; in Milton it involves deceit of the mind. For Adam the Fall in the Bible is a rather simple following of Eve; in Milton it is a purposeful act of the mind, undeceived and sensual in terms of self-projection. The sexuality of the myth beneath the legend is observed in the next biblical verse ("And the eyes of them both were opened, & they knew that they were naked, and they sewed figge leaues together, and made themselues aprons"); again Milton, through the contrast of the trees, through the linkage with Sin, and through Adam's ensuing ravishment of a willing Eve, has made both guilty.

The myth of the Fall is an explanation ultimately of the sex act and moral attitudes toward it. It is humankind's simplistic explanation of the human sex drive, the begetting and continuance of life, the morality that grew up around the family unit, and the "privacy" of the sex act and the instruments of that act (female and particularly male genitalia, as seen still in the gender-hypocrisy of today). Milton does not explore the mythic backgrounds, since what he employs basically is the biblical account that he believed was the word of God. But we, if only we would think with the bugbear of religion behind us, can understand the archetypal meanings of fruit with its female associations, of tree with its phallic form, and of fall, particularly when contrasted with the first view we have had of the pair: "Two of far nobler shape [Sin and Death are also introduced as shapes, remember] *erect* and *tall*, / Godlike *erect*" (italics added). The Fall is the formerly erect couple—literally as well as metaphorically—now reclining in sexual intercourse.[15] And despite many other positional possibilities, it is generally the man who is "superior," the second usually to be in prepared position, the one who most often acts upon the receptive, supine woman.[16] Since sexual desire is so patently fundamental to human beings and so often the cause of matters sociologically disruptive, sinfulness for the sex act must have been attached very early in time to the moral system of monogamous people. The repression of the pleasure principle is, certainly, a common means of nullifying imported guilt. The relationship of hunger and desire, of eating and sex, did not need Freud to codify it, either.

"From what arises the Godhead's ways toward us?" early people must have asked, having developed some sense of a supernatural force (or forces) to make what existed around them cogent. The answer has to lie somewhere in action not pleasing to that god, a breach of promise or of covenant or of command. For Milton and others, sin is ἀνομία or the breaking of the law,[17] and the Law of God for those in the Judaeo-Christian world means the Ten Commandments. Thus the thrust of the legend of the Fall in the Bible, when sin entered humankind's world, shifts to Moses and the Exodus, which has been argued as the central occurrence of Hebraic history, the Adam and Eve story furnishing but a meaningful prelude to the Exodus.[18] Exodus is thus likened to the Expulsion, the dissolute life of some Israelites in Pharaoh's ("Satan's") land likened to the sin of Adam and Eve. I have previously pointed out the realistic source of the mythic exodus: that is, birth from the secure world of the womb to the unknown vast world outside.[19] The expulsion from the secure world of Eden, itself a *hortus conclusus*, at the end of *Paradise Lost* is likewise such "birth," such a mythic exodus. The last line of the poem—"Through *Eden* took thir solitarie way"—is drawn from the passover Psalm 107:4. The Ten Commandments expand the basic prohibition, a logical development in a later, peopled world. But for a world populated by two, a command dealing with a relationship between those two can offer the only "law" through the breaking of which sin could enter.[20]

The law for Adam and Eve takes the form of prohibition, but importantly that prohibition denies one action (partaking of the Tree of Knowledge) while it condones another (partaking of the Tree of Life) in respects outwardly the same. The prohibition is not generic; it allegorizes the way in which an action, or thought, or set of elements can be good or evil depending upon conditions and mainly upon intent. The subdivisions of sin, Milton writes (*CD* I, xi), "are evil desire, or the will to do evil, and the evil deed itself" (YP, VI, 388). The deed itself is not evil until by wilfulness it is done. Sin "usually exists in some action. For every action is intrinsically good; it is only its misdirection or deviation from the set course of law which can properly be called evil. So action is not the material out of which sin is made, but only the 'μποκειμενον, the essence or element in which it exists" (YP, VI, 391).

The projection of the Father (as animus) into the Son (as a congeries of the anima) and its reversal is good, for it involves love; that of Satan into Sin is evil, for it involves lust. The projection of Adam into Eve lies between as it were, until his act of disobedience. The dilemma is not dissimilar to what the Son faces on the pinnacle in *Paradise Regain'd:* if he jumps to prove God's word, he will be succumbing to Satan's lure; if he stands, he is sure to fall and face death. But he stands in faith that the word of God will come to pass, and it does. Adam's dilemma is that if he eats of the fruit, he will be breaking union with God and indirectly will be succumbing to Satan's lure; if he does not eat, he can contemplate only loss of Eve (loss, that is, of his projection of self). The answer theoretically should have been to maintain faith in God (as did the Israelites in the Exodus, celebrated in Milton's very early paraphrase of Psalm 114) and see what would have happened, what miracle God would have wrought. Milton could not, of course, have written such action into his poem since she "gaue vnto her husband with her, and hee did eate," but for a believer God's omnipotence and good will could have devised some atonement and cleansing for Eve alone, or caused her to be replaced by some other helpmeet.[21] The temptation presented to Adam as a second stage recalls the second stage of temptation experienced by Abdiel, who, let it be remembered, did allow himself to be put into a corruptive position. The emphasis is again upon Adam, not Eve, and it is not her "sin" that is aggravated. Eve falls to the lures of Satan associated with *concupiscentia carnis* and *concupiscentia ocularum;* Adam falls to the lure of *superbia vitæ,* seen as a false pride in self.

What is repeatedly forgotten is that the Bible was written out of a Hebraic society, one group of which still today exalts the male and puts the female into an inferior position.[22] It is manifest that the society depicted in the Pentateuch would reflect this attitude of man's superiority over the woman and as head and master of the household. Societal beliefs, which are not restricted to the Hebraic community, cast woman as helpmeet, as mother and family center, and as commodity for man's wishes, sexual commodity being the most ubiquitous one. Societal beliefs stress woman as agent in bearing children but the male as effecting creation, the overtones of lord and master being clear. The "creation" of the Son/Jesus is an obvious case in point on the divine scale. In *Paradise Lost* Milton, in comparison to others of his time, has Eve assume a much more important role in both the redemption and the means to reversal, and that means to reversal particularly involves the principle of the anima.[23]

That *Paradise Lost* is built on dialectic is widely acknowledged. One of those sets of opposites is man/woman. Through Jung's concepts of the animus/anima we see the projection (or narcissism) of Adam's anima into Eve, that which compensates the masculine consciousness.[24] The compensatory figure for Eve is the animus. "An inferior consciousness cannot . . . be ascribed to women; it is merely different from masculine consciousness";[25] thus each has areas of nondifferentiation of the unconscious and neither can identify with an autonomous complex. Rather "The essence of the inferior function is autonomy" (68). Thus viewed, Eve's action to withdraw her hand asserts a compensatory figure, since her usual action has been to follow, not to assert at all. Adam's action to taste of the fruit asserts his compensating anima by following, by being influenced in his act not by reason but by feeling.[26] The question that animus/anima raises is, of course, the question of the differentiation of gender (and thus the opposite, nondifferentiated areas of gender) *but not with any sense of superiority or inferiority attached to either.* The sense of superiority or inferiority attached to gender is a product of a society, not something inherent in the sex, but that does not mean one should not acknowledge the differentiation that sexually different physicality and chemical structures create. (As stated before, however, such differentiations will show a range with either sex.) Most sense of superiority or inferiority, being societal rather than engendered, will depend on which elements of differentiation are deemed more worthwhile by a society.

For Jung, a representative here of society and a male, the anima produces *moods;* the animus, *opinions* (218); but both will be projected. The opposition is one largely of body and mind (or soul), suggesting for a male-oriented society the power of the brain over the heart, physical unemotionalism over emotion, strength over beauty, and even justice over mercy. The casting of Apollo as Sun and Diana as Moon, the Delian twins, was an easy assignment for the ancient Greeks, but both are needed to create the wholeness of life. The attributes of each of these gods/heavenly bodies were metaphorized into male and female characteristics by simple equations. Again life's realities and observations etched such differentiations into people's thinking, though usually, if not always, wrongly. The woman was sexual vessel, somewhat incapacitated in pregnancy and with birth and motherhood, thus central figure in the home, and source of love, mercifulness, retreat from outside harshness—that is, a kind of Edenic, safe, life-sustaining womb for children and husband as well. The man was actor in sexual life, not incapacitated by potential birth and therefore one not confined, rather one perhaps absent from the home, one who could and had to maintain livelihood for the family unit, but one too who would have to act in ways involving "justice" or correction, punishment, and the like. The false differentiations, say, in emotional values or in labor that such a former economic (thence political) state of affairs spawned is sociologically out-of-date, of course. With medical changes affecting sex, pregnancy, birth, and motherhood, and with the revisions of domestic life and the outside world of labor, we have come to a sharply different status between man and woman.

The projection of the animus in Eve as she eats of the tree brings that inside world outside into the open, making the inferior function now autonomous; the same occurs with Adam. Eve has been deceived in her thinking by Satan's falsehood and specious logic; what emerges is a projection of the animus in its male characteristic of the mind: she exercises thought without feeling. Adam has been deceived by the projection of the anima in its female characteristic of the heart after his own inadequate logic, based on incomplete knowledge, misleads him. He exercises feeling without full thought. The ironic falseness of IV, 297—

98, is well demonstrated though critically unrecognized. In both cases what has basically been suppressed up to this point has emerged. What occurs in Book X is Adam's overt unleashing of the shadow within and Eve's clear reasoning as her now shadow identification takes over. Adam's loving apostrophe of Eve in VIII, 546-59, stresses her outward beauty but also finds that "All higher knowledge in her presence falls / Degraded . . . Authority and Reason on her wait." Raphael's consternation at this breaking through of the anima foreshadows the second stage of the Fall. His emphasis on the profit of "self-esteem, grounded on just and right / Well manag'd" (572-73) operates on the belief in the superiority of reason and the superiority of the man, but it also plays with the transference that the emergence of the shadow creates. The ego comes to envy the nonego, and the self is rejected in favor of a darker side of one's personality that sees that darker side outside one's conscious. Raphael's further admonition tries to separate mere animal propagation from the true love possible for the soul of Man, and of course it is the man's fall into carnal pleasure that is depicted when fondly overcome he eats of the fruit, archetype of sexuality, and to be detailed in Adam and Eve's ensuing coupling. For Milton the significance would be that in this lustfulness the pair have become only one flesh, not also one heart and one soul (VIII, 499). (Copulation should set up an equals sign: we know that it often does not.)

Early on, at least, Milton accepts the concept in prose and poetry that man is superior and woman inferior in terms of reason, which is superior to emotion. For him Adam is an image of God, who is Wisdom, Purity, Justice, Ruler (see *Tetrachordon*, 2); "Woman is not primarily and immediately the image of God, but in reference to the man" (*Tetrachordon* 3, and compare 1 Corinthians 11 and Colossians 3:18). But she is not in any way a servant. She may, of course, be more prudent and/or dexterous, and so through natural law should govern (*Tetrachordon*, 2). But he does believe in Scripture, which told him that "from her the sin first proceeded, which keeps her justly in the same proportion still beneath" (3). The fact that the Bible appears to contradict itself according to its composite strata of accounts poses a difficulty. One report in which God is called Elohim appears in Genesis 1; it has its own inherent discrepancies. God says, "Let vs make *man* in *our* Image, after *our* likeness: and let *them* haue dominion ouer the fish of the sea,. . . . So God created *man* in *his* owne Image, in the Image of God created *hee him; male* and *female* created *hee them.* And God blessed *them,* and God said vnto *them,* Be fruitful, and multiply, and replenish the earth, and subdue it, and have dominion ouer the fish of the sea, [etc.]" (Genesis 1:26-28; italics added). This account is given by Raphael in *Paradise Lost* VII, 519-34.

In Genesis 2, however, where God is called Yahweh we read first an account of the formation of man from the dust of the ground, and man becomes "a liuing soule" (Genesis 2:6-7). We perhaps should know that the name Adam given later to this living soul comes from the Aramaic word for *red*, which was transferred to the kind of soil in the Fertile Crescent area, *red earth*, and thus *Adam*, formed from that red earth; the land of Edom has the same etymological derivation. In verses 18-24, we are told that God thought it not good that man should be alone and so he created a helpmeet for him. "And Adam said, This is now bone of my bones, and flesh of my flesh: she shalbe called woman, because shee was taken out of man. Therefore shall a man leaue his father and his mother, and shall cleaue vnto his wife: and they shalbe one flesh." Most of this account is related by Adam in VIII, 437-99. Two points are significant: This account by Adam drawn from Genesis 2 emphasizes *his* initiation of the female creation, *his* relationship with Eve, *his* perception of *his* importance and the lesser status of Eve because he precedes in creation and she derives from him. But further, this underscores that the account in Genesis 2 precedes in time the Priestly version in Genesis 1, since this male-oriented "earlier" account is seen as a correction to a more factual and reasonable account. Yet the more probable cause is that the account in Genesis 2 represents an attempt from a male-dominated and dominating society to make specific the relationships as they came to know them between the sexes and, with supposed magnanimity, to include that group of humans insufficiently denominated in the first account. Genesis 2, in other words, should be looked upon, even by believers in God's transmission of the "truth" recorded in Genesis 1, as a *man*-made account, a "fiction," if you will. How Adam can know father and mother as concepts is not explained: it indicates the social source out of which biblical accounts came to try to explain the inexplicable of the past. Such biblical accounts indicate their source in observable experience, illogical though that account may be, and here, since the man initiates birth through ejaculation, it is man who precedes woman (in addition to the significance of the male-oriented world out of which the account comes). Man is the actor, woman the receiver.

Edward Tayler has dealt with these two biblical accounts of creation, recognizing that one need not push beyond Lévi-Strauss's point that all myths formulate contraries and attempt to mediate the extremes.[27] But Rogers takes Milton to task in his remarks in *Tetrachordon* for deliberately suppressing the significance of the first account and arguing for man's precedency from Pauline restatements of the second. Not only is the first account subject to evaluation as a generalized statement that even has its own contradictions, but it seems strange to me that anyone today except the most extreme fundamentalist would not see that any of these accounts were formulated to explain what is still not fully understood: the generation of "living" matter and the differentiation of sexes for the continuance of species. (And see Chapter 13 for further discussion of the remarks in the 1645 *Tetrachordon* against the underlying concepts of the 1665 *Paradise Lost*.) The specter of religion and of the Bible is the foundation of this kind of feminist criticism. Because the Bible came out of a male-dominated society it should be clear why man is created first and given superior position, and even why God is male and why a holy trinity likened to a family finally came into religious thought as Christianity was being organized, after the spread of mystic ideas from Pythagoras and Philo Judaeus.

The helpmeet effects an amiable knot: "in matrimony there must be first a mutuall help to piety, next to civill fellowship of love and amity, then to generation, so to houshold affairs, lastly the remedy of incontinence" (*Tetrachordon*, 10). We should remember, though, that Milton is setting things up to embolden his reasons for divorce; generation, of necessity, is pushed out of prime position. A couple of pages later, in fact, he writes, "Thus we see how treatably and distinctly God hath heer taught us what the prime ends of marriage are, mutuall solace and help" (12). He does talk of the lawfulness of the marriage bed, and therefore, though unstated, he implies that generation does not need marriage, as indeed it does not. Marriage for Milton involved covenant, which we have looked at in Chapter 8. Covenant demands mutuality, it never involves command or prohibition, and it allows either party the right to reject it when the other party has abrogated any of its principles. Milton's view of marriage was idealistic, to say the least; it must be a marriage of true minds, as noted before, and must involve the opposites of love and obedience, freedom and responsibility, reason and conscience so that they are not opposites. These opposites all exist for the woman as well as the man: it is fully reciprocal. "Thus, while showing an acceptance of the belief that man is superior and woman inferior, Milton sees a more idyllic state in their being one and a potential balance between them that serves to elevate woman's position from what was and is commonplace."[28] As Diane McColley has pointed out, one should stress Eve's creation "for God in him," not "for him."

It is logical that Milton's view of marriage should lead to certain views of divorce. He had, according to his own testimony, been studying the issue of divorce before he wrote in 1643, and entries in the Commonplace Book, while not certainly dated, bear that out. It has also often been pointed out—although to the unhearing, at times—that Milton nowhere urges divorce because of desertion, a cause that might have occurred to him if Mary Powell Milton's absence from their home from around July 1642 through summer 1645 had preceded his interest in divorce and if he construed her absence as desertion. (Compare Chapter 11.) The main argument for divorce is the incompatibility of the couple; while the husband is looked upon as head of the family, the wife is also to be granted a divorce when such just cause exists. A much repeated phrase epitomizing divorce from *The Doctrine and Discipline of Divorce* (1644, 7) extends to both sexes, "with one gentle stroking to wipe away ten thousand teares out of the life of man." Milton's comment in Chapter XV of the 1644 second edition (60) does not argue against divorce for the wife to achieve help in the case of potential cruelty of person or livelihood, as it sometimes seems to be interpreted; he believes that relief should also be extended to the husband. Are the problems of alimony or child-custody for the husband much different today? He says and undoubtedly believes, however, that woman was created for man, and not man for woman; yet much of this passage is a strategy to persuade his readers—ostensibly the male Parliament of England with its male Assembly—to condone his concept of divorce. And since Milton thought of marriage as a union not of body only but of soul, he is not particularly exercised by adultery, which he takes to be only bodily. Rather, where there is not love, "there can be left of wedlock nothing, but the empty husk of an outside matrimony" (*DDD*, 1644, 15). He thus rejected *divortum a mensa et thoro* as mere separation, as well as *divortum a vinculo matrimonii*.

There would seem to be some alteration in Milton's views on divorce over the years, except that one must remember that the early tracts, particularly after the first (1643) edition of *The Doctrine and Discipline of Divorce*, were *orationes* taking a side that was unpopular and attempting to confute vituperous and slanderous charges that had been hurled against him and his arguments. At first he seems to derive argument from Mosaic law, backed up by the Gospels and Paul; he then moves away from reliance on Mosaic law, and some of this may be due to his developing ideas about covenant in the mid- and later 1640s (see Chapter 8). With his stronger break with church discipline and the emergence of his own religious precept from around 1658 on (see Chapter 15), the reliance is upon the Christian law of the New Testament, not the restrictiveness of the Mosaic books; upon grace, much less upon the Law.

We may trace an awakening of Milton to marriage in the later 1630s and early 1640s, when in the letter to an unknown friend (1637?) he spoke of those hopes and desires for house and family, and when he himself set up a domicile for his nephews. The concern of divorce may not have been far behind. His marriage and familial disruption in 1642 undoubtedly focussed attention on marriage and divorce, and even *Paradise Lost,* begun in manuscript around 1640 (there are lines in completed Book IV that had been in existence in 1642), may have had a relationship with that topic. But the Milton of the later years seems on this issue to be a mixture of the traditional male/husband and the idealist viewing liberty and grace as all people's prerogative regardless of gender.

The following chapter will explore the interference of the self on two levels: the relationships of Milton with his wives and daughters, as well, therefore, as his attitudes toward divorce; and his "diversion" from poetic aims to the mundane world of debate and government.

13

Further Interferences of the Self

Some of the manifestations of the self that Milton exhibits in the years between 1641 and 1660 are the aims of correcting conceived wrongs or wrong thinking, repression of hopes and desires, and the idealism that one can create a lasting political and social world that will only reflect change, not be changed. These are manifestations of a mother-fixation, as Chapter 11 has outlined it. Corrections of conceived wrongs or wrong thinking emerge, as numerous biographical and critical examinations of this period attest, first in the antiprelatical tracts (1641-42), which attack church administration rather than religion itself. The rejection of inter-mediaries between the individual and the godhead receives substance from oedipal relationships, urging, I would suggest, a real *imitatio Christi* of the inner being rather than the outward show that might be assigned to conformity with the church as sustained by prelaty. Milton, always the slow one, bright and able though he was, probably did not understand this from the thesis he advanced. It was perhaps not until *The Tenure of Kings and Magistrates* that he came to recognize the needed individua-tion for the establishment of the kind of being he saw as worthy, here in the realm of the governmental. The unstated philosophical principle of that tract is the development of a proper regard for self in each hu-man, which in turn will lead to a proper regard for each human for ev-ery other.[1]

The transference of such a political concept to the religious realm was to emerge in *Paradise Lost* with the "Paradise within" and to be re-stated in direct and unavoidable terms by the *imitatio Christi* theme of *Paradise Regain'd.* Here in 1649 Milton probably was realizing where thought had taken him for the great epic he hoped to create and was beginning to equate his achievements in prose with those intentions. *Eikonoklastes* and *Defensio prima* can be read to imply as much, and *Defen-sio secunda* (1654) evidences the acceptance of the thought, as Tillyard argued. But in 1649 through 1660, though not without periods of relaxation from other driving forces, *Paradise Lost* was also interfered with by other, more immediate concerns of a less religious, philosophic, and universal nature, and what became *Paradise Regain'd,* though it may have been begun in the late 1640s, was left inchoate for two more decades until other items in that mental agenda that Parker remarked (see Chapter 4) had been ticked off. It should be stressed, however, that during the 1640s when domestic and public concerns diverted full attention from Milton's great purpose, and during the 1650s when governmental activities were added to these interferences, Milton still continued to work sporadically on his poetry and on other, unprovoked prose.

Milton's concern with divorce began, as his notes in his Commonplace Book show, before his marriage to Mary Powell. That the first published argument for divorce in 1643 came at least partially as a result of his own experience in marriage and its upsetments, however, seems highly probable. While he does not consider desertion in the four tracts (five if one wants to consider the second edition of *The Doctrine and Discipline of Divorce* in 1644 a "new" book: it doubles the length of the first edition), the issues of man/woman as unified couple and the seeming incompatibility of Milton and Mary on mental and cultural levels may have set him to thinking more fully about the topic and may have fostered his basic reasons for nullification of a marriage. In his own situation there was clearly incompatibility of interests, intellect, education, age, religious persuasion, and political attitudes in as far as Mary may have reflected those matters from her father and mother. She was but a seventeen-year-old when in May (?) 1642 she and Milton married. She was thrust into a household with a thirty-three year old husband and two youthful charges, Edward and John Phillips, who were then almost twelve and eleven. Since a five and six years' difference can seem much more at that age, the plight of the young girl must have been overwhelming, even in those days when the husband was considered "master" and the wife often little more than housekeeper. These problems have often enough been cited as cause for the separation, with justification, along with reminders of the compulsive/anal personality that Milton appears to have been.

But usually circumvented are the sexual relationships that this union encountered. One partner was a thirty-three-year-old virgin, who had experienced homoerotic tendencies by all accounts, whose life and works up to that time exhibit sexual repression, and who in human relationships, as well as everything else, was dominated by idealism (not only that of the thinker but that of the anally driven[2]), and the other, a seventeen-year-old virgin. We can readily recognize the seeds of sexual disaster. The physicality of their love-making may surely have been inept, hesitant, infrequent, and guilt-related, and not only in the first weeks of that marriage, which seems to have lasted only about two months at first. May not the sexual repression we find in Milton's life be a part of the reason for saying in *Tetrachordon:* "We may conclude therfore seeing orthodoxall Expositers confesse to our hands, that by lonelines is not only meant the want of copulation, and that man is not lesse alone by turning in a body to him, unless there be within it a minde answerable, that it is a work more worthy the care and consultation of God to provide for the worthiest part of man which is his minde, and not unnaturally to set it beneath the formalities and respects of the body, to make it a servant of its owne vassall."[3]

Jung tells us that "Only the overcoming of the obstacles of reality brings the deliverance from the mother, who is the continuous and inexhaustible source of life for the creator, but death for the cowardly, timid and sluggish."[4] I suggest that Milton may have begun this process in the later 1640s with the return of Mary and the thought reflected in such prose works as *The Tenure of Kings and Magistrates*, but that he did not really achieve this stage described by Jung until the mid-1650s, after the death of his wife and the advent of his blindness. The difficult years of 1652-53 had their outward causes in death and blindness, but they may also have been the cost of having to face reality (the abrupt transition to the Protectorate in 1653 was another reality placing limits on the ideal) and being unprepared to do so. Full arrival at this stage, however, may not have been reached for a couple of years when he came to accept standing and waiting and the need not always to be doing (as Sonnets 19, 20, and 21, all written in 1655,[5] show). Now only was he able to accept the death of his second wife and their child, the coming dissolution of a government in which he had put so much hope, and the new future as creativity again took over, ego still maintained: "Now that my toil has won the richest rewards I had hoped for in this life, I do delight in them with all thankfulness, but at the same time I am earnestly seeking how best I may show not only my own country, to which I devoted all I have, but men of every land and, particularly, all Christian men, that for their sake I am at this time hoping and planning still greater things, if these be possible for me, as with God's help they will."[6]

His first marriage seems to have been arranged through the fathers, a not uncommon circumstance. It has been suggested that Milton went to Forest Hill, Oxfordshire, to collect payment on a loan by John Milton, Sr., to Richard Powell, who was repeatedly to default, but there he met and married Mary. His nephew Edward Phillips seems to have had no inkling that this was going to occur, and there is no hint of evidence that anyone from Milton's family attended. His brother Christopher and his family and their father were living in St. Laurence parish, Reading,[7] a good enough distance away. We cannot see Milton psychologically falling in love "at first sight," wooing and winning Mary, and coming to a definite decision of such a major and expectedly continued consequence, on the spur of the moment, as would seem to underlie modern critics' unstated view. An arranged marriage with some financial conditions seems a more likely answer. After all, Milton in May 1642 not only had a "family" to take care of—his two nephews—but he was in a kind of career change in that the antiprelatical tracts had been offered to the deaf ears of the public without future career hopes (*Apology* had appeared in April) and he now returned apparently to work on his major bid to fame, the great religious poem or drama, a passage of which (IV, 32-41) was written at this time.

On the part of the woman, an arranged marriage is another means of placing her as inferior, a mere instrument of the man who acquires sexual relief and a housekeeper who does not have to be paid, all in one. Milton does not present that kind of picture of himself in anything he wrote or did, although he accepted *in general* the biblical concept—both Mosaic and Pauline—that man is the superior. But looked at from Mary's seventeen-year-old point of view, this marriage offered nothing of the romantic or of the co-partner, and sexually it may have been most ungratifying. All external indicators would deny her independence if she indeed were able to assert herself ideologically and psychologically. All internal indicators that one can infer from the nonexistence of real evidence deny that she would, at this time, have been able to assert herself ideologically or psychologically. Further, the sexual therapy industry of recent times attests the importance of physical and psychological sexual compatibility for a happy married state, as well as marriage failures at least ostensibly caused by the lack of such compatibility.

The *Spaltung* available to Mary, to use Jacques Lacan's word, may simply not have been articulated to her understanding: the term means that division of being revealed between the self (as innermost part of the psyche) and conscious discourse (as seen in behavior and culture). We see no individuation here, for the symbolic order of assertion, opposition, and self-discovery necessary for being more than object seems totally absent from Mary's being except for her removal of herself from this married world and return to a *locus parentis* situation. Though this act can be construed as assertion and opposition, it delays self-discovery, and actually rejects self-assertion by return to an unalienated state. (Alienation in this psychological sense means the giving up of part of oneself to another person.) Alienation of the ego, Lacan argued, always has as corollary a sacrifice that involves truth about oneself. Mary's return to Forest Hill would have arrested individuation and may have been prompted psychologically by the father-surrogate circumstance that her husband would have presented for her. She had not progressed to a third stage of transference by which identification with the mother is possible.[8] This concept is dependent upon acceptance of the usual belief that Mary's continued stay at her parents' home was not the result of a visit that for whatever reasons persisted for three years. It does not seem logical that three years' time would have elapsed, despite parental and/or military pressures, had Mary not, at least initially, desired such separation.

Three years later she returned, but not to Milton's home in Aldersgate Street, from which she had left, now a woman of twenty years. Her husband was thirty-six and the Phillips boys were fifteen and fourteen. In the meantime her father-in-law had joined the household in April 1643, an old and ill man of about eighty-two years in 1645. Soon thereafter the family moved to larger quarters on Barbican, for apparently Mary had stayed with Milton's brother's mother-in-law, Mrs. Webber, in St. Clement's Churchyard, a good walking distance away, in the months between her return and the residential move. (Perhaps the reconciliation took place in July; the move, in September or October.) Within the year, perhaps in late June 1646, Milton's in-laws, the Powells and at least five children, were also residing at Barbican.[9] Mary and John's first child, Anne, was born in July 1646. Milton's father-in-law died before the end of the year; his father, in March 1647. His nephew Edward Phillips seems to have left the household in 1646, and the remaining Powells sometime in mid-1647. The son, Richard Powell, went abroad in March 1647, the widow, Anne, and presumably the other children were in Wheatley, Oxfordshire, by August 1647, and Milton moved to smaller quarters in High Holborn around August 1647. Mary's apparent nonresidence in Milton's home during those intervening months may only indicate that we do not have full or accurate evidence, or it may be explained by the smaller home and four people residing there with day-students also underfoot (a curious situation for husband and wife if true), or it may suggest that the reconciliation was less immediate and complete than romantic versions of it would lead one to believe.

Partially Mary's continued residence at her parents' home in Forest Hill, Oxfordshire, from mid-1642 through mid-1645 may have been due to the first Civil War, which caused Charles I's stronghold in Oxford to be under siege and fairly isolated from commerce with London. There must, at least eventually, have been communication by around mid-summer 1645, for Milton's relatives from his mother's side, William and Hester Blackborough, who resided in St. Anne's and St. Agnes's Parish, Aldersgate, or on St. Martin's-le-Grand (St. Martin's-le-Grand is a continuation of Aldersgate Street, and both are near where Milton was then residing), effected a reconciliation in their home. The romantic view that Milton was not party to the reconciliation before it occurred is unwarranted extrapolation, not too different in kind from the love-at-first-sight interpretation of their first meeting. Whether or not there had been overtures of reconciliation during the preceding three years on the part of either Mary or John or both, it is clear that a *reconciliation*—not simply a meeting—was necessary after so long a time. The blaming of Mary's mother for the separation is founded on statements in Edward Phillips's, John Aubrey's, and the Anonymous Biographer's accounts, all of which may be true but all of which may reflect, as well, male attitudes toward mothers-in-law and toward a wife's culpability whenever disruption in a marriage occurs. Certainly the "frowardness" that the Anonymous Biographer cites is insufficient to sustain its cause (her mother's inciting); the hindsight of Aubrey's saying she went to her mother without Milton's consent is unfounded speculation (and note that the husband must give consent!); and Phillips's having Milton surprised at the Blackboroughs' home and Mary's "making submission and begging pardon on her knees before him" makes for a good dramatic scene or novel.[10]

Mary's return to her parents' home should need nothing more than these facts for explanation to those experienced in the possible vagaries of early married life: a young, inexperienced woman, in charge of a previously-ordered male household and with instant family only somewhat younger than she, and with a husband almost twice as old as she, whose world of the mind and the past was so totally different, whose routines were set (particularly so for a compulsive type), and, most telling of all, who gives every indication of having experienced sexual repression, of being inexperienced sexually, and of both exalting sexual intercourse above the bodily only and thereby subconsciously relegating sex to a lesser position than the state of marriage itself.[11] The psychologically frightened young bride is not uncommon, and the role of housekeeper only would hold little interest for a young woman of seventeen. In addition one should probably consider the psychological effect of viewing Milton as a father-surrogate.[12] That Mary's mother abetted her separation is certainly a strong possibility, and the Civil War situation may have contributed in succeeding months to difficulties in communication and travel. In any case, after a few months of separation it would have been increasingly difficult to effect a reconciliation, and only a truly concerted effort by relatives and friends would have been able to alter the situation, except with the most dogged aggressiveness from either partner. Neither Mary nor John seems that kind of partner, and John's understandable aggrievement that *he* had been deserted may have been a strong deterrent to any action on his part. At the same time Mary would have been experiencing a maturation—mental, emotional, and bodily—and the avenue of divorce, even annulment, would not have been considered by the Roman Catholic Powells.

On the part of the man, an arranged marriage asserts male domination and sees the wife not as a helpmeet in Milton's sense in his divorce tracts but as a sexual object, a mother of his legitimate children, and a servant. This does not represent Milton's attitude, it is clear from any and all of his remarks in the divorce tracts, despite an acceptance of subordinationism in such social affairs, one not different from that in theological belief. But we must speculate as to why he partook of this first marriage (whether arranged or not) to begin with. In the Letter to an Unknown Friend in the Trinity MS is the key, I believe: there, perhaps in 1637, he posits what must have been his own feelings, not only an observation. "Or if it be to be thought an naturall [*inclination in me*] <pronenesse> there is <against y^t> a much more [*potent inbred affection*] potent <&> inbred <inclination> wch about this tyme of a mans life sollicits most, the desire of house & family of his owne, [w^{ch} *would soone over master the other*] to wch nothing is <esteemed> more helpfull then the early entring into credible employment, & nothing more hindering then this affected solitariness."[13] The lack of citation of a wife specifically, the clearly unromantic content of this "desire of house & family of his owne," and the personal concern with "affected solitariness," the loneliness so prominent in the divorce tracts[14] (and that word "affected" documents repression), all delineate one who wanted to be married more than wanted to marry, one who wanted the stabilizing elements of house and family in a man's life as well as a traditional and societally moral existence rather than primarily a sexual partner.

The definition of masculinity has been seen through the separation from the mother, and such individuation is inevitably a tragic process because it involves a sacrifice of ego. Males, it is said, initially seek to become autonomous, with relationship being subordinate to achievement. For one with homoerotic tendencies, like Milton, the alteration which the death of his mother would have effected had twofold significance. First, it created "alienation," by which is meant a giving up of part of oneself to achieve an identification with the father (which action we have observed in "Ad Patrem" and remarks on subordinationism), and to receive, as alienated man living outside himself, the gaze of others

upon him. These "gazes" involved the reactions to *A Mask,* his reception
in Italy (which became such a focal point for his assertion of ego in the
Second Defense), and the antagonists to his antiprelatical tracts and especially his divorce tracts (and the drawing inward which those gazes then
caused).[15] Second, it led to an awareness of his own death (as in "Lycidas") and its consummation in an asserting of himself in the social and
cultural world surrounding. The ego that emerged mirrors the dialectic
of the narcissistic identifications we have observed in Chapter 1, in-
verted. But part of the sacrificed truth for Milton lay in sexual orientation and assertion, not to be fully "alienated" until recognition when the
death of Diodati moved Milton's "double" more obviously into shadow.[16]
The remarks in the Letter to an Unknown Friend prelude the conscious
awareness of an identified sex role,[17] emboldened by surrogate parent-
hood, and finally a few years later Milton acted to assure that sex role
through his "arranged," "unromantic," and seemingly abrupt marriage.
The ego, subordinate to the self, being the center of will and identity,
constructed a persona for others' view, to protect privacy and to conceal
its shadow. The human being, as Lacan saw it, is the effect of the signifier, not its cause.

Milton's concepts of woman should be read against various studies that
have been brought forth by our contemporary attention to woman's position in patriarchal society over the years, particularly that from biblical
sources and that delineating Renaissance attitudes.[18] Maclean (66)
makes the important statement, "The earliest debates about trial marriage, divorce, and the abolition of the institution in a Christian context
of which I know are to be found in John Milton and in the conversations
of *précieuse* women as recorded by Michel de Pure in the 1650s." Important also for Milton's interrelating of Eve and Mary ("the second Eve")
and the protoevangelium announced to Eve and executed through
Mary is James Hillman's analysis of four grades of *anima* whereby Mary
spiritualizes Eve and Sophia spiritualizes Helen.[19] One way of looking at
the latter half of this paradigm is to see Adam's enamoring of his Helen
transcending into the true sapience that Eve exhibits as Sophia (in stark
comparison to her first words upon partaking of the fruit, IX, 795-97,
and Adam's ironic and sardonic lines just after *his* Fall, IX, 1017-18)
when she leads the repentance in Book X and completes the drama of
the full poem with the words "By mee the Promised Seed shall all restore," XII, 623. The seed results from the enamoring of each to the
Other, but it has transcended the merely physical and moves into pur-
posefulness and ideality.

Amid the protests and arguments against certain aspects of patriarchy by such writers as Judith Drake and Mary Astell,[20] we find the male reactions of someone like William Fleetwood.[21] Some of his words reflect ideas in Milton's divorce tracts, and he seems aware of the epic and its usual reading of Eve. He has not progressed, however, to the thinking of *Paradise Lost* that I examined in Chapter 12:

The Scripture does, in a great many places, lay most express Commands on Wives, to live in subjection to their Husbands; but I choose, in treating of this Duty, to speak to this passage in St. *Peter,* because it contains not only the *Command,* but one of the good *effects* of such *Submission,* which is a great encouragement to the fulfilling it; for when a Law carries its reason with it, it is more likely to find a good acceptance and compliance, especially with quick and disputing People, when it comes, arm'd only with its own authority and power [166]. . . . It is impossible for any company of People to subsist any while together, without a Subordination of one to the other. Where all will command, none will obey, and then there will be nothing done, but mischief [167]. . . . Though there be many Women superior to many Men, in strength of body, and abilities of mind, in fineness of parts, greatness of capacity, soundness of judgment, and strength and faithfulness of memory, yet the number of such, neither is, nor ever was, nor ever will be, great enough, to shew that Nature intended to give that Sex the Superiority over the Men: and though Use and Education might make some alteration in the case, [169] yet all the Use and Education in the World would never fit them for the performances of the great businesses above-mention'd of Trade and Merchandise, and making Wars abroad, and executing Justice at home; the abilities of managing which, are evident indications of Nature's intending to make the Men superior to the Women. [170]

On the one hand we have the commonplace view of Daniel Defoe in *The Political History of the Devil* (1726): "Mr. Milton, as I have noted above, brings in the Devil and all Hell with him, making a Feu de Joye for the victory Satan obtained over one silly Woman"; and on the other, John Tutchen ameliorating Eve's "fault" by the failing of humankind:[22]

> Their untun'd Prattle do's our Sense confound,
> Which in our Princely Palaces do's sound;
> The self-same Language the old Serpent spoke,
> When misbelieving *Eve* the Apple took;
> Of our first Mother why are we asham'd,
> When by the self-same Rhetorick we are damn'd?

A more enlightened (though not "perfect") view than Fleetwood's or the rest of the century and beyond is Robert Southey's at the end of the century: "A man of well cultivated mind will seldom find a woman equal to him while the present execrable system of female education prevails; however if he does not find equality he can make it: Woman is a more teachable animal than man: but when the man is inferior to his wife, Ignorance, Conceit, and Obstinacy, form an indivisible Trinity in Unity, which will for ever prevent his improvement."[23]

Antagonism toward Milton's view of woman and charges of misogyny have arisen from his recounting of women in *The History of Britain,* the portrait of Dalila, and the presence of only Eve and Sin in *Paradise Lost.* The distress at the omission of such biblical female heroes as Jael and Deborah from Books XI and XII and the inclusion of only the daughters of Cain as seductresses is based on a misunderstanding of what those books are doing. Milton presents a seesawing view of humans who follow the Word or who follow the satanic; he is not depicting biblical history. We are given examples of those East of Eden who choose their opposed places in eternity, using well-known types of the Bible, and then a quick overview of the Israelites (beset by right choice and wrong choice) and the progeny leading to Jesus: Abel, Cain, Seth, Enoch, Noah, Nimrod, Ham, Abraham, Isaac, Jacob, Joseph (all from Genesis); Moses, Aaron, Joshua, David, Solomon, and Jesus. Milton is not here concerned with all manner of heroic action; there is no Gideon, there is no Josiah (though mentioned in *PL* I, 418). The lust which the Fall brought into being, in Milton's grand allegory of sexuality and compulsions, is observed in the men who copy Adam "not deceav'd," and the "Beavie of fair Women" who copy Eve "nothing loath" after the Fall. Enleashed upon the world with the Fall are both vaunts of power and weakness of the flesh: both lack love (or charity, the soul of all the rest of virtuous things). The patriarchal indictment of woman as man's curse is a fact not yet eradicated from the *human* mind, and thus to indict Milton as misogynist for squarely facing the issue and portraying the misogynistic male world (which unfortunately is at times adapted by the female world or opposed by a misanthropic female world) has no real foundation of itself.[24] To minimize or not recognize Milton's contribution to the exaltation of woman and the reversing reconsideration of male/female roles is not to read but to assert prejudice and to express (though justified) bitterness at the world's disposition and nature. Unacceptable, thus, is Junke's implied accusation when she writes, "Milton is restoring for his readers the traditional misogynistic interpretation of the fall of humankind," and "it seems evident that Milton deliberately gathered the remnants of misogyny to create his symbolic triptych of Sin, Eve, and the daughters of Cain" (57).

There are various references to historic women in *The History of Britain* (1670, but written in part around 1648 and later); some are positive references and some are not, depending upon the person and what was known of her historic being. There is Godiva, a woman of great praise (YP 5, i, 386), and Eldred's first wife and sister of Canute, "a woman of much infamy for the trade she drove of buying up *English* Youths and Maids to sell in *Denmarke*" (YP 5, i, 384). The issue is not gender but what the person did in terms of politics and society. Either misread or not totally read by Milton's antagonists is: "Until *Marganus* and *Cunedagius* her two Sisters Sons, not bearing that a Kingdom should be govern'd by a Woman, in the unseasonablest time to raise that quarrel against a Woman so worthy, make War against her, depose her, and imprison her" (YP 5, i, 25). He is, of course, saying that Cordelia who "as right Heir succeeding . . . rul'd the Land five years in Peace" was worthy of such position, and that her nephews, Goneril's and Regan's sons, could not stand the idea of a woman as ruler. The statement actually comes straight out of Milton's sources, Geoffrey of Monmouth, Matthew of Westminster, and Raphael Holinshed. He writes of "*Elfled*...a martial Woman, who . . . gave her self to public affairs, repairing and fortifying many Towns, warring sometimes, dy'd at *Tamworth* the Cheif Seat of *Mercia,* wherof by guift of *Alfred* her Father, she was lady or Queen" (YP 5, i, 300), and his incidental remark about Edwin, whose "administration of justice wrought such peace over all his Territories, that from Sea to Sea, man or woman might have travail'd in safety" (YP 5, i, 203), places an equality in his expression and indeed in the concept of woman traveling about as any man might.

At times Milton is sarcastic and subtle of tone, although French Fogle, the editor of the *History* for the Yale Prose, sometimes misses the point. "[A]lso remembered [is Gurguntius Barbirus'] Wife *Martia* to have excell'd so much in wisdom, as to venture upon a new Institution of Laws. . . . In the minority of her Son she had the rule, and then, as may be suppos'd, brought forth these Laws, not her self, for Laws are Masculin Births, but by the advice of her sagest Counselors; and therin she might doe vertuously, since it befell her to supply the nonage of her Son: else nothing more awry from the Law of God and Nature, then that a Woman should give Laws to Men" (YP 5, i, 31-32). The sarcasm of the last sentence blares out surely in viewing woman's laws given to men as being the most "awry" possibility to confute the Law of God and Nature. Milton's reference to the laws of Queen Martia in the Commonplace Book, page 179, seems fully approving, along with those of Alfred and Molmutius. That laws should have "masculine" or "female" or "neuter" births indicates the ridicule of those who wrested these laws from Martia's hand (they were assigned to the Mercians in the seventeenth century). Fogle's explication misses the sarcasm and indicates a lack of adequate understanding of Milton's position concerning some women's superiority to men in a work such as *The Doctrine and Discipline of Divorce:* "That man should be in subjection to woman was to Milton, of course, a total reversal of the divine and human order" (32).

Fogle references Milton's "attitude toward the leadership of Boadicea" in this note as well. The discussion berates the Britons and Boadicea, who seems to be presented as a "distracted Woeman, with as mad a Crew at her heeles" (YP 5,i,80). The upshot of the reported battle is that the Romans slew all the men and women and horses ("About fowrescore thousand *Britans*") with only four hundred Romans dead. But preceding and following this account are "a deal of other fondness . . . not worth recital" and the conflicting histories of Gildas and Dio. As in other places in the *History,* as we have noted in Chapter 7, Milton in this section of Book II is concerned to rid historiography, even that of Dio Cassius and Tacitus, of fabulousness and incredibility; such historians "embellish and set out thir Historie with the strangness of our manners, not careing in the mean while to brand us with the rankest note of Barbarism, as if in *Britain* Woemen were Men, and Men Woemen. I affect not set speeches in a Historie" (79-80). (Milton's reference here, as Fogle points out, was to Tacitus's statement about there being "no distinction of sex among their rulers.")

Milton's sources indicated that the Britons "plainly manifested themselves to be right *Barbarians;* no rule, no foresight, no forecast, experience or estimation, either of themselves or of thir Enemies" (80). Boadicea either committed suicide or sickened and died. "*Gildas* calls her the craftie lioness, and leaves an ill fame upon her doeings," and Dio opposes the above by saying that the Romans won with difficulty and intended another battle had Boadicea not died. Milton is severe with the overconfident Britons and with Boadicea, but is he so "for her usurpation of man's proper role of military leader and for her inefficiency in military planning and exercise of command," as Fogle states (80, n. 48)?

Another comment that has been read as a putdown of woman by Milton is this: "King *Edward*...took to Wife *Edith* or *Egith* Earl *Godwins* Daughter, commended much for beauty, modesty, and, beyond what is requisite in a woman, learning" (YP 5, i, 374), and information is cited from the pseudo-Ingulf of her learning. The line may be read to say, particularly here in the context of a marriage, that a woman does not need learning to be a good wife; the emphasis is on "requisite." Negatively, that separates woman from man and implies an expected inferiority in learning but an expected beauty and modesty. Positively, it indicates that woman indeed is capable of learning (though many male readers of Milton's *History* might not agree). To raise the issue of female abilities of the mind ("contemplation" in Adam's description) rather than only outward appearance and moral being ("softness . . . and sweet attractive Grace" in Eve's) suggests the gendering of such attributes and some hint of "unusual" when woman shows "contemplation." But while the phrase can represent Milton's acceptance of the biblical superiority of man over woman, it also can represent a somewhat snide accusation against those men who think only the "requisite" is desirable for marriage and who deny woman abilities "not in Grammar only, but in Logic."

We do not know enough about Milton's three wives to place them on any line marking such abilities; all seem "dutiful" wives (that is, in the patriarchal meaning); perhaps once they had reconciled, Mary was the soulmate the divorce tracts sought, perhaps Elizabeth Minshull was as well. Betty, it can be inferred, had interest in reading and matters other than just domestic ones. There seems to be a kind of "equality" from what little we know rather than male/husband domination of a more usual nature. Yet all three wives were appreciably younger than their husband, and what inferences can be drawn must remember the age difference and the usual manifestations in relationships because of that difference.

A better guide to Milton's thinking on this issue of woman's "learning" is the evidence of his daughters. The oldest, Anne, as has been said previously, was lame, apparently mentally incapacitated in some way (a slow person?), but she was taught embroidery and was employed in that line of work, and she was married around 1675. The middle daughter, Mary, like many middle children it would appear, ran into arguments with her father because of alleged favoritism of the youngest daughter and his parental controls, and resented her stepmother. Mary too learned a sewing trade, but also to read and write and even to read Latin. She probably read to her father and wrote for him. She was alive in 1678 and unmarried. Deborah, the youngest, was apparently the favorite, and a seamstress. She too was literate, knew Latin, and read to her father and wrote for him. She married Abraham Clarke in 1674 and bore a large family, only a few of whom grew into adulthood.

The two salient points here for a mid-seventeenth century context are that the daughters had a trade by which they could support themselves and two were well educated by early middle-class standards. While people today look down on such occupations as seamstress, in Milton's day middle-class women's opportunities generally were only marriage and mothering, being a governess or a midwife, or engaging in the husband's work. The early twentieth-century condemnation of Milton's "forcing" his daughters to learn Latin and to read to him or write for him (as in S.J. Liljegren's acerbic denigrations) has reversed the point:

Milton in at least a small way (and financial status certainly may have contributed to what could be done) was seeing that his daughters could be independent and cultured. There is nothing we know that suggests that he tried to force marriage upon them, as one might conclude Richard Powell had upon his daughter Mary.

The daughters left Milton's home sometime before 1669, at which time they would have been 23, 21, and 17 respectively—not uncommon ages for children to leave home even now. The reports of family difficulties arose in depositions at the hearing in the Prerogative Court of Canterbury over Milton's nuncupative will in 1675. He was reported as talking of his "unkind children," and the daughters' attitudes are variously recounted, although Deborah spoke happily of her father in the eighteenth century when interviewed by John Ward and Thomas Birch. The evidence of Milton's domestic life with wives and daughters offers a predominance of husband-father and helpmate-parental controller, but it also indicates possible differences in the woman's role as wife and companion and as challenger of such male preserves as reading and intellectual pursuits, and particularly independence.

While such domestic issues as being husband and parent and (before 1650) being son and son-in-law come to "interfere" with Milton's achievement of his great purpose in life, they also lead to Milton's assertion of the Other within himself, if we allow the frequent psychological earmarks of the anima. The Self has developed and changed over the years, moving from the repression and narcissistic disorders and homoeroticism of the past following the death of his mother, and moving from the parent imago of his selfobject with the death of his father. There has been after 1637 and then again after 1647 the "gradual replacement of the selfobjects and their functions by a self and its functions" (as Kohut writes). This Self is less repressed, although the anality associated with repression remains, exhibits a different narcissism through achieved creativity and completed individuation, is heterosexually engaged while remnants of negativity toward the sex act remain. What the evidence of Milton's relationships with his wives and daughters points to is an empathy with the female, the dominance of the principle of Eros which, as Jung said,[25] is expressed as psychic relatedness, and for Jung this principle helps define woman's psychology. The Self becomes reblended with the mother, who was the primary object and continues as the "inexhaustible source of life for the creator."[26] The ruling principle ascribed to Man as Logos since early times continues as well, but it is no longer absolute for Milton's Self: it is tempered by and fused with Eros. The allegoric proportions of Eve and Adam which we have already looked at indicate that "contemplation" is insufficient without the practical knowledge of experience leading to wisdom. The interferences of Milton's life that occurred helped lead to such practical knowledge and thence "wisdom," but the catalyst is the mother image, the feminine within, the Other.[27]

Underlying *Samson Agonistes* and *Paradise Lost* are basic ideas of man and woman, their relationships, their mutualities, and their differences which were looked at in Chapter 12. For Milton there are the narcissistic factors presented in Chapter 1 as well as the extension of subordination-ism into human relationships. (More will be extended into the political world reviewed in Chapter 14.) Milton's personal life casts its shadow on the creative work of the 1640s, the resolutions of the later 1650s and then the 1660s. The epic, at least, was being planned, partially written, developed, and completed during those times, and the alteration in Milton's experience and self may thus reflect within the poem, even allowing some inconsistency to exist. The question of the date of the dramatic poem, however, becomes crucial: one must wonder how the personality of woman as seen in Eve, if it evidences even a modicum of Milton's attitude, can have been so differently construed *later* in Dalila. But even more bewildering are the accusations against Adam as deliberate disobeyer of God, as narcissistic emotionalist denying the contemplativeness assigned to him, and as ranting self-lover and self-deceiver that we find him in his tirade against Eve, when placed against a *later* Samson. An understanding of the four characters of these two poetic works strongly suggests an earlier and less intellective view of man and woman in Samson and Dalila, and a more perceptive and less individualistic (that is, more allegoric) analysis of Adam and Eve. A literary biography, of course, must consider such matters as the chronology of the writings and their relationship with the author's self at different points in that biography. And so, without detouring into reasoning for a dating of *Samson Agonistes* in the later 1640s with revision in the period of 1667?-1670 (such a detour has been charted from time to time in other places), I look at the dramatic poem for its reflection of the self of Milton.

The reduction of the bodily and some distaste for the bodily in marriage has been observed in the divorce tracts. Samson in the Bible succumbs to his carnal desires in his "wiving" of the woman of Timna and of Delilah, for all his protest of God's will. The situation thus used as background in the dramatic poem has consonance with the psychological author of those tracts, who would accept that such carnality could lead to the disaster that Samson's did. The main argument of Samson against Dalila, however, that a wife owes certain commitments to the husband and her marriage vows, which ostensibly remove her from her own thought and individuality, comes to agree in certain ways with Milton's idealistic views of marriage. But underneath such views is the concept of male superiority and male precedence: "But *St. Paul* ends the controversie by explaining that the woman is not primarily and immediatly the image of God, but in reference to the man" (*Tetrachordon* 3). (Milton proceeds to reduce the absolutism of that statement and to recognize that the woman may be wiser than the man.) Little attention has been given to Samson's inconsistency of action in the past and statement in the present of the dramatic poem, and in similar measure little attention has been given to Dalila's possible sincerity in the present of the work[28] against her fraudulence (in the past). Assuming that Milton was misogynistic and that Dalila has no argument for her actions in the past or sincerity in the present, critics have overlooked Samson's inconsistencies and his *dramatic* character in the poem as well as the possibility that Dalila has changed.

Such prejudged or surface readings of the dramatic poem as those that set up Samson as believer in Milton's attitudes toward marriage (as seen in the divorce tracts) and Dalila as Woman, fraudulent, enticer of Man, inferior to Man, arise often. "We scarcely need to observe that *Samson Agonistes* assumes the subjection of women, a practice to which Milton gives his unequivocal endorsement," is a given for John Guillory.[29] Thus, not considering authorial psychology or a reading of the dramatic poem as presenting other than a simplistic Samson as Good Man and Dalila as Bad Woman in Milton's eyes, he concludes that "The central panel of *Samson Agonistes* is . . . an example of . . . the 'tragic' social practice Milton called the discipline of divorce, a programmatic attempt to control the bodies of men and women . . . by disentangling them" (122). Perhaps, however, looked at anew, this central panel may offer a Dalila who is a fictive spokesperson (the material is not biblical) for a view that action for one's God and country takes precedence over all other concerns, even marriage vows. That Dalila's God and country was not Samson's and that Samson's appears to be the "true" God and analogously the politically right country for Milton has led commentators to see Dalila only negatively, to fail to recognize the basic questions underlying the whole dramatic poem—Whose God is God? Whose political world is the right political world?—and to cast the male/female issue for Milton into male chauvinistic beliefs only.

The view of Dalila as serpent appears in Samson's words and in the Chorus's final observation of her. Is this Milton's concept or that of those characters in the dramatic poem, a view of her that has been her legacy from the Bible onward? Another reading of Dalila may more meaningfully explore the wrong action based on the wrong reason though done in sincerity of belief in that reason. That, if we see Milton's poem as politically fraught (whether in the late 1640s or in the late 1660s), is more significant as an indictment of the opponents of thorough republicanism than seeing Samson as stalwart champion of the Good Old Cause that any thinking person would espouse.

But the sexual dimension and the concepts of marriage that seem to underlie the work do raise the issue of carnality, the potential evil of such ascendance of emotion over mind, the falseness that sexual desire might lead to, the belief in marriage as more than bodily, as a companionship, as a union. These basic underpinnings of the dramatic poem suggest a Milton of the period closer to the divorce tracts, one still uncertain of the beauties of married sex and rather repressed thereby, one not yet fully convinced that "female" seduction and "hostages to fortune" (to remember Sir Francis Bacon's phrase) do not deter from one's great purpose in life. Allan H. Gilbert asked, "Is *Samson Agonistes* Finished?"[30] and in that question may be some of the answer to the difficulty that readers have experienced with the work. Not "finished" when first begun but revised and/or amplified later, perhaps the received poem reflects an author whose own sexuality had been assured by wives and children *and* the "fortune" that achievement of the great purpose would bring, while remnants of a past subconscious persist.

If indeed it is "only the overcoming of the obstacles of reality [that] brings the deliverance from the mother," we can understand the intervening years of the 1650s and early 1660s as the catalyst allowing the author to fill in "in the mean while" visits "by other persons"—these are the words of the Argument to the poem that bridge citation of Manoa and the Public Officer. Dalila and Harapha are there in the Argument, but were they the full portraits we now have in an early draft working on that outline? May they not now represent both the author's subconscious and a deliverance from a mother fixation to recognize that female argument may be as worthy as male argument, that "female" seduction may more honestly be self-desire, that pride in "male" strength and fighting ability may be excessive and, as Harapha shows, unworthy? Perhaps our inability to agree on Dalila's character and hence on its reflection of Milton's attitudes, and our uncertainty of the reasons for Harapha's "effeminacy" and prissiness (though we should recognize his contrast and comparison with the proud Samson of the past), and our overlooking the unattended-to inconsistencies in Samson's actions and his speech are the result of an altered subconscious and conscious on the part of the author.

Once we allow that Dalila may indicate sincerity and that Samson's fall has been in the past a result of sexual desire and submersion of mind, we can compare Eve and Adam, where these prototypical woman and man lay out some of the actions and thoughts of all women and men and where Dalila and Samson become only types of woman and man. The union and sexual activity of Adam and Eve before the Fall has none of the indictment of sex that shows up in the divorce tracts or in the dramatic poem. Importantly, Adam in his diatribe against Eve and his self-justification, indicting not only Eve as culpable but God as well, ignores that he himself has brought on the evils that have befallen him, "Sole Author I, sole cause" (to import Samson's words, 374-76). Here the prototypical man Adam exhibits male prejudice toward woman, enticer of man, fraudulent being, the view of Dalila that continues to emerge in Samson's meeting with her, and unfortunately in many critical readings of the dramatic poem. Beneath such a portrait of Adam the man is male superiority. But this is now the postlapsarian world, and Chapters 12 and 14 here should be read to understand Milton's picture of the prelapsarian world in terms of hierarchy rather than superiority/inferiority and of the ideal postlapsarian world that the "hand-in-hand" union of male and female can be.

But it is Eve's contrast with Dalila that is most significant. Eve falls deceived by Satan and his arguments, where the hunger of noon and intellectual false reasoning lead to her succumbing; Dalila falls into fraudulence by commendable aid to her country and her god. Eve has exercised her individuality and (not unlike Abdiel) her ability to make a decision for herself, but she, like many people, is seduced by arguments of power and godlike status and pride. Dalila has not been seduced but has exercised belief in what is truth to her. The question posed to Dalila in the poem is whether or not marriage vows (or such union of two people) should always without hesitation take precedence over everything else. She has decided negatively in the past and now, if we take her as sincere, has altered her thinking, though chauvinistic Samson discounts it. Eve has forgotten Adam in her partaking of the fruit, but once fallen she shows concern for him and their union and experiences jealousy. Yet she too changes and leads Adam to true union again and to hope in the future. If Dalila represents a view of woman, it is as a woman who acts for man as seductress and, from Samson's angle of vision, one who is incapable of true union; if Eve represents a view of woman, it is as a woman who has potential to be deceived and to become man's projection of self-love and yet the source of renovation and of true union. It is difficult, I think, to see Dalila as a character conceived totally after the time of the conception of Eve as Woman; to see her as Woman more than as a character exhibiting some womanly attributes is misplaced.

Samson, particularly as contrasted with Jesus in the preceding brief epic with which the dramatic poem was published, is a character conceived as a person who may have counterparts in humankind. But Adam takes on allegorical position as holding the seeds of all that is positive and of all that is negative. Samson is "saved" by himself and the rousing motions of God's miracles; Adam is "saved" by Woman.

For *Paradise Lost* the four central feminist arguments against Milton as discriminatory author in his treatment of Eve have been these: 1) Milton's God institutes a rule of masculine authority that is static, closed, and oppressive to women, who are "excluded from heaven" and subordinated on earth.[31] 2) The structure of the family, which determines the roles of Adam and Eve in Eden, is based on bourgeois values of sexual restraint and male-dominated hierarchy.[32] 3) Eve's potentially sinister sexuality is domesticated by marriage, but the need to submit to and articulate the imperatives of the patriarchal voice silences her own voice and creativity.[33] 4) Milton's deepest sympathies are with the revolutionary artist and hero of the poem, Satan, for Satan provides women with an example of energetic, defiant, and self-created identity.[34] Answers to these criticisms have already been offered, primarily in Chapters 1 and 12: Milton's acceptance of the Bible and its male-oriented point of view of male hierarchy in parallel with divine hierarchy (this, of course, explains but does not condone); his rejection of the Satanic action (to be seen further in Chapter 14); and the need for a full and valid and perceptive reading of the poem. So many of the arguments against Milton in the poem are extensions of a superficial reading: the advancement of Satan and Eve or Sin and Eve, only, as parallel equivalents, or the lack of distinction between positive and excessive narcissism, or, so importantly, the assignment of the rather commonplace male view of the **fallen** Adam to the "message" of the poem and to Milton's deep-seated beliefs. Indeed, many of the feminist critics have, in their desire to impugn Milton, missed the positive picture of Eve that is presented and the negative picture of Adam. It is difficult to argue against such misreading when it is based on prejudice and when it is the result of the critic's dereliction of responsibility to the text.

The idealistic attitudes in the poem toward marriage and sexual intercourse that give rise to some of the criticism do suggest the influence of the author as psychological being. But it is an author who has overcome the interferences of Self and who in his position as husband and father has found an integration of Self that can accept hierarchy but not "superiorities," that can sublimate homoerotic feelings to a circle of young male students and friends, and that can experience a union through his marriage with Betty. We can wonder about the sex life of an older blind man with a younger wife. Perhaps there has been a "subordination of the phallus to the tongue,"[35] but the female world in which Milton found himself, with wife, children, and servants, may have been the only answer finally to the homoerotic, to the moral strictures of carnality, to the need for companionship and avoidance of the "lonely" life.

14

The Political Dimension

The most obvious interference in Milton's working on and completing his intended great bid for fame, the one most readily cited, was his governmental service as Secretary for Foreign Tongues to the Council of State from March 1649 through October 1659. The burden of Chapter 6 here has been that the achievement of *Defensio prima* and *Defensio secunda,* if not his other governmentally connected prose, refocussed that great bid for fame and satisfied it through instruments of education against the antichrists of the world and toward the achievement of salvation when each human's Book of Life will be read at the Great Judgment. Foundational for such achievement are Milton's own political thought and his governmental/political role, but further the political dimension of his life and works, including the poetry.

It is distressing that only a few students of Milton have been concerned with his governmental service, dismissing it as a job that took little ability other than knowing Latin (the prose works generated by his position being placed in an independent category). Just what state papers Milton worked on and the nature of his work have often been ignored because of the difficulties of attribution and, for those who have shown some concern, because of the uncertainty of texts. The falsity of the notion that the edition of *Literæ Pseudo-Senatûs Anglicani* (by John and Peter Blaeu in Amsterdam) in 1676 represents Milton's final and complete manuscript at death has been revealed by the discovery of additional state papers by, primarily, J. Milton French, Maurice Kelley, J. Max Patrick, Leo Miller, Robert J. Fallon, and me. The realization that in such other printings of papers as J. Christian Lünig's *Literæ Procerum Europæ* (1712)[1] and Giovanni Leti's *Historia, E Memorie recondite sopra alla Vita Di Oliviero Cromvele* (1692)[2] we have possibly more and more informed (perhaps even more reliable) texts than those in *Literæ,* the Skinner MS, or the Columbia MS,[3] leads to the conclusion that at present Milton's texts as written by him have not necessarily been determined for all the "authenticated" state papers, nor have all the "authentic" state papers been assigned.[4] Two recent books by Leo Miller have revised our knowledge of some of the state papers in text and in canon, as well as placed those writings by Milton into their contexts and into a more valid understanding of the nature of his work.[5] The belief that Milton was simply following orders and the language of others in his translations is fully nullified by Miller's researches and stylistic conclusions. He shows, for example, Milton's ambivalence and conflicts toward the Dutch war as an official in the government of England. In his capacity Milton of necessity would publicly acquiesce to the official actions, but a lack of agreement with those actions can be discerned even in the tone and phraseology of his official work.

While at first for Milton such governmental work may have appeared to interfere with his hopes of inculcating virtue in humankind through his writings, and while it did deflect him from pursuit of his poetic endeavors, the products of those ten years became for the idealist a more direct and practical means of achievement. One must do what one must do. And though an individual state paper might be only a perfunctory act of business, it represented the world in which ideals might also be sought often enough through contributing toward accord among people, through subtle influence on the great actions of diplomacy and governmental relationships among nations. The way something is said— and this would include the language of influence and diplomacy— Milton early had learned could be effective: the orator arguing his position (truly believed or not) could create a favorable reaction on the part of an audience. The author of *The Censure of the Rota* was right enough in epitomizing Milton's politically charged writing as showing that "you fight always with the flat of your hand like a Retorician, and never Contract the Logicall fist."[6] Extension of rhetorical skills will be seen in the state papers, particularly when they are compared with others' work in the same vein.

The watershed for Milton's political world lies in the crisis of government during the 1640s and 50s. There is a growing antagonism to monarchy as it becomes synonymous with religious and social worlds. The stark contrast between the republican frame of mind and the monarchic came to focus not only the "evil" that monarchy posed but the intertexts of liberty for these three estates. The pigeon-holed view of life came finally to disappear, but late, as usual with the anally retentive Milton, who so frequently was not a "timely-happy spirit," into the composite world of the Christian Commonwealth. The author of *The Censure*, writing in opposition to *The Ready and Easy Way to Establish a Free Commonwealth*, quotes approvingly a linkage between Milton's antiprelatical and divorce tracts and his political thoughts:

You had shown your selfe as able a Divine, as a Statesman; For you had made as politique provision for spirituall, as civill Liberty in those pious and Orthodox, (though seeming absurd and Contradictory) grounds you have laid down in order thereunto, which being rightly interpreted, do say, or by consequence inferre thus much. That the Church of Christ ought to have no Head upon Earth, but the Monster of many heads, the multitude, who are the onely supream Judges of all matters that concern him. . . . That all Christian Lawes and Ordinances have a Co-ercive power, to see themselves put in Execution, and yet they ought to be subject to every Man's will and humor, (which you call his best light) and no man to them but in his own sense. . . . That every man may do what he pleases in matters of Religion, but onely those that are in Authority, who ought not to meddle in such matters. . . . That no man can serve God, nor save his owne Soul, but in a Common-wealth, in this certainty, you go after your owne invention, for no man ever heard it before. . . . That any man may turn away his Wife, and take another as oft as he pleases, as you have most learnedly prov'd upon the Fiddle, and practic'd in your Life and Conversation, for which you have atchieved the honour to be Styld the Founder of a Sect. All this you call Liberty of Conscience, and Christian Liberty, which you conclude no Government is more inclinable, not onely to favour, but protect, than a Free Common-wealth. [11-12]

The roots of this political position lie prior to Milton's entry into the antiprelatical controversy. It was emerging, unrecognizedly, in his church-outing and in his concern for the military actions at home when he was in Italy. His own father's rebellion against the religious strictures of the grandfather lay in the unconscious; the subordinationism of son to father persisted through the individualizing years of the late 1630s, to become increasingly bifurcated between subordination and assertion of the ideals of the father. The idea at the bottom of the primitive Christian ideal of the Kingdom of Heaven which "is within you" "is that right action comes from right thinking, and that there is no cure and no improving the world that does not begin with the individual himself," according to Jung, discussing the relations between the ego and the unconscious.[7] As Milton said in *Apology for Smectymnuus*, "he who would not be frustrate of his hope to write well hereafter in laudable things, ought him selfe to bee a true Poem, that is, a composition, and patterne of the best and honourablest things; not presuming to sing high praises of heroick men, or famous Cities, unless he have in himselfe the experience and the practice of all that which is praise-worthy" (16).

James Driscoll, in a study of Milton and Jung,[8] cogently argues that "Godhead operates in a three-staged dialectical process working toward conscious totality—hence a trinity. But in its structure the Godhead is quaternal." The first stage is the Father (Sensation); the second bifurcates into the Son (Thinking) and Satan (Feeling); the third moves to the

Holy Spirit (Intuition). ("Satan" is the wrong image: perhaps "Adversary" or "Human" or "Rebel" would better enunciate the concept, including thus, as in *Paradise Lost,* Satan and Adam and Eve.) In the second stage, which correlates for Milton with the period of the late 1630s, the 1640s, and then the 1650s, there is both repression/submission and rebellion/defiance. "Ad Patrem" is an early statement of movement out of the submissive or repressive; the rebellious, with its source in feeling, follows. As well-stated in *Tetrachordon,* the demands of defiance, beginning in feeling and operating through reason, are made clear for Milton:

Although if we consider that just and naturall privileges man neither can rightly seek, nor dare fully claime, unless they be ally'd to inward goodnesse, and stedfast knowledge, and that the want of this quells them to a servile sense of their own conscious unworthinesse, it may save the wondring why in this age many are so opposite both to human and to Christian liberty, either while they understand not, or envy others that do; contenting, or rather priding themselves in a specious humility and strictnesse bred out of low ignorance that never yet conceiv'd the freedome of the Gospel. . . . Christ having cancell'd the hand writing of ordinances which was against us . . . hath in that respect set us over law, . . . to follow that which most edifies, most aides and furders a religious life, makes us holiest and likest to his immortall Image, not that which makes us most conformable and captive to civill and subordinat precepts. . . . Men of most renowned vertu have sometimes by transgressing, most truly kept the law. . . . our Saviour for whom that great and God-like work was reserv'd, redeem'd us to a state above prescriptions by dissolving the whole law into charity. [1-2]

Within this quotation we hear the acceptance of subordination and the belief that one must be a true poem, but also the centrality of feeling (charity unto all people, *caritas,* "the soul of all the rest") and its assertion through reason into rebellion. We see Milton not denying his father but rather asserting what the father has stood for, what he expressed as a father who had "bestowed no more preferable gifts, however many might have been prudent, / who trusted to his young son the common light, / the chariot of Hyperion, the reins of day, / and the tiara waving about with radiant brightness" ("Ad Patrem," 97-100).

As epitomized in the seeming opposition of father/son relationships of God and his Son and of God and Satan, one is drawn to agree with Kerrigan that the oedipal being of Milton is both celebratory and belligerent. While the ego may act as rival to the father, the ego-ideal may rise to a dominant position in the structure of conscience, delimiting the superego, or, rather, making it part of the ego-ideal. But for the Son and Satan, and thus for all sons of God, a question of the righteousness of the Father underlies relationship. This has been stated often enough as the difference between the true and the false God, and true or false or half gods—terms covering concepts and feeling. Ralph Waldo Emerson (in "Give All To Love") counseled, "Heartily know, / When half-gods go, / The gods arrive." ("Love," of course, equates "charity" here, and, as I have argued, that is the theme of *Paradise Lost*.) The Son in Book III of *Paradise Lost* celebrates the Father, surely, but prior to his offer of himself there is an underlying question about the Father's position, about his attitude toward humankind, a "First vague shadow of surmise." Belligerence is, again, not the right word, but the Son's is not a nonthinking acceptance.[9] The Father rises to the occasion and shows himself, in the Son's eyes, a whole god, the true god. This is akin to Milton's relationship with his father in "Ad Patrem," and the record of Milton's life from 1638 shows that his father rose to establish himself as whole father, true father. The Son takes on the being of the Father as his surrogate, takes on the superego of the Father, that is, in his dealings with humankind in the Creation, the Judgment, and the Incarnation. The superego of the Father has become the ego of the Son. Repeatedly in life there is the father figure who proves to be worthy of emulation, possibly even after some overt opposition, but there is also the father figure who proves most unworthy. Extremes make the point: the criminal, the wife and child abuser, the ne'er-do-well, the vanished husband and father. For the Son, the Father is All; for Milton his father is similarly worthy, enabling the son to be surrogate for the potentialities of that father, composer and rebel against establishment.

The balance of feeling and wisdom in this second stage for Milton, as well as a continuance of constraint learned at the feet of the father and the Father, can be seen in the contrast with some radicals of the time. F.D. Dow, writing of one phase of those liberal reconstructionists, says: "Many radicals in the 1640s and 1650s were certainly very liberal in their attitudes to sexual and domestic relations. Milton was not alone in advocating divorce, and many would have defended the right of a godly woman to desert an ungodly husband. . . . Some radicals did deserve their reputation for sexual libertinism. Aliezer Coppe and Laurence Clarkson advocated complete sexual freedom, the latter arguing that to the pure all things are pure, and that freedom from the guilt of sin was only achieved by being free to sin."[10] We are reminded of the sonnet "I did but prompt the age to quit thir clogs" (autumn 1645?) and Milton's analysis of some of those Dow refers to: "Licence they mean, when they cry liberty." The superego constituent of the ego-ideal persists in Milton and predicates that anyone loving liberty "must first be wise, and good."

Recent critics, particularly those who have approached authors like Milton from a position well left of center, have tried to make him a radical. The term should imply a cutting of roots, not simply reformative theory and acts or even revolutionary alteration, building upon the past and pointing to some possible return. For such critics agreement with a plank or so that seems to effect radical change places Milton within the camp of that radical group (this is true not only of the strictly political but also of the strictly religious), and so paradigms are devised that are said to define Milton's political thinking. My concern in this chapter (and this biography) is to understand the underlying political thought and its ontology (for the most part, its psychological roots). My conclusions do not place Milton within a truly radical paradigm without qualification or with unqualified inferences drawn from such placement; rather, I find his psychological being built upon acceptance of, emulation of, and accommodation to the father/God rather than upon rebelliousness. There are false fathers and false gods, but right action comes only from right reason.

I read as consonant with my statement David Loewenstein's suggestion that "however iconoclastic and radical their vision may be, Milton's revolutionary tracts never offer a fully or consistently developed philosophy of history" (5). Much of his radicalism lies in millenarian vision, which is central to numerous tracts and poems and is the lifespring of Christopher Hill's extensively influential revisionism of how to read Milton. Joan S. Bennett recognizes antinomian strains in Milton's thought and works, for instance, particularly the major poems, where antinomianism may be defined as a belief in the abrogation of Mosaic law as binding; compare Chapter 8 above. Even disregarding the libertine aspects of some, antinomians were considered radical in their political sphere. But I part company with the trend in Milton studies that sees him as radical because of his espousal of certain beliefs associated with such radical groups. Perhaps the separating point for me is that Milton does not expel all hierarchy or legal restrictions for the masses. He too frequently rejects the rabble and too much stresses the individual for me to place him in some kind of proto-Marxist position.

As Michael Wilding writes, Milton reasserts the primacy of the inner light in *Paradise Regain'd* (243), with its "stress on the primacy of the individual conscience over the pressures of external authority, the stress on the accessibility to all men of 'the Spirit of god'." Wilding understands incisively "the contradictions that arose when [Milton] renounced the attempt to establish by military means a radical Kingdom of Heaven on earth, and turned instead to the private preparations of the soul for the paradise within" (258). This is not a rejection of antiauthoritarianism or of the love of liberty or of the desire to establish a new society, but at the same time it is a recognition of a political status quo, though one needful of change. Not only is the "kingdom of God" that "is within you" (Luke 16:21) the primitive Christian ideal but its fostering is the means to achieve that Kingdom.[11]

Moving into the third stage is a transcendence when ego and reason no longer proclaim their sovereignty, or as Driscoll writes, "The light of reason turns inward upon the realm of feeling and outward to that of sensation." Since feeling is no longer self-sufficient, it "ceases its war on reason and instead offers guiding values to thought and brings refinement to sensation." Through the 1650s this is what occurs to Milton, whose personal tragedies of 1652 carry him to the renewal seen in the *Defensio secunda* of May 1654, in the letter to Philaras of September 1654, in the resolutions and calm of Sonnets 19-22 of October (?)-December (?) 1655, and in a probable return to renewed poetic writing, until 1659 and the immanence of the Restoration. The Holy Spirit (or Intuition) pervades the poet of *Paradise Lost*, who as rhetor is creator of a world imbued with good (ego) and evil (shadow), with thinking and feeling, with the need for submission to the Holy Spirit that thought and experience will bring, and with the charity in feeling that will counter the rebellion that noncharity in feeling brings. Important are the "ordinances which [are] against us" in the realm of the mundane world, making humankind "most conformable and captive to civill and subordinat precepts," and the "law" which is from God, the "whole law" finally being dissolved "into charity" by Christ. The Covenant of the Law has been transformed into the Covenant of Grace.

Up to this point in time, 1654-59, Milton has presented a political view usually in reaction to others' views or influences: it involves what I have called the negative path. For David Aers and Gunther Kress, speaking of the early prose, "Milton's orientation involves the dissolution of concrete social reality in particular human communities where, and where alone, the individual develops his specific identity and lives his life. This dissolution is rather indicative of his inability to make the advantages and limitations of his own social and economic position a topic for serious examination."[12] *The Tenure of Kings and Magistrates* (1649) presents a political view that, while it may continue to show inability to deal with his own position, nonetheless offers a positive path. That positive path, based on a conception of the Father/Son relationship, remains idealistic and divorced from some of the practicalities of the world. But it is in direct conflict with the father/son metaphor that Sir Robert Filmer argued in *Patriarcha: or, The Natural Power of Kings*, not published until 1680 but known through manuscript; this work is reflective of much thinking of the time, the King being the father to whom the son (the people) owe unquestioning allegiance and obedience. With the

Interregnum and his position in it, Milton was faced with some of those practicalities and some of the difficulties that a rather absolute position of right and wrong engenders. That Milton was not happy with the concept of the Protectorate seems clear; that he was somewhat uncertain about Cromwell appears subtly in his encomium to him in the *Defensio secunda*. As Donald Roberts remarks in his edition of this work, "Milton made the best of this bad bargain [the Protectorate], as is evident later in this tract, but it is apparent also that, though Milton accepted this *fait accompli* and genuinely admired Cromwell, he did not really like such absolutism and hoped for a change in the direction of broader-based power."[13]

What we are recognizing here is an accommodation, an adaptation of laws to circumstances, a reconcilement of law with the exigencies of life. This is what he was doing in *The Ready and Easy Way to Establish a Free Commonwealth* which, as I have said, does not try to stop the Restoration, which is certain, but to alter what might be some of its monarchic operation; it calls up a *ready* way and an *easy* way to effect a free commonwealth of representation, though the stress is on the aristocratic.[14] (While he condemns monarchy in the tract, he certainly recognized the inevitability of the Restoration.) This specific limited and mixed oligarchy was not to be brought into being, but its sense of limitation and mixture, as in Philip Hunton's *A Treatise of Monarchy* (1643), was to prevail and come to republican achievement with the ascent to the throne of William and Mary in 1689. That important year brought forth new editions of Hunton, of Edward Sexby's justification of execution of a king, *Killing No Murder*, five times, and of *Pro Populo Adversus Tyrannos: or the Sovereign Right and Power of the People over Tyrants* (an altered version of *Tenure*). A fusion of submission and revolution underscores Milton's 1660 proposal, just as it does in *A Treatise of Civil Power in Ecclesiastical Causes* (1659) and *Of True Religion, Hæresie, Schism, Toleration, And what best means may be us'd against the growth of Popery* (1673).[15]

The secretary years with their practicalities of diplomacy and dashed idealism, growing from the numerous attacks on the two *Defences* and *Eikonoklastes*, as well as the problem with the Racovian Catechism,[16] supplied the experience with the world, that dark world and wide, that seems to have been needed for Milton to move beyond the defiant to degrees of understanding, if not acceptance, of humankind. *A Treatise of Civil Power* advances Liberty of Conscience, arguing that "for beleef or practise in religion according to this conscientious perswasion no man ought be punishd or molested by any outward force on earth whatsoever" (5). Stress is upon the Holy Spirit within one, "which we ought to follow much rather then any law of man, as not only his word every where bids us, but the very dictate of reason tells us" (4-5). The transcendence to the Holy Spirit and Intuition which Driscoll posits is affirmed for the Milton of the years following experience in the real political world of men. A similar position underlies *Of True Religion*. It is what he means when he writes that "The last means to avoid Popery, is to amend our lives" (16). (Compare my remarks in Chapter 8, note 30.) Popery is viewed as political, not simply religious, demanding allegiance and obedience of the people, not unlike monarchy, though he is careful not to go that far. For Milton, then, we can understand that "True Religion is the true Worship and Service of God, learnt and believed from the Word of God only" (4).

In an amazingly misinformed study,[17] Charles R. Geist alleges that "The weakness of Milton's entire social philosophy was that he did not posit a concept of man's nature which remained constant throughout his thought" (6). I trust my reader, like me, believes that mental growth is admirable. Geist thinks that subordinationism is heresy and continues to speak of affinities with Arius, but misunderstands the whole subject, since he speaks of "gradations of essence." Little use is made of *Tenure*, and though he purports to have read Barbara K. Lewalski's work on the 1659-60 tracts, his comments would belie that.[18] "Milton's weakness as a political thinker was due to the fact that he never successfully bridged the gap between the two images because of his *idée fixe* with seminal identity" (85), the images being the form of man as the image of God and the form of government as the image of man (from James Harrington's *Oceana and Other Works* [London, 1771], 462). My previous remarks should refute that position. But Geist and I agree in part on one point: Milton's "lasting contribution to political theory was the revival of the classical paradigm of the mixed regime in its purest form before it subsequently succumbed to the empiricists" (104). But a study of *Tenure* should have altered some implications in that statement, and looking at George Sensabaugh's *That Grand Whig, Milton* should have obviated its final words. Sensabaugh summarizes the point to be made: "To this return, to this triumph of the main European tradition modified by Puritan and Whig thought, Milton made a notable contribution through his revolutionary program for man and society. . . . [H]e had contributed most significantly to the political life of England through his universal propositions on individual liberty and the nature of government—propositions which, because of his powerful rhetoric, echoed in the hearts of his countrymen until they became . . . a part of the popular consciousness and an expression of the national mind."[19]

But the political dimension of Milton's thought also appears in *Paradise Lost, Paradise Regain'd*, and *Samson Agonistes*. Satan in the longer

epic has often been cast as a rebel against a tyrannic overlord who alters
the rules at whim. For those seeing Milton as one of the Devil's party, an
equation is made between Charles I (or any monarch) as tyrant unheed-
ing of his political constituents and God the Father as abrogator of law,
and between Milton (or any other revolutionist among the regicides) and
Satan. A superficial reading of the text can advance one's cause against
perceived tyranny and yield solace for the aggrieved in the rousing
words of many of Satan's speeches. Such an interpretation, however, reveals a shoddy reading of the poem: The hierarchy of administrative
posts, which Lucifer/Satan and other archangels hold over other angels,
for example, is ignored; and the godhead of the Son is forgotten (the
"begetting" of the Son simply divides acts of the godhead between the
Father and the Son, but the Son is still God, so that no actual abrogation
or alteration of law has been made). The psychological motivation for
Satan becomes the conceived political impediment created by God, although neither that motivation nor that cause has similarity to Milton's
conceptions of liberty and hopes for governmental reforms; and Satan is
ego-driven, without high goals for his fellow angels, as opposed to the
political issues which the opponents to Charles (and monarchy) espoused and Milton sincerely believed. The poem has a strong political
dimension but it is not so simplistic as some commentators have made it.

The matter of Satan and the rebellious angels denies subordinationism, which lies at the heart of Milton's thinking. There seems to be an
unstated belief on Satan's part that he is equal with God or, if not equal,
the next best. The begetting of the Son, as he sees it, pushes him down
the ladder a notch: he is less equal. But of course he does not see himself
as equal to the other angels who are part of his regiment (except perhaps Beelzebub, who mythically is an aspect of Satan and who presents
a kind of Other for Satan—weak, naive, obedient, and subordinate).
Modern commentators want to view a sense of equality in the poem that
is not there and is not part of Milton's thinking about God, angels, or
humankind. Frederic Jameson, for instance, declares that "the poetic
narrative . . . offers testimony of the constitutive relationship between
this image of sin and of the fall and the failure to imagine genuine human equality. Eve has to fall, not because she is sinful or disobedient, but
because Milton cannot find it in himself to imagine and to give figura-
tion to an equality between the sexes that would open up into a concrete
vision of the community of free people. The poem thus illustrates and
documents, not a proposition about human nature, not a type of philosophical or theological content, but rather the operation of ideological
closure."[20] The points are accurate enough: the ideological closure that
Milton exhibits involves subordinationism and hierarchy in all divisions

of the realm of what is conceived of as being—divine persons, angels, and humans—and the need for obedience within the hierarchy, which obedience will be the natural result of love. As Raphael remarks,

> My self and all th' Angelic Host that stand
> In sight of God enthron'd, our happie state
> Hold, as you yours, while our obedience holds;
> On other surety none; freely we serve,
> Because wee freely love, as in our will
> To love or not; in this we stand or fall:
> And som are fall'n, to disobedience fall'n,
> And so from Heav'n to deepest Hell; O fall
> From what high state of bliss into what woe![*PL* V, 535-43]

The subordinationism of the Father and the Son is administrative; the hierarchy of the angels is administrative; the relationship of Adam as head to Eve as helpmeet is basically administrative also within their unfallen world. The political concept of equality simply did not enter Milton's thinking in this realm of hierarchies.

Movement upward or downward within the hierarchical structure depends upon the worthiness of the respective persons within that hierarchy. As Milton indicated in the divorce tracts and Dow wrote of some advocates for divorce, "the right of a godly woman to desert an ungodly husband" would have been defended. Such action is not dissimilar to Abdiel's challenge to Satan, his hierarchical superior, once he recognizes Satan's abrogation of Satan's position under God. "Equality" (or what can be construed as equality) exists in the essences the three persons of God are, in the essences Raphael and Michael and Gabriel are individually, and in the essences Eve and Adam are individually. They are their individual selves, just as Milton is his individual self, in matters of self, but in matters of community a hierarchy of administration cuts through. The positioning within the human hierarchy depends (or should) on abilities, and so some are leaders who take on the concerns of those who are led. The supposed abilities of the man take on a leadership over the supposed abilities of the woman in like manner. We do not like, and I hope do not accept, the stereotyping of "man" and "woman" that underlies such hierarchy. But Milton accepted the word of the Bible in this matter, and "Paul," we remember (as mentioned in Chapter 1), "ends the controversy by explaining that the woman is not primarily and immediately the image of God, but in reference to the man." He did not, as Jameson with seeming modern expectation that he might, "imagine genuine human equality." Nor does Milton, because of their political dependence on the Pope, extend toleration to Roman Catholics; nor does he concern himself at all with the Jews and their debarment from England. Indeed, it is difficult not to observe that the rabble abhorred in the "Ode to Rouse" ("the insolent speech of the multitude and even / the vicious throng of readers") or in "Ad Patrem" ("the indolent rabble," the "most detestable band") are neglected in Milton's political and governmental philosophy.

Certainly *The Ready and Easy Way* proposes an oligarchy, not a fully democratic senate. No, equality in our usual sense does not apply for Milton in the realm of political or governmental life, social or family life, or indeed religious life. Though he advances the idea that each person can interpret the Bible, he does not mean to say that all people are equal to the task and that, therefore, no ministry is necessary. His thinking had not progressed to such concepts; he simply did not turn attention to such matters, and thus we cannot competently know what his stand would have been on a proletariat, continued existence of a "rabble."

Milton's thinking goes a different way, as I have suggested for *Tenure* and remarked in Chapter 6. Probably looking only at the aristocracy and the bourgeoisie but not the proletariat, and blind to *die Lumpen,* Milton argues the need, in *Paradise Lost* but more obviously and dominantly in *Paradise Regain'd,* that humankind must change itself, must internalize the being that the Son was, must be so impervious to the evil temptations everywhere (self-aggrandizement, the thinking of "master" over "slave," and the pride and envy encountered constantly) that the institutions of government, whether national or communal or familial, would be colored by the ideal selves of their constituencies. Perhaps what is needed critically is the positive view of things—praise for those aspects of political life and male/female relationship that assert the independence and essence of each member of the group and the means to assertion and maintenance of independence and essence—rather than the negative view—the omissions of thought, the lack of logical extensions of thought, the inattention to examining and hence rejecting ideologies (including the religious) that are simply assumed as the idols of the tribe they are.

As I wrote previously, "Fortified against such temptation [as that represented by "Satan" in any guise], men can band together to maintain the law of liberty which has fortified them. The start for such idealistic life on earth . . . is the proper regard for self in every person and the proper regard of each person for every other person—the intrinsic message of *Paradise Regain'd.*"[21] What *Samson Agonistes* contributes to this concept is the depressing realization that the group mind lacks individuality when anxiety and fear and ease cloud it: it is easier not to act but to arrogate action to others, particularly God. Its counter is individual "action" and then (but only then) a banding together as a group to act collectively. The individual not only needs the proper regard for self and the selflessness toward others exhibited by the Son and finally by Samson, but also the determination to act. This will lead to confrontation, and that in turn will uncover falsity and reveal truth—at least what can at that particular time be considered truth. "The political organization . . . will, in Milton's thinking, allow humankind to keep in their ways by creating a force that will counter the opposition to their keeping in their ways."

This phrase, "keep in their ways" (from Psalm 91) will be explored for its significance in *Paradise Regain'd* in Chapter 16, but it relates to a thought laid forth in Chapter 2 concerning God's relationship with his true servants. The people under Johanan and Jezamiah expressed their hope to Jeremiah "that the Lord thy God may show us the way wherein we may walk, and the thing that we may do" (42:3), and Jeremiah had previously warned the children of Benjamin with the Lord's words, "Stand ye in the ways, and see, and ask for the old paths, where is the good way, and walk therein, and ye shall find rest for your souls" (6:16), but the doom of Jerusalem descends because the people will not obey. To regain Jerusalem and the New Heaven and New Earth (Isaiah 65:17-25; Revelation 21), Isaiah had recalled Psalm 114, "that [God] wouldest come down, that the mountains might flow down at [his] presence . . . that the nations may tremble at [his] presence!" (64:1-2) and continued, addressing the Lord, "Thou meetest him that rejoiceth and worketh righteousness, those that remember thee in thy ways" (64:5). The political organization, which may show the administrative hierarchy we have discussed, is the means to assert and maintain independence for humankind and to help it to persist in its faithful path.

Milton does not abdicate the rights of the people in that organization, as Hobbes does, but he does advocate controls and law, and in *The Ready and Easy Way* even goes so far as to encourage the use of force against a majority who would nullify liberty for all. "The whole freedom of man consists either in spiritual or civil libertie. As for spiritual, who can be at rest, who can enjoy any thing in this world with contentment, who hath not libertie to serve God and to save his own soul, according to the best light which God hath planted in him to that purpose, by the reading of his reveal'd will and the guidance of his holy spirit? . . . The other part of our freedom consists in the civil rights and advancements of every person *according to his merit*: the enjoyment of those never more certain, and the access to these never more open, than in a free Commonwealth" (88-89, 94; my emphasis). "What I have spoken," he writes, "is the language of that which is not call'd amiss *the good Old Cause*" (107).

It will be remarked that "equality" in some supramodern sense does not apply, nor does a radicalism approaching licence or any control by "a misguided and abus'd multitude." Milton is far from a conservative political thinker; for his time he was perhaps a "revolutionary" adherent to achieve republicanism and he was a "radical" in specific concepts; but he is also far from the radicalism observable in others and expected by some modern-day critics.

15

The Religious Precept

Ask someone what Milton's religion was and the immediate answer will be "Puritan." Just what a Puritan was is confused, of course, and has frequently been the subject of historical study that has pointed out the "purifying" etymology of the name. Puritans were people who wished to remove such traces of Roman Catholicism remaining in the new state church, the Anglican church as it was soon to be called, as vestment, kneeling, certain rituals, and hierarchic positions that persisted between the Godhead and the believer. The Puritan was Calvinist, but just how extreme or liberal his attitude was concerning election, predestination, biblical interpretation, and the like is not measurable since the term included many people of varying attitudes about such matters.

Largely the name, as limited from the broader Protestant, derived from reforms of practice, externals, and the church, not from differences of opinion about theology. The liturgy and its uses also sparked differences among the various Protestant groups. Much of the reason for these early puritanic enjoinders was the nebulous change that occurred in the latter half of the sixteenth century when Elizabeth and her advisers moved England out of the Roman Catholic fold into another. While the break with Rome that Henry VIII had precipitated was made firmer under Edward VI, with a backsliding under Mary, it was through the actions of the Elizabethan government that strong change occurred. Yet that change was not so firm as to deter Roman Catholic upsurges under James I, Charles I and Henrietta Maria, Charles II, and, of course, James II. Milton and his religion are a product of those years from January 1559, when Elizabeth, two months after her ascent to the throne, asserted an intention to break with Rome, through the 1670s.

In 1559 and for a couple of decades thereafter there were varying groups of Catholics: those who harked back to the medieval church, fairly unchanged; those middle-of-the-roaders who maintained adherence to the faith and yet did not defy the state church; and the recusants, few at first but dominant among the Catholics by the time of Elizabeth's death. "By 1603 the rigours of Elizabethan government policy had eliminated catholicism within the Elizabethan church, so

that catholicism was now a distinctive, separated religion."[1] That "separated"religious body expanded during the seventeenth century. At the
time Milton was beginning to emerge as an author in print with the
five antiprelatical tracts, 1641-42, the tension of anticatholicism had
generated into a political issue. "Alarm over the papists spread on an un-
precedented scale; the five major cities in England . . . were declared
to be centres of popish conspiracies; so too were many other towns
and villages."[2]

It is no wonder that Milton's sense of toleration in *Of True Religion,
Hæresy, Schism, Toleration, and what best means may be used against the growth
of Popery* (1673) did not include Roman Catholics: in his formative years
and in the years when he was specifically faced with the issue of church
administration—not theological precept, let it be noted—the Catholic
thrust beckoned a return to formerly rejected practices. Further, of
course, was the political force that Catholicism still posed in the early
1670s, despite the Thirty Years' War and the 1648 Peace of Westphalia.
It still exerts significance in sociological and hence political power
through its influence over its members' minds. And further, and even
more important, an acceptance of Roman Catholicism on a personal
level denied Milton's father and his father's rebellious action against
his father.[3]

Milton's grandfather, Richard Milton, was one of the recusants from
Oxford during Elizabeth's reign. He was excommunicated in May 1582,
and there are records of recusancy fines in later years. Milton's father,
John, is reported to have quarreled with his father over religion, apparently leaving home at least by 1583 and becoming active as a scrivener by
1590. Early accounts report that he was disinherited because of this
quarrel and that he proceeded to London for his livelihood. Is there a
residue of Milton's father's rebelliousness against his grandfather in Satan's rebellion against God, and its sublimation in his loving accedence to
his father in the Son's functioning as surrogate for the Father? "Ad Patrem" emboldens that suggestion. In Samson we have a nonunderstand-
ing son who tries to conform to the wishes of God the Father but who is
able to proceed only when he can deflect the desires and counsel of his
father, Manoa. And one way of looking at *Paradise Regain'd* is to see it as
resolving the dilemma of how to achieve using the energy of Father/Son
through the function of anima (the mother archetype), which supplies
the determining form.[4] The psychological picture of the poet that keeps
emerging is of a son much dedicated to his father, emulating him and
growing up to discharge, psychologically at least, those concerns that
were seen as the father's[5]: artistic achievement, middle-class "political"
advantage, and the true religious belief in a protestant god.

Milton was raised an Anglican, trained to become an Anglican minister, and remained an Anglican through the signing of the subscription books of Cambridge University in both 1629 and 1632, which demanded allegiance to the state church and its Thirty-nine Articles. But Anglican carried no clear denotation of beliefs or theological precepts: Milton would have been generally Calvinistic, he may or may not have entertained attitudes that smacked of Arminianism (as in Sonnet 7), and he knew (and literary research has shown employed knowledgeably[6]) the liturgy. But whether prior to 1632 he fostered separatist views or had a strong position on baptism or on other sacraments, we cannot be sure. There seems to be no change discernible through the middle 1630s with his writing of "Comus," except perhaps in some implications for the religious Anglican establishment in the Lady's lines denouncing an aristocratic world and economy. But were these, perhaps, part of the 1637 alteration that has been alluded to before?[7] With the events of 1637, if my reconstruction in Chapter 4 is correct, came a realization of argument against the Church of England, whose hierarchical system was little reformed from its Catholic source. Such realization could have remained submerged until the events of 1637 made the way things were crystal-clear. His recognition of his disability as sermonist is evident in the Letter to an Unknown Friend, and a nonconformity of thought has usually struck most people about Milton, although there is no certain evidence of it up to this point in time. Lines in "Lycidas" have often been excerpted as a digression on the clergy, but they are, rather, a statement of this realization that the church establishment in rule and authority was tainted with Catholicism and, second, an integral part of the growth of the poet, the uncouth swain.

Perspective on Milton always points to an anal retentive personality, one not only who is self-disciplined, acquisitive, and obstinate, but one who is not given to airing his accomplishments or being fully satisfied with them once they have been aired. Note, for example, the alteration of the text of *Comus* in 1645 after its first publication in 1637, of the "Nativity Ode" in 1673, and so significantly of *Paradise Lost* in its second edition. But the prose too is revised: the second edition of *The Doctrine and Disciplines of Divorce* (1644) is almost double the length of the first (1643); *Eikonoklastes* and *The Tenure of Kings and Magistrates* have additions, for the most part unimportant, however, in 1650 printings; and *The Ready and Easy Way*, within a month's time in March/April 1660, almost becomes two different books. With Parker we may remark that "Milton not only strengthened his main proposal and brought it up to date, but also amplified his attack on monarchy, reminding his readers of things they had perhaps forgotten, such as the wastefulness and corruption of court life";[8] and we can construe the first edition as being hurried into print because the Restoration was upon him. Yet there is that dissatisfaction with self that is so typical of the anal personality. And with the publication of *Paradise Lost* in 1667, Milton finally was able to release a number of items for publication well after they had been written: *Accedence Commenc't Grammar* (1669), *The History of Britain* (1670), *Artis Logicæ Plenior Institutio* (1672). Other works that saw print long after composition were *Considerations Touching the likeliest means to remove Hirelings* (probably from 1653 in rebuttal of William Prynne's *A Gospel Plea,* but not published until 1659 in promised complement to *A Treatise of Civil Power*), and the posthumous *Character of the Long Parliament* (1681), *A Brief History of Moscovia* (1682), *A Letter to a Friend, Concerning the Ruptures of the Commonwealth* and *The Present Means, and Brief Delineation of a Free Commonwealth* (1698), and *De doctrina christiana* (1825). The last, of course, may not be quite as he might have wanted it, since the manuscript indicates numerous alterations of the text over some years. This record is easily assignable to the kind of personality I suggest, and helps make cogent the career and religious convictions that finally emerged in 1637. Milton seems consistently to lag behind the "more timely-happy spirits" of his world, coming to realizations and decisions well after we might have expected another in similar circumstances to have acted. And, indeed, the continuance of the shell of his world in the 1630s demarks that personality, though inwardly there had been change.

Over the years of the 1630s, then, we see a change in Milton's attitude toward the church, from a seemingly straightforward Anglicanism to an antiprelatical position. He had been "church-outed," but there is no evidence of change in belief. Once questioning in one sector sets in, however, questioning and then revision may occur in another, and such is the case, I think, with Milton. Religion, Jung tells us, is "a careful consideration and observation of certain dynamic factors, understood to be 'powers,' spirits, demons, god, laws, ideas, ideals or whatever name man has given to such factors as he has found in his world powerful, dangerous or helpful enough to be taken into careful consideration, or grand, beautiful and meaningful enough to be devoutly adored and loved."[9] He is not talking of creed and certainly not of church. Protestantism offers the frame of the conviction that God has revealed himself in Christ, who suffered for mankind, but the liberation from the dogma and ritual of Catholicism led to the authority of the Bible (and each man's interpretation of it now becomes possible) and to the ascendancy of inner experience. Elsewhere Jung also commented that when confronted with humankind's need for dependence and security, "What can one say of the Protestant? He has neither church nor priest, but only God—and even God becomes doubtful."[10]

The Milton of the 1640s, concerned with church government, espouses Presbyterianism and then rejects it; moves into Independency with its Arminian proportions, but falls out with certain practices; and finally abjures church attendance for himself. Milton's approval of Presbyterianism was probably a short-lived stratagem to effect church reform rather than a wholehearted acceptance of principles—that is, if he even had a clear knowledge of those principles that were to emerge with the Westminster Assembly of Divines' *Confession of Faith* in 1646 (called first *An Humble Advice*). The close alliance of Presbyterians and the monarchy during the troubled period from 1644 to 1649 also could not have continued Milton in their support. Independents, basically working through congregational organization, believed in leaving doctrinal matters to individual consciences. And this was and was to be a main lemma of Milton's religion. Independence from state control was meaningful when a Them/Us relation existed, but as the state became controlled by the Independents, during the Interregnum, and there was largely only Us, the question of liberty of conscience became a question of tithing and state support of the clergy. Milton's overt antagonism toward the nonseparation of church and state, like that of others in England and America, grew belatedly; the state/church collocation should have been foreseen from the first Erastian actions of the mid-sixteenth century, but was not, causing, later, schism among former partners.

William B. Hunter suggests that the main catalyst for Milton in reexamining his beliefs (creed, religion, theological positions) was the reception given his divorce tracts in 1643-45.[11] And this may be so, particularly with the rejection of his argument for divorce in the *Confession of Faith*, which, though he is unnamed, is a direct attack upon his position: "Although the corruption of man be such as is apt to study arguments, unduely to put asunder those whom God hath joyned together in marriage, yet nothing but Adultery, or such wilfull desertion as can no way be remedied, by the Church, or Civill Magistrate, is cause sufficient of dissolving the bond of Marriage. . . . And, the Persons concerned in it, not left to their own wills and discretion, in their own case."[12]

It seems clear why Milton is tolerant of varying sects—it is the personal religion that is important, and as long as a sect does not interfere with a person's personal religion it need not be stamped out: "No protestant therfore of what sect soever following scripture only, which is the common sect wherin they all agree, and the granted rule of everie mans conscience to himself, ought, by the common doctrine of protestants, to be forc'd or molested for religion."[13] Disagreement on doctrine was not important, but doctrine not derivative from God's word and the organization that fostered a concept of infallibility for any such doctrine were reprehensible. Thus we see Milton accepting adult baptism and the salvation this sacrament held forth as available to everyone. He could be called, that is, a General Baptist on this issue, not a Particular Baptist, for whom salvation was possible only for the elect. Thus we see him reflecting certain antinomian concepts as well, such as the abrogation of Mosaic law through the New Covenant (see Chapter 8), or antinomian resistance to persecution of religious dissenters. But at no point does Milton condone the libertinism often associated with the movement. His emphasis on the internal illumination that each person experiences as the Spirit of God fills one links him with the Friends (or Quakers), one of whose central figures in the mid- and later part of the century was Milton's former student and friend Thomas Ellwood. But Milton was not a Friend; his position on militarism and soldiery is a manifest disagreement with the Friends' precepts. And what strikes some people as "libertine" and morally offensive is Milton's acceptance of polygamy, although it hardly constitutes a religious congruence with, say, the Familists and their religion of love. In *De doctrina christiana* (I, x) he is concerned to deny that scripture condemns or denies polygamy, that is all; he is not advocating it. The litany of sectarians that Christopher Hill reviews[14] indicates how Milton agreed with different groups on this point or that, but we cannot push him into any specific pigeonhole, although he came close to the Muggletonians for Hill on the basis of anticlericalism, materialism (since Milton saw *creatio ex deo* as fundamental), millenarianism, and mortalism, but also, invalidly, anti-Trinitarianism and hell internal.

The anti-Trinitarian controversy in Milton studies—so frequently and erroneously labeled Arian controversy—has had a long and still ignorantly viable life. It is not that Milton was anti-Trinitarian but that he subscribed to the nonheretical (until the Council of Nicæa) doctrine of subordinationism. In *De doctrina christiana* (I, v) he wrote, "it is certain that the Son existed in the beginning, under the title of the Word or Logos, that he was the first of created things, and that through him all other things, both in heaven and earth, were afterwards made. . . . All these passages prove that the Son existed before the creation of the World, but not that his generation was from eternity."[15] He continues that the Father and the Son are not one in *essence* and that the *essential* unity of the three persons of the Trinity is illogical. Rather, each has its own essence, but all derive from the same *substantia*, the Godhead, as does everything created. The concept of the one God equates with God the Father; the other persons of the Trinity may be called God "in accordance with the Father's decree and will," but, like all things created, they come from the *substantia* of God. This is not an anti-Trinitarian position, no matter how unorthodox it may seem to be.

Milton's language in *De doctrina christiana* evidences his worriment of the word more incisively than allowed by the superficial "Three Persons in One Indivisible God" that seems to constitute Trinitarianism for most people. Milton contended that such a statement was indefensible because of illogic and contradictory of scripture: "I have already demonstrated satisfactorily, from the agreement of spiritual texts, that when both Father and Son are mentioned, the name, attributes, and works of God, and also the divine honor, are always ascribed to the one and only God the Father. . . . Even the principal texts which are quoted as proof of the Son's divinity show quite plainly, when they are closely and carefully studied, that he is God in the way I have suggested. . . . .If Father and Son were of one essence, which, because of their relationship, is impossible, it would follow that the Father was the Son's son and the Son the Father's father. Anyone who is not a lunatic can see what kind of conclusion this is. For I have said enough already to show that more than one hypostasis cannot be fitted into one essence."[16] The statement in the *Confession of Faith* on the Trinity falls between the general, inexact catchphrase and Milton's analytic argument: "In the Unity of the God-head there be Three Persons, of one substance, power, and eternity; God the Father, God the Sonne, and God the Holy Ghost. The Father is of none, neither begotten, nor proceeding: The Sonne is eternally begotten of the Father: the Holy Ghost eternally proceeding from the Father and the Son."[17]

John Short's exposition of 1 Corinthians 15:24-28 reads Paul's words in a way that is consistent with Milton's ideas. "Therefore, while he is in no doubt that God is mediated through Jesus Christ, he never fully identifies the two. God must be supreme from first to last. It is God, and God alone, who is the alpha and the omega. Whatever the relationship in terms of communion may be between the Father and the Son, they are not in the apostle's thought identical. In respect of the work of Christ among men, for man's redemption, the relationship is one of subordination to the Father."[18] Saint Augustine is also both helpful and confusing on the issue, but yielding a seemingly much less unorthodox Milton: "For by the name Father, the Father by Himself is made known, but the name God includes Himself, as well as the Son and the Holy Spirit, because the Trinity is one God. . . . God alone makes and is not made, nor can any passive potency be conceived in Him, insofar as He is a substance, by virtue of which He is God. . . . To sum up: Whatever is spoken of God in respect to Himself and of each single person, that is, of the Father, the Son, and the Holy Sprit, and together of the Trinity itself, is to be predicated in the singular of each divine person and not in the plural. . . . [J]ust as we do not speak of three essences, so we do not speak of three greatnesses. I give the name essence to what the Greeks call *ousia*, but which we more generally designate as substance."[19]

For Milton—the later Milton at least—creation is *ex deo*, that is, from the substance that is God. When at the end of time the Son puts himself under the Father so that God will be All in All (1 Corinthians 15:28),[20] Milton interprets, there will be a bodily return of all substance to the one and only *substantia*, the Godhead, out of which creation has come. Similarly, with double meaning he wrote in *Paradise Lost* at the defeat of the rebellious angels, with reference to the Messiah's Sign in Heaven: "Under whose conduct *Michael* soon reduc'd / His Armie, circumfus'd on either Wing, / Under thir Head imbodied all in one" (VI, 777-79).

The concept of a "hell internal" that Christopher Hill refers to derives 1) from Satan's remarks, such as "The mind is its own place, and in itself / Can make a Heav'n of Hell, a Hell of Heav'n" (*PL* I, 253-54) and "Which way I flie is Hell, my self am Hell" (*PL* IV, 75); 2) from the narrator's reference to Satan, "The Hell within him, for within him Hell / He brings, and round about him, nor from Hell / One step no more then from himself can fly / By change of place" (*PL* IV, 20-23); and 3) through contrast, from Michael's prophetic voice telling Adam, "Then [with knowledge, deeds, and love] wilt thou not be loath / To leave this Paradise, but shalt possess / A Paradise within thee, happier farr" (*PL* XII, 585-87). C.A. Patrides has shown how common the "hell internal" metaphor was among writers on religion,[21] and thus Adam's "O Conscience, into what Abyss of fears / And horrors hast thou driv'n me; out of which / I find no way, from deep to deeper plung'd!" (*PL* X, 842-44) is not unusual, surely not a means of linking Milton with any sectarian group. He refers, of course, to "The second degree of death . . . called SPIRITUAL DEATH."[22] It consists "in the loss or at least the extensive darkening of that right reason, whose function it was to discern the chief good, and which was, as it were, the life of the understanding," and "in that extension of righteousness and of the liberty to do good, and in that slavish subjection to sin and the devil which is, as it were, the death of the will."[23]

What all this is meant to suggest is that the various attempts to make Milton a proponent of one creed or another are unacceptable because they are based on a tangency or two, not on a clear placement of him in any specific fold past his defection from Anglicanism. Commentators have been too eager to place Milton in a niche, find a similar thought or approach, and precipitantly pounce on a label. His religion was his own, and a description of it—which must be accordingly generalized except inasmuch as one can detail theological positions from *De doctrina christiana*—indicates that it was.

Quite simply, Milton was Calvinist, agreeing with election and predestination but also accepting renovation (and vocation) as the means to restoration through the redemption of Christ. Renovation means the state of grace to which man is brought after having been cursed and subject to God's anger; through vocation—God's invitation to fallen man to learn the way to placate and worship the Godhead—all are invited to salvation. Like the Puritan, Milton emphasized the doctrine of the Fall, the inheritance of "the sin common to all men," and the need and means of regeneration. "Ingrafting in Christ" defined regeneration for Milton, as the former person is destroyed and a new inner man emerges, restored to God's image, sanctified in soul and body, to God's service and to good works. Regeneration brings repentance and faith. A logical conclusion for this precept is that no agent is needed to bring the individual into regeneration: the internality of "Faith, . . . Vertue, Patience, Temperance, . . . Love, By name to come call'd Charitie" (*PL* XII, 582-84) is an individual matter entirely. It is most unlikely that Milton had come to such attitudes during the early 1640s when he was arguing against prelaty, but perhaps the Protectorate, the "Blue Laws" under Major-General Lambert, and the issue of liberty of conscience led him to these ideas.

We can see such ideas dimly before the end of the 1650s, but it was probably the experiences of those years that, around 1658 onward, led to the thoughts of *Paradise Lost* and *De doctrina christiana*, both apparently developed in those years of 1658-65 when fears about the Restoration did not encroach. It would have been an easy step to turn from church attendance or any other external show of religious action. The minister has his function to maintain "the primitive faith" and feed "the sheep that worship Christ," "to bring joyous messages from heaven, and . . . teach the way which leads beyond the grave to the stars" ("Elegia quarta," ll. 17-18, 92-93). But for those like Milton who recognize that way already, there is no continued need for ministerial services, not even for the preaching of the Word. If internal scripture, then, is superior, it follows that no visible church has authority over the inner scripture. And with the nullification of the church's role in administering the two sacraments that remain, baptism and the Lord's supper,[24] the church had lost for him almost all reason for being. The charity to be dispensed to those one comes into contact with, one's "neighbors," is the main topic of

Book II of *De doctrina christiana;* it is not church-related. While he acknowledges that worship be maintained, he deduces that no special day or place is required. He does not object to holding a sabbath and in a specific place, but he firmly believes that no coercion from civil authority should exist to ensnare one's free conscience, particularly by invalid recitation of scripture. Milton's church is a church of one.[25]

Two areas in which Milton's theological thought have caused consternation for some are the Incarnation and the eschatological relationship of body and soul. Milton's view of the Incarnation and the death of Christ seems to come close to Nestorianism and Monarchianism, although neither label is apposite. The relationship of the divine being and the human being in the Incarnation of the son as Jesus may be a union of the two natures (traditional and orthodox), a union of two persons (as Milton argued), a dominance of humanity and human personality in the person of Jesus (Nestorianism), or a single person as well as a single being (Monarchianism). Behind Milton's thinking is traducianism, which alleges that since the soul is substance, it was propagated from parent to child. Thus the soul as substance would die (or sleep) with the body and await reemergence at the Last Judgment. Early on, if "Lycidas" and "Epitaphium Damonis" can fully carry the weight of theological interpretation, Milton would seem to have believed that the soul did not die with the body at death. We see Lycidas and Damon both mounted high, rejecting the rainbow. But later Milton accepted the doctrine of thnetopsychism, that is, that the soul dies with the body and awaits renewal at the resurrection. Similar is psychopannychia, which taught that the soul slept until the resurrection of the body. Milton's language in *De doctrina christiana* (I, xiii) places him in the category of thnetopsychist, but he also uses the word "sleep" of the soul at death, suggesting he did not distinguish between the two concepts. This belief in the death (or sleep) of the soul is generally called mortalism and was not uncommon in the Renaissance, as Norman T. Burns has shown us.[26] The main issue, of course, between the ascent of the soul and the death of the soul is its nature, that is, its materiality.

For the Nestorian the natures of God and man were not merged; Jesus was man in whom God worked his will, as it were. There was no union of essences; instead the divine Logos took up abode in the man Jesus. Milton proceeds from his interpretation of kenosis in Philippians 2:6-8,[27] which we see reflected in 1629 in the "Nativity Ode": "That glorious Form, that Light unsufferable, / And that far-beaming blaze of Majesty, / Wherwith he wont at Heav'ns high Councel-Table, / To sit the midst of Trinal Unity, / He laid aside" (8-12); and later in "Upon the Circumcision": "for us frail dust / Emptied his glory" (19-20). If the Son fully "emptied" himself of his Godhead and was incarnated as Jesus, then we are surely on the verge of Nestorianism. But Milton hedges somewhat, saying, "Christ, then although he was God, put on human nature, and was made Flesh, but did not cease to be numerically one Christ" (YP, VI, 420). Thus Christ is thought of as not relinquishing his divine nature: he maintains "the essence itself." There is union for Milton, but the stress on the individual beings flirts with the concept that God worked through Jesus rather than that Jesus was divine. Milton, however, also contends that Jesus died in both natures (divine and human), and of course this is logical if the soul is substance and was propagated from parent to child.[28] Monarchians were anti-Trinitarian, seeing Christ either as mere man, chosen by God, and inspirited and exalted by him (he is Son of God by adoption), or as truly divine but thus indistinguishable from God the Father. Such thinking led to the heresy espoused by the Patripassians and Sabellians that the Father also suffered in the Crucifixion. Again Milton's interpretation of kenosis puts him dangerously close to the first view noted for Monarchianism, even though he was not anti-Trinitarian, as I have argued.

While there has been much attention to theological issues in Milton and some attempts to categorize his creed and church on the basis of a likeness or two, little scholarship has been devoted to Milton's religion *per se.* The best statement, though brief, is that already cited, by William B. Hunter in *A Milton Encyclopedia* (7:106-20). Another is the published dissertation by Paul Chauvet,[29] who reviewed the Anglican and Puritan contexts as well as the schismatic groups such as the Arminians, the Independents, and the Antinomians, which Milton would have known. Deriving evidence from the facts of his life and from the works, including *De doctrina christiana,* Chauvet presents a Milton who is anti-Roman Catholic, recognizes that in 1632 he was an Anglican as the signing of the Thirty-nine Articles makes clear (38), and sees him moving toward a middle position between Anglicanism and Puritanism (such as the Arminians represented) at least after 1639 and by 1645. For Milton the Bible is of prime importance. Chauvet recognizes an affinity first with Presbyterian attitudes, with Baptist beliefs, and with Antinomian thought, and thus stresses the importance of individual conscience for Milton "et que les bonnes et les mauvaises oeuvres sont également indifférentes à notre salut" (119). He discusses Milton's beliefs in toleration, separation of Church and State, and liberty of conscience. "Milton est le constant accusateur du péché et le chantre infatigable de la Rédemption. . . . mais que ce même puritanisme, en émancipant sans prudence la conscience individuelle, sapait les bases de la fois apostolique et tendait à démolir la doctrine après la discipline . . . " (211). He therefore concludes that Milton's religion is individualistic and not specifically congruent with those given classifying labels: "Le Miltonisme est, dans son essence, la religion puritaine fortement modifiée par la personnalité ultra-intense de John Milton" (243).

Religion is an escape from the unconscious, supplying the "other side," or anima. Milton's father may have been a deterrent in bringing him to realizations about himself and about his religion: the church was the world to which he was intended until 1637 when, with his mother's death, he was able to achieve some freedom of decision as well as movement. But it took two decades to traverse the road to his individualistic religion, "Le Miltonisme," as Chauvet labeled it. Taking on his father's energy in its formulated religious structure repressed his own energy (I use the term in its Jungian manifestations). As the form that such energy took in religious matters, the church was the first to be reexamined and recast, only later to take new form for Milton's own energy. "[E]verything depends on the *form* into which energy passes. Form gives energy its quality. . . . For the creation of a real value, therefore, both energy and valuable form are needed."[30] It is the father archetype that supplies energy, the anima or mother archetype that supplies form.

Through those two decades, the content which the form held also underwent reexamination and recasting. And it was with his father's death in 1647 that Milton moved into such revision, although at first the concerns were governmental, religious ostensibly only in religion-government issues such as liberty of conscience. In a way this period was a delaying action created by the transference of ego energy to the object government; only with reductive analysis (a severing of that transference) can one release that energy to achieve what was promised oneself in the past. With the period of 1658-65 and the writing of *De doctrina christiana* and *Paradise Lost,* Milton was able to forge new religious content for his new form through the exercise of his own energy. Again Jung supplies a rationale of this human experience. The adult cut loose from parents finds that "energy streaming back from these manifold relationships [of the past] falls into the unconscious and activates all the things he had neglected to develop. . . . To the man in the second half of life the development of the function of opposites lying dormant in the unconscious means a renewal."[31] In the postscript to *Defensio prima* published in 1658 Milton has given proof of this statement: "Now that my toil has won the richest rewards I had hoped for in this life, I do delight in them with all thankfulness, but at the same time I am earnestly seeking how best I may show not only my own country, to which I devoted all I have, but men of every land and, particularly, all Christian men, that for their sake I am at this time hoping and planning still greater things, if these be possible for me, as with God's help they will."[32]

But we can see the major beginning of the assertion of self in Sonnet 19, "When I consider how my light is spent," written surely in (October?) 1655, "Ere half my days in this dark world and wide," despite some attempts to place it earlier. (It is *not* "On His Blindness," of course; that is only a significant background for the tenor of the poem, which is the resolve to activate the things that had been neglected to develop when time and occasion and psychic energy should appear.) What the poem suggests is an emptying of self and the past, and a picking up the pieces of what remains to reform them in the present and future. According to James P. Driscoll, "Nothingness beneath real identity [and this is what Sonnet 19 shows us] is a necessary condition for understanding the larger self. . . . [I]t symbolizes consciousness freed from ego tyranny to gain contact with the whole self."[33] The opposites of rebellion and sublimation are rawly presented in *Paradise Lost,* perhaps because they were rawly and recently the oppositions within Milton's own two-decade experience. *Paradise Regain'd,* I have argued elsewhere,[34] was begun in the late 1640s and completed and expanded in different form after 1665. This reexamination of Milton's religion and its apparent psychological substructs suggests a reason for the poem's inchoate condition and for an alteration of content and form, and for its renewal as a work of real value beyond the influence of *Paradise Lost* and Thomas Ellwood's imperceptive reading of that epic. With *Paradise Regain'd* Milton proceeded to full assertion of his religious precept.

16

The Bible

Milton is the English author most generally acknowledged as the greatest religious poet. That opinion rests for most people on his masterwork *Paradise Lost.* What is implied is, first, the subject matter; second, the scriptural foundation and quotation of the poem; and third, the sense of religiosity imbued by it. Indeed, many people in the eighteenth and nineteenth centuries seemed to learn the substance of the Bible from the poem, often confusing the two. The archangel Uriel, for instance, who does not appear in the Bible but owes his being to Hebraic tradition, has a very important role in the poem in Books III and IV. The name appears three times in 2 Esdras (4:1, 5:20, 10:28), and in Hebrew means "Flame or Fire of God." Milton makes him the "Regent of the Sun" and identifies him with the "glorious Angel . . . whom *John* saw also in the Sun" (III, 622-23), referring to Revelation 19:17. In later rabbinical tradition he became one of the seven angels of the Presence and one of the four angelic commanders, with authority over the South. Milton employs this tradition in his description of Uriel. In the poem Uriel points out Earth to Satan in his guise as an innocent cherub, only to recognize him as one of the fallen angels escaped from Hell as Satan proceeds to infiltrate Eden. Uriel then warns Gabriel in Book IV of Satan's entrance. His function in the poem is to establish that "neither Man nor Angel can discern / Hypocrisie, the only evil that walks / Invisible, except to God alone" (III, 682-84), shortly before Eve is assaulted in her sleep by Satan appearing like Adam to her, in a foreview of the temptation in Book IX. The Uriel episode makes clear that the hypocrisy and false guise as a serpent that Satan presents to Eve in the temptation could understandably be cast as truthful by a mere human. The episode is a major element in establishing one of the themes of the poem: that deception can lead to wrong reason.

Or we might think of Abdiel, an angel totally invented by Milton. The word does appear in 1 Chronicles 5:15 as a man's name; and in *Sepher Raziel* (printed after 1700), a cabalistic conjuring book, as the name of an angel. In Hebrew it means "Servant of God." Abdiel at first mistakenly seems to join Satan in his rebellion against God, in Book V, until he realizes the thrust of Satan's assemblage of his troops. Once understanding the import of Satan's charges against God's begetting of the Son, he exercises his free will to condemn the "argument blasphemous, false and proud" and thus keep "His Loyaltie . . . his Love, his Zeal . . . unmov'd, / Unshak'n, unseduc'd, unterrifi'd" (V, 809, 898-900). One of his functions in the epic is to indicate approval of independence of thought and action (just as Eve will exercise her independence of thought and action when in Book IX she separates from Adam to undertake her chores separately);[1] another is to make clear that even with a first unknowing step toward disobedience, the exercise of free will to remain obedient can reverse that step. Adam, in contrast, partakes of the fruit of the Forbidden Tree by an unhappy exercise of his free will: "he scrupl'd not to eat / Against his better knowledge, not deceav'd" (IX, 997-98). This episode helps establish another theme: that disobedience can be wilful without deception when based on personal desires, for Adam completes the "mortal Sin Original" overcome by narcissistic feelings for "Flesh of Flesh, / Bone of [his] Bone," construed as "Femal charm." This psychological analysis of Adam and his sin which Milton creates derives from a bare biblical text stating the act and Adam's words in the previous chapter when God creates woman from his rib (Genesis 2:23).

Uriel and Abdiel, nonbiblical figures, serve Milton's aims to present the truths of the Bible and to interpret what occurred in the Fall recorded in Genesis 3, and why. Both angels are repeatedly spoken of in the eighteenth century and after as if biblical. For instance, Nathaniel Salmon in *The History of Herfordshire* (1728) likens an important landowner, William Clerk, to Abdiel: "This Protestor in a Convention of Rebel Angels, must lose some of the Beauties, unless we suppose him a Cavalier in Masque. . . . The Scripture Account of the Defection makes not the Lapsed so much as a Majority; . . . what Notion must we have of Angelic Perfection, to admit *Abdiel* could think himself alone?" (185). Daniel Defoe in *The Political History of the Devil* (1726), Part II, Chapter VII, 298, confuses Uriel and Ithuriel, apparently because of the memorable picture Milton draws of the Regent of the Sun. Ithuriel, whose name means "Discovery of God," appears as one of the angelic guard in Book IV; his spear touches the discovered Satan, returning Satan from toad to his proper shape as diminished fallen angel. Ithuriel's spear is a frequently used metaphor for miraculous action; for example, by Jonathan Swift in "Journal to Stella," Letter VIII, dated 31 October 1710. Like these other angels, Ithuriel is nonbiblical; the name is found in some cabalistic works of the sixteenth century.

While certainly readers in the years following the publication of *Paradise Lost* knew their Bible well, chapter and verse, they nonetheless evidence an appropriation of supposedly biblical matter from the poem. Frequently it is the poem that offers a prooftext, as with Cotton Mather's recommendation for "Study of the Sciences" (36) in *Manuductio ad ministerium. Directions for a Candidate of the Ministry* (1726), or the numerous quotations in Sermon XXIV, on Revelation 21:5, published in the *Arminian Magazine* for December 1790 (589-92). The poem—that is, the second half of the poem—takes as its basic texts Genesis 1-3, the Creation, covered specifically in Books VII and VIII, the Disobedience, presented specifically in Book IX, and the Judgment, denounced in Book X. The panorama of biblical personages who are types of the antitype, Christ, such as Noah, or negative representatives, such as Nimrod, is detailed in Books XI and XII, drawing on additional books of the Bible. This very selective biblical history leads up to Jesus as antitype and Christ, giving us a Noah, for example, in the Flood but not in his drunkenness (except for a later reference to Ham), and making of Nimrod one

> Of proud ambitious heart, who not content
> With fair equalitie, fraternal state,
> Will arrogate Dominion undeserv'd
> Over his brethren, and quite dispossess
> Concord and law of Nature from the Earth,
> Hunting (and Men not Beasts shall be his game)
> With Warr and hostile snare such as refuse
> Subjection to his Empire tyrannous:
> A mightie Hunter thence he shall be styl'd
> Before the Lord, as in despite of Heav'n,
> Or from Heav'n claming second Sovrantie;
> And from Rebellion shall derive his name,
> Though of Rebellion others he accuse. [XII, 24-37]

The name Nimrod in Hebrew means "rebel," and Milton's expansion on Genesis 10:8-9 interprets what he read as the implication and message of the biblical text. Aligning Nimrod with the Satanic forces unleashed on Earth through original sin, he also makes him the founder of Babylon, with its connotations of false religion and evil, since Nimrod has the beginning of his kingdom in Babel, with which Babylon was identified. (In the background for his fit audience Milton is recalling the fall and desolation prophesied for Babylon in Jeremiah 51 and Revelation 18; in its fall will be "found the blood of prophets, and of saints, and all that were slain upon the earth," verse 24.) The scathing indictment of this "rebel" against the true God displaces Milton from the rebelliousness (or radicalism) that critics have alleged. Consistently Milton fights for the Truth of the true God against the falsity of the petty images of Satan, who would limit the liberty and individualism of a person under God. This may mean the toleration of polygamy rather than its advocacy, the acceptance of certain Arminian concepts rather than an acceptance of all Arminian concepts, the belief in the advent of the Millennium without the politicization of the Fifth Monarchists.

The Bible is being interpreted, its subject matter chosen for the Truths laid bare in the poem, its integrity as two testaments manifested by the repetitions and parallels and developments of the poetic meditation. The vision on the Hill of Speculation that Michael enables Adam to see vacillates between good types and bad up to the birth of "the true / Anointed King *Messiah*," the antitype. After a rhapsodic recounting of the achievement of the Second Adam, with the bringing to pass of the protevangelium (which had been pronounced in Book X and which has led to Eve and Adam's prayer and the descent of Prevenient Grace at the end of Book X and beginning of Book XI), the poem rapidly ends with Adam's realization "that suffering for Truths sake / Is fortitude to highest victorie, / And to the faithful Death the Gate of Life," and with Michael's advice "onely add / Deeds to thy knowledge answerable, add Faith, / Add Vertue, Patience, Temperance, add Love, / By name to come call'd Charitie, the soul / Of all the rest" (XII, 569-71, 581-85). This preceding biblical content is the burden of only Books VII through XII.

That the Bible required interpretation for humankind to understand and embody its Truths is clear from Milton's attempt to reconcile various Calvinist positions in *De doctrina christiana*. Though he speaks of the literalness of the Bible, his meaning is its truth which should stand forth with literal meaning. But the varying positions on doctrine taken by strict Calvinists, by the Remonstrant group of Holland, by the group centered around Saumur, France, and the differences observable in the writings of William Perkins, William Ames, John Wolleb, all pounded home the realization that "more . . . still needed to be measured with greater strictness against the yardstick of the Bible, and reformed with greater care" (VI, 120). "Most authors," Milton writes, as noted in Chapter 2, "have relegated to the margin, with brief reference to chapter and verse, the scriptural texts upon which all that they teach is utterly dependent. I, on the other hand, have striven to cram my pages even to overflowing, with quotations drawn from all parts of the Bible and to leave as little space as possible for my own words, even when they arise from the putting together of actual scriptural texts" (VI, 122). Yet, of course, such juxtaposition creates a reading which would not necessarily be that determined by reading separated texts, and when one moves to direct confrontation with a public audience, as in a sermon or a poem, interpretation and presentation are unavoidable.

Milton's equation of the office of the pulpit and the vatic author in *The Reason of Church-Government* is often cited, and the need to dress Truth elegantly so that "those especially of soft and delicious temper . . . will . . . look upon Truth herselfe" (I, 817-18) is explicitly stated. In a Latin elegy to his former tutor Thomas Young, written in 1627, when Young was pastor to the English merchants in Hamburg, Milton observed the same equation and need when he spoke of those "whom provident God himself has sent . . . , and who bring joyous messages from heaven, and who teach the way which leads beyond the grave to the stars" (92-94). The minister is needed to bring God's word to the people. Milton believed that "God has revealed the way of eternal salvation only to the individual faith of each man, and demands of us that any man who wishes to be saved should work out his beliefs for himself." Accordingly he admonishes, "Do not accept or reject what I say unless you are absolutely convinced by the clear evidence of the Bible" (VI, 118, 124). But of course that "clear evidence" depends on its being that same "evidence" for one person as it is for another, and the minister, poet, definer of Christian doctrine presents the Truth he sees in the evidence, though logically others may see a different Truth.

While the Bible presents literal Truth for Milton, it must be rendered understandable and meaningful by a ministry to those less capable of comprehending. It may require accommodation—by the poet, for example—best furnished through such figures as Uriel, Abdiel, and Ithuriel: the slyness of the devil professing truth (through Uriel), the need to assert freedom of will that follows right reason (through Abdiel), and the miraculousness that God can work (through Ithuriel). This position flies in the face of such Calvinists as Theodore de Bèze and his followers at Geneva, although Calvin himself did not eschew literary creation. For Bèze only a cautious exegesis of Scripture, revealing its Truth, was proper.[2] Milton's frequent demurrals from assertion of self as author and his hope in the inspiration of the Celestial Patroness should be read against this background.

Paradise Lost, particularly, and *Paradise Regain'd* present biblical truths elegantly dressed for those especially of soft and delicious temper. They build upon what the reader would be expected to know from the Bible but present it in such a way that its message is explicit and, so important, memorable. The expansion and interpretation of the Temptation in the Wilderness in the brief epic, drawn from Luke 4:1-13 and also recounted in Matthew 4:1-11 and Mark 1:12-13, presents not only the rejection of the lures of the flesh (and gluttony) in "man shall not live by bread alone" (the first temptation), and the rejection of worldly kingdoms (and covetousness) in "Get thee behind me, Satan" (the second temptation), and the rejection of the devil (and pride) in "Thou shalt not tempt the Lord thy God" (the third temptation), but offers for the astute reader the deep and wide-ranging significations of these temptations. The poem presents both the understanding of what the Messiah is, thereby delineating his ministry, and the nature of and means to salvation for all humankind.

Jesus is seen, first, to develop his selfhood; that is, he shows himself one who is not afraid to be himself and to accept a subordinational position. Second, he develops the arms of his great warfare against the devil, Faith and Works, through obedience and love of others. In *Paradise Lost* Milton had contrasted Satan's arms, Sin and Death (XII, 430), and the Son's defeat of Sin and "death for Man," which Adam should "the benefit imbrace / By Faith not void of works" (XII, 425-27). Jesus in his ministry will nourish the soul by the Word, reemphasizing that man does not live by bread (for the body) alone; he will continue the patience exhibited in the second temptation, rejecting the externals of wealth and power and mundane glory; and he will exemplify faith in God and God's word, as he does in the third temptation when, precariously on the spire of the temple at Jerusalem, he stands firm. Of course, he would have fallen, but God sends ministering angels to save him as it had been promised to those who say of the Lord, "He is my refuge and my fortress: my God; in him will I trust" (Psalm 91:2). The specific text of this psalm, which Satan fraudulently, incompletely quotes during the temptation reported in the Gospels, is: "For he shall give his angels charge over thee, to keep thee in all thy ways. They shall bear thee up in their hands, lest thou dash thy foot against a stone" (Psalm 91:11-12). The miracle God would work for those who are his true servants was always in Milton's mind. As we saw in Chapter 2, it is the central point of his first extant poem, "A Paraphrase upon Psalm 114"; lack of such faith—not his disobedience—is the major failing of Adam.

Third, and most important, Jesus in *Paradise Regain'd* lays bare the way to live one's life, not simply by emulating him, the Son, but by so internalizing the lessons of the temptations that one will be able to face any assault from the devil.[3] The poem interprets and expands the gospel text of the Temptation in the Wilderness, making it a rite of passage for Jesus from his baptism and youth to his ministry. With the Son's Faith demonstrated, the poem ends with the angelic chorus's "Hail Son of the most High, heir of both worlds, / Queller of Satan, on thy glorious work / Now enter, and begin to save mankind." In the meantime, "hee unobserv'd / Home to his Mothers house private return'd" (IV, 633-35,

638-39). Mythically the action of the poem corresponds to the rite of confirmation, known in some form in all cultures. It is as much Ike Mc-Caslin's conquering of the wilderness in William Faulkner's "The Bear" as it is Stephen Dedalus's finally leaving Ireland to become the artificer of his race in James Joyce's *A Portrait of the Artist as a Young Man*. The Truths of the Bible will repeat generation after generation.

Certain biblical content is the burden of Books VII-XII of *Paradise Lost*, as noted, but not of Books I-VI because there is so little that is direct. For the War in Heaven in Books V and VI Milton's primary biblical authority was Revelation 12:7-9: "And there was war in heaven: Michael and his angels fought against the dragon; and the dragon fought and his angels, and prevailed not; neither was their place found any more in heaven. And the great dragon was cast out, that old serpent, called the Devil, and Satan, which deceiveth the whole world: he was cast out into the earth, and his angels were cast out with him." The episode of Sin and Death in Book II, but reprised in the building of the bridge from Hell to Earth in Book X, so that sinners would have easy passage, comes from James 1:15: "Then when lust hath conceived, it bringeth forth sin; and sin, when it is finished, bringeth forth death," to which Milton added the two beasts of Revelation 13, the chapter after that just quoted, concerned with the Devil's expulsion. And it is in the first, less biblical half of the poem that Satan seems to dominate for many readers and for critics who would cast him as hero of the poem.

Such critics are not reading the poem very perceptively. The line may be highflown oratory with rousing sounds, but can anyone really believe that Satan means it when he calls himself "One who brings / A mind not to be chang'd by Place or Time"? There are, of course, numerous instances in the poem when he does change his mind, but even so such absolutism is illogical, nonexperiential, and a horrendous concept. Satan is not directly built upon biblical texts, other than those I have cited; he is Milton's personification of the devil, the Old Serpent, Evil, based on what can be drawn from the history of interpretation of the Bible texts, and with the residue of the fallen Lucifer, of whom Isaiah says, "How art thou fallen from heaven, O Lucifer, son of the morning," continuing to recount his attempt to be like the Most High and his being doomed to hell, to the sides of the pit.

Milton's poem contributes to the equation of the devil and Satan (the text in Revelation creates the juxtaposition as well), but most people are quite unaware that Satan does not appear in the Bible until the Book of Job (except for one mention in 1 Chronicles 21:1).[4] Satan, whose name in Hebrew means Adversary, acts as adversary in Job, not as the devil. There is some adversariness in *Paradise Lost* (the word is used seven times), but Milton has expanded and interpreted his various texts to create a psychologically strong characterization of what today we have often called an antihero, remembering such as Dostoievsky's Underground Man, as well as what personifies false pride and envy. Critical objections have been leveled against the Satan of *Paradise Regain'd* by those comparing him with the figure in the longer epic because he is not a psychologically strong character. But of course he wouldn't be: he is like the Satan of Job, and the Book of Job permeates the brief epic. He is called Adversary once at the beginning and he calls the Son Adversary once toward the end. He is only a foil for Milton to establish the Truths which the Son demonstrates. The seven uses of the word in *Paradise Lost* also indicate his adversariness to God and Man, but the character becomes more than that in the longer epic: he becomes the devil and the Old Serpent.[5]

We can see from these remarks why and how Milton occupies a position as great religious poet, and how the subject matter, personages, and religiosity of his poetry present the Truths he knew from the Bible, though interpreted and elegantly dressed. Indeed, one need not be of any particular religious persuasion, in fact not even religiously inclined, to understand and appreciate such truths and make them a part of one's individual being. One of Milton's important techniques in developing these reader attitudes is quotation and allusion, and repetition of quotations and allusions in similar or contrastive contexts. Let us look at three such examples in *Paradise Lost:* the figure of Moses, and the texts of Psalm 2 and 1 Corinthians 15:28. These texts delineate the mediatorial roles of Christ.

The proem to Book I, foreviewing the full poem, reads in part:

> Sing Heav'nly Muse, that on the secret top
> Of *Oreb,* or of *Sinai,* didst inspire
> That Shepherd, who first taught the chosen Seed,
> In the Beginning how the Heav'ns and Earth
> Rose out of *Chaos:* Or if *Sion* Hill
> Delight thee more, and *Siloa*'s Brook that flow'd
> Fast by the Oracle of God; I thence
> Invoke thy aid to my adventrous Song [I, 6-13]

The references are to Moses as Prophet (that is, one who foresees and shows the people the way to a new world), to David the King (who sits on Sion Hill), and to Jesus (who healed the blind man at the pool of Siloam—John 9:7). These denote the prophetic, kingly, and priestly roles of the Son as Messiah, made explicit by Milton in *Paradise Regain'd* through his treatment of the three temptations. As poet, Milton asks the

Heavenly Muse to aid him in his great argument "To assert eternal Providence, and justify the ways of God to men," with these three roles underlying his song. The contexts of those roles will appear throughout the epic in various guises and forms: Moses as prophet who leads his people out of bondage as God miraculously parts the waters of the Red Sea; the reign of the anointed Son and the vain imitation of the petty kings of the earth; and the end of time when God will be All in All.

James Sims in *The Bible in Milton's Epics*[6] lists sixty allusions to the book of Exodus in *Paradise Lost;* we need only look at a few to conclude the integral place of Moses' prophetic role in it. The first major reference to the Exodus occurs in I, 306-11: "the Red-Sea Coast, whose waves orethrew / *Busiris* and his *Memphian* Chivalry, / While with perfidious hatred they pursu'd / The Sojourners of *Goshen,* who beheld / From the safe shore thir floating Carkases / And broken Chariot Wheels" (cf. 14:23-30). Soon after this Moses is specifically named: "As when the potent Rod / Of *Amrams* Son in *Egypts* evill day / Wav'd round the coast, up call'd a pitchy cloud / Of *Locusts,* warping on the Eastern Wind, / That ore the Realm of impious *Pharaoh* hung / Like Night, and darken'd all the Land of *Nile*" (I, 338-43; 10:12-15). Note that Milton presents Moses in his filial role, "*Amrams* Son," an ideological construction discussed before in Chapter 2. It suggests something about Milton's relationship with his own father, and in the epic it underscores the subordinationism of not only the Son to the Father but of Eve to Adam, and on through all generations, supernal or human. Significantly and ironically, of course, Death is not subordinate to *his* father, although dependent upon Satan's making "all things" the "prey" of daughter and son.

Not long after this second citation of Moses and the Exodus from the bondage of Pharaoh, the failure that ensued in the new land and new beginning is recalled: "Nor did Israel scape / Th'infection when thir borrow'd Gold compos'd / The Calf in *Oreb* (I, 482-84; 12:35; 32:4). All three citations in Book I are keyed to identify Satan and Pharaoh, Satan's bondage of humankind with Pharaoh's bondage of the Israelites. I have elsewhere discussed the parallels of the Mosaic exodus and Adam and Eve's Expulsion,[7] and the failure of the new beginnings in time. The Exodus is narrated, of course, in the view of biblical history that Michael presents to Adam in Book XII, 151-269. The prophetic, ministerial role Moses plays is explicitly set forth in this narration: he proclaims the revelation:

> But the voice of God
> To mortal ear is dreadful; they beseech
> That *Moses* might report to them his will,

> And terror cease; he grants what they besaught
> Instructed that to God is no access
> Without Mediator, whose high Office now
> *Moses* in figure beares, to introduce
> One greater, of whose day he shall foretell,
> And all the Prophets in thir Age the times
> Of great *Messiah* shall sing. [XII, 235-44]

Moses acts as mediator with God and prepares his people for the new life in Canaan. It is a role we can ascribe to Milton as poet, setting up a narration for his readers that mediates God's presence and looks toward the Incarnation of "One greater," whose day Moses has foretold and whose work is awaited in lines 4 and 5 of *Paradise Lost:* "till one greater Man / Restore us, and regain the blissful Seat."

With the completion of the Judgment in Book X, the Heavenly Audience hymn the song of Moses: "Just are thy ways, / Righteous are thy Decrees on all thy Works" (X, 543-44; Revelation 15:3, "And they sing the song of Moses the servant of God, and the song of the Lamb, saying, Great and marvellous are thy works, Lord, God Almighty, just and true are thy ways, thou King of Saints"). The Judgment has shown the just ways of God to men. Or rather it *should* be the telling expression of Milton's success in achieving his great argument. But is it so? Do all readers read the same? Apparently not. It is the "one greater Man" who will reveal God's Eternal Providence.

The kingly and priestly roles, denoted in Psalm 2 and in 1 Corinthians 15:28, reinforce Milton's success in asserting Eternal Providence when rightly read. The important text of Psalm 2 is the linchpin of the action as Milton attempts to explain Satan's rebellion. It reads, verses 6 and 7: "Yet have I set my King upon my holy hill of Zion. I will declare the decree: the Lord hath said unto me, Thou art my Son; this day have I begotten thee." Construing the begetting of the Son announced in Book V as creating a new chain of command (Satan and many critics keep forgetting that the Son *is* God, though a different aspect from that of the Father), Satan becomes envious, allows his false pride to soar, moves to rebel, and in that instant Sin is born of his mental being (she is described in parallel with the mythic birth of Athena from Zeus, from the left side of his head). Satan is presented as seeking kingship and the supposed accoutrements of kingdom throughout: the beginning of Book II has him "High on a Throne of Royal State" and in Book IV he believes "Divided Empire with Heav'ns King I hold . . . and more then half perhaps will reigne" (111-12).

But the psalmic text preceding puts it all in perspective: "Why do the heathen rage, and the people imagine a vain thing? The kings of the earth set themselves, and the rulers take counsel together, against the Lord, and against his Anointed, saying, Let us break their bands asunder, and cast away their cords from us. He that sitteth in the heavens shall laugh: the Lord shall have them in derision." The first pointed use of this text in the poem is satirically ironic; it is Belial "with words cloath'd in reasons garb / [Counseling] ignoble ease, and peaceful sloath, / Not peace," who says: "he from heav'ns highth / All these our motions vain, sees and derides" (II, 190-91). And Sin, trying to separate Satan and Death from armed encounter, exclaims, "O Father, what intends thy hand . . . / Against thy only Son? . . . and know'st for whom; / For him who sits above and laughs the while / At thee ordain'd his drudge" (II, 727-32). Milton is asking his reader to recall the allusion and recognize the meaningful contrast between the "only Sons" and their fathers' attitudes toward them. Next, when God the Father in Book V observes the "foe . . . who intends t' erect his Throne / Equal to ours, throughout the spacious North," the Son answers, "Mightie Father, thou thy foes / Justly hast in derision, and secure / laugh'st at thir vain designes and tumults vain" (V, 724-37). But Satan always appropriates, or tries to appropriate, things to himself that are conjoined with God. In Book VI, when on the second day of battle the rebellious angels are winning through their discovery of gunpowder and cannon, "Satan beheld thir [the faithful angels'] plight, / And to his Mates thus in derision call'd. / O Friends, why come not on these Victors proud?" and the narrative voice tells us, "So they . . . Stood scoffing . . . eternal might / To match with thir inventions they presum'd / So easie, and of his Thunder made a scorn, / And all his Host derided, while they stood / A while in trouble; but they stood not long" (VI, 607-9, 628-34). The final reprise of the psalm reaffirms the kingly role of the Son when the "Anointed King *Messiah*" is envisioned by Michael: "he shall ascend / The Throne hereditarie, and bound his Reign / With earths wide bounds, his glory with the Heav'ns" (XII, 370-72).

But perhaps the most significant biblical text for the full poem, its full thrust and message, is that describing the eschatological priestly role of the Son: "And when all things shall be subdued unto him, then shall the Son also himself be subject unto him that put all things under him, that God may be all in all" (1 Corinthians 15:28). The text appears most strategically and significantly in Book III as the Son's offer of sacrifice is praised by the Father, in Book VI just before the Son ascends in the Chariot of Paternal Deitie and again as the rebels are defeated and expelled and the loyal angels return, and through expression consonant with the now postlapsarian world, in Book XII as the Expulsion occurs. The biblical text accords with Milton's belief in *creatio ex Deo*, rather than *creatio ex nihilo:* all creation is from the *substantia* of God, though each thing created, the Son included, has an individual and separate *essentia.* In Book III the Father in his great prescience says, at this focal point in humankind's redemption, and recalling Psalm 2: "Then thou thy regal Scepter shalt lay by, / For regal Scepter then no more shall need, / God shall be All in All" (III, 339-41). As the fall of Satan is about to occur, the Son, also alluding to Psalm 2, takes on his Father's will: "Scepter and Power, thy giving, I assume, / And gladlier shall reign, when in the end / Thou shalt be All in All, and I in thee / For ever, and in mee all whom thou lov'st" (VI, 730-33). The graphic *ins*—"All *in* All," "I *in* thee," "*in* mee all whom thou lov'st"—remind us that there is only one *substantia*, God's, and that at the end of time all will return to that one substance who is God. The echoing use of the biblical text less than fifty lines later, just after the defeat of Satan, plays upon the same graphic concept, while punning doubly: "the great Ensign of *Messiah* blaz'd / Aloft by Angels born, his Sign in Heav'n: / Under whose conduct *Michael* soon reduc'd / His Armie, circumfus'd on either Wing, / Under thir Head imbodied all in one" (VI, 775-79).

Here at the beginning of what will bring human existence, the eschatological role of the Son is prophesied, compressing all time into a single instant, which is the concept of time for God. The return of "all whom God lov'st" is metaphorized as Michael (who is cognate with Hermes in his role as conductor of the dead to the afterlife), under the sign of Messiah, leads back ("re-duces") the faithful angels to become body to the Head, who is God; they are reduced (in size) to fit all together into the One. And then, as human time begins with the descent from Eden, Eve, in what is most significantly the last speech in the poem, restates the protevangelium with clear allusion to the 1 Corinthians text: "though all by mee is lost, / Such favour I unworthie am voutsaft, / By mee the Promis'd Seed shall all restore" (XII, 621-23). And we are naturally drawn back to the opening lines: "till one greater Man / Restore us, and regain the blissful Seat." Eve's last word is that overwhelming word "restore," impossible until "one greater Man" appears, demanding that humankind emulate him.

The poem is an amazing achievement. One reads and reads and still finds further examples of this technique of quotation and allusion and their repetitions, all designed to communicate the Truths of the Bible that Milton knew and wanted to share. Might Milton have said with Walt Whitman, "Failing to fetch me at first keep encouraged, / Missing me one place search another, / I stop somewhere waiting for you"?

17
Milton and 1674

He was only sixty-five, an age many of us can look forward to as our removal to Sarasota or Coronado or Woodstock, Vermont. He had not even reached the promised biblical age of three score and ten or come close to the symbolic full life of a hundred days which he alluded to in "when I consider how my light is spent." He was living in Artillery Walk, Bunhill Fields, where he had been since around 1669, about nine or ten blocks from where he had been born on Bread Street and even nearer to five other locations where he had made his home in the intervening years. Aside from his years in Cambridge, his travel to France and Italy and Geneva, his parental residence in Hammersmith and Horton, and a trip to Oxfordshire from which he was to emerge a married man, we cannot be sure that he ever travelled outside the compass of the environs of the City of London and the City of Westminster. These areas, as well as Hammersmith, are today all part of the Greater City of London. Indeed, his geographic world was rather confined, outside of which was the dark world and wide.

The house he lived in was large enough for him to be taxed for four hearths in March of 1674, a somewhat commodious house we would conclude. He seems not to have rented out part of it, as was common then. The household regularly included only his wife, Betty, the former Elizabeth Minshull, some thirty-one years his junior, and a servant, Elizabeth Fisher. But there were some visitors: his brother Christopher from time to time; his last amanuensis, Daniel Skinner, but how often we do not know; his servant's sister, Mary Fisher, who also served; a yeoman, Richard Hayley, to whom he lent £40; allegedly a twenty-one-year-old admirer, Jonathan Hartop, who lent him £50, though we do not believe it; the Danish resident official Marcus Gioe (or was it Simon de Petkum acting for Gioe?); a Mr. Wright, who later became a clergyman and a doctor; John Dryden, and perhaps Edmund Waller. Not many but we may infer others: his nephew Richard Milton, though not his brother Christopher's other children; perhaps his nephew Edward Phillips; his friends Thomas Ellwood and Edward Millington, the bookseller who had given him refuge from government agents in 1660 and who discovered the memorandum from Arthur Annesley, Earl of Anglesey, concerning the authorship of *Eikon Basilike;* Andrew Marvell; Cyriack Skinner, the so-called Anonymous Biographer, who remembered that "he in great serenity spent his time"; perhaps his publishers Brabazon Aylmer and Samuel Simmons, or their agents; and his physician, who was probably his friend Dr. Nathan Paget, a second cousin of his wife.

These total not many visitors, and some called only once. But friends and relatives forget the old—and when they are blind and incapacitated, as he was with the gout, the visits become trying for all. His daughters did not put in an appearance, and we cannot really be sure about his sister Anne Phillips's boys. Edward's inaccuracies in his account of his uncle's last year have led us to doubt that he got to London that year, although the assumption that he helped in the revisions of *Paradise Lost,* published in this year, suggests otherwise. Of course Phillips may not have contributed to the second edition, or maybe it was prepared earlier—in 1670? or at least well before its publication as the Faithorne portrait or its revision by William Dolle, has suggested to some. What all this means, of course, is that we do not really know what was happening in those years, and inferences about composition and publication and general activities based upon such assumptions are not very reliable. Further, we have always thought that John Phillips was estranged from his uncle back around 1652 and never darkened his door again. But we do not really know. What work has been pursued on John Phillips has been subject to that assumption, and so the conclusions have not been cogent. Phillips, in so many ways, was his uncle's literary ward. His political astuteness and lampooning and his alleged escapades seem little evidence of a split.

Still, the few possible visitors would not have disturbed the great serenity. Did death or life or the world outside? At least others also passed on who were important to him or to us: Jean Chapelain, who had discussed the Salmasian affair in letters to Salmasius's son and to Nicolas Heinsius; and Edward Hyde, Earl of Clarendon, who died a month later on what would have been Milton's birthday, December 9. Though Clarendon did not cite Cromwell's Secretary for Foreign Tongues in *The History of the Rebellion and Civil Wars*—and there is no reason why he should have, much as that may be difficult for some to grant—he knew of the author of *The Doctrine and Discipline of Divorce* and *Defensio prima,* as letters show, and he rejected the antimonarchic views of Salmasius's opponent in two other letters of 1653. Ironic it may seem that this man who was so involved in the infamous murder of the government agent Anthony Ascham—the subject of State Papers in 1650 and a revision in the

second edition of *Eikonoklastes* the same year—should die on the day
that would have been Cromwell's secretary's anniversary of birth. In
most ways, though, Milton had always remained in the background, despite some attacks as divorcer and Commonwealth man; he was even little cited in the many discussions of the infamous attack on the late king's
alleged prison meditations and prayers. He simply was not important in
the long view of history; he was not a leader, he was not a theorist; he
was but a worker in the vineyards.

And there were Robert Herrick and Thomas Traherne and Robert
Fletcher, also deceased in 1674, and Milton's correspondent Jean de La-
badie, and Sir Walter Walker, who had been a fellow student at Christ's
College. Probably Milton knew nothing of any of these deaths; possibly
he paid little attention to the comings and goings of life. What topics did
subtend whatever conversation there was? Politics? Literature? Censorship? Finances? But amid death and dying, life also abounds, and it began this year for Nicholas Rowe and Isaac Watts. An author's
immortality lies in his works or, as "On Shakespear" attests, in his readers, not in his menial tasks in the flood of history. It was Charles Gildon
who first pointed out in 1714 in *A New Rehearsal, or Bays the Younger* that
Rowe had joined those who would not willingly let die the masterwork
Paradise Lost. "Tamerlane" (1702), "The Fair Penitent" (1703), "Jane
Shore" (1714), and "Lady Jane Grey" (1715) all owe debts, all proclaim
inheritance from the epic poem. Directly we have Rowe's words, in his
account of the life of Mr. William Shakespeare in his landmark edition of
The Workes in 1709, of his knowledge and appreciation of the
seventeenth-century giant. And in 1706 Watts was to acknowledge his
appreciation and debt in *Horæ Lyricæ:*

> There Milton dwells: The mortal sung
> Themes not presum'd by mortal tongue.
>   New terrors, or new glories, shine
> In ev'ry page, and flying scenes divine
> Surprize the wond'ring sense, and draw our souls along.
> Immortal bard! Thus thy own Raphael sings,
>   And knows no rule but native fire:
> All heav'n sits silent while to his sov'reign strings
>   He talks unutterable things:
> With graces infinite his untaught fingers rove
>   Across the golden lyre:
>   From ev'ry note devotion springs;
>   Rapture, and harmony, and love,
>   O'erspread the list'ning choir.

Soon the immortal bard and opponent of licensing was to have major effect on such creative spirits as Rowe and Watts, on Sir Richard Blackmore and Alexander Pope, on James Thomson and Thomas Gray, and on pamphleteers such as William Denton and Samuel Johnson and Thomas Hunt, and on historians such as Sir James Tyrrell. But in 1674 readers' commendations could be seen only in the great work of a John Dryden or the inferior poetizing of a Thomas Flatman. New editions of works with critical allusions appeared—Henry Foulis's *The History of the Wicked Plots and Conspiracies of Our Pretended Saints,* pages 4 and 24; Henry Hammond's *Workes,* pages 457-58 of *A Letter of Resolution to Six Quæres*—and new publications continued to report oppositions to the divorcer, apologist for the Commonwealth, and defamer of Charles—Vincent Placcius' *De scriptis et scriptoribus anonymis atque pseudonymus syntagma,* in the individual volume *De scriptoribus occultis detectis tractatus duo,* Chapter III, Item CXXV, page 35. But the man and his achievements were little recognized. The great serenity was probably not interrupted by talk of opponents, by talk of appreciators. Nor would he have bothered, I am sure, to have Flatman read aloud to him or worry about Bishop Richard Meggott's sermonizing on the desecration of kingship. But it is perhaps sentimentally too bad that he did not know that a man by the name of Ellis prepared a list of most of his published works, or that Dryden told Charles Sackville, Lord Buckhurst, that "this man cuts us all out and the ancients too."

In 1674 there seems to have been little to sustain a drooping spirit and raise a sense of immortality other than the observation some twenty years before that his noble task of defending liberty was sufficient to lead him through the world's vain mask. But outside the dark and small world of his home, the dark and wide world was going on in its usual course. Liberty defended did not ensure liberty for anyone. The Peace of Westminster between England and Holland was enacted on February 9, 1674, and England withdrew from the war against France ten days later. But the German Diet soon voted war against France, with Spain, the Holy Roman Empire, and the Pope joining them. And Sweden invaded Brandenburg and Prussia. Words echo: "Let *Euclid* rest and *Archimedes* pause, / And what the *Swede* intends and what the *French*," though observed also twenty years before. Glanvill, and Boyle, and Newton were preparing their further important treatises, not resting indeed, and Thomas Burnet was getting ready within the decade to oppose the kind of orthodoxy underlying *Paradise Lost* and "Naturam non pati senium."

But did this current war that breeds endless war enter the serenity of Artillery Walk—*Artillery* Walk? Or was this time one ordained by mild

Heaven and fully disapproved as to care or worry about justice and injustice? Cyriack's grandsire on the Royal Bench, Sir Edward Coke, had meted out justice for the people by his unfavorable decisions against James I, but in 1655 things of justice were not always observable, and in 1674 where was Coke's justice? or the world's liberty? Is not the nearest way to solid good for the community the learning by the individual of individual strength and accomplishment and use of ability, after which one refrains from superfluous burden when God has sent a cheerful hour, though it stretch into days and years?

Probably Milton concerned himself little with that dark and wide world outside rushing to gain power and to lose it, and philosophizing on values of the ancients and the moderns, the presence of God or his deistic retreat, the complexity of the world as evidence of God's power or evidence of his indifference. A different, if not new, world of thought and government was beckoning not too far off in 1674, but the gradual rise of the people and the less gradual dominance of mechanistic philosophy were, I think, not the concerns of the retired polemicist and poet.

The activities of friends and relatives may have impinged on the long days created by blindness and gout to give subjects for talk at least. Brother Christopher, Sir Christopher, was reappointed a member of the Inner Temple parliament, and here he resided during stays in London, although his official home was Ipswich. Christopher and his son Richard transacted various pieces of legal business, following along John Sr.'s financial course, the world of law and finance little appealing to the scrivener's other son. Daniel Skinner was graduated from Cambridge in February and became a junior fellow at Trinity College the following October. The stage was set for Skinner's difficulties for being associated with the antimonarchist and for urging publication of so-called seditious material. The stage was perhaps set, too, for the poetic manuscript workbook to find its way into its still present resting place in the Trinity College Library at Cambridge, as a kind of bribe. Thomas Agar, the nephew and namesake of his Royalist brother-in-law, who had died the year before, married Mary Bolles, daughter of the very prominent barrister and landowner, Sir Robert Bolles. His former student, Richard Jones, was created first Earl of Ranelagh and was appointed constable and governor of Athlone. The interrelations with prominent Royalist and landowning people are startlingly persistent in the life of the defender and publicist of the Good Old Cause. It seems to be an extraordinary example of the division possible between one's physical world and one's intellectual conclusions, a division given little credence in studies of the current political or sociological or academic world.

Milton's conversations with Betty may have flitted over these matters, but they could not have touched on the marriage on June 1 of his daughter Deborah—the youngest and favorite—to Abraham Clarke, a weaver, at St. Peter and St. Kevin's Church in Dublin. He was not to know of it or of its issue of seven sons and three daughters, of whom only two sons and one daughter reached adulthood. The family line itself was to disappear well before the first centenary of his death. Probably his brother-in-law Richard Minshull's sally into the financial world was noted. Richard, a framework knitter of Wistaston, gave a bond to Robert Cudworth and, apparently successful in the world of finance, was to be instrumental six years later in acquiring a lifetime interest for his sister in a house and farm in Brindley, using her inheritance as base, so it would seem. But the most recent work of his nephew Edward Phillips, the *Theatrum Poetarum*, licensed in 1674 though published the next year, might have been mentioned along with other recent publications of note, such as friend and former pupil Thomas Ellwood's *Forgery No Christianity*. In this year too Anthony Wood's *Historia et antiquitates Universitatis Oxoniensis* appeared, with its allusion to Milton in John Fell's "Editor Lectori." In turn this work led to John Aubrey's notetaking of the lives of prominent men with some attachment to Oxford, in preparation for Wood's *Athenæ Oxonienses*, the only means through which we have learned of the poet's incorporation at Cambridge's sister university. And with hindsight we may note that Louis Moréri's *Le grand Dictionnaire historique*, which later was to include a biassed, acerbic entry castigating the opponent of royalism and Roman Catholic defenders of royalism, received its first edition. On the positive side was the building of the Theatre Royal in Drury Lane, which was to become the scene of John Dalton's triumphant 1738 adaptation of "A Mask," thereafter always to be called "Comus."

These are mundane things, but the world of 1674 was mundane to a blind and sickly man whose day brought back the night for those others in this world who had not yet brushed away the tears from their eyes. The true account had been recorded. Of his own work, what could 1674 hold? Little that was new, though probably a few of what we today would call acceptance slips and rejection slips. For his writing and publishing efforts—if indeed they were truly his—succeeded and failed. Momentous as we look back was *Paradise Lost. A Poem in Twelve Books. The Second Edition Revised and Augmented by the same Author,* commended in Latin verse by S.B. and in English couplets by friend and colleague Andrew Marvell. Who was S.B.? Samuel Barrow? a medical doctor? a friend to the author? We don't know at all, despite some absolute statements by various of the poet's biographers. Marvell's decision not to compete prosodically with the poem being praised both subtly praised that prosody by its own standardization and condemned Dryden's request to tag the lines, when he visited the retired author, perhaps along with Waller.

The Stationers' Register, under April 17, 1674, tells us that what was to be called "The State of Innocence, and Fall of Man" was on its way, although three years elapsed before it was made available. Perhaps, as has been suggested before, the revisions of the epic were made prior to 1674, a year that may have held less of the poet's own work than we suppose. Did the new *Paradise Lost* sell well? Probably it did better than its earlier form, reissued five times within three years, but the 1675 reissue of the revision implies that it did not sell well either. Its reputation to 1688 agrees, despite a new edition in 1678. We like to assume that masterworks are immediately recognizable by their inner glow—like Havelock the Dane—but the poetry of the subject of this book was little read and known in these days until a concerted effort out of Christchurch in 1688 produced a beautiful folio, enhanced by illustrations and sustained by a long list of subscribers. It became one of the first English works accorded such honor. Finally the reputation of the poet took off, while infamy of the Commonwealth man, the accuser and defamer of Charles the First of sacred memory, continued unabated and grew into a chorus with a new edition of *Eikonoklastes* in 1690. Had 1688 not seen this gilt-edged publishing event, led by John, Lord Somers, Francis Atterbury, and Henry Aldrich, how long might it have been before England recognized its own? And what would have been the history of eighteenth-century poetry? In 1674 there was nothing to prognosticate what reputation the future held for the dying poet.

The only new work of the year was a translation, *A Declaration, or Letters Patents of the Election of This Present King of Poland John the Third, Elected on the 22d of May last past, anno dom. 1674,* published in July. Was this done for money? Was it because the commoner-made-king appealed to the translator's sense of political justice? Was it because his publisher, Brabazon Aylmer, a couple of months before was trying to, in a way, exploit the blind man who had attempted things not done before in prose or rhyme? At least Aylmer seems to have been thwarted in one publishing venture, and settled in May instead for *Epistolarum Familiarium.* Since these personal letters were few—only thirty-one in number—we are told that this volume is *Liber Unus,* but it is unlikely that there ever was hope for a *Secundus.* Other letters just were not available, and in over three hundred years only a very few more have been discovered. Aylmer himself lets it be known that the volume has been made into a more acceptable size (there are 148 pages of text in this small octavo) by the addition of some incidentally-found prolusions from the author's adolescent college years.

Possibly the last two items—*A Declaration* and the *Familiar Letters*—owe their light of day entirely to the failure of Aylmer to get the State Papers published, or so we suppose. Moses Pitt, however, seems also to have expected to publish these papers. The last amanuensis, Daniel Skinner, found himself possessed of a manuscript of the State Papers, but troubles ensued, although finally a quite different manuscript was published in 1676 in Amsterdam, with Aylmer and Pitt out in the cold. To assume, of course, as most people seem to, that this 1676 text is authoritative is to display ignorance of the facts; nor can one assume Skinner's manuscript to be authoritative, and there were other collections of the papers, as well. Many seem to have been trying to capitalize on the infamy of the Cromwellian era in the 1670s, but what close connections any of this had with the Secretary for Foreign Tongues who produced the papers are speculative. Maybe Aylmer was just trying to get in on a good publishing bet, wound up with a new translation (its author unstated), a collection of different letters and prolusions, and another item, *A Brief History of Moscovia,* not printed until 1682. The reason for delay is unclear, since books on Russia had been rather popular through the decades before and after the author's death, but the lack of sales value in the author's name during these same years may have been a major reason. Another work apparently associated with the State Papers around 1674 and in the possession of Skinner was *De doctrina christiana,* partially copied over in the immediately preceding years though possibly not altered since the earlier 1660s. Too frequently the document is lumped with the State Papers, and what seems true of them is assumed for the theological treatise. In any case, it disappeared until 1823, and we can only speculate on the foundation of Skinner's partial repenning that it received any attention from its author in 1674.

But there are a few other items. Did Betty dispose of the manuscript workbook of the minor poems which we have so often mentioned before? To whom? To Skinner? Had it disappeared into his or someone else's hand before 1674? Perhaps in 1673, when the second edition of the minor poems was printed? If true, is this some evidence that Skinner was the producer of the copy-text? Did Thomas Ellwood come into possession of some of Cromwell's papers that Cromwell's secretary owned in 1674, or earlier? We have their publication and this provenance through Ellwood stated in 1743. And what of the Commonplace Book soon to be scribbled o'er by Sir Richard Graham, Lord Preston, and to disappear for two hundred years?

While there may have been some negotiations concerning publication, little new or revised composition seems to have taken place. The serenity indeed may have been overwhelming; the feeling of "I've done what I was able to and there is no more" may have blocked out any other hopes. Milton's legacy had been cast for those of us who would receive. The offering to God—his true account—had been made. Probably the personal concerns from July onward were rather preparations for death and disposition of properties. His estate was promised his wife, so his servant Elizabeth Fisher deposed. He may have made arrangements for what came to be small inheritances for his daughters, or at least Christopher and his son Richard made such arrangements, and he may also have planned bequests to his brother's children, or so Christopher deposed. The litigation began in December and ended some months later, probably not to anyone's satisfaction. Oral wills offer many avenues for antagonism, and poor memories, or convenient ones, smooth no turbulent waves of the past.

His death, we may infer from all the accounts, confused though they are, came at night, either on Sunday, November 8, or after midnight on Monday, November 9. His servant tells of his retirement for the night and the discovery of his passing the next morning. She says it was a Sunday, but we shall probably never really know whether the moment lay before or after midnight struck. He was buried next to his father in the chancel of St. Giles, Cripplegate, a short distance from his last residence. Burial occurred on Thursday, November 12, and over a century later was disturbed and desecrated, as Philip Neve tells us in his *Narrative of the Disinterment of Milton's Coffin* (1790).

Edna St. Vincent Millay once wrote, in "Elegy Before Death,"

> There will pass with your great passing
> Little beauty not your own
> Only the light from common water
> Only the grace of common stone.

But the light and grace which commonness gives off may be the only kind that persists through shadow and through dust. At least one reader has been shown that the subjected plain is the only world of water and stone worth bothering about.

The Commonplace Book

The first major division of entries in the Commonplace Book given by James Holly Hanford (that is, authors entered before 1639 and all in Milton's hand) records three subject-matter groupings. First, there are Milton's studies of the history of the early church and church fathers, personages and events important to the history of the early Christian period in and around Greece, and Byzantine history (Nos. 1-5, Group I; Nos. 6-7, 10-11, 14, 17-29, Group II). (Hanford notes that No. 29 may date from 1639 or later, and Mohl specifically—and, I think, correctly—says "after 1639.") These studies detail Milton's remarks in the letter, for they carry him through that time when the Eastern empire disappeared, covering the last periods of "Greek" history: the Principate, the Dominate, and Byzantium. This reading may thus be dated up to November 1637. Histories of earlier Greece are not recorded in the Commonplace Book. It is important to note that the citations from Group I volumes are frequently to later sections, suggesting that the earlier sections may have been read prior to the inception of the Commonplace Book. Citations from No. 1, Eusebius's *Historia Ecclesiastica*, in ten books, are taken from Book III, Chapter 30; V, 1; VI, 42; VII, 7 and 30; X, 7. But those from III, 30; VI, 42; and VII, 30 were made together at the beginning of 109, indicating that Milton had at least proceeded through Book VII before writing this entry. Citations from No. 2, Eusebius's *Vita Constantini*, in five books, are taken from II, 77; III, 18 and 58; and IV, 24.

Citations from No. 3, Socrates' *Historia Ecclesiastica*, in seven books, are taken from I; I, 6 and 11; III, 16; V, 22; VI, 8; and VII, 25. (An entry from Socrates on 111 is numbered 91 by Hanford, who lists it as of uncertain date; reference is to I, 15. It is later than No. 12 on this same page, and handwriting dates it 1639 or after.) The earlier references are incidental or they appear to have been remembered and checked for location once Milton had come across something similar in another text. Citations from No. 4, *Historia Miscella*, in twenty-four books, are taken from XII and XIII. Citations from No. 5, Procopius's *De bello Persico*, are both taken from Book II; this work appears in *Historiarum Libri VIII,* which consists of two books on the wars with Persia, three on the wars with the Vandals, and three on the wars with the Ostrogoths. Nos. 4 and 5 deal with matters chronologically close to the plateau mentioned by Milton in his letter to Diodati. There is unfortunately no evidence that Milton read the two further histories in the volume by Procopius.

Second, there is Milton's study of the history of the West from Diocletian to the fall of Rome and from the invasion of the Lombards to the end of the thirteenth century (Nos. 8-9, Group II). This reading may therefore be dated up to November 1637 by the information in the letter. Mohl is not quite accurate when she writes, "In a letter to Diodati, dated September [i. e., November], 1637, Milton says he has finished reading Sigonius" (YP I, 376 n.). Milton does not cite any specific authors, but Sigonius was the author of *De occidentali imperio,* cited on 182, and of *De regno Italiæ,* cited on 183, 220, and 240. And third, his reading included Dante, Boccaccio, and Ariosto (Nos. 12-13, 15-16, Group II). These have no connection with Italian history, as noted in the letter, of course, Dante and Ariosto having surely been read before 1637, and often.

Mohl has offered more specific dates of entry for the works numbered 1 to 29 by Hanford. On the basis of the suggested dating for the beginning of the Commonplace Book (ca. September 1637) and the evidence of handwriting, we can suggest still further revised dating. Milton early employed a Greek *e* in his handwriting; he began to use an Italian *e* around November 1637 (as in the manuscript of "Lycidas"); increased usage is in evidence until the practice is mixed, and continued until the Italian *e* was more frequent and then from 1639 consistent. A very few Greek *e*'s do creep into manuscript materials during 1639 and later. In the following table I assign "1637" to those entries showing only Greek *e;* "1637-38" to those showing mixed practice; "1638" to those showing many more Italian than Greek *e*'s; "1638-39" to those showing only an occasional Greek *e;* and "1639 or after" to those showing only Italian *e.*

Chart of CPB Entries

Work	Page	Dating (Mohl)	Revised Dating
1	53	1635-37	1638-39
1	105	1635-37	1637
1	109 (2)	1635-37	1637
1	109	1637-38	1637
1	177	1635-37	1637
2	55	1635-37	1637
2	181 (2)	1635-37	1637
3	53	1635-37	1637
3	55	1635-37	1637

3	61	1635-37	1637
3	109 (3)	1635-37	1637
3	151	1635-37	1637
3	181	1635-37	1637
4	181	1635-37	1637
4	181	1635-37	1637-38
5	151	1635-37	1637
5	230	1635-37	1637
6	150	1637-38	1637-38
6	182	1637-38	1637-38
7	220	1637-38	1637
8	182	1637-38	1637
9	183 (2)	1637-38	1637
9	220	1637-38	1637
9	240	1637-38	1637
10	181	1637-38	1637
10	220	1637-38	1637
10	240	1637-38	1637
11	240	1637-38	1637
12	12	1635-38	1637
12	16	1635-38	1637
12	70	1635-38	1637
12	111	1635-38	1637-38
12	160	1635-38	1637
13	191	1637-38	1637
14	191	1637-38	1637
15	182	1637-38	1637
16	151	1637-38	1637-38
17	71	1637-38	1637-38
17	109	1637-38	1637
18	106	1637-38	1637
19	106	1637-38	1637
20	109	1637-38	1637-38
21	241	1637-38	1638
22	109	1637-38	1637
23	4	1637-38	1638-39
23	241	1637-38	1638
24	13	1637-38	1638
25	181	1637-38	1638
26	109	1637-38	1637
27	182	1637-38	1637
28	109	1637-38	1637
29	109	after 1639	1639 or after

Certain revisions need explanation. Despite his early reading of Eusebius (1), Milton apparently made a later reference to this work on 53; the work contains four Italian *e*'s and one Greek *e*. Probably the second citation of *Historia Miscella* (4) on 181 is 1637; one Italian *e* appears. The

entry from Dante (12) on 111 is from "Paradiso"; the other four entries
(12, 16, 70, 160) are from "Inferno," thus making the slightly later date
understandable and implying contemporaneous reading (rereading?) as
he made entries. The entry from Clement (17) on 71 comes from page
730 of *Opera,* but that on 106 (18) refers to page 158, and that on 109
(17) to page 448. Again we may conclude contemporary reading as entries were made, and Milton would seem not to have read the latter part
of *Stromata* until after November 1637. The reference to Cyprian (21) on
241 is a casual remembrance, entered after the remarks on Tertullian
(23), not an entry made during reading. Although entries from Tertullian (23-25) on 13, 181, and 241 should not, on the basis of handwriting, be dated other than 1638, that on 4 definitely dates later than the
foregoing (perhaps 1639) since only one Greek *e* appears: "esse" (first
"e").

The dating which handwriting suggests for Severus (6), Clement
(17), Cyprian (20), Tertullian (23-25), and Sozomen (29) shows that Milton had not completed his study of early church history or his reading of
the church fathers (neither Eastern nor Western) until after November
1637. Dated 1639 or later are references to other church fathers: Lactantius (30-32), Theodoretus (88), Basil (89), Chrysostom (90), Socrates
Scholasticus (91), and Gregory of Nyssa (92). (Mohl dates the entry of
Theodoretus on 53 "1635-39," that on 243 "after 1639.") Actually this
unit of reading goes beyond the merely historical; Milton continued to
pursue this material because of its general information and use. Likewise Byzantine and early Roman history were not closed items, at least
for entry: references to Codinus (96) and Frontinus (97) appear after
1639. As Hanford noted, Nos. 15 and 27 were entered with or after No.
8, and Nos. 13 and 15 are contemporary. This seems to indicate that Milton was reading (probably we should say rereading for the first) Dante
and Boccaccio around November 1637. The notes from Ariosto followed
soon after; other Italian Renaissance entries from Berni (81), Tasso (94),
and Tomasini (80) date from 1639 or later. Milton's probable rereading
of Dante and Ariosto during 1637-38 may have resulted from his search
for literary themes and models and further inspiration.

Languages in the Commonplace Book

Notes entered in the Commonplace Book are in Greek, Latin, Italian, French, and English, and were derived from Milton's reading of texts in those languages. Direct quotations—some, mere words—are cited in all five languages, according to the language of the text; comments and paraphrases appear in Latin, Italian, French, and English. At first glance there seems to be no principle behind the use of language by Milton in entering notes other than quotations except for a preference for Latin and English.

Greek was usually used for direct quotations only; there are twelve citations. Four times, one or two specific words are given in Greek, amid Latin, only one of which comes from a Latin text (Bede, No. 34, 181); once Greek is used in a marginal note alongside a Latin entry from a Latin text (Lactantius, No. 32, 14). (Both Hanford and Mohl assign the Bede entry to Holinshed because Milton adds after "Bede.": "et ex eo Holinshed." But the quotation comes from Bede, and Holinshed merely cites him as source in the margin. The date is 1639 or after in any case.) Texts in Greek or in Greek and Latin are noted or commented upon forty-three times in Latin and three times in English. These include Eusebius (1, 2), Socrates (3, 91), *Historia Miscella* (4), Procopius (5), Evagrius (7), Gregoras Nicephoras (10), Clement (17, 18), Ignatius (22), Justin Martyr (26, 27), Decrenus (28), Sozomen (29), Aristotle (40), Löwenklau (75), Theodoretus (88), Basil (89), Gregory of Nyssa (92), and Nicetas Acominate (106). Löwenklau and Nicetas Acominate will be considered under Latin texts as well. One of the English comments refers to Aristotle's *Ethics* (40), being an addition to Smith, 182, the only English being the single word "See." Another (Basil, No. 89, 185) lies amid many entries in English, being connected to the preceding note, which cites the definition of a tyrant in Smith, by the phrase, "and Basil distinguishes a tyrant from a K. breifly thus." There are two other notes from Basil entered in Latin. Apparently at times Milton was influenced by related materials; it is probable that these notes were added at the same time or shortly after the preceding notes to which they are related. The entry of a Greek text into an English comment (Nicetas, No. 106, 249) was made by Amanuensis D, who also produced a note in Latin and quotation in Italian from Dante (105). Milton may have dictated English because this entry discusses "The evill custom in England, of seising all shipwracks as forfeit" etc.

Of these entries from Greek texts, I have dated twenty-nine as 1637, two as 1637-38, and one as 1638-39. Seven appear to be from 1639 or after: Socrates, No. 91, 111; Basil, No. 89, 55, 57, and 185; Aristotle, No. 40, 182 (specifically 1639-41); and Theodoretus, No. 88, 53 and 243. (Hanford listed the Theodoretus entry on 53 as of uncertain date; Mohl gives 1635-39. But the handwriting makes clear that 1639 or after is correct.) Likewise the citation from Bede (and Holinshed) on 181 is dated 1639-41. Perhaps, therefore, the undated entry from Gregory of Nyassa, No. 92, 109, which fits the edition of 1639, should be dated at this time also (1639-41), since the only Greek texts cited in the Commonplace Book after that time are Löwenklau (1643-44, four entries), which is in Latin with some Greek, and Nicetas Acominate, entered by Amanuensis D in English and dated after 1647, the date of the edition used, which included both a Greek and a Latin text. Mohl gives "ca. 1665" for the Nicetas entry, but see my remarks concerning Amanuensis D.

There are five quotations in French: one from Girard (53) on 61, which is largely quotation introduced by a Latin phrase; one from Girard (53) on 110, which is almost entirely quotation; one from Commines (54) on 110, which is entirely quotation; one from Girard (50, 53) on 186, introduced by a comment in English and with bibliographic references in Latin; and another from Girard (53) on 186, also introduced by a comment in English. The two entries on 110 have brief marginal notes in English. Other entries from texts in French (Du Chesne [42], Girard [50, 53], Commines [54], and Gilles [55]) are written in Latin (nine) or in English (thirteen): Du Chesne (42), three in English; Girard (50, 53), six in Latin and eight in English; Commines (54), two in Latin and two in English; and Gilles (55), one in Latin. In other words, Milton employed French very seldom in the Commonplace Book and then only for quotation. The reason for using Latin or English seems to be indeterminate, although surrounding entries or perhaps other texts Milton was reading contemporaneously may have influenced the decision. Du Chesne's volume on the British Isles, for instance, was being read and noted at the same time that Milton was working through Holinshed and Camden.

Texts entered in the Commonplace Book in Italian are: Ariosto (16), Berni (81, 99), Boccaccio (15), Boccalini (79), Boiardo (100), Costanzo (109), Dante (12, 13, 105), Guicciardini (93), Machiavelli (43, 101, 102), Sarpi (49), Savonarola (33), Tasso (94), Tassoni (78), and Villani (95). Italian quotations appear twenty-seven times, of which twelve were written by amanuenses: Ariosto, 151, with Latin comment; Berni, 71, 182, 187, all with Latin comment; Boccalini, 189, with Italian comment and Latin marginal note; Boiardo, 77 and 187, both with Latin comment; Costanzo, 5, with Latin comment, and 248, with Italian summary; Dante, 111 and 197, both with Latin comment; Guicciardini, 182 and 190, the latter with Latin comment; Machiavelli, 177, with Latin comment, 182, 185, with Latin marginal note, 195 (2), one with Latin marginal note, 197, with Latin comment, 242, with English title, 245, and 246 with Latin comment; Sarpi, 109 and 179, both with English comment; Savonarola, 179, with Italian comment; Tasso, 71, with Latin comment; Tassoni, 189 (2); and Villani, 12, which is primarily quotation. Other Italian texts have entries in Latin (twenty-five instances) or in English (one instance). Unlike Greek and French, Italian is used for comment, paraphrase, or summary as well as quotation; like the Greek and French texts, Latin is also used for comment or entry; and like the French texts, English is also used for comment or entry. English was employed only after 1639 and then generally when British materials (as from Holinshed) were also being noted.

As would be expected, texts in English are quoted and entered in English with only the following exceptions: there are five Latin entries for Stow (15, 57, 72, 181, and 184), apparently because of the influence of Malmesbury, entered or read at the same time. Another possible exception is on 181, where the Latin with Greek entry has reference to Holinshed, but is from Bede. Three Latin notes or marginal notes are added to English entries: Stow, 242; Campion, 74; and Purchas, 57 (referring to a Latin text).

Latin texts are quoted and entered in Latin with a few exceptions. Malmesbury has English entries on 53 and 73; Camden, on 186, 220 (4), and 242; Sleidan, one on 181; Jovius, 13; Thuanus, both English and Latin on 182, and English on 183; Cuspinian, one on 181; and Nicetas, a Latin and Greek text, entered in English on 106 by Amanuensis D. These either deal with English subjects or are entered amid or along with English texts. Hanford's suggested reference to Spelman on 183, in English, is probably incorrect and is instead, as Mohl suggests, a reference to a topic in the lost theological index.

In all, therefore, Milton entered notes from Greek, Latin, Italian, French, and English books; he quoted in those languages from those books; he generally made entries from Greek, Latin, Italian, and French books in Latin; at times, and after 1639 when he was working with English texts, he sometimes entered notes in English from Latin, Italian, and French volumes; he also paraphrased or summarized Italian materials in Italian; and he generally used English for English, although at times Latin was employed.

Dating of the Plans

For a discussion of the spelling process referred to here, see pp. 144 and 322n.5.

The first draft of *Paradise Lost* (top lefthand column), page 35, was put down first, followed closely by draft two (top righthand column). These drafts, with their various additions, but excluding "other Tragedies . . . Abram in Ægypt," show five pertinent spellings with "e," none without "e." All other spellings may also be early. Next, Milton seems to have written the third draft of *Paradise Lost*, page 35 (twelve words with "e," one without "e"), followed shortly afterward by its additions (three words with "e") and "other Tragedies,"[1] page 35 (no significant words). Again, all other words may be early. Perhaps around the same time, not much later certainly, Milton began to jot down subjects on page 36; the material at the top lefthand column, excluding the detail under "Thamar" ("where . . . attempted"), and at the righthand column, down to "Comazontes . . . or the Rioters," have two words with "e," none without "e." All other words may also be early. If Milton was considering primarily a poem about Arthur in 1639 and early 1640, these materials, which show his perusal of the Bible from its first verses onward, page by page, in search of possible subjects, were probably entered around mid-1640 (April?-September?).

The first entries of subjects from British history, pages 37 and 38, may have been made from later 1640 (September?), being completed about the time page 39 was being worked on (observe handwriting, pen, and ink), that is, around March (?) 1641.[2] Since these subjects are all concerned with earlier British history, progressing only up to the Norman conquest (cf. his remarks on this point in *Reason* cited in the text), the entries would date from the earlier part of his reading of the histories. The numerous references to the church fathers entered in the Commonplace Book after his return from the Continent perhaps lie in 1639 to early 1640, and the entries from the British histories probably began thereafter, from middle 1640 onward. The subjects in the Trinity MS were probably put down after some historical reading. The original entries on page 37 evidence twelve words with "e" and six without "e," their additions having four with "e" and two without "e." Those on page 38 show seven words with "e" only. Other spellings may be early, except "Bithric" (written after "Bithrick" and probably "Brightrick"), which is perhaps an "error" since "-ck" was used until the middle of 1644.

During this same period, from ca. late 1640 (September [?]- February [?]), Milton continued to note biblical subjects on page 36. In the righthand column, beginning with Ruth and then 1 Samuel, he entered "Theristria" down to "Rehoboam 1 Reg 12," left room for the insertion of the prose outline of "Abias Thersæus" (note pen, ink, handwriting, smaller spacing between the lines, smaller and cramped letters, and line slant), and continued with "Imbres or the Showrs" through "Ahab 1 Reg 22." Next the detail under "Thamar" was probably added; note reference in righthand column to "Tamar. 2 Sam. 13." There is one pertinent spelling with "e."

Around March (?) 1641 Milton seems to have begun the outlines on page 39; these were apparently copied from some original worksheets. "Abram from Morea" has eight words with "e" and nine without; "Baptistes," four with "e," two without; "Sodom," nine with "e," eight without; and on page 40 the continuation of "Sodom" has eight with "e," six without. Totals for these outlines are twenty-nine words with "e" and twenty-five without. Here the odd spellings "com," "discours," perhaps "divers," "som," the first "thir," and "wher" come through, as they do in the first three pamphlets (May-July 1641). Later and perhaps by May 1641 Milton made additions to "Baptistes," one word with "e," eight without; in this appear "cours" and "els." His spelling without "e" seems almost stabilized now, for only the usual "some" comes through as the first word of the addition; but this also shows that relapses did occur. These totals of the retention and omission of "e" are similar to totals in the first three pamphlets, allowing for some change of odder forms by the compositor: *Reformation,* 751 with "e," 340 without "e"; *Episcopacy,* 211 with "e," 80 without "e"; *Animadversions,* 730 with "e," 251 without "e."

The change of pen and ink separates the succeeding entries from the "Baptistes" additions. Around the middle of 1641 Milton completed page 36 as we now have it: in the righthand column he copied the prose outline of "Abias Thersæus" and added "beginning at the synod . . . glory be &c.," "(See Lavater . . . seducing," and "wher is . . . religion"; later "Asa . . . Idol," "[D]ura . . . Dan. 3" and "Hesechia . . . Ægypt" were added. The outline for "Abias Thersæus" has two words with "e" and three without; the rest of these entries together show six without "e,"[3] including "fals" and "wher." Perhaps the words with "e" arose from the earlier copy from which Milton took the outline. Just after the time Milton was writing his first three pamphlets (July-November 1641), he may also have been thinking of other subjects for a drama and developing the newest draft of *Paradise Lost*.[4] At this time he probably entered more subjects on page 40 (one without "e"), "Adams Banishment," page 40 (four with "e" and six without "e"), the title "Adam unparadiz'd" and the addition to the beginning of the latter outline on page 40; the two additions at the bottom of page 40 (one without "e"); the addition on page 41 (three without "e"); and the Scotch subjects on page 41 (five without "e").[5] The increased, but not fully consistent, deletion of "e" accords with the mixture of practice seen in the first three pamphlets. The totals here are four words with "e" and sixteen without "e." The four words with "e" found in the fourth *Paradise Lost* draft may be a result of transcription from a slightly earlier copy. The first occurrence of "pre-" comes through in "Adam unparadiz'd" though "præ-" is found in the addition to "Baptistes," page 39. The date of change must lie in middle to later 1641: although no spellings with ligatures are found in *Reformation* (May 1641), probably having been changed by the compositor, one comes through in *Animadversions* (July 1641), but none are subsequently found in later written material, including *Reason* (January 1642). This apparent date of change helps place "Adam unparadiz'd" in the last half of 1641.

Remaining entries in the Plans section of the Trinity MS were probably put down in the latter half of 1641 or in 1642. In two general groups, the entries consist of the additions to "Sodom" and the two brief religious outlines on page 41. The addition to "Sodom" on page 39 ("with the preist"), that on page 38, that on page 40 (four words without "e") continued on page 41 (three words with "e"), and the new title on page 40, entered in two writings, constitute the earlier group. The words with "e" are probably oversights, as they appear in the apparently rapidly written continuation of the addition to "Sodom," although the addition itself gives only spellings without "e." Milton, perhaps annoyed that it had overflowed to the next page, which was being otherwise used, seems to have wanted to be quit of the addition. That he was making errors of haste is seen by the rewritten "firie" and the misdrawn line on page 40. These words indicate that Milton still, in the latter half of 1641, sometimes wrote both forms. (Note also the slip with "howre," Sonnet 9, line 13, written ca. 1643.)

The final two outlines show three and two pertinent words without "e." "Moabitides" gives the preferred "drivn," and "Christus patiens," the odd "receav," both of which date from at least the middle of 1641:

neither *Reformation* nor *Episcopacy* gives "-ceav," but *Animadversions* (July 1641) does. "Moabitides," Numbers 25, was first noted as a possibility on page 36. "Christus patiens" shows that during this earlier formative period Milton not only thought of poems on *Paradise Lost* and Samson but also was working up materials with Christ as the central figure. Although there is nothing to require a specific date for this outline, "Christus patiens," which should be connected with the subjects on Christ on page 40, written around late 1641 ("Christ born" is an addition after the others), probably was entered not too long afterward. Thus the terminal date for the latter group may be early 1642. Of *Paradise Lost* he says, "this Subject for Heroic Song Pleas'd me long choosing" (IX, 25-26). But since this choice had been made by 1642, at which time Edward Phillips tells us he saw the verses from Book IV, lines 32-41, he had probably completed the slight jottings of subjects and outlines found in the Trinity MS, despite his development of at least two more subjects thereafter. The "long choosing," I believe, refers to the vacillation between not only specific subjects but also kinds of subjects and forms as reflected primarily here in the Plans section of the Trinity MS.

An outline summary of the probable dating and order of the plans follows; in parentheses are given the number of words with "e" and the number without "e":

I. middle 1640
  A. earlier in period
    1. p. 35, draft one of *Paradise Lost*   (1, 0)
    2. p. 35, draft two of *Paradise Lost*   (4, 0)
    3. p. 35, draft three of *Paradise*
      Lost   (12, 1)
    4. p. 35, additions to draft three   (3, 0)
    5. p. 35, "other Tragedies"   (0, 0)   (20, 1)
  B. later in period
    1. p. 36, left column, "The Deluge . . . Thamar"   (1, 0)
    2. p. 36, right column, to "the Rioters"   (1, 0)   (2, 0)
                                                                      (22, 1)

II. late 1640-early 1641
  A. during period
    1. p. 37, British subjects in order   (12, 6)
    2. p. 38, British subjects in order   (7, 0)
    3. p. 37, additions   (4, 2)
    4. p. 38, additions   (0, 0)   (23, 8)
  B. during period
    1. p. 36, right column, "Theristria" to "Rehoboam 1 Reg 12"   (0, 0)

2. p. 36, right column, "Imbres . . . Ahab 1 Reg 22"   (0, 0)

3. p. 36, left column, detail under "Thamar"   (1, 0)   (1, 0)

                                                   (24, 8)

III. early 1641-middle 1641
   A. earlier in period
      1. p. 39, "Abram from Morea"   (8, 9)
      2. p. 39, "Baptistes"   (4, 2)
      3. p. 39, "Sodom"   (9, 8)
      4. p. 40, "Sodom" continuation   (8, 6)   (29, 25)
   B. later in period
      1. p. 39, additions to "Baptistes"   (1, 8)   (1, 8)

                                                   (30, 33)

IV. middle 1641-later 1641
   A. earlier in period
      1. p. 36, right column, "Abias Thersæus . . . good &c."   (2, 3)
      2. p. 36, right column, "wher . . . religion"; "beginning . . . glory be &c."; "(See . . . seducing")   (0, 3)
      3. p. 36, left column, "Elias in the mount" to "by Jeremiah"   (0, 2)
      4. p. 36, left column, "Asa . . . Idol"   (0, 0)
      5. p. 36, left column, "[D]ura . . . Dan. 3"   (0, 0)
      6. p. 36, left column, "Hesechia . . . Ægypt"   (0, 1)   (0, 1)

                                                   (2, 9)

   B. later in period
      1. p. 40, more subjects   (0, 1)
      2. p. 40, "Adams Banishment"   (4, 6)
      3. p. 40, "Adam unparadiz'd"; addition to beginning   (0, 0)
      4. p. 40, two additions to "Adam unparadiz'd" at bottom   (0, 1)
      5. p. 41, addition to "Adam unparadiz'd"   (0, 3)
      6. p. 41, Scotch subjects   (0, 5)   (4, 16)

                                                   (6, 25)

V. late 1641-early 1642
   A. earlier in period
      1. p. 39, addition to "Sodom"   (0, 0)
      2. p. 38, addition to "Sodom"   (0, 0)
      3. p. 40, addition to "Sodom"   (0, 4)
      4. p. 41, addition to "Sodom"   (3, 0)

5. p. 40, title for "Sodom"	(0, 0)	(3, 4)
B. later in period		
1. p. 41, "Moabitides"	(0, 3)	
2. p. 41, "Christus patiens"	(0, 2)	(0, 5)
		(3, 9)

Notes

1. The Roots of Being

1. *The Life of John Milton* (London: Macmillan, 1881-94), 6 vols., vol. 7, Index.

2. *Milton: A Biography* (Oxford: Clarendon Press, 1968), 2 vols.

3. Lacan makes a distinction between metaphor (Freud's "condensation") and metonomy (which involves displacement). Metaphor represents the "nodal point" (*Knotenpunkt*) that acts to allow multiple interpretations, thus joining metaphoric function to signifying representations. These incremental repetitions allow for expanding signifying representations in Milton's life and psychology. See the notes by Anthony Wilden in Lacan's *The Language of the Self: The Function of Language in Psychoanalysis* (Baltimore: Johns Hopkins Press, 1968), 109-10 n. 53, 115-16 n. 70, and 118-22 n. 80.

4. But see two rather recent studies that help remedy this situation: Archie Burnett's *Milton's Style: The Shorter Poems & Samson Agonistes* (London: Longman, 1981) and Thomas N. Corns's *The Development of Milton's Prose Style* (Oxford: Clarendon, 1982), as well as those that have engaged a reader-response.

5. Douglas Bush, *John Milton: A Sketch of His Life and Writings* (New York: Macmillan, 1964), 32. "Ad Patrem" (so dated) is cited to suggest such decision in 1631/32.

6. *The Life of John Milton* (Oxford: Oxford Univ. Press, 1983), 161.

7. William W. Kerrigan, *The Sacred Complex: On the Psychogenesis of Paradise Lost* (Cambridge: Harvard Univ. Press, 1983), 27.

8. The word "virgin" appears thirteen times in "Comus," "virginity" three times; "chaste" is used five times, "unchaste" once, "chastity" seven times. Comus means virginity when he tempts the Lady: "List Lady be not coy, and be not cozen'd / With that same vaunted name virginity" (737-38); and the Lady means the contrast between the two concepts when she responds: "To him that dares / Arm his profane tongue with contemptuous words / Against the Sun-clad power of Chastity, / Fain would I something say, yet to what end? / Thou hast nor Ear, nor Soul to apprehend / The sublime notion, and high mystery / That must be utter'd to unfold the sage / And serious doctrine of Virginity" (781-87). See also the uses of "chastity" in the Elder Brother's speech, ll. 420, 425, 440, 453, which emphasize the concept as epitomized by Diana, and the lines of Sabrina, "Shepherd 'tis my office best / To help insnared Chastity" (908-9). We might note that the Trinity MS records pertinent changes in l. 826: "Sabrina is her name a virgin goddesse" > "a virgin chast" > "a virgin pure."

Poetic quotations are from my edition of *The Complete Poetry of John Milton*, rev. ed. (New York: Doubleday Anchor, 1971). The prose is quoted from original editions and *Complete Prose Works of John Milton,* gen. ed. Don M. Wolfe (New Haven: Yale Univ. Press, 1954-82), 8 vols. in 10; referred to as the Yale Prose (YP). Latin prose texts and at times their translation are taken from *The Works of John Milton,* gen. ed. Frank Patterson (New York: Columbia Univ. Press, 1931-38), 18 vols. in 21; referred to as the Columbia Milton (CM). The Trinity MS is cited from William Aldis Wright's facsimile edition (Cambridge: Cambridge Univ. Press, 1899).

9. See Barbara Breasted, "*Comus* and the Castlehaven Scandal," *Milton Studies* 3 (1971): 201-24; and Leah S. Marcus, "The Milieu of Milton's *Comus:* Judicial Reform at Ludlow and the Problem of Sexual Assault," *Criticism* 25 (1983): 293-327, revised and condensed as "A 'Local' Reading of *Comus,*" 66-85, in *Milton and the Idea of Woman,* ed. Julia M. Walker (Urbana: Univ. of Illinois Press, 1988).

10. Recently William B. Hunter has questioned Milton's authorship of this work. While he cites evidence that raises telling questions about the production and provenance of the manuscript—and these may impinge on authorship—my ensuing remarks here and elsewhere indicate like theoretical and religious positions between Milton and *De doctrina christiana* when the Latin is the source of the text. Professor Hunter notices what seem to him to be some differing beliefs, but these seem to disappear when comparison is made with the Latin. I thus continue here to assign the work to Milton and accept that assignment, but the reader should be alert to the question of authorship. (See William B. Hunter, "The Provenance of the *Christian Doctrine*," *Studies in English Literature* 32 (1992): 129-42, with responses by Barbara K. Lewalski [143-54], John T. Shawcross [155-62], and Hunter [163-66]. I cite translations of *De doctrina christiana* by Charles Sumner [1825], basically the text given in CM, and by John Carey, printed in YP.)

11. Heinz Kohut and Ernest S. Wolf, "The Disorders of the Self and Their Treatment: An Outline," *Journal of Psycho-Analysis* 59 (1978): 414.

12. See ibid., 416.

13. See Heinz Kohut, "Forms and Transformations of Narcissism," *Journal of the American Psychoanalytic Association* 14 (1966): 257 ff.

14. See ibid., 245. James W. Earl has meaningfully discussed "Eve's Narcissism" in *Milton Quarterly* 19 (1985): 13-16, employing the work of Kohut and Lacan as well. He does not call this object love an antithesis to narcissism; it becomes the female's resolution of narcissism. In an unnecessary cuteness, he writes that "what *Eve* needs is a *baby,* to satisfy her desire as she satisfies Adam's." Previously he epitomized Milton's "theory of narcissism" as the bearing of an image like oneself (Eve's bearing "Multitudes like thyself," IV, 474). As he notes, Freud theorized female resolution of narcissism "into object-love only in mothering." My disagreement (as well as with the quotation from Kerrigan, 70 n. 5) is that he sees Eve *transferring* "some of her narcissism to Adam, her first Other." Earl genderizes the "direction" (as it were) of narcissism: the man sees the woman as self-object (with its libidinous dimension), as a surrogate for the mother-object, and as his other self, whereas Eve (as first woman) narcissistically cathects *her* own image, thence transferring part to her Other. No thought is given to the recognition of the Other, after she has met the Other, as her image-giver. The point is, rather, that Eve's vision in the pool depicts first a pre-

narcissistic stage (one engaging a kind of auto-eroticism as she first, like the baby, draws back from the image) which then reaches a narcissistic stage (herself) to move soon afterward to an object-choice (Adam); the process, however, is really a refinding of the object-choice, which is the primary narcissism. (See Jean Laplanche, *New Foundations for Psychoanalysis*, trans. David Macey [Oxford: Basil Blackwell, 1989], 68 ff.) Laplanche (74 ff.) is concerned to expose the Freudian confusion of reducing sexual evolution to self-preservation, a differentiation important in the point I am trying to make. In *Paradise Lost* the narcissistic relationship of Adam to Eve and Eve to Adam produces sexual evolution to mutual love; but the assertion of the idealized parent imago for Eve (Adam and what he is conceived of being) is fraudulently thwarted by the phallic Satan, who redirects her assertion by eliciting self-preservation on her part, and the ensuing nonmutuality for Adam (in his love for Eve) reverts to narcissistic self-preservation on his part. It is not a sexual matter of a man's being gratified through sex but the woman only through mothering. The protoevangelium promises self-preservation to both through progeny simply understood and through defeat of evil in time. It does not offer Eve, or Adam for that matter, a narcissistic resolution of sexual desire. The blatant sexism of Earl's reading also implies the need for lustful carnality for birth to occur ("there are no solutions to the problem which avoid the Fall," he writes).

15. Kohut, 266. For a pertinent reading of the Son, see my *Paradise Regain'd: 'Worthy T'Have Not Remain'd So Long Unsung'* (Pittsburgh: Duquesne Univ. Press, 1988), esp. 63-68.

16. See Kohut, 268.

17. Heinz Kohut, *The Analysis of the Self: A Systematic Approach to the Psychoanalytic Treatment of Narcissistic Personality Disorders* (New York: International Universities Press, 1971), 124.

2. A Biographical and Literary Overview to 1645

1. Rime royal is a seven-line stanza in iambic pentameter, rhyming a b a b b c c; Milton makes the last line an alexandrine.

2. As in the citations of Exodus 19:18-19; 1 Samuel 5:3-4; Job 38:6-7; Psalm 85; Isaiah 6:6-7; Ezekiel 8:14; Matthew 2:18; Luke 2:7-20; Philippians 2:6-8; 1 Thessalonians 4:16; 2 Peter 3:12; Revelation 3:18 and 20:2-3.

3. See "Areopagitica as a Scenario for Paradise Lost," 121-41, in *Achievements of the Left Hand: Essays on the Prose of John Milton*, ed. Michael Lieb and John T. Shawcross (Amherst: Univ. of Massachusetts Press, 1974).

4. YP 4, i: 624, trans. Helen North.

5. In his Commonplace Book, Milton, following Aristotle, divides his entries into an "Index Ethicus" (relating here to the moral issues involved in "ecclesiastical liberty"), an "Index Œconomicus" (domestic matters), and an "Index Politicus" (civil matters). Such earlier schematization gives validity to his 1654 claim for his prior writing.

3. The Lady of Christ's

1. Edward Le Comte in "Sly Milton: The Meaning Lurking in the Contexts of His Quotations" (English Studies Collection: East Meadow, N. Y., 1976), 11 n.

34, questions my reading of line 216: "This might be interesting if *gestans* meant 'riding,' which it does not. All other Milton editors agree on the sense of the line, of which a literal translation is, 'and bearing the joyful shades of the leafy palm.'" But others' translations are not accurate, even if they agree with the sense of Le Comte's; e.g., Merritt Y. Hughes's "and with shadowing fronds of joyous palms in your hands"; or Douglas Bush's "and, with shadowing branches of the joyous palm in your hands." (See *John Milton: Complete Poems and Major Prose* [Indianapolis: Odyssey Press, l957], and *The Complete Poetical Works of John Milton* [Boston: Houghton Mifflin, 1965] respectively.) The line is "Lætaque frondentis gestans umbracula palmæ." For *gestans* to be the present participle of the active verb *gesto* (meaning "bearing," "carrying") there must be an object; Hughes's and Bush's translations are thus clearly inexact. Further, they both reverse the nouns and their modifiers. *Læta* ("happy") must modify *umbracula* ("bowers"), which is a plural neuter accusative. The problems that translators have had with the line have arisen from their misconstruing *gestans*. Le Comte's translation having Diodati bear "joyful shades" does not make sense: one does not carry a "shade," nor does one carry a "shady place" or "bower." That is why Hughes and Bush mistranslate, in order to have him carry palm fronds or branches, which would create the "shadowing." But Le Comte's translation also misses the difference between *umbra* ("shade") and *umbraculum* ("any thing that furnishes shade," "a shady place," "a bower," "an arbor"). *Frondentis*, which is the present participle of *frondeo* (meaning "putting forth leaves") and not some form of *frons* ("frond" or "branch" as Hughes and Bush translate it), is in the genitive and modifies *palmæ*. Literally, the phrase is "of leafy palm," where it is genitive of material, thus indicating that the *umbracula* are made up of palm leaves. Le Comte's translation makes "the joyful shades" the result "of the leafy palm," which is the sense of Hughes's and Bush's translations. *Gesto* as a neuter (that is, intransitive) verb means "to ride," "to be carried about" (as in a carriage) for pleasure despite Le Comte's positive statement apparently to the contrary. (I use for reference Lewis and Short's *A Latin Dictionary* [Clarendon Press, 1962], 814.) The phrase "Lætaque . . . gestans umbracula," when *gestans* is construed as neuter, says, "being carried about in happy bowers" or "riding in happy bowers" where the accusative follows a verb of motion which is treated as a transitive verb. (Cf. 237d and 238 in Allen and Greenough's *Latin Grammar,* rev. ed. [Boston, 1895].) We say, for instance, "I ride the bus" when what we really mean is "I ride on or in the bus," even though many have falsely construed the verb *ride* in that construction as a transitive and *bus* as a direct object, a meaningless reading. The problem for Milton's poetic line comes from the differing meanings attached to *gesto* when truly transitive and when neuter, and simply the fact that it has two such different uses and meanings. The allusion to palms, in any case, leads us to see Diodati as joining the heavenly host of Revelation 7.9. Compare also the remarks by John K. Hale, "Sion's Bacchanalia: An Inquiry into Milton's Latin in the *Epitaphium Damonis*," *Milton Studies* 16 (1982): 115-30.

2. The metaphor implies that Milton already accepted creation *ex deo*, which he was to make a focal point in *Paradise Lost*, for return for man means return to unification with the substance of God. Accordingly Michael leads back ("reduces") the faithful angels who are "Under thir Head imbodied all in one" (*PL* VI, 779).

3. A type of this ultimate marriage appears in Milton's seventh sonnet when he concludes that whatever he achieves in life will be the result of his own worthiness and action and of God's grace upon him, as we have seen. It lies central to *Comus* as we have already noted, for the Lady evinces resistance to the lures of the Satanic and maintains her chastity of mind (soul), but only through the divine agency of Sabrina can she be freed bodily: "If Vertue feeble were, / Heav'n itself would stoop to her."

4. But compare his relationship with Beelzebub: "Sleepst thou Companion dear, what sleep can close / Thy eye-lids? and remembrest what Decree / Of yesterday, so late past the lips / Of Heav'ns Almightie. Thou to me thy thoughts / Wast wont, I mine to thee was wont t' impart; both waking we were one" (*PL* V, 673-78). Here he is asserting maleness, or, indeed, playing God; but the tone and language suggest a homoerotic attitude, which both denies a maleness like that of God the Father and implies an assertion of latent femaleness. The tone of disapproval accompanying the passage, like that in "In quintum Novembris" (ll. 90-101), where Satan bids the Pope rise, is not uncommon in the homosexual personality that feels guilt at its own sexual orientation. Angels, however, were reputedly bisexual and capable of assuming either form. (Plato's *Symposium* recalls much of this traditional lore that tries to rationalize sexual differentiations.) When, on the second day of battle, Satan reveals his discovery of gunpowder and development of cannon (note also the relationship between imagery of war and of love), it is in male and sexually aggressive terms; see *PL* VI, 482-90, 558-91, and Michael Lieb, *The Dialectics of Creation: Patterns of Birth and Regeneration in Paradise Lost* (Amherst: Univ. of Massachusetts Press, 1970), 116-17. Satan's overt sexualism implies a disorientation (understandable in terms of antiheroics) and an assertion to convince himself of his male attributes and capabilities.

5. The "weeping" is metaphoric, of course; the poem is the "wept sepulchre." Milton ends the poem by saying, "neither do [literal] tears for you befit, nor shall I shed them more. Away, my tears" (ll. 202-3). He alludes to Revelation 12:4 (as also at the end of "Lycidas," l. 181, and *PL* XII, 645): "And God shall wipe away all tears from their eyes; and there shall be no more death, neither sorrow, nor crying, neither shall there be any more pain; for the former things are passed away."

6. "Gate" is a yonic symbol, that is, a symbol implying the vagina and entrance. Natural openings (mouth, anus) function similarly, both as symbols and as surrogates.

7. See, for the most extensive and illuminating literary discussion of this metaphor, Stanley Stewart's *The Enclosed Garden* (Madison: Univ. of Wisconsin Press, 1966).

8. Much as religious minds dislike this characterization of the Son, one need point out only that the Father loved the Son so much, and the Son the Father, that they begot the Holy Spirit. We might also note such Christ figures as Nathanael West's Miss Lonelyhearts, Dostoevski's Sonia or Alexis, and Shakespeare's Antonio. "Feminine" attributes depend on the previously cited male concepts of "worthiness" and on the female's role as mother.

9. In the Letter to an Unknown Friend in the Trinity MS.

10. H. R. Hays in *The Dangerous Sex: The Myth of Feminine Evil* (New York: Putnam's, 1964; Pocket Books, 1966, 1972), Chap. 17, "The Bosom Snake,"

diiscusses Milton's "passively homosexual potential." Hays errs on some biographical statements and proceeds on some questionable (though not unusual) interpretations of the works, but infers that Milton's sexual orientation had its effect on "Comus," *Paradise Lost,* and *Samson Agonistes,* as well, obviously, as his personal life and the divorce tracts.

11. See Donald C. Dorian's *The English Diodatis* (New Brunswick: Rutgers Univ. Press, 1950) for full biographical treatment, which, however, does not consider such psychodynamic matters as those raised here.

12. See CM, 12:292-95.

13. See YP, 1:337 n. 1 (ed. W. Arthur and Alberta Turner; trans. Robert D. Murry).

14. For a full discussion see Leo Miller, "Milton's Clash with Chappell: A Suggested Reconstruction," *Milton Quarterly* 14 (1980): 77-87.

15. CM, 12:207. He had previously written: "It is not pleasant constantly to submit to the threats of a stern tutor / and to other things which are foreign to my nature" ("Elegia prima," ll. 15-16).

16. CM, 12:241 (and 238).

17. The translation in CM obscures the point; see Phyllis B. Tillyard's translation in YP, 1:284. While Milton does mean physical combat between men and manual labor, he also puns obscenely. See also the important study of this prolusion as a salting by Roslyn Richek in *English Literary Renaissance* 12 (1982): 103-31 (esp. 127-31).

18. Compare, for example, William Riley Parker's statement, "His reaction to a nickname may be another instance of misjudging friendliness, although we know too little of the circumstances to be sure. Nicknames are informal tributes of recognition, sometimes cruel but often ironically affectionate. . . . It is inconceivable, however, that his widow regarded it as a slur or as evidence of unfriendliness; one must assume that her husband had told her the anecdote with a masculine chuckle" (*Milton: A Biography,* 43).

19. The translation that has suggested that Milton had additional poems awaiting Diodati's judgment is simply ignorant of Latin; the *quoque* goes with *Te* (in addition to Christ, that is), not with *meditata.*

20. In *The Sacred Complex,* William Kerrigan, with reference to an earlier version of this chapter, asserts that Milton "was not a homosexual" because that "runs contrary to the regularities of his character manifested by the bulk of his writings" (49). Kerrigan feels that "Had Milton found himself primarily and continuously attracted to men, he would have acted on this attraction at some point in his life." I have, of course, been misread badly: there is a great difference between homoeroticism and homosexuality. I do not say that Milton was "a homosexual" and I certainly do not say that he found himself "primarily and continuously attracted to men." My remarks so far, and in the remainder of this chapter, are concerned with personality, and I suggest that on the spectrum between modal maleness and modal femaleness (as those terms are usually connoted) Milton as a youth fell somewhere past center on the femaleness side. At no point do I talk of Milton and "men," only of his relationship with Diodati. At no point do I imply "primary" or "continuous" "attraction." I say and imply none of these things because there is no evidence that I am aware of for them (and, besides, I do not believe them to be true). Apparently I must reiterate: the ev-

idence I have adduced, as cited here, suggests that Diodati was apparently homosexual and was a "male" dominating type, that Milton experienced a homoerotic attitude toward Diodati and was a more "female" personality type, and that there *may* have been some overt sexual actions between them. This does *not* make Milton "a homosexual" or attracted to "men." It is not an uncommon occurrence between younger men and between younger women, most of whom pass through such a stage into heterosexuality, which then persists without change and without residue from an earlier phase. My remarks on the Italian poems, of course, counter any thought that I had tried to cast Milton as one "primarily and continuously attracted to men."

21. "Milton's Italian Sonnets: An Interpretation," *University of Windsor Review* 3 (1967): 27-33. In such an interpretation the name "Aemilia" would imply one worthy of emulation or one who is a rival (as in the opposition between human and divine love).

22. Hays points out that Milton's first marriage (to Mary Powell) was to one not of his own political and religious persuasion (a kind of "foreign" wife) just as Samson was to choose outside his nation. While the appeal of exoticism for most people is pertinent, yet psychologically such choosing implies a subconscious desire to thwart the success of such union. Theories of complementarianism may help account for Milton's attraction to Aemilia, but the association with Diodati—also Italian and in physical appearance different from Milton—suggests that subconsciously Aemilia, whether real or fancied for purposes of this poetic sequence, was a surrogate for Diodati.

23. What the reader should do, of course, is return to these poems and read them in this suggested light to see whether such a view is tenable. For me, this view does stand up in such rereading and leads to important differences in understanding of the sequence. It nullifies the seeming problem of double addressees (the lady and Diodati); it makes more understandable the references to divine love and spiritual need with which the poems are punctuated; and it poses the real uncertainty about the sequence—that is, confusion between human (bodily) love and divine (spiritual) love that underlies attitudes in "Comus," the divorce tracts, and *Paradise Lost*. It may be well to exalt the bodily to a union with the spiritual (as seen in Adam and Eve's innocent love), but the rejection of bodily satisfaction of and by itself serves to describe a "sinfulness" for sex and thus a major failing of the author of such pamphlets as *The Doctrine and Discipline of Divorce*.

24. Probably "Arcades," the Greek translation of Psalm 114, "On Time," "Upon the Circumcision," "At a Solemn Music," "Lycidas," "Ad Patrem," and perhaps "Philosophus ad regem." Whether it was in the fall of 1637 that he firmly rejected a clerical career and adopted a poetic one is discussed in Chapter 4. Nevertheless, "Ad Patrem," written in March 1638 (although some would date it much earlier), seems to most scholars to corroborate such a decision.

25. See *The Prose of John Milton*, gen. ed. J. Max Patrick (Garden City: Doubleday Anchor, 1970), 604-7.

26. See also William B. Hunter, *Milton's Comus: Family Piece* (Troy, N. Y.: Whitston, 1983). In 1631 Mervin Touchet, Lord Audley and Earl of Castlehaven, second husband of the Countess of Derby's daughter Lady Anne, was brought to trial, found guilty, and executed for having his wife and her daughter (and his

daughter-in-law) raped by a servant (while he watched) and for committing sodomy with two of his male servants. "Comus" is not a lurid retelling of the distasteful events for the audience (as some recent critics seem to view it) but an idealistic consolation that such perverse action does not alter the sanctity of the person whose mind does not accede to such action. This point has sociological and psychological importance in today's world, where such victimization occurs frequently.

27. Note also the Elder Brother's "So dear to Heav'n is saintly chastity, / That when a soul is found sincerely so, / A thousand liveried angels lackey her" (ll. 435-55). An article complementary to the present remarks is Irene Tayler's "Say First! What Mov'd Blake? Blake's *Comus* Designs and *Milton*" in *Blake's Sublime Allegory,* ed. Stuart Curran and Joseph Anthony Wittreich, Jr. (Madison: Univ. of Wisconsin Press, 1973), 233-58. Tayler cogently argues that "Blake saw the lady's encounter with Comus as the product of that frightened girl's fantasy: her bondage, the bondage of sexual fears; her release, the release from them" (235). While we see the additions to the masque that set forth the doctrine of chastity espoused by the Lady a bit differently, we agree that the Lady—and we may substitute Milton—"reached maturity by breaking free of her benighted state of self-isolating fear of her own desires" (248).

28. The reference to masturbation is obvious enough as a polarity to mutual sexuality, but Milton's citation of it should be noted. It is rejected by Comus, arguing in "reason's garb," as unsavory ("morally offensive"), hardly an adjective that the Satanic Comus would credit. The mutual sexuality is clearly heterosexuality.

29. My disagreement with E.M.W. Tillyard's reading of these revisions will be evident; see "The Action of Comus," with an addendum, in *Studies in Milton* (London: Chatto and Windus, 1951), 82-99.

30. Milton contrasts Adonis's wound; a boar had gored him in his side. The contrasting sexes of Adonis in the mortal heaven and Psyche in the superior heaven owe their being to concepts previously raised in this chapter: the male as exerciser of maleness; the female (whether man or woman) as exerciser of femaleness.

31. Milton's first published work was "On Shakespear" in 1632 as previously noted, and his second was *Comus,* 1637 (i.e., early 1638). Both were anonymous, possibly a further sign of his anal-retentive personality.

32. Ernest Sirluck's discussion of some of these matters in "Milton's Idle Right Hand," *Journal of English and Germanic Philology* 60 (1961): 749-85, is faulted by antagonism toward certain controversies (generally chronological hypotheses advanced by Parker), but his examination of Milton's attitude toward virginity (or celibacy, as he calls it) is most significant, for he sees it as inhibitory of achievement in marriage and creative activity.

33. See William B. Hunter, Jr., "Some Speculations on the Nature of Milton's Blindness," *Journal of the History of Medicine* 17 (1962): 333-41; reprinted in *The Descent of Urania: Studies in Milton, 1946-1988* (Lewisburg: Bucknell Univ. Press, 1989), 184-92. Various conjectures of the cause have been set forth; for example, Lambert Rogers ("John Milton's Blindness: A Suggested Diagnosis," *Journal of the History of Medicine and Allied Sciences* 4 [1949]: 468-71) cogently argued that it was a suprachiasmal cystic tumor of the pituitary gland. Blindness

has often been associated psychologically with castration. Samson, who is finally galvanized to act by "inward eyes," is a good example; the cutting of his hair reinforces the psychodynamic significance of the blinded hero.

34. November 2 and November 23; see W. Arthur and Alberta Turner in YP, 1:325 n., for redating of the month. I quote from my translations in *The Prose of John Milton,* 607-9 and 610-12.

35. Note in the second letter this remark: "I did indeed, since it had been so agreed, long expect your letters; yet, in fact, never having received any, I did not, believe me, on that account allow my old good-will toward you to cool in the least; rather that same excuse for delay which you used in the beginning of your letter I had anticipated already in my own mind that you would offer, and that rightly and consistently with our relationship."

36. See Rose Clavering and John T. Shawcross, "Milton's European Itinerary and His Return Home," *Studies in English Literature* 5 (1965): 49-59, for a full examination of the problem. Numerous discussions have emerged over the years concerning the date of knowledge of Diodati's death. Two problems almost all of these arguments have not engaged are, first, what Milton said in *Defensio secunda* in Latin, not what is said in English translations of the passage by Edward Phillips or a modern translator; and second, where Milton would have received mail and when. The translations have suppressed the subtleties of Milton's words and introduced others that are inaccurate, and the vagaries of mail delivery and the uncertainty of Milton's itinerary and its timing are ignored. Indeed, to what address or person or group might a letter have been sent to him in Italy? There was none except the embassy at Venice.

37. CM, 8:127. The explanation for his remaining in Venice a month, despite the news he may have received there, may be that the feast of the Ascension, a major festival in Venice at that time, occurred on June 2; but he was in Geneva on June 10, when he inscribed Camillo Cardoyn's album, and such fast travel may not have been possible then.

38. "The care of the flock left behind" ("Epitaphium Damonis," ll. 14-15) suggests that his sister Anne may have died between April 1638 and May 1639 and that the flock were his nephews Edward and John Phillips, who joined his household soon after his return. Ralph Hone's argument ("New Light on the Milton-Phillips Family Relationship," *Huntington Library Quarterly* 22 [1958]: 63-75) that Anne was alive on December 29, 1639, on the basis of a real estate document of that date, is most questionable. The reference in the document simply repeats the wording of the previous deeds; Anne did not sign or witness the document. Her death is the only reasonable answer for the boys' actually living with Milton. Perhaps this was the main communication that Milton received in Venice, the information about Charles being additional.

4. Decision to Become a Poet

1. William R. Parker, *Milton's Contemporary Reputation* (Columbus: Ohio State Univ. Press, 1940), 60 n. 4. The reader should also see Parker's remarks in *Milton: A Biography,* passim. Related to this acceptance of Milton's consistent aims is the consistency seen in ideas and the imagery and language sustaining those ideas. See such studies as Edward S. Le Comte's *Yet Once More: Verbal and*

Psychological Pattern in Milton (New York: Liberal Arts Press, 1953); Jean-François Camé's *Les structures fondamentales de l'univers imaginaire miltonien* (Paris: Didier, 1976); and Armand Himy's *Pensée, mythe et structure dans le Paradis Perdu* (Lille: Publications de l'Université de Lille, 1977). Indeed, that has been part of the thesis of Chapter 2 of this biography. As Robert Ellrodt argues, there is a "changelessness" in the "structures of Milton's mind [that] dictate the choice of perspective, poetic form, and syntax" ("Milton's Unchanging Mind and the Early Poems," *Milton Quarterly* 22 [1988]: 59-62).

Yet there is also development and growth, and an awakening to things going on around him (including his religious and political world) and in him that bring consciousness out of its subconscious state. "An important disclosure of the poet's psychic life and literary ego, *Epitaphium Damonis* is an early instance of Milton's autobiographical impulse, a habit of self-examination reflected time and again throughout his works, in writings as diverse as the *Familiar Letters* and *Samson Agonistes* and *Paradise Lost*" (193) is the significant conclusion of Albert C. Labriola, whose understanding of Milton's continuing but developing self is seen in his title, "Portraits of an Artist: Milton's Changing Self-Image"; *Milton Studies* 19 (1984): 179-94.

2. Merritt Y. Hughes, ed., *Paradise Regained, the Minor Poems, and Samson Agonistes* (New York: Doubleday, 1937), xvii. See also John Spencer Hill, *John Milton Poet, Priest and Prophet: A Study of Divine Vocation in Milton's Poetry and Prose* (Totowa, N. J.: Rowman and Littlefield, 1979).

3. *The Reason of Church-Government Urg'd Against Prelaty* (London, 1641 [1642]), 39.

4. Cited in Chapter 3.

5. *Reason of Church-Government*, 38.

6. Cf. Parker's comment on "Elegia sexta" as poetic prognosticator, *Milton's Contemporary Reputation*, 60-61 n. 4.

7. Milton's not taking orders in 1632 does not rule out the possibility of a career in the church, as any reader of the Seventh Prolusion knows. He was eager to take flight over all history and regions of the world in order to improve wisdom and morals—concerns more of the cleric than of the seventeenth-century poet.

8. Kester Svendsen, in "Milton's *On His Having Arrived at the Age of Twenty-three*," *Explicator* 7 (1949): item 53, gives a similar reading as paraphrase 1. "It" in line 13 refers to "inward ripenes" specifically, since "All" would include such "inward ripenes." Cf. also Romans 12:3, 6: "For I say, through the grace given unto me, to every man that is among you, not to think of himself more highly than he ought to think; but to think soberly, according as God hath dealt to every man the measure of faith. . . . Having then gifts differing according to the grace that is given to us, whether prophecy, let us prophesy according to the proportion of faith."

9. We do not know certainly when "On Time," "Upon the Circumcision," and "At a Solemn Music" were written, but see Chapter 5.

10. The usual date of 1631, based on the reference to his "three and twentieth year," was challenged by William R. Parker ("Some Problems in the Chronology of Milton's Poems," *Review of English Studies* 11 [1935]: 276-83), who argued that Latin reference to age would indicate that the whole of the year in

which Milton would have been twenty-three would have elapsed. Thus he dated the sonnet around December 1632. More recently William B. Hunter ("The Date of Milton's Sonnet 7," *English Language Notes* 13 [1975]: 12-14; reprinted in *Descent of Urania,* 179-83) reasserted 1631 as the date on the basis of his nonordination as deacon shortly after his twenty-third birthday as would have been normal had he been offered "some certain place where he might use his function" (Church Canons of 1604). See Hunter's remarks in *Milton's Comus: Family Piece,* 11-12, and 21 n. 2. Thus the sonnet may have been composed actually in early 1632 well before December; probably it was composed as the time advanced for a decision about where he would be and what he would be doing after the master's degree had been granted on July 3. Perhaps it should be dated in the interval between his birthday, December 9, 1631, and the beginning of Hilary term in January 1632.

11. *Defensio secunda,* CM, 8:121.

12. Translation of Thomas R. Hartmann in *The Prose of John Milton,* 19.

13. See Chapter 5 for discussion and dating.

14. See H. A. Barnett, "A Time of the Year for Milton's 'Ad Patrem,' " *Modern Language Notes* 73 (1958): 82-83, and my article, "The Date of Milton's 'Ad Patrem,' " *Notes & Queries* 204 (1959): 358-59.

15. Referring to "*Phoebus* repli'd, and touch't my trembling ears" (l. 77), Lowry Nelson, Jr., writes in *Baroque Lyric Poetry* (New Haven: Yale Univ. Press, 1961), 66: "Why is it in the past? To begin with, the past tense informs the reader that the question stated in the present tense ['What boots it . . . To tend the homely slighted shepherds trade,' etc., ll. 64-66] as a part of the performance of the poem, was in reality first asked in the less remote past, presumably just after the death of Lycidas."

16. The prophetic tag "yet once more" (Hebrews 12:25-27) has allusive reference to the Second Coming after which all tears will be forever wiped from man's eyes (Revelation 21:4 and line 181 of "Lycidas"). It "signifieth the removing of those things that are shaken . . . that those things which cannot be shaken may remain," as St. Paul states it. See for discussion Joseph A. Wittreich, *Milton and the Line of Vision* (Madison: Univ. of Wisconsin Press, 1975), 117-19; Michael Lieb, " 'Yet Once More': The Formulaic Opening of *Lycidas,*" *Milton Quarterly* 12 (1978): 23-28; and Lieb, "Scriptural Formula and Prophetic Utterance in *Lycidas,*" 31-42 of *Milton and Scriptural Tradition: The Bible into Poetry,* ed. James H. Sims and Leland Ryken (Columbia: Univ. of Missouri Press, 1984). In writing "Lycidas" Milton has been able to shake off those things that deter humankind from the right path, such as injustice and frustration, so that those things that are ultimately meaningful and effective, such as achievement of godly worth, may remain.

17. Elizabeth Hanson reviews the Orpheus legend and Milton's employment of it in "Lycidas" and *Paradise Lost* VII in "To Smite Once and Yet Once More: The Transaction of Milton's *Lycidas,*" *Milton Studies* 25 (1990): 69-88. She sees the proem to Book VII as revealing anxiety over feminine weakness and ferocity, as in the legend "corporeal feminine fury destroys the order established by Orpheus's masterful masculine poetic voice" (78). With his failed rescue of Eurydice, Orpheus has separated himself from female society, seeking homosexual comforts; the women, returning, dismember him, and it is thus "Orpheus's

own poetic mastery that produces his destruction." In "Lycidas," therefore, with Phoebus's admonition (ll. 76-84) and "the dear might of him that walkt the waves" (l. 173), we see Milton's finally aligning himself with the voice of authority (God) within him. Hanson concludes that the proem in the epic rejects the mother-figure in the rejection of Calliope (an earthly symbol) for the father-figure through Urania (a heavenly symbol of the Almighty Father). (The sexual overtones of the Orpheus legend and Milton's use of it raise issues pursued in Chapters 3 and 11.)

18. "Ad Patrem," ll. 68-70, 56, 57.

19. James Holly Hanford, *A Milton Handbook,* Fourth Ed. (New York: Appleton-Century-Crofts, 1946), 168.

20. Milton first wrote "nothing sed" in the Trinity MS, and this is the reading of 1645. He crossed out "nothing," however, and put "little" in the margin in the Trinity MS, and this is the reading of the first edition of 1638. How did "nothing" get printed in 1645 when the copy text seems to have been a copy of 1638 with later alterations based on the Trinity MS? Did the preparer of copy for 1645 err in picking up "nothing" and changing "little"? or did Milton reverse himself again and decide that "nothing" was more accurate? The fact of the matter is that something was said against the actions of the grim wolf—witness Prynne, Bastwick, and Burton. It was "little" but not "nothing." I cannot believe that Milton reversed himself, and I chalk up the 1645 reading to a not very astute amanuensis, one who missed a number of errors in the 1638 text and a number of revisions in the Trinity MS after 1637.

21. See Helen Darbishire, "The Chronology of Milton's Handwriting," *The Library,* 4th Series, 14 (1933): 229-35. Perhaps "Ad Patrem" was written to accompany a presentation copy of *A Maske.*

22. "Ad Patrem," ll. 101-3.

5. Preparations

1. See William B. Hunter, "The Date and Occasion of *Arcades," English Language Notes* 11 (1973): 46-47; revised as Chapter II, "The Creation of *Arcades*" in *Milton's Comus: Family Piece,* 11-22.

2. See Christopher Grose's " 'Unweapon'd Creature in the Word': A Revision in Milton's Letter to a Friend," *English Language Notes* 21 (1983): 29-34, for the significance of "word" rather than "world" as given in YP, 1:319. While Grose does not offer a specific date for the letter, his remarks are in accord with my proffered dating of Milton's decision to be a poet.

3. In his signature for the bachelor's degree in the University Subscriptions Book at Christ's College, January 1629, reproduced in Samuel Leigh Sotheby's *Ramblings in the Elucidation of the Autograph of John Milton* (London, 1861), facing 124.

4. Students of Milton have not always paid attention to the dating of the Trinity MS, and some have not accepted the dating offered here. Mashahiko Agari in "A Note on Milton's Trinity MS," *English Language Notes* 22 (1984): 23-26, examined the *á* (*a* with a downstroke) which he does not find in "Lycidas," although it does appear in "Arcades" and "Comus" and on the pasted leaf of "Comus." He thus concludes that the materials entered in the manuscript prior to "Lycidas" (November 1637) must date from some years before. The *á* appears in

the article *á* in "Arcades" four or five times and in *ánd* once; but the poem also shows one or two occurrences of *a* without the downstroke and nine of *and*. The two drafts of the letter have sixteen or seventeen occurrences of *á* and eight or nine occurrences of *a;* one of *ánd* and three of *and*. In the odes *á* is found in "On Time" once and *ánd* in "Upon the Circumcision" twice; *a* appears four times and *and* nine times. Note that in "Upon the Circumcision," ll. 20 and 22, the down-stroke appears, but in l. 24 it does not. (The word *and* begins the line in each case.) The transcriptions of "On Time" and "Upon the Circumcision" would seem to follow the working out of "At a Solemn Music," which in its three and a half drafts does not show an *a* with a downstroke. "Comus," not including the pasted leaf or the last page, has 38 occurrences of *á* and 2 uncertain; 45 of *a* and 3 uncertain; 7 of *ánd* and 107 of *and*. The pasted leaf shows 1 *á* and 2 examples of *a*, and 6 of *and*. The last page (the revised epilogue) has 4 examples of *and*. "Lycidas" gives *a* 4 times (plus one occurrence in the headnote added after 1639) and *and* 79 times—all without the downstroke. The full statistics, if the use of the downstroke is significant, as Agari believes, indicates mixed practice with movement toward not using it rather than dating years prior to the time "Lyci-das" and some of the revisions to *Comus* were being written down.

William B. Hunter in "Problems in the Trinity College Manuscript of *Co-mus*," *Milton Quarterly* 19 (1985): 61-71 (revised as "A Bibliographical Excursus into the Trinity Manuscript," *Descent of Urania*, 246-60), reasserts traditional dat-ing on the basis of what he sees as the nature of the assembling of the text of the masque and the ordering of the manuscript sheets according to watermarks. I find the reordering of leaves partially acceptable, but with influence on the dat-ing. Professor Hunter seems not to understand that a folio quire (which this workbook would seem to be, as normally it would have been at that time) has only 25 leaves; thus his worry that thirteen leaves have watermarks and only twelve do not is unfounded. I would suggest that his ordering (see 248) should be as follows:

1w	14	15	27w	21w
2	13w	16w	26	
3	12w	17	6w	
4	11w	18w	24	
7w	10	19	22w	
8	9w	20w	5	

"W" means that a watermark appears; 23 and 25 are the remaining leaves of a separate quarto gathering that has been bound in; and 6, 26, and 27 are blank. This ordering accepts the displacement of leaf 5 (with Sonnets 8-10) and of leaf 6 (reordered with other blank leaves), but places an extra leaf (as in quires) within the natural fold of the second gathering of six leaves. Leaf 21 records the Scotch subjects, etc., on the recto and is blank on the verso. The alternation of watermarks in the second gathering is normal, that in the first (as in Hunter's arrangement) is unusual for 3/12w.

The matter of the recensions of text on the pasted leaf must await a more detailed account. My disagreement with the conclusion that the basic transcrip-tion of the masque in the manuscript was earlier than 1637 rests not only on those recensions (and others) but on the handwriting of which Hunter is forced to conclude, "He may have begun to use it [the Italian *e*] in the later summer of 1634 when he was assembling his text of *Mask*, and the change may not have been complete even when he left for Italy in 1638" (259). S.E. Sprott in his edition of *A Maske; The Earlier Versions* (Toronto: Univ. of Toronto Press, 1973) both misunderstands and ignores certain textual evidence of the masque's manuscript revisions in his aim to reestablish the traditional dating of the poem in its basic received form as 1634 (some revisions being acknowledged as dating from 1637) and to reconfirm the Bridgewater MS as produced in 1634. The textual discussion is too involved and detailed for examination here, demanding a full and separate treatment.

Cedric Brown, for the most part accepting Sprott's conclusions, has looked at both "Arcades" and "Comus" in *John Milton's Aristocratic Entertainments* (Cambridge: Cambridge Univ. Press, 1985). He would assume that Milton initiated none of the changes in the Bridgewater MS (see "Appendix: The Authenticity of the Bridgewater Manuscript and the Idea of the Censor," 171-78), dating it 1634 and not pursuing the evidence of relationships with the Trinity MS versions. But its text lies clearly between the basic transcription in the Trinity MS and revisions found therein. In "Chapter 6: 1634 and 1637—Texts, Epilogues, Audiences," 132-52, Brown concedes the revisions in terms of intentions, being little concerned with the occasion for Milton's 1637 reconsideration of his text. (The majority of revisions occurs in the temptation scene and the epilogue.) In two other articles he questions the dating of the transcription and development of "Arcades" in the Trinity MS in terms of the dances performed after the verses and the connotations of "rises" and "appears" in post-performance; see "Milton's Arcades: Context, Form and Function," *Renaissance Drama* 8 (1977): 245-74, and "Milton's 'Arcades' in the Trinity Manuscript," *Review of English Studies* 37 (1986): 542-49. He apparently has misread what I have suggested concerning "rises" and "appears." I do *not* read "rises" as post-performance. My argument in "The Manuscripts of 'Arcades'," loc. cit., observed that the text is a transcription, thus representing what was written prior to transcription (although some revisions are made in the process of transcribing), and that later alterations were made. "Rises" occurs because it was the "original" text; whether machinery was or was not used in the first (1634) performance does not matter: the expectation that it would be used was in the text. Brown does acknowledge that "appears" is a later change. My contention is that the revision was made when Milton was reexamining such works as "Arcades" and "Comus" in 1637 or after, in an effort to transform stage production for a viewing audience into poems for a reading audience. The handwriting of "appears" and the new title of "Arcades" is that from after Milton's return from Italy rather than before he went abroad.

The significance of the dating of "Comus" as 1634 or 1637 can be seen in such articles as George William Smith, Jr., "Milton's Revisions and the Design of *Comus*," *ELH* 46 (1974): 56-80, and John Creasor, "Milton's *Comus:* The Irrelevance of the Castlehaven Scandal," *Notes and Queries* N.S. 31 (1984): 307-17, both of which assume 1634 as the date of the received text. The problem of "virginity" and "chastity" raised here in Chapter 1 depends, of course, on what date one gives to the received text and what one purports to be the text of the September 1634 performance. (Like Creasor, Brown minimizes the effect of the Castlehaven scandal on the text.)

None of the aforementioned articles pays any attention to the works and their dates in terms of Milton's biography, psychological development, poetic career, or the like. (See also Creasor's "Editorial Problems in Milton," *Review of English Studies* 34 [1983]: 279-303; 35 [1984]: 45-60.)

5. There is an undated copy of "On Time" in a poetical miscellany in the Bodleian Library (Ashmole MS 36, 37, f. 22v), with (earlier?) variations from the printed text. The poem has been dated as early as 1631. This manuscript has been entered in my bibliography of Milton in the seventeenth century under 1633 to place it before the entry of the Trinity MS, which is listed under 1634 for reasons set forth in the foregoing discussion. See *Milton: A Bibliography for the Years 1624-1700* (Binghamton: Medieval & Renaissance Texts & Studies, 1984), Nos. 34 and 35.

6. The dating of "Ad Patrem" has been advanced in Chapter 4 as March 1638, although other times have been suggested. "The Fifth Ode of Horace" has been given a range of years between 1628 and 1648.

7. See my identification in "Notes on Milton's Amanuenses," *Journal of English and Germanic Philology* 58 (1959): 29-38. Questions about this identification apparently remain for some Miltonists. The identification rests mainly on assigning the handwriting of the prefatory statement in the manuscript of *A Satyre Against Hypocrites* (1655) to John Phillips, who wrote the poem and seems to have signed the preface. This hand also makes corrections within the scribal text. Unpublished questions have been raised about Phillips's being the autographer of this preface only because no other firm example of his hand is known.

8. This identification, first made by William R. Parker, has frequently been questioned. Maurice Kelley believes that in a communication to him Parker later questioned this identification himself on the basis of the biographer's formation of *f*, which formation could not be found in what manuscripts there are in Skinner's authenticated hand. Professor Kelley has kindly sent me a xerox of Parker's note: "I have another letter by Skinner, of the same year, but containing no 'f' that sits on the line." To me this seems insufficient evidence to withdraw the identification, since letter formation at different times and under different circumstances may be different.

9. *Achievements of the Left Hand,* Appendix, 367, 372, 391 n. 155.

10. See "The Arrangement and Order of Milton's Sonnets," *Modern Philology* 18 (1921): 475-83.

11. See also Kelley's "Milton's Later Sonnets and the Cambridge Manuscript," *Modern Philology* 54 (1956): 20-25.

12. I cannot agree that the quarto gathering was begun only to supply Milton with a fair copy, since the transcriptions of Sonnets 11-17 and "On the Forcers of Conscience" were certainly readable and usable, unless there was some other purpose, such as a new edition, at that time.

13. Cf. my remarks in *Achievements of the Left Hand,* Appendix, 331.

14. *Reason,* 37.

15. Letter to Charles Diodati, dated Nov. 23, 1637, *The Prose of John Milton,* 611.

16. Discovered in 1874, the Commonplace Book was first published by Alfred Horwood in facsimile in 1876, in an edition in 1876, and in a corrected edition in 1877. CM 18 prints the original languages and a translation; Ruth Mohl gives an English translation of the work in YP 1. Dating of the entries was undertaken by James Holly Hanford in "The Chronology of Milton's Private

Studies," *PMLA* 36 (1921): 251-314, reprinted in *John Milton Poet and Humanist* (Cleveland: Press of Case Western Reserve Univ., 1966), 75-125, and revised by Mohl in her aforementioned edition. See also Mohl's *John Milton and His Commonplace Book* (New York: Frederick Ungar, 1969).

17. Milton asked Diodati to send him Giustiniani's history of Venice.

18. See my remarks in *Achievements of the Left Hand*, Appendix, 372-73. "Perhaps the theological index was begun during the period when Milton was engaged in antiprelatical controversy (from mid-1641 on) or later when he moved into discussion of divorce (from mid-1643 on) or even later still when he may have been working on poetic statements of his ideas of man's fate and of true liberty (from 1646 on)."

19. Ibid., 370.

20. The so-called Anonymous biography (Cyriack Skinner's), published by Helen Darbishire, *The Early Lives of Milton* (London: Constable, 1932), 33. See note 8, infra.

21. See my discussion in "Notes on Milton's Amanuenses," but compare note 7, infra. Leo Miller's judicious review of the identity of this amanuensis leaves the question unanswered, as it must be until further evidence is discovered. See his *John Milton & the Oldenburg Safeguard* (New York: Loewenthal Press, 1985), Chapter 32, 293-95.

22. See note 9, infra.

23. See Darbishire, *Early Lives*, 8.

24. Parker, *Milton: A Biography*, 2:925 n. 19.

25. See my "Notes on Milton's Amanuenses" for possible assignment to John Phillips.

26. See William R. Parker, *Times Literary Supplement*, September 13, 1957, 547, and note 8, infra.

27. See remarks in the Anonymous Life in Darbishire, *Early Lives*, 25.

28. *Defensio secunda*, YP 4, i:613-14, trans. Helen North. The notes by Donald A. Roberts are often suspect of inexactness and interpretative error. We should also remember that *Defensio secunda* was written in 1654, seventeen years after the time Milton is recounting, and, more importantly, that these comments are in refutation of his antagonist's scurrility.

29. *The Prose of John Milton*, 611.

30. Refer to the data recorded by Parker, *Milton: A Biography*, 814-15, n. 90, and the inferences therefrom.

31. See Louis L. Martz's persuasive argument for seeing *Paradise Regain'd* as kin to Vergil's *Georgics* in *Poet of Exile: A Study of Milton's Poetry* (New Haven: Yale Univ. Press, 1980), Appendix 1, 293-304; and Anthony Low's *The Georgic Revolution* (Princeton: Princeton Univ. Press, 1985), Chapter 7, "Milton and the Georgic Ideal," 296-352.

32. All the poems eventually published in 1645 had been written except Sonnets 8-10 and the Latin poems of the Italian sojourn (five items) and "Epitaphium Damonis."

33. Cf. also ll. 95-96, "What father could bestow a greater gift, or Jove himself, / with the exception of heaven, if he had given all?" See also Chapter 1 here.

34. Cf. also the concern with fame in the manuscript letter: "a desire of honour & repute & immortall fame seated in the brest of every true scholar."

35. Lines 35-38 read: "Spiritus & rapidos qui circinat igneus orbes, / Nunc quoque syderis intercinit ipse choreis / Immortale melos, & inenarrabile carmen," rendered in the CM as: "At this instant too the fiery spirit that flies round and round 'mid the swiftly whirling orbs is singing, himself, amid the starry choirs, singing a never-dying melody, a song beyond all describing." Douglas Bush reviews the varying interpretations of the "fiery spirit" in *A Variorum Commentary* (New York: Columbia Univ. Press, 1970), 1:245-46. Clearly the fiery spirit is singing and thus is a personification. It is the "fiery" sun, Apollo, who was also the God of music and poetry, flying round and round the starry choir with "never-dying" melody. Taking the spirit to be the Empyrean or "the soaring mind of man" or "the cherub whose songs harmonize with the music of the spheres" or "the Platonic soul of the world" or an "interfused and sustaining spirit and mind" or, worse yet, as "Milton's own disembodied spirit," is simply bad reading.

36. See also Edward Chaney, *The Grand Tour and the Great Rebellion: Richard Lassels and 'The Voyage of Italy' in the Seventeenth Century* (Geneva: Slatkine, 1985).

37. See Clavering and Shawcross, "Milton's European Itinerary." The Latin is: "In Siciliam quoque & Græciam trajicere volentem me, tristis ex Anglia belli civilis nunius revocavit: turpe enim existimabam, dum mei cives domi de libertate dimicarent, me animi, causâ otiosè peregrinari" (85, edition of 1654).

38. There is also a distich by "Selvaggi." The name may mean "the uncultured one"; that is, it may be anonymous or pseudonymous. Chaney, however (see n. 36), cogently argues that this is David Codner, who used the name Matteo Selvaggio, a rendition of the cognomen "Savage"; see his Appendix III, 244-51. What we might suppose is that all these tributes were communicated to Milton by his friends while he was in Italy. It seems unlikely to me that Milton would have attached "Selvaggi" to the distich or not identified the author had this not been the name under which the epigram was sent. The distich is the source of John Dryden's often-printed epigram on Milton, first published under Robert White's portrait printed in the fourth edition of *Paradise Lost* in 1688. The thought that Milton in his epic combines Homer and Vergil and thus surpasses both becomes the basic neoclassical view such as we find in Joseph Addison's critique on the poem.

39. See Rose Clavering and John T. Shawcross, "Anne Milton and the Milton Residences," *Journal of English and Germanic Philology* 59 (1960): 680-90.

40. See Parker, *Milton: A Biography,* 304 and 930 n. 40, and 368 and 966 n. 47.

41. See also ibid., 838-39 n. 2.

42. See Erich Neumann, *The Origins and History of Consciousness,* trans. R.F.C. Hull (Princeton: Princeton Univ. Press, 1954).

43. *Psychology and Religion,* 2d ed., in *Collected Works* (Princeton: Princeton Univ. Press, 1969), 11:157. The first edition (New Haven: Yale Univ. Press, 1938) presents a significant idea for a fuller understanding of *Paradise Lost* when Jung writes of *"the God within,"* "the essential identity of God and man, either in the form of an a priori identity, or of a goal to be attained by certain practices or initiations" (72). In *Mysterium Coniunctionis,* 2d ed., in *Collected Works* (1970), 14:531, Jung notes that "he is no hero who never met the dragon," a variation surely on he who can boast "a fugitive and cloister'd vertue, unexercis'd &

unbreath'd, that never sallies out and sees her adversary, but slinks out of the race, where that immortall garland is to be run for, not without dust and heat" (*Areopagitica*, 12).

44. See the very important article by Michael Lieb, "Milton's 'Dramatick Constitution': The Celestial Dialogue in *Paradise Lost*, Book III," *Milton Studies* 23 (1988): 215-40. Cf. also Lieb's " 'Hate in Heav'n': Milton and the *Odium Dei*," *ELH* 53 (1986): 519-39. In "Reading God: Milton and the Anthropopathetic Tradition," *Milton Studies* 25 (1990): 213-43, Lieb examines the passability of God the Father in the Bible and *Paradise Lost* and that of the Son, which is indicative of both the passability of the Father and of humankind. One might view the dilemma for humankind as the recognition of the Father as self, approachable only through the ego of the Son and control of the id of the satanic.

45. Kerrigan discusses this point differently by stressing the oedipal complex, which he understands as developing celebration and defiance against the father. This leads him to draw parallels in *Paradise Regain'd* as Satan, giver of gifts, wishes to be worshipped, to become as it were the Son's Father. "Somewhere at the ground of the imaginative act that created this Satan . . . was the image of John Milton, Sr., fixed in the unconscious of a troubled oedipal son" (115). For the celebratory, Kerrigan examines "Ad Patrem" and the way in which the positive "lent its veneration to the Miltonic God" (116). He develops in his book the concept of a "sacred complex," one in which the superego is refashioned so as not to be collapsed into the ego; it is akin to what I call the idealized identity. The place of the mother here involves an internalization, an assimilation into oneself: "a mother who does not tempt or retard, but rather propels her son to the paternal identification that resolves the oedipus complex and organizes his autonomy" (107-8). With this should be compared my reading of the brief epic: "What I have suggested is that *Paradise Regain'd* depicts the allegory of Man's achievement of the Paradise within, first, by full knowledge and acceptance of Self, which implies an awareness of Godhead and the Spirit of God within one, thereby assuming the energy of the Father, and, second, by rejection of the bodily, the material, the worldly [error corrected] as Goods, which implies renunciation and passivity, thereby assuming the meekness of the mother. . . . .The poem thus initiates him from being mere Man into being the man-God. His return to his mother's house as womb symbol is entirely appropriate, for assertion of manness is now behind him"; "The Structure and Myth of *Paradise Regained*," *The Laurel Bough*, ed. G. Nageswara Rao (Delhi: Blackie & Son, [1982]), 8.

46. The genitive epithet in the phrase "forth rush'd with whirlwind sound / The Chariot of Paternal Deitie" (VI, 749-50), as the Son begins to vanquish Satan on "the third sacred Morn" of the War in Heaven, should particularly be remarked. Michael Lieb, who has made an exhaustive study of God's chariot, which has been equated with the vision of Ezekiel 1, a vision that foreshadows the Last Day, has told me that the epithet appears nowhere else. Milton emphasizes by it the fact of the Son's acting as surrogate for the Father, stressing thus the omnipotence that belongs only to God the Father. As Lieb also remarks, however, the word "chariot" does not appear in the Hebrew rendering of Ezekiel 1 or the Geneva or King James versions either; instead it derives from the apoc-

ryphal Ecclesiasticus 49: 8 ("Ezeckiel saw the glorious vision, which was shewed him vpon the charet of the Cherubims"), from which the Septuagint rendered Ezekiel 43:3 as "the appearance of the chariot which I saw," as opposed to "the vision which I saw." Ecclesiasticus had apparently picked up 1 Chronicles 28:18, "the chariot of the cherubim," which refers to the Ark of the Covenant. (The Geneva Bible glosses: "the merciseat which couered the Arke, which was called the charet because the Lord declared him selfe there.") The Chariot, which is described in lines 751-59 of *Paradise Lost* VI in accord with Ezekiel's vision, is equated by Ezekiel with "the likeness of the glory of the Lord." Milton's line thus suggests—for he knew the biblical passage well—that true glory is to be achieved only through paternity worthy of deification by a son: such a father may be anyone who has admirably, praiseworthily been father to a son and led him to proper precepts. The glory is to be sought through the idealized identity of the father taken on by the son. Milton puts the words into the mouth of Raphael, whose name literally means "the medicine of God," "God has healed," and we can understand that Milton is enhancing the tradition of the Chariot with a personal reminiscence. See also Lieb's "Milton's 'Chariot of Paternal Deitie' as a Reformation Conceit," *Journal of Religion* 65 (1985): 359-77. See also John Peter Rumrich's study *Matter of Glory: A New Preface to Paradise Lost* (Pittsburgh: Univ. of Pittsburgh Press, 1987). As Rumrich remarks, "Adam and Eve failed to glorify God and consequently have lost their original glory" (132). Through their act of nonglorification they have become emptied of *kabod*, that is, great reputation and substantial entity.

But one wonders whether some influence has not come from Elisha's words at the death of Elijah, who ascended to heaven in a whirlwind (2 Kings 2:12 and 13:14): "My father, my father, the chariot of Israel, and the horsemen thereof!" We noted Psalm 114 in Chapter 1; and Parker remarks (1:19): "This seems a conventional patronymic, a mere genealogical flourish, until we reflect that Abraham's father, Terah, like the poet's grandfather Milton, was an 'idolater', whereas Terah's devout son, like the poet's own father, had the faith to obey when called to go out into a place which he was to receive for an inheritance." The "blest seed" of Abraham is Jacob (later Israel), whose progeny were led out of indolent and evil Pharian fields in the great Exodus, just as the Son leads men out of the grasp of Satan, defeating him and his cohorts through his ascent with whirlwind sound in the Father's chariot, and just as Elisha takes on the mantle of Elijah in a whirlwind by means of the chariot of Israel, and just as Milton hopes to lead forth men to understand God's great Providence by following the precepts learned from his father.

47. Driscoll, *Identity in Shakespearean Drama* (Lewisburg: Bucknell Univ. Press, 1983), 169, and see also 156. Driscoll's book has helped focus many of the ensuing remarks on Milton's "identities."

48. Cf. my *With Mortal Voice: The Creation of* Paradise Lost (Lexington: Univ. Press of Kentucky, 1982), 84-90.

49. See Ruth Mohl, "The Theme of *Paradise Lost*" in *Studies in Spenser, Milton and the Theory of Monarchy* (New York: Columbia Univ. Press, 1949; rptd., New York: Frederick Ungar, 1962), 66-93.

50. Neumann, 415.

6. The Left Hand and the Great Purpose

1. *Milton's Sonnets*, ed. A.W. Verity (Cambridge: Cambridge Univ. Press,1895), Appendix I, 67-69.

2. E.M.W. Tillyard, 131. See also Tillyard's discussions in *Milton* (London: Chatto and Windus, 1930; revised, New York: Barnes and Noble, 1967), particularly noting, "The *Defensio Secunda* is . . . the turning-point of Milton's literary life, the work in which he found his true strength after his utmost weakness. It is further the one prose work that sprang directly from the mood which first conceived *Paradise Lost*" (pp. 163-64); H.J.C. Grierson's *Milton and Wordsworth: Poets and Prophets* (Cambridge: Cambridge Univ. Press, 1937), especially, "It was not till he had written *Defensio Secunda* (1654) that the idea of a national historical poem was abandoned, as being in a way completed" (47); and Tillyard's *The Miltonic Setting, Past and Present* (London: Chatto and Windus, 1957), where he writes: "I grant it that the praise Milton bestows on Cromwell and the rest in *Defensio Secunda* fulfilled after a fashion an earlier pledge to exalt the apostles of English liberty, but it points to Milton's reluctance to abandon utterly *any* plan he had made and not to any long-sustained intention to crown his plan with a great poem" (68).

3. See "A Survey of Milton's Prose Works" in *Achievements of the Left Hand*, 291-391.

4. Letter to Henry Oldenburg (YP, 4, ii: 866).

5. Ida Langdon, *Milton's Theory of Poetry and Fine Art* (New Haven: Yale Univ. Press, 1924), 8.

6. Criticism has emphasized their universal message but has also filled in the temporal background of at least most of the tracts, and most recently has been examining the rhetorical arts employed. See such studies as Arthur Barker, *Milton and the Puritan Dilemma*, 1641-1660 (Toronto: Univ. of Toronto Press, 1942); John X. Evans, "Imagery as Argument in Milton's *Areopagitica*," *Texas Studies in Language and Literature* 8 (1966): 189-205; W.E. Gilman, *Milton's Rhetoric: Studies in His Defense of Liberty* (Columbia: Univ. of Missouri Press, 1939); Barbara K. Lewalski, "Milton: Political Beliefs and Polemical Methods, 1659-60," *PMLA* 74 (1959): 191-202; Barbara K. Lewalski, "Milton on Learning and the Learned-Ministry Controversy," *Huntington Library Quarterly* 24 (1961): 267-81; Keith W.F. Stavely, *The Politics of Milton's Prose Style* (New Haven: Yale Univ. Press, 1975); Joan Webber, *The Eloquent "I": Style and Self in Seventeenth-Century Prose* (Madison: Univ. of Wisconsin Press, 1968); as well as essays in *Achievements of the Left Hand*.

7. He writes: *"the often copying of it hath tri'd my pen to give my severall friends satisfaction, and brought me to a necessitie of producing it to the publick view"* (*A Maske Presented At Ludlow Castle*, 1634 [London: Printed for Humphrey Robinson, 1637], A2-A2v.

8. Examples are numerous, but I might cite Robert Fletcher whose *Ex otio Negotium* did appear in 1656, and yet even Douglas Bush, in *English Literature in the Earlier Seventeenth Century 1600-1660* (Oxford: Clarendon Press, 1945; revised, 1962), nowhere mentions his name. See D.H. Woodward's modern edition of *The Poems and Translations of Robert Fletcher* (Gainesville: Univ. of Florida Press, 1970).

9. See Tillyard's discussion in *Studies in Milton,* already cited.

10. First set forth in my "Milton's Decision to Become a Poet," *Modern Language Quarterly* 24 (1963): 21-30.

11. Hill, 28.

12. See Langdon, passim, and John Diekhoff, ed., *Milton on Himself* (New York: Oxford Univ. Press, 1939), passim, for many examples and some discussion of Milton's statements of his beliefs and aims.

13. *Reason,* 37.

14. Others have pointed out Milton's educative purpose; see, for example, William Allan Neilson, "On Milton's Conception of Poetry," *Studies in the History of Culture, The Disciplines of the Humanities, American Council of Learned Societies* (Menasha, Wisc., 1942), 156-60; Langdon, 8; Grierson, 71 ff. Neilson generalizes (157), "Throughout [his work] the intention to teach seems not to be denied."

15. *Of Prelatical Episcopacy* (London, 1641), 3.

16. Compare "For I did not avoid the toils and dangers of military service without rendering to my fellow citizens another kind of service that was much more useful and no less perilous. . . . Indeed I congratulate myself and once again offer most fervent thanks to the heavenly bestower of gifts that such a lot has befallen me—a lot that seems much more a source of envy to others than of regret to myself," *Defensio secunda,* trans. Helen North, YP 4, i: 552-53.

17. *Animadversions upon the Remonstrants Defence, against Smectymnuus* (London, 1641), 38.

18. *Defensio prima,* trans. Donald MacKenzie, YP, 4, i: 537.

19. *An Apology against a Pamphlet call'd A Modest Confutation* (London, 1642), 16.

20. "Milton and the Poetics of Defense," 184-85, in *Politics, Poetics, and Hermeneutics in Milton's Prose,* ed. David Loewenstein and James Grantham Turner (Cambridge: Cambridge Univ. Press, 1990).

21. See "The Theological Context of Milton's *Christian Doctrine,*" 269-87, in *Achievements of the Left Hand.*

22. In the second draft this becomes: "due & tymely obedience to that command [from] in the gospell set out by the terrible seasing of him that hid the talent" (7).

23. *ME,* 8:48-51.

24. "Milton's Sonnet 19: Its Date of Authorship and Its Interpretation," *Notes & Queries,* N.S. 4 (1957): 442-46.

25. Dayton Haskin, paper presented at the Modern Language Association Convention in 1984.

26. "By some measures the author of *Paradise Lost* was not a particularly philosophical man" (266-67), but "when we are invited to reach into Milton's representations and make our own sense of them, . . . *Paradise Lost* transcends philosophy as we have come to know it" (270-71) is the not unlike conclusion of William Kerrigan in "Milton's Place in Intellectual History" (*The Cambridge Companion to Milton,* ed. Dennis Danielson [Cambridge: Cambridge Univ. Press, 1989).

27. *Milton: A Biography,* 1:258.

28. Emphasis is on the two adjectives since time was essential in March/April 1660; he is not saying *ideal* or even *preferable* way to establish a *free*

Commonwealth. In the background lies James Harrington's ideal and yet very practical economic "utopia," published in 1656 as *The Common-Wealth of Oceana:* Harrington's emphasis on equality of land ownership is not different from the Lady's remarks in "Comus" that "If every just man that now pines with want / Had but a moderate and beseeming share / Of that which lewdly-pamper'd Luxury / Now heaps upon som few with vast excess, / Natures full blessings would be well dispens't / In unsuperfluous eev'n proportion" (768-73). With equality of landholding will come equality of power, and that is what a commonwealth is, according to Harrington.

For the work as an anti-utopian jeremiad, see James Holstun, *A Rational Millennium: Puritan Utopias of Seventeenth-Century England and America* (Oxford: Oxford Univ. Press, 1987), 246-65, and Laura Lunger Knoppers, "Milton's *The Readie and Easie Way* and the English Jeremiad," 213-25, in Loewenstein and Turner.

29. *The Prose of John Milton,* ed. Patrick, 526.

30. "The Higher Wisdom of *The Tenure of Kings and Magistrates,*" 142-59, in *Achievements of the Left Hand.*

31. See Leo Miller's *John Milton among the Polygamophiles* (New York: Loewenthal Press, 1974).

32. George F. Sensabaugh, *That Grand Whig Milton* (Stanford: Stanford Univ. Press, 1952).

33. William Haller, *The Rise of Puritanism* (New York: Columbia Univ. Press, 1938), 289-90.

7. Education as Means

1. Joseph Addison, "An Account of the Greatest English Poets," in John Dryden's *The Annual Miscellany: For the Year 1694. Being the Fourth Part of Miscellany Poems* (London, 1694), 321-23.

2. Thomas Yalden, "On the Reprinting of Milton's Prose Works," in Robert Anderson's *The Works of the British Poets* (London, 1795), 7:762-63.

3. Paul M. Dowling rejects traditional thinking about Milton's *historia* (and historiography) in *Areopagitica,* viewing it (as he says of Herodotus) as a marshalling of "the particulars," some of which are false or inaccurate, "in order to allow the more perceptive of his readers to reflect on certain universal questions which the particulars suggest." See "Milton's Use (or Abuse) of History in *Areopagitica,*" *Cithara* 23 (1983): 29, and also 35. In that tract, however, Milton is engaged in argument rather than reportage, and thus the emphasis is not on factual recitation, as Dowling reminds us, but on the author's intended meaning.

4. Raphael Holinshed, *The Firste Volume of the Chronicles of England, Scotlande, and Irelande* (London, 1577), Book VI, Chapter 12, reprinted as *Holinshed's Chronicles: England, Scotland, and Ireland* (London, 1807), 1:667.

5. *The History of Britain* (London, 1670), Book V, 201.

6. Book V, I, 272. See p. 274 for the continuation of the account of Edmund's death.

7. (Philadelphia, 1856), 1:40.

8. An important study of Milton's volume by Nicholas von Maltzahn, appearing after this manuscript had gone to press, is independently in agreement

with my remarks and suggestions in this chapter, and should be consulted for a thorough review of the issues; see his *Milton's* History of Britain: *Republican Historiography in the English Revolution* (Oxford: Clarendon Press, 1991). His discussion of Milton's correction of earlier British histories is particularly noteworthy. He argues, however, for the writing of the first three books (as well as most of the fourth) in the first months of 1649 and before mid-March, discounting the statement of Theodore Haak dating the inception earlier.

9. "Milton on King James the Second," *Modern Language Quarterly* 3 (1942): 41-44.

10. Locke MS c. 44, "Adversaria Physica," f. 63v.

11. See Brady's *A True and Exact History of the Succession of the Crown of England* (1681, reprinted in *An Introduction to the Old English History* [1684], with a reference to *Defensio prima;* Howell's *Medulla Historiæ Anglicanæ* (1679); and Sheringham's *De anglorum gentis origine* (1670), which shows research into Anglo-Saxon documents and which prints passages in runic letters. The author of the preface to Howell's book, T.N., speaks of the "Historiographer" and stresses not overwhelming the reader with material and detail and not entertaining him with romances. Earlier in *An Institution of General History* (1661), Howell remarked: "nor shall I take that freedom to mix fiction and history together" (A3).

12. "Survey of Milton's Prose Works," 342-43, in *Achievements of the Left Hand*. I summarize the view of Eugene Laurence in *The Lives of the British Historians* (1885), 376-80.

13. Austin Woolrych argues for a date of composition for the *Digression* (that is, *The Character of the Long Parliament*) in 1660 soon after the second version of *The Readie and Easie Way* (April), on the basis of its disillusionment, a feeling he finds inconsistent with what would have been Milton's attitude in 1648. (I think the psalm translations of April 1648 as well as Sonnet 15 in August 1648, which shows hope but also anxiety, belie Woolrych's position.) He assigns its nonpublication in the 1670 *History* to the editor. See "The Date of the Digression in Milton's *History of Britain*," *For Veronica Wedgwood These: Studies in Seventeenth-Century History*, ed. Richard Ollard and Pamela Tudor-Craig (London: Collins, 1986), 217-46. Von Maltzahn dates the *Digression* in early 1649 as part of Book III. He argues that Sir Roger L'Estrange was the editor of the 1681 edition (see pp. 5 ff.).

14. *Milton's Library* (New York: Garland Press, 1975).

15. Chapter V of *Reconsiderations: Literary Essays* (Cambridge, 1920), 105-27.

16. "For Milton, all knowledge bears moral significance. In this respect, he is more medieval than modern in his viewpoint. Yet his picture of the natural world was far less consistent, more scientifically accurate, and therefore more problematic, than a medieval man's," in John Rumrich's words (*Matter of Glory,* 72).

17. School, college, and university texts were those of the ancients, most notably Sacrobosco and Aristotle: "For academic purposes, that physical universe was the traditional geocentric universe of Sacrobosco. Only slowly was an awareness of the Copernican theories and their accompanying mathematics beginning to exhibit itself"—Harris F. Fletcher, *The Intellectual Development of John Milton* (Urbana: Univ. of Illinois Press, 1961), 2:469. Raphael's reference to the Copernican system, amid his Ptolemaic explanation of the universe (*PL* VIII, 122 ff.),

may have been a late addition to the poem. While the Ptolemaic system provided an important metaphor for the epic in its centralizing of man and his world, the lack of much attention to the "new" science may reflect earlier first writing when such knowledge was not Milton's. As Kester Svendsen remarked, "Aside from Raphael's discourse, nearly all astronomy in Milton refers to a geocentric universe" (*Milton and Science* [Cambridge: Harvard Univ. Press, 1950], 48).

8. Covenant: Sacred and Profaned

1. For a general discussion of the matter, see Jane Lane (Elaine Kidner Dakers), *The Reign of King Covenant* (London, 1956).

2. So noted by A.H. Drysdale, *History of the Presbyterians in England: Their Rise, Decline, and Revival* (London, 1889), 314. In *Tetrachordon* (1645) Milton wrote: "*I saw, and was partaker, of your Vows and Cov'nants, Parlament of England*" (A2), but see also "On the New Forcers of Conscience" (early 1647?).

3. "For if our personal religion were not in some degree dependent on ourselves, and in our own power, God could not properly enter into a covenant with us," CM, 15:215, trans. Charles R. Sumner. John Carey's more exacting translation in Maurice Kelley's edition in YP, 6:398 reads: "Obviously if religious matters were not under our control, or to some extent within our power and choice, God could not enter into a covenant with us."

4. See his entry on "Covenant Religion," *ME*, 2:91. My differences with what may be inferred from this statement (whatever the author's intent) will become clear.

5. "No understanding man can bee ignorant that Covnants are ever made according to the present state of persons and of things; and have ever the more general laws of nature and of reason included in them, though not express'd. If I make a voluntary Covnant as with a man, to doe him good, and he prove afterward a monster to me, I should conceave a disobligement" (36).

6. "Let who so will interpret or determine, so it be according to true church-discipline; which is exercis'd on them only who have willingly joind themselves in that covnant of union" (14).

7. For example, it is not pursued by C.A. Patrides in *Milton and the Christian Tradition* (Oxford, 1966), despite an extensive discussion of grace, or by Maurice Kelley in *This Great Argument* (Princeton, 1941), despite a summary of Book I, Chapters XXVI-XXVIII of *De doctrina christiana* on the covenant of grace (172-78). Kelley does cite parallels in *Paradise Lost* XII. A most important and most illuminating exception is Joseph E. Duncan in *Milton's Earthly Paradise* (Minneapolis: Univ. of Minnesota Press, 1972), especially 132-47.

8. William Perkins, *A Golden Chaine* (London, 1591), Chapter 19.

9. This is basically Jewish rather than Christian. C.A. Patrides notes in *The Grand Design of God: The Literary Form of the Christian View of History* (London, 1972), 4-5: "Jewish writers chose invariably as their theme God's covenant with Israel. That covenant is an explanation—'the shadow of the future thrown back on the past'—of God's constant efforts to safeguard Israel." The quotation comes from Alfred North Whitehead in *Adventures in Ideas* (Cambridge, 1933), 82.

10. Translated by Theodore Haak (London, 1657), note to Deuteronomy 18:15: "*Moseh* stood between God and the people in the Covenant of the Law,

Gal. 3.19. so is Christ the onely Mediator between God and his people in the Covenant of Grace."

11. Comparison with Chapter 3, "Concerning God's Eternal Decrees," of the contemporary *Confession of Faith* of the Westminster Assembly (first published as *The Humble Advice of the Assembly of Divines . . . Concerning a Confession of Faith* in 1646) is instructive for the various issues regarding covenant mentioned here. See also questions 22 and 32 of the "Larger [or Longer] Catechism."

12. William Ames, *The Marrow of Sacred Divinity* (London, 1642), 55 (Chapter X, item 33).

13. See 2 Corinthians 3:6-18 and Hebrews 8.

14. *Covenant: The History of a Biblical Idea* (Baltimore, 1969), 188.

15. Ibid.

16. Compare Hebrews 9:11-22.

17. Ames, 114 (Chapter 24, items 13-14).

18. While the Sumner translation is often inexact, Carey's translation is often insufficiently literal for critical use. Milton specifically used "foedus," that is, covenant, here.

19. Milton thus rejects unilateral covenant and in so doing reinforces his rejection of the prohibition as a covenant.

20. The implications here led Duncan to talk of a covenant of redemption (132-47).

21. See also C.A. Patrides, "The 'Protevangelium' in Renaissance Theology and *Paradise Lost*," *Studies in English Literature* 3 (1963): 19-30.

22. Parker, 1:487-91, reviewed some of Milton's ideas in *De doctrina christiana*.

23. For example, Wollebius speaks of a covenant of works (*The Abridgment of Christian Divinitie* [London, 1650], 1, viii, 55), and he calls the Trees a double sacrament (ibid., vii, 55).

24. The Old Testament prophetic covenant offers promise through Nathan to David (2 Samuel 7:5-17), through David's continuing dynastic reign (2 Samuel 23:5, Psalm 89:28-29), through the prophetic-messianic expectation of Isaiah 11:1, 10, and through the New Covenant of Hosea 2:18-23 and the renewal of the Old in Ezekiel 20:34-38. David as true shepherd is the burden of, for example, Jeremiah 23:4-5 and Ezekiel 37:24, and the covenant in the heart the message of Jeremiah 32:39-41.

25. Michael Lieb, "*Paradise Lost* and the Myth of Prohibition" in *Eyes Fast Fixt*, ed. Albert C. Labriola and Michael Lieb, special issue of *Milton Studies* 7 (1975): 233-65. For further discussion of prohibition and other concerns of this chapter, see Lieb's *Poetics of the Holy: A Reading of Paradise Lost* (Chapel Hill: Univ. of North Carolina Press, 1981), passim.

26. Compare the discussions cited in Heinrich Heppe, *Reformed Dogmatics Set Out and Illustrated from the Sources*, rev. and ed. Ernst Bizer, trans. G.T. Thomson (London: George Allen and Unwin, 1950), 291 ff. Theorists cited, unlike Milton, accept covenant prior to the Fall. The basic definition of Johannes Henricus Heideggerus (*Corpus Theologiae* [Zurich, 1700], 9:29) fits Milton's view: "The law of nature is defined as the divine law by which God first imbued Adam, and in him the common nature of rationally endowed man, with the knowledge of what is honourable and base," but the remainder of the definition which alleges that man is "bound" to pursue or avoid, Milton does not accept.

27. Compare my discussion in *With Mortal Voice*, 21-32.

28. Christ's offices in *Paradise Regain'd* are discussed by Barbara K. Lewalski in *Milton's Brief Epic: The Genre, Meaning, and Art of Paradise Regained* (Providence: Brown Univ. Press, 1966), 182 ff.

29. Milton (XVI, 165) and Heppe (609-10) note that baptism answers to circumcision and the Lord's supper to the Passover under the Mosaic dispensation. Milton states his concept of sacrament definitively: "a sacrament is a thing to be used, not abstained from . . . a pledge, as it were, and memorial of obedience" (CM, 15:115). Clearly it is a sign of faith by man toward God under the covenant of grace (CM, 16:165). Milton would agree with Heppe (591) that a sacrament is not a *res sacra* (a sacred thing) but a *res sacrans* (a thing that consecrates).

30. This concept underlies the message of *The Tenure of Kings and Magistrates:* "Milton's contribution to political theory appears in points of counsel . . . [e. g.] 1. educate man to judge more objectively, without the false thinking of custom or self-interest, . . . 4. develop a proper regard of each man for every other. . . . Milton's contribution is fundamental to an improved political world rather than tangible structures, laws, and principles." See "The Higher Wisdom of *The Tenure of Kings and Magistrates*" in *Achievements of the Left Hand*, 155-56.

31. William B. Hunter, "John Milton: Autobiographer," *Milton Quarterly* 8 (1974): 100-104 (reprinted in *Descent of Urania*, 100-105), seems to err in this way by dividing religion at the time into the purely Calvinistic and the Arminian.

32. See Kelley, YP 6:77-79.

33. "Upon the eternal testament of the Father, upon the likewise eternal vow of surety by the Son and upon the pact between Father and Son rest God's covenant of grace with the elect. . . . 'The covenant of grace is a gratuitous agreement between an offended God and certain offending men, in which of His grace and sheer good pleasure and to the same sobered believers God has assigned righteousness and life in the same Christ the Mediator, and these in turn, by promising to produce faith and sobriety to God through the grace of Christ, obtain from Him righteousness and the right to expect life' " (Heppe, 382, quoting Heidegger, 11:8).

34. Calvin wrote, "God equipped man's soul with a mind, with which to discern good from evil, righteous from unrighteous, and to see by the previous light of reason what must be followed or fled from. . . . To this He joined the will, with which lies choice" (*Institutio Christianæ Religionis* [Berlin, 1834], 1, xv, 8). Choice is to direct appetite and control all organic movements, will thus assenting to the control of reason. Therefore, freedom of will is seen as willing good. See Heppe, 242.

35. Heppe, 388, citing Cocceius, *Summa Doctrinæ de Foedere et Testamento Dei* in *Opera*. Tom. VI (Amsterdam, 1673), VII:215, 223.

36. Unjustifiedly, he says this differently, creating a false impression: "his belief that from eternity God bestowed on man a freedom of choice, and that consequently not all divine decrees are absolute" (83).

37. Dennis Danielson in "Milton's Arminianism and *Paradise Lost,*" *Milton Studies* 12 (1978): 47-73, comments, "Although it would not be right to claim that Milton was in any sense a 'card-carrying' Arminian, there is no doubt that the term can be applied meaningfully, especially to his later writings" (47). While I commend Danielson's discussion of ideas in the poem, I cannot agree that Mil-

ton reversed his theological position and "was himself arguing an Arminian position against what he had previously accepted as the truth. This truth had been set down in 1647 in the Westminster Confession" (61). See later. This attitude is based on seeing Milton's earlier critical remarks on Arminians as espousing "the truth" and his later statements in *De doctrina christiana* as espousing Arminianism, rather than viewing his position as basically consistent and independent. (See also a revision of this article in Danielson's *Milton's Good God: A Study in Literary Theodicy* [Cambridge: Cambridge Univ. Press, 1982].) In a recent unpublished paper in which he argues that "Calvinism and Arminianism . . . came to mean something different in Milton's later years," Danielson suggests that Milton's views did not change so much as expand and "that the theological opinions Milton set forth in *Christian Doctrine* and in *Paradise Lost* concerning election, predestination, grace, and free will are Arminian in the doctrinal sense of that term." With this position I have no disagreement.

Mary Ann Radzinowicz in *Towards Samson Agonistes: The Growth of Milton's Mind* (Princeton: Princeton Univ. Press, 1978) engages in a lengthy discussion of "Arminianism and *Samson Agonistes*," 339-47, posited on the "heresy" of contingent predestination. Shocking is her mention of "Milton's 'heretical' Arianism or subordinationism" (340), which she links with his " 'heretical' Arminianism," accompanied by the usual repetition of his alleged change in belief. Her argument appears to be dependent on an inadequate understanding of free will in Calvin, Arminius, and Milton, inexactness in discussing election in Arminius and Milton, and the weighted and inaccurate use of the word "heresy."

38. Another category to which Milton has been recently assigned, the Antinomian, also should be voided. Milton at no point argues the nullification of the Law; it is, rather, replaced as representative of the covenant of grace by a new covenant of grace, one working through spirit rather than through commandment. Certainly there are affinities in Milton's position with antinomian emphasis on the higher status of devotion of heart over compulsion of law, but never does he proceed to a doctrine of exemption from moral law.

39. "The Theological Context of Milton's *Christian Doctrine*" in *Achievements of the Left Hand*, 273. Hunter also evidences the disagreements of Milton's systematic theology with that of the Arminians.

9. Moves toward the Great Purpose

1. See John T. Shawcross, "*Epitaphium Damonis:* Line 9-13 and the Date of Composition," *Modern Language Notes* 71 (1956): 322-24; and "The Date of the Separate Edition of Milton's *Epitaphium Damonis*," *Studies in Bibliography* 18 (1965): 262-65. Sergio Baldi in "The Date of Composition of *Epitaphium Damonis*," *Notes & Queries* 25 (1978): 508-9, in refutation of the preceding, argues that only one harvest of wheat occurs in Italy. Milton wrote: "And now twice was the stalk with its green ear rising / and twice were the yellow harvests being counted in the barns, / since the last day had swept Damon beneath the shadows, and still Thyrsis was not present, namely, love of the sweet Muse was keeping that shepherd in the Tuscan city." The tenses of the verbs are imperfect and the context places Milton still in Florence for two plantings and harvests of wheat before his return. He left England in April 1638 and returned in August 1639, and Diodati

was buried on August 27, 1638. He may thus be talking of a harvest in 1638 during the summer, a planting in fall 1638, a planting in spring 1639, and a harvest in summer 1639. While apparently spring-sown wheat is not considerable in Italy, yet the country is a favorable place for its growth, particularly toward the north and west, in comparison with other Mediterranean countries; it has different lengths of growing season. (See Naum Jasny, "The Wheats of Classical Antiquity," Johns Hopkins University Studies in Historical and Political Science, Series 62, No. 3 [1944], especially 59-60, 72.) Fall-sown wheat is perhaps more successful in the north and west (ibid., 77). While wheat harvest in Italy is generally around June (see Peter Tracy Dondlinger, *The Book of Wheat* [London: Kegan Paul, Trench, Trubner, 1908; rptd., 1973], 77), there is an extended harvest because of the varied plantings. The harvest of the summer of 1638 may have actually occurred by the time of Diodati's death in August, but it would have occurred during Milton's stay in Italy. In any case, the remark refers to a time before Milton left Florence to go to Venice.

2. See also John M. Steadman's edition of the outlines for tragedies in YP 8, Appendix A: 539-85, and James Holly Hanford's notes on the "Paradise Lost" and other scenarios, Appendix B, 586-96.

3. See *Arthurian Legend in the Seventeenth Century* (Baltimore: Johns Hopkins Press, 1932). Cf. Malcolm M. Ross, *Milton's Royalism* (Ithaca: Cornell Univ. Press, 1943), 54-56, and John M. Steadman's entry in *ME*, 1:85-90.

4. Note British subject, No. 24: "Alfred in disguise of a minstrel discovers the danes negligence sets on with a mightie slaughter about the same tyme ye devonshire men rout Hubba & slay him. / A Heroicall Poem may be founded somwhere in Alfreds reigne. especially at his issuing out of Edelingsey on the Danes. whose actions are wel like those of Ulysses."

5. See my article "One Aspect of Milton's Spelling: Idle Final 'E'," *PMLA* 78 (1963): 501-10, and dissertation, "Milton's Spelling: Its Biographical and Critical Implications" (1958), New York University, where the following revised discussion appears as Chapter VIII, 190-200. The primary key to dating the Plans in the manuscript is Milton's omission of the redundant "e," but there are many exceptional spellings (e.g., "raigne"). However, words of one syllable and words of two syllables with the stress on the second syllable, ending in "-ffe" or "-sse" only, retain the double consonant and the "e" until 1643; I accordingly omit these ("passe," "Duffe") from my totals here. Milton may have omitted the "e" on "divers" in accord with the spelling principle under consideration or in accord with today's differentiation of words; thus I do not include the single occurrence in the Plans. His practice with "hous" and like words is questionable.

6. Actual examination of the facsimile is imperative to follow the discussion in Appendix C. Commentaries on the manuscript do not indicate the order of entry, except for the few remarks in Harris F. Fletcher's second volume of *John Milton's Complete Poetical Works Reproduced in Photographic Facsimile* (Urbana: Univ. of Illinois Press, 1943-48), 12-15, which are often erroneous, and some notes by Steadman in YP, 8:539-85. It should be observed, since Fletcher seems to raise the question, that the present order of at least these seven pages of the Trinity MS is correct. Pages 35 and 36 are recto and verso of one leaf, as are pp. 37 and 38. Page 38, since it contains a note positioned for insertion on p. 39, was the verso leaf adjoining recto p. 39. Page 40, the verso of p. 39, faced opposite

p. 41, since the latter contains a note positioned for insertion on p. 40. Thus we have the definite order: pp. 35-36, 37-41. Page 35, showing earlier mature handwriting, early spelling practices, and three early drafts of "Adam unparadiz'd," must have preceded the other pages.

7. See Allan H. Gilbert, "Is *Samson Agonistes* Unfinished?" *Philological Quarterly* 28 (1949): 98-106, and William Riley Parker, "The Date of *Samson Agonistes*," ibid., 145-66, and "The Date of *Samson Agonistes*: A Postscript," *Notes & Queries*, N.S. 5 (1958): 201-2.

8. Thomas Ellwood, *The History of the Life of Thomas Ellwood* (London, 1714), 233-34.

9. See my discussions in "The Chronology of Milton's Major Poems," *PMLA* 76 (1961): 345-48, and *With Mortal Voice*, Appendix, 173-77.

10. Over all is the admonition of Psalm 2:2, 4: "The kings of the earth set themselves, and the rulers take counsel together, against the Lord, and against his Anointed. . . . He that sitteth in the heavens shall laugh: the Lord shall have them in derision." The text underlies the fabric of the poem; see II, 190-91, 731; V, 718, 735-37; VI, 600-609, 783-84; X, 488; XI, 816-18, 385-420; and cf. Chapter 16 here.

The sexuality of the cannon and its phallic disclosure through the rebellious angels' ranks (see VI, 569-84: "Pillars laid / On Wheels" graphically represent penises and testicles) perhaps plays on the dichotomies of war and love (Mars and Venus), both here perverted by Satan. The male concepts of and emphases on maleness we have observed in Chapter 3 appear in the description and unite war and sexual prowess.

11. *On the Composition of Paradise Lost* (Chapel Hill: Univ. of North Carolina Press, 1947).

12. J. Milton French, ed., *The Life Records of John Milton* (New Brunswick: Rutgers Univ. Press, 1958), 5:17.

13. See Darbishire, *The Early Lives*, 9 (from Bodleian MS Aubrey 8, f. 68b) and 46 (from *Atheniæ Oxonienses* [London: Printed for Tho. Bennet, 1691], 1:883).

14. Darbishire, 29 (from Bodleian MS Wood D.4, f. 143, the so-called "Anonymous Life").

15. Edward Phillips, ed., *Letters of State, Written by Mr. John Milton* (London: Printed in the Year, 1694), [liii] ("Catalogue") and xxxix ("Life"). Second reference in Darbishire, 75.

16. Darbishire, 185 (from "The Life of John Milton" in *A Complete Collection* [Amsterdam, 1698], 43; reprinted separately by John Darby in 1699).

17. See notes and introduction in Fletcher's facsimile edition, vol. 4, and French, 5:29.

18. Parker, 2:1138. The date on the present title pages (which are partially identical) seems to have been originally MDCLX according to its being centered, with X and I separately added slightly out-of-line with the rest of the date and creating a noncentering. The signature I of the *Samson Agonistes* title page was added after the X and the I of the date were added since it is centered on the full date. (Parker is inaccurate.) Clearly some error in setting the date occurred and some correction was made. The compositor may have set MDCLX in simple error, but such a simple error is more readily understood if it should have been

MDCLXX rather than MDCLXXI. I see no visual evidence that the date was originally set as MDCLXX or MDCLXI; rather, the fonts of the existing title pages suggest that the date was first MDCLX, that X from a different font was added out-of-line, uncentering the date, and that I from the basic font was then added, in line with the added X.

19. Pp. 233-34. Further discussion of dating will be found in my *Paradise Regain'd: "Worthy T'Have Not Remain'd So Long Unsung."*

20. The assumption that *Paradise Lost* was not completed until Milton had moved to Chalfont St. Giles is just that, an assumption. Should Amanuensis D ever be identified, we may have some evidence for dating the manuscript, which was emended by several hands, including Edward Phillips's, some while before it was employed for the first edition.

21. Walter MacKellar, ed., *A Variorum Commentary on the Poems of John Milton*, Vol. 4: *Paradise Regained* (New York: Columbia Univ. Press, 1975), 4 and n.

22. Parker, 1:616.

23. Fletcher, 4:8-11.

24. Lines 779-806 do not appear in the Trinity MS; ll. 350-65 were worked out on a scrap of paper which was attached to the MS but which is now missing; ll. 672-78, 688-706, 679-87 appear on the pasted leaf (with numerous examples of Italian "e," which Milton adopted in fall 1637). Verbal changes occur, for example, in ll. 291 and 409 (in 1637), 781 (in Milton's hand in the Pforzheimer copy of the 1637 edition), 214 and 605 (in 1645); etc.

25. In his later years Milton brought forth a number of earlier works: *Accedence Commenc't Grammar* (June? 1669), *The History of Britain* (November? 1670); *Artis Logicæ* (May? 1672); "At a Vacation Exercise," "On the Death of a Fair Infant Dying of a Cough," and "Apologus de Rustico et Hero" in *Poems* (November? 1673); and *Epistolarum Familiarium Liber Unus* (with the College Prolusions, May 1674). We owe the seven prolusions to the publisher Brabazon Aylmer's desire to fill out the volume of letters. In 1658 Milton published "Sir Walter Ralegh'"'s *The Cabinet-Council,* the manuscript of which he owned and which he discovered apparently in looking through older papers he held. During late 1655-58 he may have returned to fairly steady work on *Paradise Lost,* incorporating earlier writings (as discussed by Gilbert) found at this time among his various papers. In 1665-66 his return to unpublished manuscripts, prompted by Ellwood's question perhaps, yielded items for each year from 1669 through 1674.

26. I have previously identified Ellwood as the amanuensis who wrote out the receipt for payment of royalty from Samuel Simmons, April 26, 1669.

27. See Parker's speculations, 1:614-15.

28. Compare my discussion of "The Genres of *Paradise Regain'd* and *Samson Agonistes:* The Wisdom of Their Joint Publication" in *Composite Orders: The Genres of Milton's Last Poems,* ed. Richard S. Ide and Joseph Wittreich (*Milton Studies,* 17 [1983]: 225-48). See also Wittreich's " 'Strange Text!': 'Paradise Regain'd . . . To which is added *Samson Agonistes,*" 164-94, in Neil Fraistat, ed., *Poems in Their Place* (Chapel Hill: Univ. of North Carolina Press, 1986).

29. See "Chronology of Milton's Major Poems" (cited in n. 14). Parker (2:1140) suggested a date of ca. 1656-58 for the inception of the work as a drama.

30. See *Toward Samson Agonistes,* Appendix E: "The Date of Composition of *Samson Agonistes,*" 387-407. Since Radzinowicz misreads my statement about the arrangement of *Samson Agonistes* in my revised edition of the poetry (xviii n. 7), I am not surprised that she thinks me "indifferent to Milton's biblicism" or unnoticing of the postulation of "an original poem following Matthew's order of Christ's temptation in the wilderness, to change to Luke's order, and a final bracketing of Luke's account within a Jobean framework" (398). Clearly she has closed her mind to such a possibility; I have not. See William B. Hunter's "The Double Set of Temptations in *Paradise Regained," Milton Studies* 14 (1980): 183-93 (reprinted in *Descent of Urania,* 261-70), which independently explores such a possibility.

31. Ibid., 407.

32. *Milton and the English Revolution* (New York: Viking Press, 1977), Chapter 31, "*Samson Agonistes:* Hope Regained," 428-48; see also Appendix I, "The Date of *Samson Agonistes,*" 481-86.

33. I dismiss as insubstantial the suggestion of composition in 1660-61 advanced by A.S.P. Woodhouse in "*Samson Agonistes* and Milton's Experience," *Transactions of the Royal Society of Canada,* Third Series, 43 (1949): 169-75.

34. This altered reading of *Paradise Lost* demands two revisions of what seem to be standard views: First, covenant does not operate in *Paradise Lost* until the protevangelium is stated in Book X and it is accepted by Adam and Eve as the book ends. The Father's pertinent discussion in Book III is focussed as futural; its actualization is seen in Books XI and XII as some keep the covenant and some do not, and as some attest to their inelectability and others act through inward grace to achieve hope of election—the predestinated such as Noah and Elijah. The Father's words are not a gloss on Adam and Eve and the ensuing action of Book IX. The subject of the poem—man's disobedience—is reemphasized as a test of humankind's commitment to God's command, as a demonstration of a human being's free will, and as the aberration of the natural law within that person, which aberration accounts for the depravity of humankind after the Fall. The subject of the poem does not involve covenant as mutual act. Rather, the basic truth is advanced that command ultimately achieves less than mutual agreement. It is a lesson for all people in their lives, especially, Milton would say, in their political lives and their married lives. God, of course, has foreknown this truth.

Further, typological reasoning and expression cannot exist in Books I through IX, except as God the Father foresees. While Mary is referred to as the second Eve in V, 386-87, this is so only "Long after." Eve is not yet a type, but the narrator makes certain for the reader, here and there, the significance of personages and events within Man's time frame (which does not begin until Adam and Eve leave Paradise). This realization is validated, I believe, by the statement made immediately upon pronouncement of the protevangelium (X, 179-81) as the narrator establishes the antitypes of the Son and Mary when he remarks, "So spake this Oracle [the Son acting for the Father], then verifi'd / When *Jesus* son of *Mary* second *Eve,* / Saw Satan fall" (X, 182-84), followed by a restatement of the protevangelium: "Whom he shall tread at last under our feet; / Eevn hee who now foretold his fatal bruise, / And to the Woman thus his Sentence turn'd" (X, 190-92). The types of the Old Testament appear in Books XI and XII, which proceed up to the mortal existence of the antitype, after which the poem rapidly ends. (My disagreement with the major thrust of William Madsen's *From Shadowy Types to Truth* [New Haven: Yale Univ. Press, 1968] is evident.)

35. Remark Eve's "but till more hands / Aid us, the work under our Labour grows, / Luxurious by restraint" (IX, 207-9), spoken not long before Satan's assault.

36. The possibility, however, is glanced at in Chapter 12, n. 14, above.

37. For a full discussion of the narcissistic sins in the epic, see Jean Hagstrum, *Sex and Sensibility* (Chicago: Univ. of Chicago Press, 1980), 41-46.

10. A Biographical and Literary Overview to 1674

1. See Jackie Di Salvo, " 'The Lord's Battells': *Samson Agonistes* and the Puritan Revolution," *Milton Studies* 4 (1972): 39-62, and Joseph Wittreich, *Interpreting Samson Agonistes* (Ithaca: Cornell Univ. Press, 1986). Wittreich would differ strongly with the concept of renovation which I stress for Samson (often talked of as "regeneration" in the past).

2. See "The Higher Wisdom," *Achievements of the Left Hand,* 144: "Milton wrote *The Tenure of Kings and Magistrates* not to argue against adherents of the king but against those who align themselves with reform yet draw back as consequent acts, dictated by reason, arise."

3. See the important but unfortunately unacknowledged discussion by Robert Thomas Fallon in *Captain or Colonel: The Soldier in Milton's Life and Art* (Columbia: Univ. of Missouri Press, 1984).

4. See Michael Fixler, *Milton and the Kingdoms of God* ([Evanston]: Northwestern Univ. Press, 1964).

5. His residence there is the only one of many still standing. Ellwood, the Friend, was not very far away in Old Jordans, a center of the religious group. He and his family, as well as William Penn and his family, are buried on the property there.

6. Kohut and Wolf, 416.

7. Kohut, "Forms and Transformations," 244.

8. See ibid., 257 ff.

9. Ibid., 268.

10. Reference is to Matthew 11:29-30, a text important for Sonnet 19, "Take my yoke upon you, and learn of me . . . For my yoke is easy and my burden is light"; and Ecclesiastes 12:1-2, "Remember now thy Creator in the days of thy youth, while the evil days come not, nor the years draw nigh, when thou shalt say, I have no pleasure in them; / while the sun, or the light, or the moon, or the stars, be not darkened, nor the clouds return after the rain." Verse 1 is echoed in *Paradise Lost* VII, 25-27, and Verse 2 in Sonnet 22.

11. Milton is alluding to Ecclesiastes 9:1 ("For all this I considered in my heart even to declare all this, that the righteous, and the wise, and their works, are in the hand of god") and Luke 1:78-79 ("The dayspring from on high hath visited us, / To give light to them that sit in darkness and in the shadow of death, to guide our feet into the way of peace").

12. See Maurice Kelley's review of the evidence in *Seventeenth-Century News* 11 (1953): 29.

13. Unfortunately the Variorum Commentary ignored the historical circumstances that a date of 1655 would pose for the sonnet, largely through the editor's nonobjective presentation of the various views of the dating and meaning of the poem. Related to this has been the further question of the date of Sonnet 22, which reads: "this three years day these eyes, though clear / To outward view of blemish or of spot, / Bereft of light thir seeing have forgot"; it would seem to have been written around December 1655 and thus is seen to be inexact if Milton's total blindness was around February 1652. Dating of Sonnet 22 has thus ranged into earlier years and, if 1655, earlier months; the Variorum comment is, "The phrase, if it was to have any meaning at all, would be approximately accurate, say within a month or two," and "The first line and indeed the whole sonnet imply an anniversary as the occasion of composition, the arrival of a particular and unforgettable day (or short space of time) associated with his realizing the fact of total blindness" (2, ii: 481, 483). Perhaps the fact that this is poetry has been forgotten?

A recent article by Jonathan Goldberg, "Dating Milton," 199-220 in *Soliciting Interpretation: Literary Theory and Seventeenth-Century English Poetry,* ed. Elizabeth D. Harvey and Katharine Eisaman Maus (Chicago: Univ. of Chicago Press, 1990), places Sonnet 19 "against a range of Miltonic self-productions. Thus, most of this essay reads Milton's prose, to find there the subjects, the various Miltons, whose traces remain to disturb the possibility of determining a single Miltonic 'I' or a single moment of its writing in sonnet 19" (200). While I believe we can fairly well determine the moment of writing and recognize in that the significance of the historistic reaction of the narcissistic "I" behind it, I find Goldberg's point one that should constantly be remembered as we read the autobiographical statements that punctuate all of Milton's work, prose and poetry. The self-representation of the great defender of liberty through the writing of the *First Defense* that is given in Sonnet 22 (a work that Goldberg does not review) offers a Milton that is close to the Milton of Sonnet 18 or 19 but quite different from that of the proem to *Paradise Lost* VII. Ego persists in all these representations, as in the autobiographical section of the *Second Defense,* which Goldberg treats at length; but it is also an ego that is not the ego-ideal sought, or else is a fictional ego-ideal by way of suppression or aggrandizement of self, or else is the self and its functions that have replaced the selfobject and its functions, or else is, as in Sonnet 22, an "ideal ego." Goldberg seems to have limited himself to the review of Sonnet 19 given in the Variorum Commentary (though, of course, supplemented by more recent scholarship); recognition of the historical moment against which Sonnet 19, I argue, was written, offers another "chance" upon which Milton's self-presentation capitalizes as well as "the discontinuities which it suppresses in order to make this construct" (218).

14. See "Milton's Sonnet 19: Its Date of Authorship and Its Interpretation," *Notes & Queries* 4 [202] (1957): 446 n. 17.

15. See No. XI, "Ego-ideal and ideal ego," *Freud's Papers on Technique, 1953-1954,* 129-42, for various concepts in this paragraph. In *Collected Papers: Authorized Translations under the Supervision of Joan Riviere* (New York: Basic Books, 1959), vol. 2.

11. Interferences of the Self

1. See Peter Du Moulin, *Regii sanguinis clamor ad coelum* (The Hague, 1652), 9. Du Moulin had picked up the reports of Milton's rustication in Lent Term, 1626, through some altercation with his tutor, William Chappell, and he knows of his trip to Italy; but the errors of fact and time may suggest deliberate fabrication.

2. For these statements see *Pro Populo Anglicano Defensio Secunda* (London, 1654), 81-83; the translation is that of Helen North in YP, 4, i: 612-14.

3. See 114-15 of Carl Jung's *Two Essays on Analytical Psychology* (New York: Meridian Books, 1953), "The Archetypes of the Collective Unconscious."

4. Kerrigan, 56.

5. See "The Action of *Comus*," *Studies in Milton*, 82-97.

6. *The Feminine Reclaimed: The Idea of Woman in Spenser, Shakespeare and Milton* (Lexington: Univ. Press of Kentucky, 1986), 195-96. One of the first subjects feminist theory should study is what Estella Lauter and Carol Schreier Rupprecht have engaged in *Feminist Archetypal Theory* (Knoxville: Univ. of Tennessee Press, 1985). To counter the nearly exclusive male archetypal world fostered by Carl Jung and his disciples, we need gender studies that will reassert the "truths vital for the survival of the human race," as Annis V. Pratt puts it in "Spinning Among Fields: Jung, Frye, Levi-Strauss and Feminist Archetypal Theory," *Feminist Archetypal Theory*, 134. An important study in this regard is Christine Downing's *The Goddess: Mythological Images of the Feminine* (New York: Crossroads, 1981). Hera, for example, is seen as standing "for the transition from in-one-self-ness to *hiero gamos*, in response to a vision of a *coniunctio* that is neither dissolution nor battle" (92); somewhat like Milton's Eve leaving Eden, we might note, she "represents that in virginity which longs for conjunction as part of its own nature and that in *coniunctio* which looks back nostalgically toward in-one-self-ness as part of its own nature" (93).

7. Carl Jung, *Answer to Job* (Princeton: Princeton Univ. Press, 1958), trans. R.F.C. Hull, 83.

8. But compare John Creasor, "Milton's *Comus:* The Irrelevance of the Castlehaven Scandal," *Notes & Queries* N.S. 31 (1984): 307-17.

9. *The Great Mother: An Analysis of the Archetype*, trans. Ralph Manheim (Princeton: Princeton Univ. Press, 1963), 166-67 and n. 42.

10. Eros is related to woman, for Jung, and Logos is ascribed as man's ruling principle, as in Milton's two lines from *Paradise Lost* recalled earlier.

11. Carl Jung, *The Archetypes and the Collective Unconscious* (Princeton: Princeton Univ. Press, 1980), 85, 87.

12. Jung, *Two Essays*, "The Relations between the Ego and the Unconscious," 240.

13. Jon Harned in "A Psycho-biographical Reading of *Lycidas*," *CEA Critic* 48/49 (1986): 24-31, sees the father raising Milton to achieve a restatement of his own success.

14. Jung, *Two Essays*, "The Relations between the Ego and the Unconscious," 247.

15. "The Structure and Myth of *Paradise Regain'd*," 10.

16. Jackie Di Salvo, "Intestine Thorn: Samson's Struggle with the Woman Within," 211-29, in *Milton and the Idea of Woman*.

17. Carl Jung, *Psychology of the Unconscious*, trans. Beatrice M. Hinkle (New York: Moffat, Yard and Co., 1921), 360.

18. John A. Phillips, *Eve: The History of an Idea* (New York: Harper and Row, 1984), 170-71.

12. The Personal World: Man and Woman

1. *The Enchanted Palace: Some Structural Aspects of Paradise Lost* (Stockholm: Almqvist & Wiksell, 1967), esp. 95-98, 114-16. The number thirty-three denotes Christ. Qvarnstrom points out that Adam's warning to Eve just before the Fall (IX, 343-75), which he says is the only *speech* of this length, implies the ultimate need for Christ and his crucifixion because of what is presently to happen.

2. "The Significance of the Phallus," *Écrits, A Selection*, trans. Alan Sheridan (New York: Norton, 1977), 281-91. Compare Purvis Boyette's "Something More about the Erotic Motive in *Paradise Lost*," *Tulane Studies in English* 15 (1967): 19-30. He concludes: "the erotic motive . . . is firmly established in Milton's metaphysical understanding of the male-female principle. . . . Male and female are both the facts and the metaphors whereby men and women discover themselves in the experience of difference moving toward reconciliation" (30).

The reprise of the hand-in-hand motif as the poem ends and Eve and Adam leave Paradise reinforces the symbolism and psychological epitome just discussed. It is Michael who joins their hands, now that they are chastened to a new world and new life, thus emphasizing the reversal of the subtraction of love (the "logos" of God) from their future sexual encounters. The phallus is still the signifier. But a signifier, Lacan contended, is that which represents the subject of another signifier: the phallus has signified the mysterious knot, it came to signify only desire by the Fall, and it now has become the representation of the mysterious knot once more but with the symbolic implication that woman and man not "hand-in-hand" will yield phallus as agent of desire only.

3. Another way of looking at this much discussed moment, from what might be thought Milton's point of view, is that it does set up the testing of virtue, a sallying forth from cloistering to meet the Adversary (see his remarks in *Areopagitica*), a necessary act to galvanize one against the assaults of temptation. In this case, however, the victim is so innocent that the guile of the tempter (who persists today hundredfold) can easily deceive, as it does repeatedly still.

4. *The Muse's Method: An Introduction to Paradise Lost* (London: Chatto and Windus, 1962), 111. The implied meaning of the motif for Milton is observed in his translation of Psalm 85: "Mercy and Truth *that long were miss'd* / Now *joyfully* are met; / *Sweet* Peace and Righteousness have kiss'd / *And hand in hand* are set" (v. 10, ll. 41-44).

5. The motif echoes and is based on Milton's conception of the true union which is possible for two individual essences (or three in the case of the Trinity); while they remain individuated, they can fully merge into one (as in coition or as in a true marriage of minds). He argues for divorce when that true union has not occurred, when there is only bodily union but not a union of souls or minds.

The nuances of language in *Paradise Lost* are particularly telling for the full understanding of Milton's ideas and attitudes in these matters of love, marriage, genderization, and humankind's means to recapture true union. The reader should pursue this matter in such works as Kathleen Swaim's *Before and After the Fall: Contrasting Modes in Paradise Lost* (Amherst: Univ. of Massachusetts Press, 1986) and two articles by Hideyuki Shitaka, "Man's Mutuality, Love, and Language in *Paradise Lost*," *Hiroshima Studies in English Language and Literature* 30 (1985): 25-35, and "Degeneration and Regeneration of Man's Language in *Paradise Lost*," *Studies in English Literature* (The English Literary Society of Japan), 62 (1985): 17-33. Shitaka details Milton's subtle use of seemingly simple verbal patterns (such as between the uses of 'thou' and 'me'), and notes, "Adam answers nothing to Eve's last words of love, but his action is more eloquent: he takes again his wife's hand, the pledge of their mutual love, when they go out into human history as we know it, full of trials" (*Hiroshima Studies*, 34).

Milton's concept of ideal marriage and of heterosexual activity, as seen particularly in the divorce tracts, appears interestingly in Annabel Patterson's "No Meer Amatorious Novel?" 85-101 in Loewenstein and Turner. The "ideal and disinterested self" is distinguished from "a confessedly self-interested author" whose "self-division" seems to rest on equating heterosexual activity with animalism, physical labor, and slavery. (See also Edward Le Comte, *Milton and Sex*, 29-30, to which she refers.) "Milton's allusions to sexual process" set up a synonymy "with the novel as a category of thought, as a genre" (99). In this same volume Stephen M. Fallon ("The Metaphysics of Milton's Divorce Tracts," 69-83) shows how Milton "invokes monism to hold out to the godly the prospect of an ideal sexual life" (69); "The loveless but sexually active couple 'grind in the mill [with apparent remembrance of Samson] of an undelighted and servil copulation'," quoting *The Doctrine and Discipline of Divorce*, 2d ed., 15.

6. *The Troublesome Helpmate: A History of Misogyny in Literature* (Seattle: Univ. of Washington Press, 1966), 144.

7. "Patriarchal Poetry and Women Readers: Reflections on Milton's Bogey," *PMLA* 93 (1978): 368, referring to *A Room of One's Own* (New York: Harcourt, 1929), 118. The essay was reprinted with a few small differences as "Milton's Bogey: Patriarchal Poetry and Women Readers" in Sandra M. Gilbert and Susan Gubar, *The Madwoman in the Attic: The Woman Writer and the Nineteenth-Century Literary Imagination* (New Haven: Yale Univ. Press, 1979), Chapter 6, 187-212, 667-71. It is the first essay in a section entitled, "How Are We Fal'n?: Milton's Daughters."

8. Joan Malory Webber brilliantly destroyed Gilbert's article in "The Politics of Poetry: Feminism and *Paradise Lost*," *Milton Studies* 14 (1980): 3-24. Diane Kelsey McColley discusses critics (male as well as female) who have found Eve "fatally frail or innately perverse," "vain and obstinate, and Adam weak and uxorious" before the Fall. See *Milton's Eve* (Urbana: Univ. of Illinois Press, 1983), 3.

9. A most instructive examination of this issue is A.B. Chambers's in "The Falls of Adam and Eve in *Paradise Lost*," *New Essays on Paradise Lost*, ed. Thomas Kranidas (Berkeley: Univ. of California Press, 1969), 118-30. "This allegory [of Adam and Eve] and psychology [of temptation] must strongly have suggested to Milton's mind the probability of the biblical Eve's fall as the deceived reaction of mankind's flesh and carnal reason to a mental sophistication with which it is unprepared to deal. They must also have pointed toward the probability of Adam's fall as a knowledgeable assent of the mind to a temptation it self-consciously re-

fuses to reject. They suggested, in short, that Adam was not deceived but that the woman was" (129).

10. The description of Eve's creation in VIII, 437-90, is the golden section of the poem (that is, a position of the narrative roughly .618 into the poem), the artistic focal point. In the first edition the exact golden mean is lines 6519-20; that is, present lines VIII, 444-45: "I, ere thou spak'st, / Knew it not good for Man to be alone." This became the central fact of the myth, of life, and of the poem. See *With Mortal Voice*, 24-32, for my discussion of love as the theme of the epic. (I use the word "theme" correctly: it does not equate "subject.")

11. *The Sacred Complex*, 230-45.

12. "thee chiefly, who full oft / Thy self in me thy perfect image viewing / Becam'st enamour'd, and such joy thou took'st / With me in secret, that my womb conceiv'd / A growing burden" (II, 763-67).

13. Jean Hagstrum likewise points out that love is both good and evil (46) in his thorough examination of "Milton and the Ideal of Heterosexual Friendship" in *Sex and Sensibility*, 24-49.

14. He does, however, set the stage for Adam *not* to partake of the fruit and thus makes Adam succumb through his own character and free will. Dennis Danielson in "Through the Telescope of Typology; What Adam Should Have Done," *Milton Quarterly* 23 (1989): 121-27, examines the way biblical typology could have allowed Adam to be the first Christ (just as Christ is "the last Adam," 1 Corinthians 15:45), offering himself for the now fallen Eve, "to die for," not "to sin with." The fallen Eve's exclamation "O glorious trial of exceeding Love, / Illustrious evidence, example high!" (IX, 961-62), as Danielson points out, parodies the angelic response to the Son's offer to die for humankind, "O unexampl'd love, / Love no where to be found less then Divine!" (III, 410-11). But Adam does not exhibit charity (love toward others); he exhibits self-love, and Milton, not simply reciting the Genesis story, allegorizes how an act involving "sinfulness" (when not induced by fraud, as with Eve) is an act of the self, one's self-love or one's self-hate (as with the "self-tempted, self-deprav'd" Satan), not any charitable act or concern for one's neighbor. Sin arises from humankind's indwelling and is rejected by Christ's altruistic *agape*. Of course, typology does not exist as a concept at this point in time, coming into being only with the statement of the protevangelium (see Chapters 8 and 9): Adam, indeed, had he been the first Christ, would have obviated typological thinking, not only because a second Christ would have served a different function from what he does but because Adam would have become an antitype of truly "unexampl'd love" to be emulated rather than a mere human whose "unexampl'd love" (self-love) is so frequently, unfortunately, emulated.

Arthur Miller's quip, "Where choice begins, Paradise ends. . . . The apple cannot be stuck back on the Tree of Knowledge," epitomizes the problem: choice sets in motion action that cannot ever be thoroughly and completely reversed. Compare also his rendition of the myth in his play "After The Fall."

15. In Sonnet 4, addressed to Diodati, the poetic voice says, "I . . . now have fallen where upright man sometimes entangles himself" succumbing to "foreign beauty" and "song that could well mislead the laboring moon / . . . and from her eyes shoots such great fire." The "laboring moon" of the Lapland witches

connected with Sin in Book II and *"Eve,* whose Eye darted contagious Fire," as the first lustful action begins in Book IX, are interestingly reprised pictures.

16. The symbol of the serpent as phallus and Eve's succumbing to sexual desire (the fruit suggesting a yonic symbol) in the first stage is explored by Wolfgang E.H. Rudat in "Milton, Freud, St. Augustine: *Paradise Lost* and the History of Human Sexuality," *Mosaic* 15, No. 2 (1982): 109-21. The holding forth of the fruit to Adam by Eve and his being overcome by female charm, which however is his projected self, in the second stage repeats the first stage as sexual indulgence.

17. *De doctrina christiana* I, xi; YP, 6:382. He is quoting 1 John 3:4.

18. See Harold Fisch, "Hebraic Style and Motifs in Paradise Lost," in *Language and Style in Milton,* ed. Ronald David Emma and John T. Shawcross (New York: Ungar, 1967), esp. 38, and Eric Voegelin, *Order and History,* vol. I of *Israel and Revelation* (Baton Rouge: Louisiana State Univ. Press, 1956).

19. See *"Paradise Lost* and the Theme of Exodus," *Milton Studies* 2 (1970): 3-26. Reprinted, with revisions, in *With Mortal Voice,* Chapter 11, 119-38, 189-91.

20. "Sin," personified, comes into existence from the left side of Satan's head, similarly, at the moment he breaks the "law" of God under which the angels existed; see II, 749-58, and Raphael's description of the stimulus in the assembly in Heaven (V, 600-615).

21. The curious legend of Lilith in Hebraic folklore might be noted. She was supposedly Adam's first wife, existing well before the creation of Eve. The Hebraic version meliorates the Semitic myth of an evil female spirit who attacked children in the night as well as men sleeping alone. Contrastively, Eve's name comes from a verb meaning to bring into existence, to give life to ("Mother of Mankind"). Lilith apparently comes from a word meaning *night,* and thence comes to mean *night-hag.* She is associated with darkness, Sheol (Hell), and the womb in a nonregenerative sense.

22. One might compare Keith L. Sprunger's information on women in the seventeenth-century Reformed Church in *Dutch Puritanism: A History of English and Scottish Churches of the Netherlands in the Sixteenth and Seventeenth Centuries* (Leiden: E.J. Brill, 1982). "Only John Smyth, the Anabaptist, allowed a place for women in congregational discipline and censures. During the 1630s, however, the issue was raised anew and became a point of controversy in some churches," 324-25. See further 333-34.

23. For other articles on the foregoing controversy, see Allan H. Gilbert, "Milton on the Position of Women," *Modern Language Review* 15 (1920): 7-27, 240-64; William Haller, " 'Hail Wedded Love'," *ELH* 13 (1946): 79-97; Marcia Landy, "Kinship and the Role of Women in *Paradise Lost," Milton Studies* 4 (1972): 3-18; and Barbara K. Lewalski, "Milton on Women—Yet Once More," *Milton Studies* 6 (1974): 3-20. I find the often combative discussion of "Milton on Sex and Marriage" by David Aers and Bob Hodge *(Milton Studies* 13 [1979]: 3-33) generally distorted: for example, of IV, 738-43, they write, "The happy couple were 'laid': Who by? Adam is not seen to be doing anything, in this totally unfrank description. Eve does not 'dart contagious fire': she just does not actually refuse. Does she lie there and think of England, as Victorian wives were supposed to do?" (28). The essay is reprinted in David Aers, Bob Hodge, and Gunther Kress, *Literature, Language and Society in England, 1580-1680* (Dublin:

Gill and Macmillan, 1981), as Chapter 6, 122-51, 206-10. And one is exasperated by Edward Le Comte's curious *Milton and Sex* (New York: Columbia Univ. Press, 1978) despite its frequent valid statements, such as "What follows [in Book X] is an all-too-natural marital quarrel, with points scored on both sides. It is *not* an expression of Milton's hatred for women. Samson and Dalila, also married, also quarrel. That is not proof positive of the poet's misogyny either" (100). One must frown when the nettling tone of that paragraph carries over into such questionable inferences as: "In any case . . . there can be no doubt of the shattering impact of the precipitous first marriage. It shattered an idol. The girl did not live up to his expectations—and perhaps no girl could have. . . . There was a split in the author from then on, first revealed in the divorce tracts, which were not meant to tell a tale but did" (119). Does no one but Robert Graves look at the situation from Mary's point of view?

24. Jung, *Two Essays*, writes: "So long as the anima is unconscious she is always projected, for everything unconscious is projected"; the anima is most easily projected upon a woman (207). The projection of the animus is discussed on 219.

25. Ibid., 217.

26. Adam has not fallen at this point, is still sinless, but remark the parallel with Eve's relation to herself in the pool sequence, which had led some inadequate readings of the poem to argue that she had fallen before the Fall, even though the narrative voice says just before her Fall that she is "yet sinless" (IX, 659).

27. Edward W. Tayler, *Milton's Poetry: Its Development in Time* (Pittsburgh: Duquesne Univ. Press, 1979), 4-5, 3.

28. John T. Shawcross, "Milton's Views on Women," *ME*, 8:174. For a full discussion of this topic, see John Halkett, *Milton and the Idea of Matrimony: A Study of the Divorce Tracts and Paradise Lost* (New Haven: Yale Univ. Press, 1970).

13. Further Interferences of the Self

1. See "The Higher Wisdom of *The Tenure of Kings and Magistrates*," 155 and passim.

2. Among the manifestations of the anal personality are meticulousness, ceremonialism (that is, repeated acts in exactly the same order and form under seemingly similar circumstances), and an idealism that believes that perfection may be achieved and maintained through such meticulousness and ceremonialism.

3. *Tetrachordon* (1645), 10.

4. Jung, *Two Essays*, 428.

5. The question of the date of Sonnet 19 is reviewed in Chapter 10.

6. Postscript to *Defensio prima* (1658), 171; translation by Donald MacKenzie. The "hoping and planning" was occurring in 1658, but also, as I have suggested, from late 1655, after *Defensio pro se* of August, with minor "interference" from governmental activities and other personal matters taken in stride.

7. They were residing there by August 27, 1641, when Christopher's daughter Anne's baptism occurred, and a muster Roll of October 21, 1642, indicates their continued presence at the time of Milton's marriage.

8. A major problem with psychological theories has been that they generally have been written by men about men. I here employ a concept written concerning men, who, having moved into a second stage of transference, acknowledge the law of the father and thus are enabled to move into a third stage of identification with the father through a passing of oedipal urges as a result of "normal" sexual achievement and its accompanying assertions of being. Women, perhaps, need to acknowledge the "law" of society before moving into identification with the mother. But of course that "law" is man- (not woman-) made, and leads to indefensible attitudes of woman's inferiority to man, to sexual misconceptions of the efficacy of virginity (also transferred biblically to man), and to misplaced gender applications. See Jane Tibbets Schulenburg's "The Heroics of Virginity: *Brides of Christ and Sacrificial Mutilation*," 29-72 of *Women in the Middle Ages and the Renaissance: Literary and Historical Perspectives,* ed. Mary Beth Rose (Syracuse: Syracuse Univ. Press, 1986), as well as other essays therein, for some terrifying means to resist such "law" of society.

9. Parker (1:303) notes that Christopher Milton's family, upon leaving Exeter in April 1646, were back in London, possibly staying briefly at Mrs. Webber's and/or possibly at Milton's house.

10. See Darbishire, *The Early Lives,* 22-23, 2-3, and 66-67, respectively.

11. Building on a combination of antagonistic tradition toward Milton (and some unfounded extrapolation) and on reading *Paradise Lost* and *Samson Agonistes* biographically, the discussion of H.R. Hays in *The Dangerous Sex,* Chapter 17, "The Bosom Snake," 158-67, points to the ideal and yet potentially distasteful in the sex act in Milton's remarks in the divorce tracts: "a conversing solace, & peacefull society is the prime end of mariage, without which no other help, or office can bee mutual, beseeming the dignity of reasonable creatures, that such as they should be coupl'd in the rites of nature by the meer compulsion of lust, without love, or peace, wors then wild beasts" (*Colasterion,* 14). But Milton's confutation of his anonymous critic involves his stress on the solace of marriage (union) whereas the author of *An Answer to a Book, Intituled, The Doctrine and Discipline of Divorce* (1644) had argued "that solace . . . is not the main end of mariage or conjugall society, is very plain and apparent," and since "man ordinarily exceeds woman in naturall gifts of minde, and in delectablen[e]sse of converse . . . the solace and meetnesse of a helper to *Adam* which is spoken of, was not that which you seem to speak of as contrary to discord only, but is a solace and a meetnesse made up chiefly as of different Sexes, consisting of Male and Female" (12). Milton is not calling the sex act pollutional; he is saying that engagement in the sex act between two people who are not mutually committed (loving) makes the act only copulation, a relieving of lustfulness, as can be observed in certain animals. He is separating at opposite poles an ideal of marriage and the otherwise "prostitutional." He is, I think, assigning all nonmarried sex to what would be construed as prostitutional. His age (with the exception of some betrothed sexual activity) did not ostensibly experience the thinking of more recent times in regard to unmarried sex: for the female engaged in nonmarried sex, there was sinfulness as also in adultery; for the male, there might be pardon or even the exoneration of natural urges and of a need to know about such things.

James G. Turner in *One Flesh: Paradisal Marriage and Sexual Relations in the Age of Milton* (Oxford: Clarendon Press, 1987) sees a struggle on Milton's part between a vision of Eros and Genesis, whereas in the divorce tracts "Milton could not incorporate sexuality into the ideal without tension, violence, and open disgust" (232) but in the epic "intimacy is a course of delight rather than horror" (233). Milton's "imagination responds generously . . . to the ecstatic egalitarian love of 'one flesh' as well as to patriarchal love of superior and inferior" (285): "Proper self-knowledge . . . involves the discovery of the human capacity for egalitarian love, instituted in Paradise" (284).

12. We do not know when Richard Powell was born. His first son was baptized on June 10, 1621, and Parker assigns a birthdate of 1601? for Anne Powell. It is thus possible that in 1642 Mary's father was only around forty-two, less than ten years older than Milton himself.

13. Square-bracketed, italicized words were deleted; words in pointed brackets were added, usually above the line.

14. "Loneliest," "loneliness," or "lonely" appear in the prose only in *The Doctrine and Discipline of Divorce*, 16 occurrences, and *Tetrachordon*, 7 occurrences. In the poetry "loneliness" occurs in *Comus*, 404; "lonely" is found 5 times, including Adam's significant lines: "Thy going is not lonely, with thee goes / Thy Husband, him to follow thou art bound; / Where he abides, think there thy native soil" (*PL* XI, 290-92). It does place the husband in foremost position, and we have recorded this common belief (note "bound" here, which indicates that this condition is a result of the Fall) on Milton's part in Chapter 11, but the emphasis, as in the divorce tracts, is that the compatibly married pair will not be lonely because they are together: the solitariness of the unmarried life predicates loneliness for Milton. It is not unequivalent to an incompatible marriage.

15. See my forthcoming essay "Allegory, Typology, and Didacticism: *Paradise Lost* in the Eighteenth Century," in *Enlightening Allegory*, ed. Kevin I. Cope (New York: AMS Inc., 1992), for an examination in *Paradise Lost* of the Satanic gaze, which Regina Schwartz discusses as "a powerful patriarchal symbol." "Milton understands the temptation *as* the temptation of voyeurism—that is, the temptation to polarize power" (93), as she clearly shows. See "Rethinking Voyeurism and Patriarchy: The Case of *Paradise Lost*," *Representations* 34 (1991): 85-103. What I suggest for Milton's biography is the polarization of power that those "gazes" created for him and his frequent withdrawal from the power play.

16. See Mitchell Walker, "The Double: An Archetypal Configuration," *Spring: An Annual of Archetypal Psychology and Jungian Thought* (1976): 165. A double is "a soul figure with all the erotic and spiritual significance attached to anima/us, but of the same sex, and yet not a shadow." "Epitaphium Damonis" should be read again with this in mind. Milton makes such remarks pertinent to anima as "Quis fando sopire diem, cantaque solebit?" (43, "Who will be wont to lull my time with speaking and singing?"). The shadow that this double fully becomes by the end of the poem (that dangerous dark side of personality) can be understood in the frequent "Quid te, Thyrsi, futuram est?" ("What is to become of you, Thyrsis?") and the assertion of ego in answer ("dubito quoque ne sim / Turgidulus, tamen et referam" (159-60, "I question also that I may not be vain, and yet that I may recite"). The shadow is to have effect in *Paradise Lost;* Louise

Schleiner argues that "male sociability" underlies various episodes, that "paradisal intimacy" is "definedly male" (51), and that Eve, successfully incorporated into the "pastoral 'new created World' of male intimacy" (50), "could become male to only a limited extent" (51). See "Pastoral Male Friendship and Miltonic Marriage: Textual Systems Transposed," *LIT* 2 (1990): 41-58.

17. See Walker, 165, 174.

18. See such studies as Phyllis Trible, "Depatriarchalizing in Biblical Interpretation," *The Jewish Woman: New Perspectives* (New York: Schocken Books, 1972), 73-114; Raphael Patai, *The Hebrew Goddess* (Philadelphia: KTAV Press, 1976); Ian Maclean, *The Renaissance Notion of Woman* (Cambridge: Cambridge Univ. Press, 1980); and Virginia Mollenkott, *The Divine Feminine; the Biblical Imagery of God as Female* (New York: Crossroad, 1983).

19. See *Anima: An Anatomy of a Personified Notion* (Dallas: Spring Publications, 1985).

20. See Drake's *An Essay in Defense of the Female Sex* (London, 1696), formerly assigned to Astell, and Astell's *Some Reflections upon Marriage Occasion'd by the Duke & Dutchess of Mazarine's Case; Which is also consider'd* (London, 1700), both of which were frequently reprinted.

21. See *The Relative Duties of Parents, Husbands, Masters, and Children, Wives, Servants, Consider'd in Sixteen Sermons* (London, 1705). I quote from Discourse [Sermon] VII on 1 Peter 3:1-2. Fleetwood, a celebrated preacher and zealous Whig, was a descendant of the Fleetwood family of Hesketh, Lancashire.

22. Defoe, *Political History of the Devil* (London, 1726), Chapter VIII (I quote from a 1772 edition, p. 95), and Tutchen, *The Foreigners. A Poem.* Part I (London, 1700), 8-9.

23. Letter XV, February 2, 1796, in *Letters Written During a Short Residence in Spain and Portugal* (Bristol, 1797), 267.

24. Cf. William Shullenberger, "Wrestling with the Angel: *Paradise Lost* and Feminist Criticism," *Milton Quarterly* 20 (1986): 69-85, and Anna K. Juhnke, "Remnants of Misogyny in *Paradise Lost*," *Milton Quarterly* 22 (1988): 50-58.

25. Carl G. Jung, "Civilization in Transition," in *The Collected Works of C.G. Jung*, trans. R.F.C. Hull (Princeton: Princeton Univ. Press, 1970), 10, paragraph 255.

26. Carl G. Jung, *Psychology of the Unconscious*, trans. Beatrice M. Hinkle (New York: Moffat, Yard and Co., 1916), 360, 428.

27. Important essays related to the preceding discussion are Jim Swan, "Difference and Silence: John Milton and the Question of Gender," *The (M)other Tongue: Essays in Feminist Psychoanalytic Interpretation*, ed. Shirley Nelson Garner, Claire Kahane, Madelon Sprenznether (Ithaca: Cornell Univ. Press, 1985), 142-68; Christine Froula, "When Eve Reads Milton: Undoing the Canonical Economy," *Critical Inquiry* 10 (1983): 321-48; and John Guillory, "From the Superfluous to the Supernumerary: Reading Gender into *Paradise Lost*," *Soliciting Interpretation: Literary Theory and Seventeenth-Century English Poetry*, ed. Elizabeth D. Harvey and Katharine Eisaman Maus (Chicago: Univ. of Chicago Press, 1990), 68-88. Froula writes that Eve's temptation is "to cease respecting one authority fetish of an invisible power and to see the world for herself" and that "Adam's fantasy of Eve's subordinate creation dramatizes an archetypal womb envy as constitutive of male identity," the latter being based on the rib as phallus

and the life-creating function of Eve's womb. One should also remark that the serpent-figure of Satan in the temptation is also phallic and Eve's partaking of the womblike fruit indicates the initiating action of the first authority fetish, which is then replaced by a different invisible power allowing for recognition of another authority. Adam will maintain his phallic fantasy in his diatribe against Eve in Book X (as will many men) but Eve will understand the fusion of authorities in the protevangelium. However, some like the daughters of Cain persist in acceptance of the authority fetish.

28. But see the important discussion of John C. Ulreich, Jr., in " 'Incident to All Our Sex': The Tragedy of Dalila," in *Milton and the Idea of Woman,* ed. Julia M. Walker (Urbana: Univ. of Illinois Press, 1988), 185-210.

29. John Guillory, "Dalila's House: *Samson Agonistes* and the Sexual Division of Labor," *Revisiting the Renaissance: The Discourses of Sexual Difference in Early Modern Europe,* ed. Margaret W. Ferguson, Maureen Quilligan, and Nancy J. Vickers (Chicago: Univ. of Chicago Press, 1986), 106-22, 338-44.

30. Allan H. Gilbert, "Is *Samson Agonistes* Unfinished?" *Philological Quarterly* 28 (1949): 98-106.

31. See, among others, Marcia Landy, "Kinship and the Role of Women in *Paradise Lost,*" *Milton Studies* 4 (1972): 3-18, and Gilbert, "Patriarchal Poetry and Women Readers."

32. See Jackie Di Salvo, "Blake Encountering Milton: Politics and the Family in *Paradise Lost* and *The Four Zoas,*" 143-84, in *Milton and the Line of Vision,* ed. Joseph A. Wittreich (Madison: Univ. of Wisconsin Press, 1975).

33. See, among others, Stephanie Dematrakoupoulos, "Eve as a Circean and Courtly Fatal Woman," *Milton Quarterly* 9 (1975): 99-107; Marcia Landy, "Milton and the Modern Reader," *Milton Studies* 9 (1976): 3-36; Froula; and Swan.

34. See Froula.

35. Guillory, "Dalila's House," 119.

14. The Political Dimension

1. First reported by Leo Miller in *Notes & Queries* 17 (1970): 412-14. Most important is Miller's demonstration of more cogent texts, dates, and addressees supplied by Lünig's versions.

2. The significance and full listing of the state papers cited herein was first indicated in "A Survey of the Prose Works" in *Achievements of the Left Hand,* Leti's biography having been dismissed by Walter Abbott in his edition of Cromwell's letters in 1937-47.

3. The Skinner MS in the hand of Daniel Skinner, apparently Milton's last amanuensis, will be found in the Public Record Office (London), SP 9/194; the Columbia MS, in the hand of an unidentified scribe, is owned by Columbia University (New York City), MS X823 M64/S52.

4. It is clear that a new, complete, up-to-date edition is needed, recording all variants and offering what appears to be a defensible text for each state paper (and each version of those state papers that underwent various uses to different governments). The editions of the state papers in CM and YP are inadequate on many counts. Before a new edition is completed, at least three major studies are

required: the Cromwellian government's relations with the Dutch, which Miller has studied for the years 1651-54; with the Danish; and with the Portuguese. Robert J. Fallon has a forthcoming book on the English relations with various governments including the Dutch, Danish, Portuguese, and Spanish. Index 2 of *Milton Bibliography,* 1624-1700, lists the appearances of the seemingly "authenticated" and possible state papers in manuscript and print up to 1700, including versions of documents that Milton did not produce (such as some of those of the Spanish manifesto) but one version of which he did apparently have his hand in.

5. See Leo Miller, *John Milton & the Oldenburg Safeguard* (New York: Loewenthal Press, 1985) and *John Milton in the Anglo-Dutch Negotiations, 1651-1654* (Pittsburgh: Duquesne Univ. Press, 1992).

6. Anonymous, *The Censure of the Rota Upon Mr Miltons Book, Entituled, The Ready and Easie Way to Establish A Free Common-wealth* (London, 1660), 13.

7. Jung, *Two Essays,* Part I, "The Relations between the Ego and the Unconscious," 238.

8. *The Unfolding God of Jung and Milton* (Lexington: Univ. Press of Kentucky, 1992).

9. See Michael Lieb's "Milton's 'Dramatick Constitution': The Celestial Dialogue in *Paradise Lost,* Book III," *Milton Studies* 23 (1987): 215-40, for a full discussion of the Son's manipulation of the Father.

10. F.D. Dow, *Radicalism in the English Revolution, 1640-1660* (Oxford: Basil Blackwell, 1985), 71.

11. References within these two paragraphs are to Loewenstein, *Milton and the Drama of History: Historical Vision, Iconoclasm, and the Literary Imagination* (Cambridge: Cambridge Univ. Press, 1990); Hill, *Milton and the English Revolution* (New York: Viking Press, 1977); Bennett, *Reviving Liberty: Radical Christian Humanism in Milton's Great Poems* (Cambridge: Harvard Univ. Press, 1989); and Wilding, *Dragons Teeth: Literature in the English Revolution* (Oxford: Clarendon Press, 1987). See von Maltzahn, 40 ff., for what I would suggest is Milton's non-democratic attitude in "relation of the few and the many," his "effort to restrict the true 'populus' to the fit minority."

In a forthcoming study entitled, "The Good Old Cause," Annabel Patterson examines such ideas as those raised by the preceding volumes and by this chapter. I sincerely thank Professor Patterson for allowing me to read her important study and to learn from it. She stresses the radical implications of the republican movement observable in Milton's work, with particularly telling evidence from *Paradise Lost* VII, 484-89, which speaks of the ant (emmet): "Pattern of just equalitie perhaps / Hereafter, join'd in her popular Tribes / Of Commonaltie." Thus looked forward to is "the transformation of the many-headed multitude into a large, literate, industrious, self-determining working class." Such a prophecy does involve a radicalism not only for his but also for our time in its economic and social concerns. Milton's thinking here is a development (I would say "advance") out of and over earlier sociopolitical statements (such as the Lady's words in *Comus*), but perhaps still remaining is the hierarchy of God/queen ant and the implied hierarchy of *"just* equalitie."

12. David Aers and Gunther Kress, "Historical Process, Individual and Communities in Milton's Early Prose," in *1642: Literature and Power in the Seventeenth Century,* Proceedings of the Essex Conference on the Sociology of Literature, July 1980, ed. Francis Barker et al. (Univ. of Essex, 1981), 298-99.

13. Donald A. Roberts, ed., "A Second Defence of the English People" in YP (1966), 4, i: 638 n. 380.

14. See the excellent discussion of this tract by Austin Woolrych in the Introduction to YP (1980), 7:187-88, 214-18.

15. The so-called companion piece to *A Treatise, Considerations Touching The likeliest means to remove Hirelings out of the church,* was probably written in 1652/53 and slightly revised in 1659; see William B. Hunter's introduction to his first edition of the tract in *The Prose of John Milton,* ed. Patrick, 475-76. Emphasis in this tract opposed to tithing is on freedom for minister and parishioner alike, with a rather radical disclaimer for the need of a learned ministry, a position that can hardly be called accommodated.

16. Part of Milton's accommodation lay in his role as licenser for the Cromwellian government from December 16, 1649, through 1652, despite his arguments in *Areopagitica.* One item licensed was a Socinian tract espousing certain heretical positions, including antitrinitarianism, *Catechesis Ecclesiarum quæ in Regno Poloniæ & ducatu Lithuaniæ* (Racovia [London], 1651). Milton was dismissed from his post after the arrest and investigation of its printer, William Dugard. Lieuwe van Aitzema noted on March 5, 1652, that Milton told the investigating committee he had authorized publication because of his belief "that men should refrain from forbidding books" ("dat men geen boucken behoorde te verbieden"). See J. Milton French, ed., *The Life Records of John Milton* (New Brunswick: Rutgers Univ. Press, 1954), 3:206.

17. *The Political Thought of John Milton* (London: MacMillan, 1984).

18. See Chapter 6, n. 6, for citations of Lewalski's important essays.

19. Sensabaugh, *That Grand Whig, Milton,* 204-5.

20. Frederic Jameson, "Religion and Ideology," in Barker, *1642,* 335-36.

21. Shawcross, *Paradise Regain'd,* 127. The remainder of this paragraph summarizes some points made in that study; see especially 119-20, 126-27.

15. The Religious Precept

1. Alan Dures, *English Catholicism, 1558-1642* (London: Longmans, 1983), 39.

2. Ibid., 84.

3. See also my discussion (and rejection) of Milton's "Alleged Roman Catholicism" in *ME,* 2:26-27. Many of the issues here that involve Milton's thinking, particularly in *Of True Religion,* are examined in my essay " 'Connivers and the Worst of Superstitions': Milton on Popery and Toleration," forthcoming.

4. See my essay "The Structure and Myth of *Paradise Regain'd."*

5. Compare Carl Jung's remark in *Aion (The Collected Works of Carl G. Jung* [Princeton: Princeton Univ. Press, 1968], 9, pt. 2:109): "the God-image is immediately related to, or identical with, the self, and everything that happens to the God-image has an effect on the latter." The view of "Ad Patrem" presented in Chapter 4 is consistent with this reading of this statement.

6. See Thomas B. Stroup, *Religious Rite and Ceremony in Milton's Poetry* (Lexington: Univ. of Kentucky Press, 1968), and Hunter's book on *Comus,* already cited, among others.

7. The passages read: "Shepherd I take thy word, / And trust thy honest offer'd courtsie, / Which oft is sooner found in lowly sheds / With smoaky rafters, then in tapestry halls / And courts of princes, where it first was nam'd, / And yet

is most pretended" (321-26), and "If every just man that now pines with want /
Had but a moderate and beseeming share / Of that which lewdly-pamper'd
Luxury / Now heaps upon som few with vast excess, / Natures full blessings
would be well dispens't / In unsuperfluous eev'n proportion" (768-73). In the
first instance the manuscript of the poem (in the Trinity MS, that is) shows alterations being made as Milton wrote; the second is preceded by extensive revision, which is made on the pasted leaf, definitely in 1637. Both seem odd
passages to have been presented before the Bridgewaters in 1634.

8. *Milton: A Biography*, 1:556.

9. Jung, *Psychology and Religion*, 5.

10. Jung, *Two Essays*, 215.

11. See *ME*, 7:107.

12. *The Confession of Faith* (London, 1651), Chapter XXIV, Section VI, 53; it
appears on 44 of the 1646 expanded version of *An Humble Advice*.

13. *A Treatise of Civil Power* (London, 1659), 34-35.

14. In *Milton and the English Revolution*, esp. 100-116.

15. YP, trans. John Carey, 6:206.

16. Ibid., 233, 238, 264.

17. I quote from the thirty-two-page first edition of *An Humble Advice* (London: Printed for the Company of Stationers, [1646]), Chapter II, Section 3, p. 8.

18. *The Interpreter's Bible* (New York and Nashville: Abingdon-Cokesbury
Press, 1953), 10:238. See also Timothy J. O'Keeffe, *Milton and the Pauline
Tradition: A Study of Theme and Symbolism* (Washington, D.C.: Univ. Press of Amer-
ica, 1982).

19. *The Fathers of the Church: Saint Augustine, The Trinity*, trans. Stephen
McKenna (Washington, D.C.: Catholic Univ. Press, 1963), Book V, Chapter 8,
186-87. For clarification of the terms *ousia, hypostasis*, and *substantia*, see C.A. Pa-
trides, *Milton and the Christian Tradition*, Chapter 1, esp. 16-20, and William B.
Hunter, "Some Problems in Milton's Theological Vocabulary," *Harvard Theological Review* 57 (1964): 353-65. See also William B. Hunter, C.A Patrides, and Jack
Adamson, *Bright Essence: Studies in Milton's Theology* (Salt Lake City: Univ. of
Utah Press, 1971), and Peter A. Fiore, *Milton and Augustine: Patterns of Augustin-
ian Thought in Paradise Lost* (University Park: Penn State Univ. Press, [1981]).
See Michael Baumann, *Milton's Arianism* (Frankfurt: Verlag Peter Lang,
1987), for an out-of-date and uninformed restatement of Milton's "heresy."

20. The 1611 Authorized Version reads: "And when all things shall be subdued vnto him, then shal the Sonne also himselfe bee subiect vnto him that put
all things vnder him, that God may be all in all." See also *PL* III, 339-41, and VI,
730-33. In *The Interpreter's Bible*, Clarence Tucker Craig writes in his exegesis
(10:240) that "Though an English reader might assume that all the world of phe-
nomena was to be absorbed into the ultimate reality of God, that certainly was
not the expectation of Paul. He did not believe in the loss of individual consciousness by absorption in the world soul."

21. See Patrides, *Milton and the Christian Tradition*, 111-15, 174-78.

22. *De doctrina christiana*, I, xii; YP, 6:394.

23. YP, 6:395.

24. See ibid., 573: "If, then, any believer can preach the gospel, so long as
he is endowed with certain gifts, it follows that any believer can administer bap-

tism"; and ibid., 557: "I do not know why ministers should forbid anyone except themselves to celebrate the Lord's Supper."

25. The term has been used before. Its sense can be inferred from remarks of Milton's being "Church-outed" (*The Reason of Church-Government*, 41); it is more implicit in *Considerations Touching the likeliest means to remove Hirelings out of the church* (1659) where he speaks of "the true freedom of Christian doctrin and church-discipline subject to no superior judge but God only" and of Christ, "who hath promisd . . . both his holy spirit and his own presence with his Church to the worlds end" (142, 144). Cf. John S. Tanner's "Milton Among the Mormons" in *Ringing the Bell Backward*, ed. Ronald G. Shafer (Indiana, Pa.: Indiana Univ. of Pennsylvania Imprint Series, 1982), 123-32.

26. *Christian Mortalism from Tyndal to Milton* (Cambridge: Harvard Univ. Press, 1972).

27. "Who being in the forme of God, thought it not robbery to bee equall with God: / But made himselfe of no reputation, and tooke vpon him the forme of a seruant, and was made in the likenesse of man. / And being found in fashion as a man, he humbled himselfe, and became obedient vnto death, euen the death of the Crosse." See also Michael Lieb, "Milton and the Kenotic Christology: Its Literary Bearing," *ELH* 37 (1970): 342-60; republished in *The Sinews of Ulysses: Form and Convention in Milton's Works* (Pittsburgh: Duquesne Univ. Press, 1989), Chapter 4, 38-52.

28. "For if Christ really died, then both his soul and his body died . . . on the same day. As for his divine nature, it is more questionable whether that also succumbed to death. A lot of passages in the Bible make his divine nature succumb to death along with his human nature, and they seem to do so too clearly for it to be explained away as mere idiomatic parallelism" (*De doctrina christiana*, I, xvi; YP, 6:439).

29. *La religion du Milton* (Paris: H. Didier, 1909).

30. Jung, *Two Essays*, 58.

31. Ibid., 71.

32. YP, 4, i: 537, trans. Donald C. MacKenzie.

33. *Identity in Shakespeare*, 135. Also interesting in connection with Milton's sense of Patience in this poem is Driscoll's remark (141): "But if evil's facticity gains acute, personal reality, it shatters the roseate armor of our anthropomorphic cosmologies and leaves patience the sole defense against madness. Job is the pattern of all patience; faith is the substance of his patience." Samson, of course, has exhibited some amount of impatience, and thus not true faith, in contrast to the Son in *Paradise Regain'd*.

34. "The Chronology of Milton's Major Poems," 356. See also my discussion in *Paradise Regain'd*, Chapter 2, 9-28.

16. The Bible

1. See Diana Treviño Benet, "Abdiel and the Son in the Separation Scene," *Milton Studies* 18 (1983): 129-43, and " 'No Outward Aid Require': A Note on Eve in Separation," *ANQ* 2 (1989): 90-94.

2. See Catharine Randall Coats, *Subverting the System: D'Aubigné and Calvinism*, Sixteenth Century Essays & Studies, Vol. 14 (1990), for a full discussion.

Agrippa d'Aubigné offers clear example of the "authorization of self" in "prideful" literary creation.

3. See my study of *Paradise Regain'd*.

4. That is, in English translation the name Satan appears first in 1 Chronicles and second in Job, but in Hebrew it also appears in Numbers 22:22, 1 Samuel 29:4, 2 Samuel 19:22, and 1 Kings 11:25 where it is translated as "adversary." The word comes from the Aramaic meaning "to be remote," particularly "from the truth and the way of God." A form of the word, Sitnah, occurs in Genesis 26:21, where it means "hostility" or "hatred," as a footnote to the text gives it. See *A Hebrew and English Lexicon of the Old Testament*, ed. Francis Brown, S.R. Driver, and Charles Briggs (Oxford: Clarendon Press, 1907), 966 (known as the BDB from the editors' last names). Of importance also, as Michael Lieb has pointed out to me, the word "Satan" in the opening chapters of Job refers not to the name of a being but to the title of an office occupied by that being. Emphasis is thus on function rather than his being adversary or slanderer. "The Satan" (hassatan) is one commissioned to "run to and fro" and "rove about," as in Job 1:7, without any of the later negativities associated with the name of the being. (See Walter L. Michel, *Job in the Light of Northwest Semitic* [Rome: Biblical institute Press, 1987], 1:16, for discussion.)

5. In *Naming in Paradise: Milton and the Language of Adam and Eve* (Oxford: Clarendon Press, 1990), John Leonard looks at Satan's name as "enemy" in *Paradise Lost* and notes its employment as "accuser" (and this important meaning in Job and *Paradise Regain'd*). "Adversary" (which he does not mention) is the more usual rendition and encompasses both these other terms, with basically an active role of opposition implied in "enemy" in the longer epic and with a more passive role of "accuser" or what we popularly call "devil's advocate" in the shorter. The difference between "enemy" and "accuser" is exactly the difference between the Satans of the two epics. The name "accuser" appears for Satan in *PL* IV, 10 ("The Tempter ere th'Accuser of man-kind"; mentioned by Leonard) and is transferred to Eve by Adam in *PL* IX, 1182 ("but I rue / That errour now, which is become my crime, / And thou th'accuser"). It was used of Satan in Revelation 12:10 ("And I heard a loud voice saying in heaven, Now is come salvation, and strength, and the kingdom of our God, and the power of his Christ: for the accuser of our brethren is cast down, which accused them before our God day and night"). But it appears as well in a feminine form in Ezra 4:6, where the "adversaries of Judah and Benjamin" are frustrated by hired counsellors, who wrote unto Ahasuerus "an accusation" against them. Strangely, Leonard does not even mention Uriel or Ithuriel, or indicate any attention to Michael Lieb's discussion of Holy Name (171-84) in *Poetics of the Holy*, a revised version of his study in *Harvard Theological Review* 67 (1974): 321-39.

6. James Sims, *The Bible in Milton's Epics* (Gainesville: Univ. of Florida Press, 1962).

7. See *With Mortal Voice*, 119-38.

Appendix C: Dating of the Plans

1. The word "other" was added after the "British Trag." were begun on p. 37. Subjects on p. 36 and the drafts on p. 35 did not require that "Adam in

Banishment," etc., be classified. Note that "Tragedies" is capitalized, thus showing that "other" was added. These titles must have been entered after draft three was titled "Paradise Lost," since one is "Adam in Banishment," and before "The Deluge. Sodom" or "Abram from Morea" were put down.

2. It should be noted that pp. 36 and 37 face each other: biblical subjects on one side, historical subjects on the other. Milton's use of a columnar arrangement for the first two drafts on p. 35 and for the first entries of p. 36 place them together, and apart from the British subjects of p. 37, written in full-page lines.

3. This total includes one word no longer decipherable in the manuscript; see Steadman's transcription, 556.

4. The line around the addition to "Sodom" on p. 41 indicates that the Scotch subjects and the addition to "Adam unparadiz'd," p. 41, had already been indited when the former addition was made. The lack of a line, merely a bracket for position, and the full-page writing of the latter addition show that "Moabitides" and "Christus patiens" had not yet been made. This addition to "Adam unparadiz'd" on p. 41 was written after the two on p. 40; if it had been first, it would have been inserted at the bottom of p. 40 just as these two were. Being added last, however, but being inserted in a position in the outline preceding these two, it was placed on the half-blank p. 41 opposite its inserted position.

5. Fletcher remarks that the reference to a "former draught" at the end of "Adam unparadiz'd" is "more probably . . . to a draft no longer in existence than it is to one of the three extant outlines" (15). Although draft four was apparently copied from some intermediate work piece (as were the prose outlines on p. 39), it is an expansion of draft three on p. 35, as a parallel comparison will show.

Index